# RETIREMENT CHOICES

## for the time of your life

# RETIREMENT CHOICES
## for the time of your life

### JOHN HOWELLS

**Illustrations and Maps by Noni Mendoza**

San Francisco

Gateway Books


Research Director: Sherry Pastor
Edited by Patrick Totty
Cover designed by Ed McElligott

**Library of Congress Cataloging-in-Publication Data**

Howells, John, 1928-
  Retirement choices for the time of your life.

  Bibliography: p.
  Includes index
  1. Retirement, Places of — United States. I. Title.
HQ1063.H685 1987     646.7'9     87-82188
ISBN 0-933469-03-9


Printed in the United States of America
10  9  8  7  6  5

## Dedication

This book is dedicated to all those lively, enthusiastic retirees who unselfishly helped fill in the details of this endeavor. Seeing how these people create adventurous and interesting life styles somehow makes a person look forward to growing old, look forward to enjoying the "time of your life."

# TABLE OF CONTENTS

# INTRODUCTION

## *Retirement Choices*

Two years ago, my friend Don Merwin and I addressed our-selves to the problem of finding economical, pleasant retirement situations for people with limited budgets. We looked for places where a couple might live a dignified, stimulating life, yet get by without digging into their savings. Since we both knew and loved Mexico, we began writing CHOOSE MEXICO, a book that shows a couple how to live on a minimum of $400 a month in a pleasant climate, among interesting people. Of course, living in Mexico isn't for everyone. Many readers wanted something similar to CHOOSE MEXICO, but in a situation that didn't require learning Spanish and living in a foreign country.

It turns out that there are places in the United States where you *can* live on a budget, sometimes for less than you pay for rent in some cities. And, clearly, there are places where the climate is bearable, and where living on Social Security payments doesn't necessarily mean existing at a poverty level. Because of the high cost of living in the United States, the $400 a month figure might be difficult, if not impossible, to attain here, yet there are many places in the United States that are definitely affordable. Other localities, while not particularly inexpensive living, are certainly possibilities for those who are willing to watch the budget more carefully. There are also some rather exciting alternatives for retirement living that are available to anyone with a little creativity and a modest budget.

There are many books on the market offering to help you plan for retirement, dealing with how to face that trauma of making the decision to retire, how to deal with your "inner self" or how to take care of yourself financially and physically during your retirement. No doubt, there are many who can benefit from this kind of advice. But this book assumes that you know enough to exercise regularly, eat nutritious foods and that you understand the necessity of taking care of your body. If you haven't learned these things by this time of your life, a book isn't going to help you. This book assumes that you have done the best you can financially, and that you will consult experts in the field of finance for estate planning and stock market strategies. It would be presumptuous of me to offer you advice on things of this nature, or on how to prepare yourself psychologically for your new life; the world has far too many self-styled "financial experts" and amateur therapists as it is.

Other books present little more than long lists of cities and towns, full of statistics on population, the mean and average temperatures, annual precipitation, elevation and employment prospects. They list the number of motels in the town and local tax information. In doing research for my previous two books on retirement alternatives, I found that while statistics and charts can be helpful, they are difficult reading and don't tell the full story. For example: at the mouth of the Amazon River, right on the equator, statistics show that the average temperature is 81 degrees and the highest temperature ever recorded there was a mere 91 degrees. It sounds nice, but humidity, insects and other nasty conditions make it all but unlivable. As the saying goes, "a nice place to visit but..."

This book will keep charts and statistics to a minimum, although some will inevitably creep in. Most statistics are readily available from an atlas or an almanac. The *number* of people living in a town isn't as important as the *kind* of people they are. Are they friendly? Are they the kind of people you will feel comfortable with?

Population statistics can tell you things like which cities have the least population per square mile. For example: cities like Fargo, North Dakota, or Duluth, Minnesota, are 40 times less crowded than Honolulu or San Francisco. Yet, how many people from Honolulu or San Francisco give serious thought to retiring in Fargo or Duluth? Which towns might offer highest quality, year-round living?

As far as job prospects go, this book is for people thinking about *retirement*, not employment. True, many retirees like to earn extra money for part-time work; they are willing to work for very little just to have something to occupy their time. In a pleasant area, where there are a lot of retirees, the result is invariably an oversupply of help and depressed wages. So, if you need to work to survive, then an inexpensive retirement area isn't the place for you. The reason some locales are inexpensive is because wages are low, therefore prices and rents are forced down to be competitive. As a rule, the best retirement areas pay the least wages. But, the bright side of this picture is that if you need to hire someone to help around the house, wages will be affordable. If you need to work for the sake of work itself, far better to get involved in volunteer activities. We'll discuss this in detail later on.

Statistics on winter temperatures, altitude and precipitation tell you something, but even more important is the cost of a comfortable life-style in a particular town. The most expensive retirement areas are naturally wonderful places to live. But people who can afford to retire in Palm Beach can afford to live just about anywhere in the world they choose. They don't need a book to help them decide on alternatives. Statistics on state taxes are included at the back of the book. But let me stress that making retirement choices on the basis of sales tax, income tax or property assessments is irrational--unless you are in an extremely high tax bracket, in which case you don't need advice on affordable retirement alternatives. More important than the tax rates is the quality of living.

I don't mean to downplay the anxious questions that most people have about retirement. Clearly, a certain amount of trauma is connected with that inevitable day when you accept the gold plated watch and the "So long, pal," from your fellow workers. It's going to be a different world out there, a different life, probably with less income to live that different life. You have a lot of decisions to make. These decisions could ultimately determine whether your retirement is unsatisfactory, satisfactory, or wildly successful.

This book will try to help you with these decisions by presenting you with a range of retirement alternatives. In doing research, I traveled well over 20,000 miles throughout the United States, personally visiting retirement communities, interviewing retirees, real estate people, government agencies and retiree organizations. In addition, I traveled uncountable miles through Latin America and Europe doing research on my other books. Even with all this travel, I found it impossible to visit *every* possible retirement location. And, were it physically possible to go everywhere and if it were desirable to cover them all in one book, the result would have been a book with a single paragraph or even a lonely sentence about each town. Instead, I decided to visit places that are typical of an area and write in a little more depth.

All of this research led me to this conclusion: There is no *one* perfect place or arrangement that suits everyone. Each person's needs and dreams are different. This book, therefore, presents you with many ideas from which to compose your ideal pattern of life. The years ahead of you are often called "Golden Years," the "Years of Opportunity," or any number of euphemisms. They can be that and more. It's all up to you.

CHAPTER ONE

# *The Time of Your Life*

During the depression years of the 1930s, the birth rate dropped dramatically. It dropped to the point where experts predicted that the population of the United States--then about 125 million--would fall to around 87 million by the year 2000. Well, obviously the experts were wrong. With the "baby boom" of the postwar period, population zoomed, and it looks as if the experts will miss their mark by nearly 200 million.

In the intervening years, we've seen several amazing changes in our life-styles, our standard of living and our outlook toward aging. Those who were born in the depression years and just before are now approaching a time of life when retirement is not a far-off dream, but a looming certainty. With the large group of "baby-boomers" crowding at their heels (the ones the experts of 50 years ago failed to predict), many feel the pressure of retirement. The oldest members of the "baby boom" generation are already in their 40s. Before long, many of us are going to make some decisions. We need to seriously consider our options for the coming years, and this book will examine some of these options.

## PLANNING FOR THE "TIME OF YOUR LIFE"

These next few paragraphs may be the most important ones in this entire book. I am going to try to raise your level of awareness of where you are in your life and try to shake some attitudes and assumptions you may have about retirement.

People seem to fall into two categories when it comes to retirement planning. On the one hand, some refuse to think; they refuse to consider the consequences of aging. Since they are vigorous at age 62, they push aside any thoughts of a time when they may not be quite as active. And, at the other extreme, there are those who assume that since their parents passed away at age 70 or that, because the average age of death is somewhere in the early 70s, the end is near. They sit around and brood over the shortened odds, expecting to go any minute.

The fact is, people are living longer and longer. According to the insurance companies, a person retiring at the age of 62, has an average life expectancy of another 19 or 20 years. This includes those who die from automobile accidents, too much booze and cigarettes or being shot by jealous lovers. What few people stop to consider is that the fastest growing age group in this country is over 80! Therefore, a person of retirement age who takes care of himself physically, drives cautiously and who is careful in his or her choice of lovers has every right to plan on living another 20 to 25 years.

## TWENTY-FIVE PERCENT OF YOUR LIFE!

Think about this for a minute. Another 20 to 25 years is at least *one-fourth of your life*! And, since you won't have to fight in the job market any longer, you now have one-fourth of your life left to enjoy a new way of living. Exciting, isn't it? With such a big chunk of your future at stake, you can't afford to plan haphazardly.

As you read this book, try to keep in mind that you aren't planning for just the next few years, but for a possible 20 or 25 years-- maybe even more! Therefore, when you plan on retiring to that ranch in Oregon or that fishing boat in the Caribbean, keep in mind that after a decade or so, you might want to fall back into a less vigorous life-style. You can make plans accordingly. On the other hand, I've interviewed any number of 80-year-old-plus retirees who can run circles around most 65'ers. Keeping fit is part of the scheme, of course.

Planning for this fourth quarter of your life isn't only the responsibility of the husband. Much serious thought should be given to where the wife is going to be 20 or 25 years down the line. For example: Are you thinking of that farm way out in the country? Yet, you've always let your husband do the driving and you don't know how to drive? Better learn, now. Will you be happy carrying on with the many chores of a country place in the event that your husband should be disabled, or even gone? Look around your new community for a pleasant retirement home, just in case.

Officials and administrators of retirement programs agree that one of the biggest mistakes of retirees is they don't figure far enough in the future. Avoid this shortsighted planning by making contingency plans. Figure on the long haul.

## POLITICAL CLOUT

If the fastest growing group of voters is people in their 80s, that means their children are either retired or about to retire. And, it's a recognized fact that older voters are much more inclined to vote than young people. Figures show that 70 percent of folks over 50 vote regularly, whereas only about 30 percent of younger people utilize the ballot box. What does this mean in terms of politics? Plenty!

Politicians see the clear handwriting on the wall, that there is a growing block of voters out there who need to be wooed. As more and more retirees move to Oregon, California, Arkansas, Florida and Texas, these blocks of voters become quite important. With "sunbelt" states gaining more retirees every day, the balance of power is slowly but surely moving into the hands of older voters. The result will be more politicians espousing the cause of elderly voters, improvements in medical care and other services. The politicians will react, providing elderly voters band together for mutually beneficial goals. This is particularly easy to see in some communities of Oregon and Florida, where 40 percent and more of the residents are over 60 and 20 percent of the residents are retired. When there is a need for a new resource center, or a home-care program, these communities get action! Don't misunderstand, these things aren't going to come about automatically; they happen only when the elderly organize and make their demands known.

Another interesting thing about living where there are lots of retirees is that the local merchants see many hundreds of thousands of dollars in Social Security and pension checks pouring into the local economy. Most of it is spent locally. Merchants and real estate brokers seem to run most towns and cities politically, so you can see how important your money and your votes are to them.

## POLITICAL ACTION

Okay, so you are just starting to think about retirement; you aren't even 60 yet. Don't get the idea that service centers,

Alzheimer's programs, Medicare and Meals on Wheels are just problems for the aging. Someday, all too soon, *you* will be in need of these things. It's in your own selfish interest to join with the elderly in demanding decent medical care and dignified living conditions for everyone. It's a disgrace and a scandal that the United States is the only modern country in the world that tries to abandon its citizens after they leave the work force. The elderly citizens of this country have worked all their lives, paid taxes, fought for their country, have done everything right and proper. And yet, they see cutbacks in Medicare. They are told that Social Security is "going broke" and that we "can't afford" decent medical care. This is ironic, because Social Security is not only paying its way, but it's beginning to build up a huge surplus. It's one of the few, if not the only, sectors of the government which is doing so.

Why is it that the government expects the Social Security Administration to be self-supporting? Is the Department of Agriculture self-supporting? Is the Immigration and Naturalization Service self-supporting? Does the Department of Defense stop buying $700 toilet seats because we "can't afford" them? This is nonsense.

An example: In spring of 1987, the Agriculture Department gave over $100 million to dairy farmers to kill some of their cattle. Many farmers received over a million bucks apiece to slaughter their animals so that the government wouldn't have to pay more money in subsidies and price supports, and taxpayers wouldn't have to buy the surplus cheese and store it in caves. (The irony of this is that there are new methods of milk production which will soon replace the former production.) Did we hear any complaints coming from the Congress or the White House about this program "not paying its way?" Of course not. Not only did the Department of Agriculture shell out big money to slaughter cows, but it refused to give the cattle to countries like Mexico where children seldom get a chance to drink milk. Yet, at the same time our politicians dish out millions to buy surplus milk and cheese and pay farmers to kill cows, they scheme ways to cut Medicare and Social Security payments. How do you like those apples?

As a lifelong taxpayer, as a senior citizen or future senior citizen, you owe it to yourself to fight for your right to dignity in your old age. By the year 2000, it's estimated that there will be nearly 35 million persons in this country over age 65. If Medicare continues to be weakened, the plight of the retired can become serious indeed. Especially critical are home health care services. With adequate home care, about 2.5 million people can be kept out of nursing facilities. Not only would this save about two-thirds of the cost of institutional care, but the patients can live much fuller and more satisfying lives in their own homes.

## WHAT HAPPENS AFTER RETIREMENT?

An important consideration for many people facing retirement is: Where am I going to live? For some, this won't be difficult, for they've never dreamed of living anywhere but in their own neighborhood, near their children and grandchildren, friends and next-door neighbors, whom they've known for years.

But for others, the choice is not that simple. Even if they feel that they enjoy the social or family setting they're in presently, there are other factors that can undermine this enjoyment. One of the biggest worries of most potential retirees is the question, "How am I going to afford it?" After years of earning a living wage, a retired couple suddenly finds itself facing reduced income, but not reduced expenses. Surely, there are other places in the country where rent and utilities are not so high?

There *are* reasonable places to live, as we shall see.

Another goal of many retirees is to escape dreary winters, shoveling snow and chipping ice; or perhaps to flee the steamy, hot summers of the hometown for a cool, seashore setting. This makes sense in more ways than one, because weather extremes are bad for your health, as well as your disposition. Furthermore, escaping the burden of high utility bills can help ease the expenses of retirement.

The decision to move away on retirement is not an easy one. The decision is also not one that should be put off until the last minute. Even if retirement is several years away, you won't be wasting your time by reading through this volume and looking about for some alternatives for enjoyable, affordable retirement living. We will examine various parts of the world with the goal of finding a place where you can live a comfortable, dignified and interesting life. Who knows, that ideal place may be where you are now living--but we will also present some options for those who choose to live "at home" but vary their lives with some part-time living in other places.

## SHOULD YOU MOVE WHEN YOU RETIRE?

It turns out that about 75 percent of people retiring in the U.S.A. *don't* move; they end up staying in the same town where they've lived most of their lives. There are many good reasons for this, the most common being that it is easier to just stay put than to get involved in a move. Other reasons are social: Not wanting to leave a setting in which they are comfortable and have children, friends and relatives living nearby.

This is an important reason for staying put. However, it might be worth your while to examine your social life closely and see if there are other factors that might override this. For example: Many people's social contacts are determined by and closely entwined with their jobs. With eight hours a day (plus lunch) working with the same people year after year, and possibly socializing with them after work, it's easy to become part of a work-related social set. Then, upon retirement, your work-related friends have a tendency to fall away. Your interests aren't similar any more, your goals are different and often the old friends are too busy with work and making friends with the new employees to have time for you.

You might also discover that the friends you had at work were acquaintances you were *forced* to make because of your job, not necessarily friends of your choosing. For many retirees, one of the exciting prospects of moving to a new community or new situation is the chance to make an entirely new set of friends and begin a social life anew. You have to examine your personality closely to see how you and your spouse feel about this. Do you have the sense of adventure to make a new beginning?

Staying near children, grandchildren and other relatives is another valid reason for "staying put." If you are close to your family, see them every day and wouldn't think about being separated from them even for short periods, then you probably won't get much from this book, anyway. But people often find that visiting close relatives a couple of times a year keeps the family spirit alive, whereas too many visits create tensions. The old proverb about "absence makes the heart grow fonder," carries more than a grain of truth in many cases. Only you can decide whether it's true in your case.

## DON'T WAIT UNTIL YOU RETIRE

It is never too early to begin thinking about your retirement alternatives. Some people I know have started in their 40s and early 50s, and find it exciting to spend their vacations sampling various places both here and abroad. As they enjoy a week on the beach, or a vacation in the mountains, they also check the place out as a possible place to live. "Would we want to live here?" they ask each other.

Some already know their ideal retirement location. "Why wait," they ask, "why not buy our retirement house now?" If their target area is in a desirable location, they have no trouble renting the house they buy there, letting tenants help pay for what will one day be their retirement home. When the final day comes, the place could be almost paid for.

You should be absolutely certain about your choice before you invest heavily, however. A better alternative for many is to rent for a time before tying themselves down. Doing a pre-retirement testing in several different locations makes good sense. There's also a big question as to whether you should buy at all. Later we'll discuss the advantages and disadvantages of being a property owner. The big plus in renting is that you are free to change your mind about your "ideal" retirement location whenever you choose. If you discover that the summers are a bit too hot, or the winters too cold, you simply make a move without being encumbered with a mortgage or resale problem.

## HEALTH AND RETIREMENT

The commonly told tale of elderly people dropping dead when they retire has become a part of American folklore. We've all heard of someone who, after 40 years on the job, retires, then keels over with a myocardial infarction a couple of months later. In fact, a study back around 1980 clearly showed a correlation between newly retired people and occurrence of heart attacks. But the study failed to take into consideration that 25 percent of all retirements are because of bad health in the first place. If you take any group of people with a quarter of them already on their last legs, and measure it against a healthy group of people, it would be astounding if the sick group didn't have more heart attacks. Then, in 1985, another study was conducted in which only healthy workers taking retirement were measured against those still working. This study showed that there was no significant difference between the groups insofar as the incidence of heart attacks.

People are living longer today. One reason for this is the fairly recent recognition that regular exercise is a must to keep in shape. A doctor friend of mine, a heart specialist, came originally from Greece. When he arrived here about 30 years ago, he was puzzled by the high number of cardiac problems among the American population. It was much, much higher than in his native land. The doctor became convinced that the generally sedentary customs of the U.S. population accounted for this high rate of heart disease. "In Greece, everybody walked instead of driving an auto for every little errand," he explained. "They got plenty of exercise. But many of my colleagues scoffed at me, maintaining that *diet* was the culprit in this country."

Then, after a few years, a physical fitness trend gained momentum and soon swept across the nation. A general awareness of the benefits of exercise began to grow. Jogging and bicycling became popular, as well as other forms of moderate exercise. At the same time, heart failure rates began dropping, until they had declined about 20 percent, particularly among people who exercise regularly. "Think of that," the doctor said to me with a smile. "If that keeps up, heart doctors will be out of business." But the interesting thing is that in Greece, with a gradual rising of the standard of living, more and more people are driving or taking taxis instead of walking. "Now, their rate of heart disease is approaching ours," the doctor said with a satisfied nod of his head. "I was right all along; exercise was the key."

You don't need a book on retirement to remind you of the benefits of regular exercise, but it is worthwhile mentioning that some climates lend themselves better to exercise programs than others. When half the year is too cold to go outside, and the other half too hot, a retiree can find himself spending his days inside in front of the TV instead of jogging, walking or gardening. "It's too cold outside," they complain, "or it's too hot." I recall a few years ago when my wife and I had to spend part of a year in Ann Arbor, Michigan. During the winter, all our friends spent their free time indoors, watching televised football games. There was nothing to do outside, unless it was shoveling snow or trying to get the car started. Then, when spring came along, I looked forward to getting out in the open air and enjoying the gorgeous sunny days. To my dismay, our friends refused to leave their TV screens--after all, now it was baseball season!

I would be very interested in seeing a study done that compared healthy people who retire from a freezing winter climate to a mild one, to those healthy people who retire at home and spend the winter indoors. My guess would be that the ones who elect to move will live longer. That is, unless the retirees have become so addicted to TV that they spend their time on the sofa in their new location just as they did before.

When looking at your alternatives, the idea of a new life-style which encompasses exercise should be one of your top considerations. You should consider this even if you choose to stay in your home community.

## ALTERNATIVES

What are your choices? First of all, you can stay right where you are living right now, or move to another location in your area. As I pointed out earlier, 75 percent of the people stay put. Another choice is to move away entirely, to that beach town you've always loved, or to a lakefront cottage with a boat dock and fishing pier. A third choice is a combination of living where you are now for the most pleasant parts of the year, and selecting a distant winter or summer location in which to enjoy comfortable temperatures and a new set of friends for part of the year. The possibilities are unlimited and exciting.

We will look at many different retirement possibilities in this book. Our emphasis will be on pleasant, dignified living, in a moderate to warm climate, where a couple could, if necessary, get by on Social Security as a minimum expenditure. This may come as a surprise, but it can be done. Since the average Social Security payment for a retired couple is $833 a month, that means an income of over $10,000 a year. This effectively cuts off many communities from our study, since in some localities, just your rent could easily top $10,000 a year. Unless there is something very special about that place, it probably isn't worth it.

Of course, in any town, you can spend just as much as you can afford, and more, but I believe it's important to know that you *can* manage on a budget if necessary. Some places described will be relatively expensive, but worth considering if the reader can afford it. Even if you can't afford to live there, it's worthwhile knowing about them, in case you wish to settle within easy visiting distance. You might even want to rearrange your budget to permit living there.

When thinking about your retirement choices, it's well to examine your reasons for wanting to move. The retirees who responded to our survey gave the following reasons: Getting away from weather extremes; finding a more affordable place to live; moving closer to a son, daughter or other family members; going somewhere where they can engage in a hobby or pastime, such as fishing, hunting, gardening, swimming, racetracks, etc. Many stated a desire to make a new life, with new friends, a new start in life. By far, the question of mild weather and affordable living costs leads the list.

CHAPTER TWO
_____

*Planning for the Future*

Retirement time. It's coming for most of us, and we ought to be prepared to get the maximum from our "golden years." In the long run, retirement is just as pleasant and enjoyable as you make it. So making your plans and preparations as soon as you can makes a lot of good sense. But there's more to retirement planning than simply choosing a place to live. It's more complicated than that.

## CHOOSING YOUR RETIREMENT PARADISE

Let's assume that you've weighed all your pros and cons about moving away during your retirement, even if it's only for part of the year. We'll further assume that the pros tipped the scale on the side of moving. Your job now is to match your life-style with the ideal geographical location. That's not to say that you can't *change* your life-style. That in itself can be an exciting adventure. Certainly, if you're moving from a winter-bound climate to a beach setting, your mode of living can change in many ways--you will have more days in the year in which to exercise out of doors. There will be many pastimes available to you that aren't available at home. This is particularly true if you choose to live in an area where there are active senior citizens groups, where there are numerous organized activities and social events.

There can be pitfalls in making haphazard changes. You must examine your personal inventory of likes, dislikes, finances, abilities and handicaps when making a choice. For example: One couple I interviewed moved from their home in Milwaukee to buy a small farm in the Missouri Ozarks. The 22 acres, complete with house, barn, garden, pasture and woods, cost only $21,000. Financially, it was perfect, because after paying cash for the property, they still had over $100,000 in profit from the sale of their house in Milwaukee. Although Ozark winters are anything but balmy, they are mild compared to Milwaukee's, and the couple had always dreamed of leaving the city and becoming gentleman farmers.

Things turned out to be not so idyllic. The couple discovered that they were "outsiders" in the eyes of the natives. People were polite and tried to be neighborly, but both sides found it difficult to bridge the cultural gap. The new couple's accent sounded odd to the local people. Their interests were very different. The newcomers missed having good TV reception, a choice of movie theaters, supermarkets that stay open on Sundays and weekend bridge parties. The social life in the nearby town consisted of two taverns and an active Baptist church. Nobody in town knew how to play bridge and the couple weren't Baptists. When I interviewed them, the farm was up for sale, and they were thinking about moving to Hot Springs, Arkansas, where there are active senior citizens groups, and plenty of people with similar interests in life, including bridge games.

Another example of good planning going awry: A friend of mine, when he retired, decided he had enough of the fierce winters in Chicago. He looked around the country, then decided to move to California. My friend was nationally known and respected in his field; people from all over would come to him to ask his opinion, seek his advice or simply spend a pleasant evening with him and his wife. In California, they selected a large house on a redwood-shaded hillside in the mountains near Los Gatos. He added a guest cottage and built a charming building to display his extensive library. The setting was beautiful, no more ice and snow, a perfect place for the couple to entertain their friends and visitors.

They were all set up to receive guests, but nobody came. Whereas people from Cleveland or Omaha might have thought nothing of traveling to Chicago to visit my friend--particularly if business carried them there anyway--making a trip to California was something they thought about once in a blue moon. Instead of having judges, authors, political activists and nationally-known figures as house guests, even their children grudgingly made the trip out West, solely because of the Christmas holidays. Because their house was hard to find, tucked away in the hills, the new friends they made in California rarely bothered to drive up to see them. Had they rented for a year, they would have saved themselves a lot of loneliness and frustration. Had they not been the kind of people who need the stimulation of important visitors, they might have been happy to make friends with their nice, but ordinary, neighbors.

A final example of short-range planning is the couple from Cleveland who chose southern Oregon as their retirement base. Both 62 and in great physical condition, they saw no reason why they couldn't fulfill their lifelong dream by buying a few acres about 15 minutes' drive from Grants Pass. They had always wanted a place with some cows, chickens and a garden. They knew they could grow most of their food, keep expenses down and have a great time in the process. At first it worked out perfectly, although they discovered that cows needed more than a couple of acres to grow fat on. Forget the cows. They grew so much food the first year that they tried to give it away to their neighbors. Since their neighbors also had garden produce to give away, they resolved to cut back on the garden the next year. Edna had always been a city girl, and had never bothered to learn how to drive. Her husband's chauffeuring had always done just fine, so the lack of bus service in rural Oregon didn't bother them.

Things went along smoothly for a few years, until Larry suffered a heart attack and died. Suddenly Edna found herself stuck out in the country with no way to get into town for groceries or medicines. They had made few friends around the sparsely settled countryside; she had no one to depend on for help. Totally unprepared for this turn of events, she had to sacrifice the farm in order to return to Cleveland. There she became a burden on her children. Had she learned how to drive and to become independent, and had she and her husband made a circle of friends and contacts among other retirees, the story would have ended much differently.

## MAKING A SURVEY

All of the above problems could have been avoided had the couples done a careful survey of their new localities. Of utmost importance is matching a town or city with your personality. There is no one perfect place for retirement that suits everyone. Selecting the ideal location is a highly subjective, personal decision. Admittedly, I am biased *toward* warm climates. This bias comes not only from my love of sunshine and warm weather, and my hatred for freezing weather, but also from my conviction that having to stay indoors for long winter months contributes to a sedentary life-style that avoids outdoor activities and essential exercise. This is clearly not a healthful situation. Perhaps equally tragic is the loss of weeks and months of your remaining life as you huddle in front of a television set, dulling your brain and your senses with intellectual garbage.

Another bias I have is toward places where there are fulfilling things to do and interesting people to cultivate as friends. During my glorious days as an itinerant newspaper printer, I worked on 40 daily newspapers and more than my share of small-town weeklies. Highlights of my travels were the people I met along the way and the fun things I found to do in each town. If I didn't like a place, I quickly moved on to a better town. I worked in big cities and in small towns. I enjoyed both.

There is a stereotype of small towns as being super-friendly places. Generally, this is true--that is, people often nod at strangers with a "good morning," when they pass them on the street, and small-town folks are famous for coming to a neighbor's assistance when help is needed. But this doesn't necessarily mean the smaller the town the friendlier the people. There's a point where a town can be so small that people who weren't born there will forever be considered outsiders, even intruders. Unless you are a hermit by nature, trying to settle into a tiny, closed community can be quite uncomfortable.

Let me share with you a personal experience. I once accepted a position on a small-town weekly newspaper in a beautiful, northern California town, a mountainous fisherman's paradise. I moved there with my family. It was a great job: Good pay, excellent working conditions and prestigious enough (I thought) that making close friends would be relatively easy. Wrong. This was a railroad town, with most people dependent on the Southern Pacific for a livelihood, one way or another. It turned out that unless a person was born in the town, or had a position with the railroad, he would be an outsider no matter how long he lived there. Yes, people smiled and nodded when we passed on the street. But no one ever invited us to their homes, to their card parties or to any other social activities. Even our children were considered outsiders at school since they hadn't started out in kindergarten with the rest of the in-crowd.

Once I grew tired of trout fishing (my wife hated fishing), there was nothing left to do. Statistics had painted a lovely picture of this town. Living costs were low, wages sufficient; climate, recreation and health care scored statistically perfect. But living there turned out to be boring.

Therefore, my third bias is against statistics. If you choose a retirement location on the basis of statistics, you usually end up with small, rural towns where the quality of life may be much different from what you might wish for. Just because you can buy a house for under $30,000 doesn't mean you will be happy living there.

A case in point is the list of most desirable retirement locations selected by a popular retirement handbook. The book is packed with useful statistical information on over 100 potential retirement locations. Using these statistics, the authors ranked the locations from best to worst. Included in the towns surveyed were such unlikely places as Hamilton-Bitteroot Valley, Montana; Brattleboro, Vermont; and Penobscot Bay, Maine. (Unlikely for me, because of my bias against sub-zero weather.)

Listed below are the top 15 places for retirement in the United States, according to the aforementioned book, with research based on statistics:

1. Brevard, N.C.                        (pop. 5,323)
2. Asheville, N.C.                       (pop. 59,000)
3. Clarkesville-Mount Airy, Ga.         (pop. 2,028)
4. Crossville, Tenn.                     (pop. 6,394)
5. Lexington-Fayette, Ken.              (pop. 210,000)
6. Las Cruces, N.Mex.                    (pop. 52,500)
7. Harrison, Ark.                        (pop. 9,567)
8. Roswell, N.Mex.                       (pop. 47,000)
9. Camden-Penobscot Bay, Maine          (pop. 4,584)
10. Cookeville, Tenn.                    (pop. 21,000)
11. Bar Harbor, Maine                    (pop. 4,124)
12. State College, Penn.                 (pop. 34,600)
13. Bull Shoals, Ark.                    (pop. 1,518)
14. Biloxi-Gulfport, Miss.             (pop. 169,000)
15. Hot Springs, Ark.                    (pop. 38,100)

*Statistically* these places come out on top because of a combination of factors: Climate, housing costs, economics, personal safety, health care and recreational-cultural assets. Yet, I see only three or four towns of these top 15 that come close to fitting my personal notions of retirement edens. How about you? What happened to California? Florida? Texas? South Carolina? Arizona? Statistically, if the top place to retire in the whole United States is *Brevard, N.C.*, why are there only 5,323 people living there?

Look at some of the other places that come out on top statistically in the retirement sweepstakes: Bull Shoals, Arkansas (pop.

1,518); Harrison, Arkansas (9,567); Clarkesville, Georgia (1,348); Mount Airy, Georgia (670); Bar Harbor, Maine (4,124); Penobscot, Maine (1,104); or Crossville, Tennessee, (6,394). Perhaps it's just my warped sense of humor--but don't you sense something funny at the thought of packing up your furniture, winter clothes and snow shovels to move to the metropolis of Penobscot, Maine--trying to squeeze into that already crowded town of more than 1,100 people? Or to third-ranked Mount Airy, Georgia--where almost 700 inhabitants are probably braced with gritted teeth against the onslaught of potential retirees?

Look over the above list, and ask yourself, "Would I fit in?" If you originally come from a small town--especially a small southern town--maybe you would. But if you are a city person you might have a difficult time adjusting to small-town life. Few or no supermarkets, poor TV reception, narrow and stifled political situations. I happen to like eating out at least once a week. What kind of gourmet restaurants can I expect to find in a town of fewer than 1,500 people? *Any* restaurants at all?

Ask yourself: "Do I like freezing weather and shoveling snow?" Except for Gulfport-Biloxi, the top 15 recommendations listed as statistically best all require hefting a snow shovel at least part of the winter. Now, some people may love snow, ice, slush and other frozen things. As for myself, I've scraped all the ice from my windshield I intend to. If I already lived in snow country, and wanted to move away, I certainly wouldn't waste a great deal of time investigating Kalispell, Montana, or Winnipesaukee, New Hampshire as destinations. Same for Barneagat Bay, New Jersey. It's tough enough to pronounce or spell them, much less face winters there.

The point is: Cheap living isn't necessarily quality living. A person who is tied to a limited budget can be even more miserable in an unpleasant place, whereas a person with unlimited funds can probably find happiness wherever he goes, even in Penobscot, Maine. The trick is to match your life-style with your budget and find someplace where you will be happy--not look for the cheapest place in the country. Don't do it by statistics; do as I did, go there and look it over in person!

## MY RETIREMENT SELECTIONS

Below, I present my own list of 15 good retirement locations. They aren't ranked from best to worst. (I see no point in listing the worst places to retire.) They aren't even ranked at all other than alphabetically. They are simply 15 localities where I am convinced that I could make a pleasant, interesting life for myself and my spouse. These happen to fit our particular needs and desires. Your needs can and probably will be different, so your list will likely be much different.

| | |
|---|---|
| Aiken, South Carolina | (pop. 35,000) |
| Albuquerque, New Mexico | (pop. 362,000) |
| Baton Rouge, Louisiana | (pop. 250,000) |
| Clarksville, Tennessee | (pop. 58,200) |
| Ft. Myers, Florida | (pop. 39,700) |
| Grants Pass, Oregon | (pop. 17,000) |
| Hot Springs, Arkansas | (pop. 38,100) |
| McAllen, Texas | (pop. 79,000) |
| Ojai, California | (pop. 6,816) |
| Orlando, Florida | (pop. 145,000) |
| Paradise, California | (pop. 32,000) |
| Reno, Nevada | (pop. 108,000) |
| San Diego, California | (pop. 1,000,000) |
| Tucson, Arizona | (pop. 382,000) |

There are many, many more fine retirement towns in the United States, so many that it was hard to make a list of my favorite 15 places. Very difficult. Each of the towns featured in this book held certain attractions to me, and were places where I felt that others might enjoy, as well. But notice that most of the 15 towns listed have a few things in common: Mild climates, accessibility to recreation, adequate health care and enough population to offer good shopping, restaurants and varied social opportunities.

## SOCIAL LIFE AFTER RETIREMENT

Assuming that you are a normal, non-misanthropic individual, chances are that you enjoy friends and social activities. Therefore, it's essential that you choose a community where you can "fit in" without much trouble. A great first step is to investigate senior citizens services and organizations. Some communities have excellent set-ups for senior citizens, while others have almost none. Unless you've determined that you are definitely the independent type, you will need a support group--maybe not today or in the next few years, but eventually.

An important program, available in the more active retirement areas, is R.S.V.P. (Retired Senior Volunteer Program). There is no finer way to introduce yourself to your new community than by joining R.S.V.P. You not only get to meet other active people and provide valuable public service, but you also find out firsthand what services will be available for you when *you* begin to slow down. The typical R.S.V.P. group can provide you with volunteer opportunities in many areas: Nursing homes, libraries, schools, city and county government, hospitals and important community service organizations like the Red Cross, YMCA, Humane Society, United Way, museums, Meals on Wheels and almost any other kind of service you can think of.

There are programs for visiting house-bound or bedridden seniors, taking them shopping or shopping for them. Volunteers set up food banks to make sure no one goes hungry, and phone banks, where friendly voices answer telephones to provide information, assistance and reassurance programs for the housebound elderly. These things are crucial to making it possible for people to remain at home instead of having to enter a nursing home. By helping others, you have the opportunity of doing something very worthwhile and satisfying and, someday in the distant future, you will know how to get help for yourself. Maybe you have never been the "do-gooder" type. Well, look at it this way: By volunteering, you are helping yourself in a very selfish way, by learning about the community and making friends in the process.

One R.S.V.P. program that I investigated in Grants Pass, Oregon, has over 500 volunteers serving in more than 80 agencies. This is a lot of people, when you consider that Grants Pass only has about 17,000 population. An important side effect to all this activism by senior citizens is an awareness of themselves as a group, and an activism in local politics. It turns out that over 20 percent of the population of the county in the Grants Pass area is retired. And it also turns out that older citizens tend to vote more often than the younger set. By voting their interests as a bloc, they can make their voice known in local politics. If they wanted to, they could probably control the local government. When you have that many voters expressing their opinion at the polls, the city and county politicians sit up and take notice.

Some states and communities have other special service organizations that can be very important to you somewhere down the line. An example of this is Linkage, a program of the California Department of Aging, which is administered by the local Senior Citizens

Councils. This program, largely staffed by volunteers, is aimed at helping those who have special needs, particularly those whose health or other problems make it difficult for them to remain at home. Volunteers deliver meals and home medical equipment, do home safety repairs, provide homemaker services, legal services and transportation. In addition they provide an invaluable respite care program: For those who are confined to bed with a family member to care for them, the Linkage program sends someone to care for the disabled person while the caring family member gets a break, a chance to get away for a few hours.

Just how good these programs are depends on the community, and how well organized the senior citizens are. For this reason it's important to investigate *all* aspects of the community before making a decision to move there permanently.

Another entry point into the local scene is membership in one of the traditional fraternal or service clubs. Almost every town has organizations like Kiwanis, Elks, Moose and AARP chapters. AARP (American Association of Retired People) often has sub-chapters of special interest groups, such as retired educators clubs. You might consider joining one of these organizations *before* retirement, so you can immediately enter a support group the day you walk into town. Being a member of the Elks or VFW gives you opportunities for social activities, dances, social programs and meeting new people.

Getting involved makes it possible to check out things for your compatibility. You'll see how you are going to "fit in" with your new neighbors and with the structure of the new town. This is particularly important for those leaving behind a large support group of friends and work associates. Even for those with a limited circle of friends, the loss of pals and neighbors could be rather traumatic. In any event, here is an opportunity to start over, to begin from scratch, and perhaps for the first time in your life, to pick and *choose* your new friends, instead of simply accepting them from those with whom you work.

CHAPTER THREE

# *Weather and Crime Climates*

Everyone seems to have different ideas of what ideal weather means. Some people love hot weather, even humid, muggy weather, and they hate cold. Others don't mind a little coolness, but cannot tolerate heat. The exciting aspect of retiring is that, for the first time in your life, work doesn't dictate where you live--you can *choose* your ideal climate. Springtime in Ohio is fantastic, and fall in Connecticut is gorgeous. Winters in Palm Springs or Palm Beach can be as perfect as you can expect, unless you decide on Acapulco, Cancun or somewhere else in the tropics. (That's not as crazy as it sounds, as you shall see later on.) You can choose any climate you wish, or even make a combination choice.

Personally, I like a combination living arrangement. I choose to spend my summers in the cooler parts of the United States, then head as far south as I can afford for the winter. I used to go to Mexico or Costa Rica for the winter, to take advantage of the warm weather and the low cost of living. But lately I've been wintering in Buenos Aires or Montevideo and then summering at my home in Northern California. Do you have to be rich to do this? Of course not. This kind of retirement living *is* affordable--as you will see later on in the book. But this life-style isn't everyone's "cup of tea." Your requirements for choosing a retirement haven will probably be far different from mine.

In doing research on this book, I placed an emphasis on areas where the winter climate isn't so severe that heating bills gobble up more money than food bills, and also areas where retirees can live comfortably on a limited budget. This means that many parts of the country are eliminated from this book. This isn't to say that Minnesota, Maine or Manitoba aren't great places to live, particularly in spring, summer and fall, but they are also great places to be *from* when the temperature hits double-figures below zero. For what it costs to heat a house in North Dakota for a winter, you could rent a beach cottage on a sandy Caribbean beach and have enough left over to stock the refrigerator with coconut-rum coolers.

However, no matter how selectively you choose, almost every climate has some kind of drawback. Places which are warm in the winter tend to be hot in the summer. And, pleasant summers often mean cooler winters. So, for year around living in one place, you will necessarily need to make some compromises. Studying the weather charts in the back of this book will help.

## AFFORDABLE RETIREMENT

Some places are eliminated from the book because they are too expensive. Of course, some costs are pretty much the same wherever you go. Grocery store prices, for example, vary little, because most items are nationally distributed and priced. Local produce and meats may be lower in some localities, but that's about all. The same is true of clothing, gasoline, appliances and other items that are sold nationally. You have no control over these expenses. But where prices do vary, and where you do have some choice, is in *rent, utilities* and *services*. Together, these items can make the cost of living either affordable or send it out of sight.

In the town where I like to spend my summers, near San Francisco, the rent for a nice, two-bedroom apartment starts at $950 a month. You might find something cheaper, but you wouldn't want to park your car on the street overnight in that neighborhood. On the other hand, I know a couple who live in a really nice apartment in El Paso, Texas, for only $250 a month compared to my $950. That leaves them with $700 a month left over to buy food and other expenses. Because wages are low there, they can afford a cleaning woman to come in once a week. Their essential living expenses are covered for what *rent alone* might cost elsewhere!

The cost of services is almost totally dependent upon wages. In the San Francisco Bay area, for example, a cleaning woman can demand $10 to $12 an hour; an automobile mechanic, $24 an hour; a roof repairer, $17 an hour; and a plumber, $37 an hour. Yet a few hours' drive away--in Paradise, Calif.--wages like this are unheard of. I own a small house there that needed a new roof last summer. The roofer I hired worked like a madman for $7 an hour. He apologized for charging so much; he knew that the two young men who were working on the yard were only getting $4 an hour. As you might suspect, the cost of maintaining or repairing your automobile will be substantially lower in a place like that. Low wages for restaurant help keep the price of meals down. A restaurant dinner which might come to $18.50 in San Francisco or New York can cost half that or less in a low-cost area.

## SAMPLE BUDGET

In researching this book, I sent questionnaires to retired couples, to local retiree organizations and to chambers of commerce, asking, in part, how much money they (or the people they know) spend each month for various items. This helped to discern the cost of living in a town much more accurately, I believe, than figures from the U.S. Department of Labor's Price Index. Average figures for the whole community do not reflect the special circumstances of retirement.

One thing became apparent quite early in the survey: The cost of living varies widely between individuals. Some couples reported they spend as little as $150 a month for food, others over $300. One couple reported rent as low as $50 a month (for a mobile home park), another paid over $1,000 a month. Some, those living full-time in RVs, paid almost nothing in rent--they know where to live for free.

It's an impossibility to come up with an ideal budget for everyone. But to get an idea of how a budget could change with retirement, I asked a couple living in Harbor, Ore., to make a comparison between their present living costs and those before retirement. Previously, they lived in Sacramento, Calif. He had worked as bank employee, she as a sales clerk. They rented out their house for a small positive cash flow and moved to Harbor where they bought a ten- wide mobile home with an expansion living room for $9,500. They sold one of their automobiles. On page 38 is a comparison of their monthly expenses.

| at home | | in retirement | |
|---|---|---|---|
| FOOD | $200 | FOOD | $200 |
| RENT (house payment) | 650 | RENT | 105 |
| UTILITIES | 125 | UTILITIES (incl in rent) | |
| AUTO PAYMENT | 175 | AUTO PAYMENT (car paid) | |
| INSURANCE (2 cars) | 66 | INSURANCE (1 car) | 33 |
| GASOLINE | 60 | GASOLINE | 20 |
| DRY CLEANING | 35 | DRY CLEANING | 10 |

TOTAL BASIC EXPENSES......$1,311    RETIREMENT EXP.. $368

There are other expenditures, of course, but these they consider their basic ones. However, there are other savings in retirement, such as: they don't eat out as often, don't need to buy as many new clothes, and Sue doesn't spend nearly as much in beauty shops. On the other hand, there are added expenses for travel and hobbies that they didn't have before. "We have a boat now," Kenneth said. "Between that and my fishing gear, I manage to spend a few bucks." He added that Sue is into ceramics and tole painting. "She spends her money that way. But we can afford it, so we never complain." Eventually, they'll have to buy a new car, and they haven't figured that into their budget.

"Our biggest savings are on housing and utilities," Sue pointed out. "Here we don't need an air conditioner. Things like sewer, garbage, water and electricity are included in our rent. Instead of paying property tax, we just pay for a license plate every year, which costs about the same as our automobile plates."

## MATCHING YOUR INTERESTS

The example of the bridge-playing couple from Milwaukee (Chapter 2) who moved to a farm in the Ozarks illustrates part of the problem. You and your spouse need to examine your hobbies, interests and the kinds of interests that you might like to develop. Moving to Montana because the husband loves to hunt grizzlies is sure to create tensions if the wife's idea of retirement fun is collecting seashells and suntans. This retirement business isn't one person's retirement; if you are married, the retirement is as much hers or his as it is yours.

You also need to examine your social needs. Do you make friends easily? If so, you will have a wider latitude of places to move. If you fit into new situations easily, you could have a lot of fun making friends in localities where others would feel lonely. Of course, if you're the kind of people who don't need much social contact, then you could very well enjoy living in social isolation, for example, as the only "Yankee" in a "Deep South" community.

But most people need friends and acquaintances for social contact. Many find that the social atmosphere is best where there are many other retirees living. In these settings, typically, you will find valuable services provided by the community, and, there will be scads of organized activities with people with similar interests. Ideally, though, you will try to make friends with people of all ages, and with varying interests, otherwise you could end up in a stagnant social situation.

## A "GOOD" RETIREMENT SPOT

If you have decided that you would like to change locations, and if you are tired of cleaning snow off sidewalks, and if you can get by without having your kids and grandkids clinging onto you, or you onto them--then let's start thinking about alternatives.

The criteria for good retirement places in this book are:
1. Affordable places (preferably, where Social Security can cover essentials)
2. A mild winter climate (where winter heating costs are minimal)
3. Places where crime is at a minimum and where the retiree can feel secure
4. Places where there are other retirees and active retiree organizations
5. Places where your life can be one of quality and dignity.

Some of the above criteria will, of course, carry more importance for some people. If you have a higher than average retirement income, your range of choices will be wider, and perhaps the concern about utility bills or rents won't be as significant. But the other criteria will certainly interest you. Furthermore, should the ideal location be one where a retiree can get by on a minimum budget, then someone with a generous budget will do that much better.

## COST OF LIVING

The U.S. Government is very much interested in the cost of living. It spends a lot of time and money collecting information on how much it costs to live in various communities. The U.S. Department of Labor publishes a monthly statistical survey that is used by businesses and labor organizations to figure salaries and variable price structures. A lot of data in this section comes from this report.

Government researchers have determined that the average family spends about 33 percent of its income for housing and about 20 percent on food. You might measure these against your income, and see how close they come. Note that when we talk about income, we mean *after* taxes, what you have left after everyone has had a bite at the old paycheck. Another thing to keep in mind is that when I claim that a person can live in a certain area for a certain amount of money, I am referring to *basic, essential costs.* That is, housing, food, transportation and normal necessities of life. What you spend on fancy automobiles, electronic gadgets, Caribbean cruises, luxury clothing and things like that is impossible to predict.

Rand McNally's *Places Rated Almanac* places emphasis on the cost of living and economic outlook for various cities. While this is quite helpful for someone thinking of going someplace else to work for a living, this doesn't necessarily apply to someone wanting to *retire.* In their ratings, the book dwells on items like job growth, income growth and factors affecting employment possibilities. So, a city with reasonable rents and a nice climate, but with slow prospects for jobs, could rank way below a city where rents are sky high with salaries to match.

For this reason, Eugene, Oregon (a great town for retirement) ranks dead last in Rand McNally's economic study, yet cities like Midland, Texas, and Atlantic City, New Jersey, make the top 10! Midland, because of the oil boom there, and Atlantic City because of the gambling casinos. I personally wouldn't live in either place, except at gunpoint. (Since the book rated Atlantic City the fifth worst in terms of crime, I would imagine that gunpoint isn't too great an exaggeration.)

Yet, I highly recommend Eugene, Oregon, as a place for retirement. The very fact that economic conditions *aren't* booming is one of the desirable things about Eugene. Housing isn't out of sight, prices are reasonable and chances are it's going to stay that way.

## HOUSING EXPENSES

By far, the biggest variable in retirement planning is housing. A house that sells for $350,000 in Litchfield, Conn., might go for $65,000 in Eugene, Ore. An apartment renting for $1,000 a month in Cleveland can be had for less than $300 in Corpus Christi, Texas. If you are thinking of cutting the costs of retirement, housing is probably the first place to look. You might argue, "But, my house payments are low and my house is almost paid for. I couldn't possibly cut housing costs!" You may be right, but just for the fun of it, take out your calculator and let's do some figuring.

First, calculate how much equity you have in your house; how much cash you could walk away with if you sold out. Remember, you probably would qualify for the one-time $125,000 tax exemption, so your taxes may be minimal, or none, on your profit. Next, figure how much monthly income your equity would bring you if you invested it in quality utility stocks or non-taxable municipal bonds. This is your *potential equity income*. To this amount, add the cost of insurance, taxes, mortgage interest and average maintenance expenses. This then, is the true cost of living in your "low-cost" home. After all, the capital you have sitting in your equity is just that, *capital*, and you have to account for the income your capital is losing by not being invested elsewhere.

I know a couple who did these calculations and were astonished to learn that the *potential equity income* would not only pay the rent on another house, but would cover their food, clothing and transportation bills, with some left over for savings, to boot. They bought the house 30 years ago for a song, and at today's absurdly high prices, they could finance their retirement from the sale of their house, totally, without touching their Social Security or company pension money!

Another alternative for the homeowner: Figure out how much you could rent your house for. Sometimes the amount of rent you receive would pay for a nice retirement place, plus something left over for expenses. This isn't a bad idea anyway, because it gives you a chance to see just how you like retirement in a particular location without having to burn any bridges in the process.

## UTILITY BILLS

You have little control over many expenses. Food bills, clothing, and appliances, for example, will pretty much be the same no matter where you live. Moving away won't cut those substantially. But there's one item in your budget which can be cut dramatically: Heating and cooling your home. Some friends of mine who live in suburban St. Louis spend up to $250 a month in the wintertime for heat, and nearly $200 in the summer for air conditioning. Their place is small and well insulated, or the costs would go even higher. If you live in ice-and-snow country, you don't need to be reminded about utility bills. On the other hand, I have friends who live in a frame beach cottage in Santa Cruz, California; their monthly utility bills never top $35, winter or summer. It almost never freezes there, and summer evenings are so cool they use an electric blanket year-round.

Now, take your utility bills and add them to your rent or to your house payment (plus your *potential equity income*), and you now have a figure that shows just how much it costs to live in your home. Unless you already live in one of the areas this book recommends, you may find that you could live somewhere else and pay the rent and utilities, buy groceries and eat out a couple of times a week on the same amount of money.

"So I save money on heating," you say. "How about air conditioning in the summer? Wouldn't it be a wash?" You do have a point there, particularly if you live in a muggy, high-humidity place like Houston. But most of us who are approaching retirement age can remember the old days when air-conditioning was something you found only in movie theaters and classy department stores. We survived then, and I don't particularly recall any great hardship.

Because I spend my summers in parts of California where summer temperatures rarely require air conditioning, I've become accustomed to going without it on all but the few days when it's necessary. I rarely use my automobile's air conditioner because it's nicer to roll down the windows and enjoy a warm breeze. So it always comes as a surprise when I visit friends in the Midwest or the South to see how they insist on living in a rigidly controlled, 72-degree climate in the winter and even cooler, down to 68 degrees, in the summer. With the introduction of affordable air conditioning, most folks have come to depend on it. They never open their windows, winter or summer; the heating-cooling system has to work around the clock. I have friends in Tennessee who keep their house so cool in the summer that I wear a sweater when I'm visiting them. They think I'm strange when I prefer to sleep outside on the deck where I can enjoy fresh, natural air instead of breathing something that's been mechanically treated, re-conditioned and chilled.

There are places, of course, where an air conditioner is a must to make life easier on those sweltering days of summer. But, there are also places in this world where air conditioning is *not* mandatory. This is particularly true in areas of low humidity. Even in hot, desert climates, an inexpensive "swamp cooler" does the trick for most people. I personally prefer its refreshing, breezy feeling to refrigerated and recirculated air.

In the final analysis, air conditioning costs are something you can control, but heating costs are beyond your control. When the temperature outside drops to below zero, you had better have a good supply of fuel oil on hand. It isn't a matter of being uncomfortable, it's a matter of life or death. But when the thermometer nudges past 80 degrees, maybe that's the time to enjoy a cool drink under the shade tree, or a refreshing plunge in the swimming pool.

## WHAT TO LOOK FOR IN A CLIMATE

I've always found it interesting that winters in Kennewick, Wash., are so profoundly different from those in Ann Arbor, Mich. Kennewick is much farther north, and one would think that winters would be more severe, yet that's not true at all. For example, in the winter, temperatures in eastern Washington can drop to close to zero at night, but the moment the sun comes out, things begin to warm up. By noon, it's usually shirt-sleeve weather. Yet, in Ann Arbor, it can be 12 below zero at the coldest part of the night, and despite a beautiful, sunshine-drenched day, it can stay at 12 below, all day long!

Although being farther north has its effect on climate, there are other things that enter into the weather picture. Michigan's problem is a combination of snow reflecting away the sun's heat, humidity and being in the heart of the continental mass, where prevailing winds bring only more cold from the high plains and lakes to the west.

Relative humidity, elevation, wind patterns and nearness to the ocean all play an important part in determining the climate. It's worthwhile to consider all these when making your retirement choice. Let's take humidity. If you've ever made a trip cross-country, you've noticed the differences in humidity. When you cross the Rocky Mountains, going west, you find that you are in a very dry climate.

Relative humidity is the amount of moisture air carries compared to the maximum it can carry without becoming rain. High or low relative humidity is important in many ways. Obviously, if you suffer from arthritis or some condition which is aggravated by humidity, you will be looking for a warm, dry area. But relative humidity has a great deal to do with temperatures and with how you perceive temperatures.

For example: When the humidity increases, your body feels the cold more, and the heat more as the temperature rises or falls. Because moisture tends to draw heat and retain heat, you find that winter temperatures around the Great Lakes feel much colder than a similar temperature in Colorado. Then, in the summer, because your body can't cool itself as well in damp air, you feel the heat much more. It's the old proverb: It ain't the heat, it's the humidity.

Take a look at the humidity information presented on the next page. This chart illustrates the dramatic difference that a little humidity can make in your life. Of course, these perceived temperatures are entirely relative. There is no accurate way to measure how something *feels*. But there is no question that warm air, holding more moisture, gives the feeling of higher temperatures. For example, a 90-degree air temperature can make the body perceive the temperature as much higher, or much lower, depending on the amount of moisture in the air. (Other weather charts are in the Appendix.)

At 15 percent humidity, typical of many western desert environments, a 90-degree day will be perceived as 86 degrees in relative comfort. But a 75 percent reading, common in many parts of the East, will be perceived as 109 degrees. In other words, your body will think that it's over 20 degrees hotter in more humid climates.

There are a couple of reasons for this. One is that the body's cooling system is based on evaporation from the skin, and the higher the humidity, the less efficiently the body can give off moisture. The second reason is that damp air holds heat longer. This is the reason that dry desert climates can be hot during the daytime, but cool off rapidly the moment the sun goes down. Furthermore, cool air which is dryer appears to be warmer than the same temperature in a damp climate. A 45-degree evening in Reno, Nevada, can be quite pleasant with just a light sweater, whereas the same temperature in Florida can drive everyone indoors to turn up the thermostats. For this reason, it's important to consult the relative humidity when checking out temperature statistics for a given location. People who are used to damp climates shouldn't assume that places with high temperatures and low humidity are going to be insufferably hot, and neither should people from dry climates take it for granted that 90-degree days are going to make for perfect golf games.

Humidity can also have an effect on health. Too much is known to bother people with some kinds of rheumatism or arthritis,

ACTUAL TEMPERATURE

| RELATIVE HUMIDITY | 70 | 75 | 80 | 85 | 90 | 95 | 100 | 105 | 110 |
|---|---|---|---|---|---|---|---|---|---|
| 0 | 64 | 69 | 73 | 78 | 83 | 87 | 91 | 95 | 99 |
| 5 | 64 | 70 | 74 | 79 | 84 | 88 | 93 | 97 | 102 |
| 10 | 65 | 71 | 75 | 80 | 85 | 89 | 85 | 100 | 105 |
| 15 | 65 | 71 | 76 | 81 | 86 | 90 | 97 | 103 | 108 |
| 20 | 66 | 72 | 77 | 82 | 87 | 92 | 99 | 106 | 112 |
| 25 | 66 | 72 | 78 | 83 | 88 | 94 | 101 | 109 | 117 |
| 30 | 67 | 73 | 78 | 84 | 89 | 96 | 104 | 113 | 123 |
| 35 | 67 | 73 | 79 | 85 | 90 | 98 | 107 | 118 | 130 |
| 40 | 68 | 74 | 79 | 86 | 92 | 101 | 110 | 123 | 137 |
| 45 | 68 | 74 | 80 | 87 | 94 | 104 | 115 | 129 | 143 |
| 50 | 69 | 75 | 80 | 88 | 96 | 107 | 120 | 135 | 150 |
| 55 | 69 | 75 | 81 | 89 | 98 | 110 | 126 | 142 | 158 |
| 60 | 70 | 76 | 82 | 90 | 100 | 114 | 132 | 149 | |
| 65 | 70 | 76 | 83 | 91 | 102 | 119 | 138 | 156 | |
| 70 | 70 | 77 | 84 | 93 | 105 | 124 | 144 | | |
| 75 | 70 | 77 | 85 | 95 | 108 | 130 | 150 | | |
| 80 | 71 | 78 | 86 | 97 | 112 | 136 | 156 | | |
| 85 | 71 | 78 | 87 | 99 | 117 | 142 | | | |
| 90 | 71 | 79 | 88 | 102 | 122 | 148 | | | |
| 95 | 71 | 79 | 89 | 105 | 127 | | | | |
| 100 | 72 | 80 | 91 | 108 | 133 | | | | |

PERCEIVED TEMPERATURE

and can aggravate lung problems and people suffering from chronic bronchitis, things of that nature. Extremely dry climates can dry up the skin, cause nosebleeds and dry up the nasal passages uncomfortably. Some people have difficulty when switching between humid and dry climates; it can take them a few days or weeks to adjust.

A final item to keep in mind is that the prevailing westerly winds are almost always blowing across the Pacific, bringing tempering winds and steady temperature across the western part of the United States. This means that beach towns on the Pacific will tend to be cooler during the summertime, and warmer in the winter than beach towns on the Gulf Coast or the Atlantic. If you enjoy hot summers at the beach, the Pacific coast isn't for you. The ocean's influence is felt even as far away as the Sierra Nevada, where daytime temperatures in the winter can become springlike, with soft or melting snowpacks, while on the other side of the continent, noontime highs below freezing are common.

## ANY CRIME-FREE AREAS?

Sorry, that will never happen. As long as there are people walking around on the face of the earth, and as long as there are laws, there will be people breaking laws. A few years ago, an Oregon criminologist thought he'd found an exception to this rule. Statistics showed two places in the Portland area with no reported juvenile delinquency for several years. On investigation, the criminologist discovered that the first location was a "skid row" neighborhood where there were plenty of winos and lots of crime, but no juveniles. The second location was an affluent community where the residents didn't have a police department--they hired guards instead. So the conclusion of the study was: In order to have juvenile delinquency, you must have: 1. juveniles and, 2. police to arrest them and file arrest reports. Once again, statistics don't tell the whole story.

According to the FBI, there is a crime being committed every two seconds in the United States (Uniform Crime Reports, 1982, 1983). If my calculations are correct, that would mean over 15 million serious crimes a year. If all these crimes were spread out evenly among the population that means one in 15 people last year would have been either: murdered, raped, robbed, assaulted, burgled, swindled or had their car stolen. Over a period of five years one out of three people you know (including yourself) should have had one of these horrible things happened to them. I'm not going to argue with the FBI about their statistics, but that one seems out of line to me. Have you or one of your two neighbors been robbed at gunpoint or murdered in the last five years? Dealing with car salesmen doesn't count as a major crime, although perhaps it should. The reason for these discrepancies is that the same people get involved in crimes over and over, while others almost never. A lot depends on where you live and how you live.

Crime rates vary widely within a given community. It should be obvious that the urban centers of most large cities are also centers of crime statistics, but a few miles away, sometimes even a few blocks away, the picture is entirely different. But the high crime areas' statistics are averaged into the entire picture, making the entire city look as if it were dangerous. For example, in Manhattan, a walk through the Bowery is enough to scare the socks off me, while a stroll along Park Avenue can be rather pleasant and not at all anxiety provoking.

Many downtown areas are populated with "street people" and pitiful derelicts who have been given a handful of pills and discharged from mental health hospitals. Wandering about "skid rows" and loitering in the city center, these highly unstable, often violent, characters get into trouble over and over again. Each time they punch, victimize or kill one another, the statistics rise for the entire town, even though it's the same people. For some reason, these people rarely venture from the downtown area, leaving the suburbs and fringes of the city virtually crime-free in comparison.

Therefore, the suburbs and the smaller cities are the places where I prefer to live. I'm firmly convinced that the presence or absence of close-knit family groups has a lot to do with crime. In a locality where everyone knows everyone else and their families, people tend to behave more civilized. But of course, the major factor in the United States is the use of drugs. Addicts often need to steal to support their habits; some authorities estimate that up to 80 percent of crime today is drug related. When we were children, and when our families left the family possessions unguarded, we didn't have a drug problem.

## BEWARE OF STATISTICS!

The fallacy in using statistics while looking for low-crime areas is that the statistics don't tell everything, and sometimes they indicate things that aren't true. For example, East St. Louis--according to FBI statistics--ranks in the upper two-thirds of the country as far as safety is concerned. The FBI study ranks East St. Louis ahead of Monterey, Calif. (where I am living while writing this book). From these statistics it would appear that East St. Louis is a relatively safe place to live, while Monterey is dangerous.

Now, Monterey is a quiet, middle-class to upper-class area, where many people (including myself) don't bother to lock the doors at night. Robberies and rapes are so rare that they make front-page news when they do occur. On the other hand, East St. Louis is a total disaster area, a ghetto of the worst kind. Downtown businesses have long been abandoned and boarded over. Crime is so bad there that the police warn motorists not to stop for red lights if you can help it; a waiting car is an invitation to a thug to pull a gun on you. Still, using FBI statistics, East St. Louis looks like a calm, law-abiding town.

How can this be? For one thing, as the FBI itself points out, only about half of the crimes are ever reported, and in the case of places like East St. Louis, I suspect that not a quarter of the crimes are reported. Why bother to report an assault or a mugging, when the police can't do anything about it in the first place?

How could the Monterey area report a higher crime rate than East St. Louis? The answer lies in the statistics themselves. People in Monterey report all crimes, even those which in East St. Louis would seem irrelevant. A tricycle theft in Monterey is considered serious. Furthermore, Monterey police vigorously investigate *all* complaints and make arrests (no matter how minor the infraction), thus increasing the statistics.

Where crime statistics bulge radically in Monterey is in the area of larceny and theft. Monterey reports twice as many arrests for offenses such as shoplifting as does East St. Louis. That shouldn't be surprising, since shoplifting is a small problem in a city where most of the stores are boarded up and abandoned. One bright spot in East St. Louis crime statistics is a low rate of automobile theft. Car thieves much prefer to steal cars elsewhere, something without crumpled fenders and broken windshields.

## SOME CRIMES MORE SERIOUS THAN OTHERS

The most important question to you as a potential resident of a town is the *kind* of crimes in that community. Some crimes don't affect your life, even tangentially. Which crime presents more danger to you, shoplifting or street violence? Unless you are a storeowner or a shoplifter, you worry more about violence.

Many small city newspapers include a police report somewhere in their back pages, listing all of the actions of the police department and court cases. Reading these reports is a much better way than statistics for getting the essence of the kinds of crimes in a community. A small-town newspaper can list local crimes, but larger daily papers would have to devote several pages to the subject. Here are crime excerpts taken from the Apalachicola, Fla., daily paper. Names and case numbers have been removed to protect the suspects' rights.

The Apalachicola Police Department reported a day's activity as follows: A 25-year-old man was charged with not having an oyster transporting permit. A 36-year-old man was charged for possession of less than 20 grams of cannabis. Another man was arrested for being intoxicated. One man was charged with possessing untagged oysters; another with having unculled oysters. One desperado was apprehended without a decal on his boat, while three criminals were caught oystering on a closed day; another hunting from a roadway.

As you can see, Apalachicola police are kept quite busy coping with this crime wave. Fortunately, they manage to make an example of criminals who run around with unculled or untagged oysters, thus discouraging other lawbreakers from imitating this sorry example of lawlessness. Unfortunately, police in larger cities haven't been as successful in suppression of crime. In many big cities, serious crimes, such as murders, seldom make the front pages of the newspapers. Often they don't even make the inside pages, unless the murder is committed with exceptional creativity, or upon some well-known personality. We will admit, however, most big city police departments have kept illegal oystering to a minimum.

## IS CRIME RELATED TO POVERTY?

A common mistake is to equate crime with poverty alone. Many of you readers are old enough to remember the depression years. You remember when people were *really* poor; when hobos would knock on your back door to ask for handouts, when hungry people stood in breadlines, when a man might work for 25 cents an hour, just to put food on the table. If you remember this, you will probably also remember that there was very little crime.

Most people didn't lock their doors at night. I don't recall my parents *ever* locking our front door; if they had, I would have been in trouble, because I never had a key to the house! Poverty isn't the cause of crime, criminals are. The secret is to go someplace where the crime rate is low, regardless of the affluence of that place. Unfortunately, car salesmen can be found anywhere you go, so that kind of crime is difficult to avoid.

Well, then what *does* cause crime? Big cities, young people, drugs. Crime rates vary greatly even within the same state. Binghamton, N.Y., for example, is 20 times less criminal than New York City, at least according to the FBI reports. The murder rate there is 1.2 per 100,000 as compared to the Big Apple's 20.8 per 100,000. *Places Rated Almanac* ranks Binghamton as number 16 in crime safety. Maybe it's even safer, because many crimes aren't even reported in New York City.

CHAPTER FOUR
_____

## *Making Choices*

Your job now is to dig out the atlas and start poring over maps. You have a wide range of places from which to choose. The idea is to tailor your location to your needs. Do you suffer from arthritis or rheumatism? Hay fever? Then you need to think about a warm, dry climate. Do you and your spouse enjoy fishing or hunting? Skiing? Arts and crafts? There are plenty of places from which to choose.

Because of our arbitrary limitations of climate and affordability, we will be looking at a limited part of the United States, and later on, other parts of the world. Not all places will have Palm Beach winters, and not all places will enjoy cool San Francisco summers. The climate and living conditions in the mountains will be quite different from the seashore. There are even large differences between sea shores: The Pacific gives you a totally different climate from the Gulf Coast, which in turn is different from the Atlantic. Hopefully, you will be able to use this book to find just the right combination for you.

It would be nice to give a complete list of every possible retirement site in the world, but of course, this is impossible. The book would be so large you would need three husky stevedores to carry it home from the bookstore. Instead, what I've tried to do here is to give examples of towns in various parts of the country, examples that will be representative of life-styles in that particular area. An entire book could be written about any one of the divisions here: West Coast, Southwest Desert, Gulf Coast, Florida, East Coast and mid-South, but a lot of the descriptions would be repetitive.

## ALTERNATIVES

Part of your decision-making process, once you've determined the kind of weather you need, is to decide which life-style you want to pursue. Among your alternatives are:

1. Moving permanently to another location, either renting or buying.
2. Moving to a hot winter climate, and then to a cooler summer climate with a second home.
3. Staying home during the summer, and escaping the winter by:
   a. Going to a warmer place in the U.S.A. or,
   b. Going to Latin America for the winter.

By far the most common tack taken by retirees is to simply stay put. Since I am basically a vagabond, my option is to travel, to spend the better seasons of the year enjoying the beauty of my favorite places in the United States or Canada (or Europe, for that matter), then enjoying a second summer in South America (see Chapter 16). Obviously, that isn't for everyone. Many people become upset without some stability in their lives. But, if you aren't the type that has to live in a house that you "own," you might consider doing a test winter in Florida or California or even Mexico, someplace where it is warm enough in the colder months that you can savor what it feels like to be *retired* there.

There's an additional benefit to doing things on a trial basis to begin with. You have an opportunity to do what I've stressed in all my other writings on retirement: *Try it before you buy it!* You might find that you like your new retirement site well enough that you will decide to buy a home and move there permanently. Or, after a couple of months, you might discover that you hate it.

## TRAVEL-RETIREMENT

One couple I interviewed told of the travel mode of retirement that they have enjoyed the last five years, and how they manage it. Originally from the Midwest, they weren't sure whether they wanted to live in the desert or on the ocean. So they rented out their home, bought a motor home and headed for Las Vegas to try out desert living. They loved the winter they spent there, but when summer, with its 100-degree heat approached, they decided to try

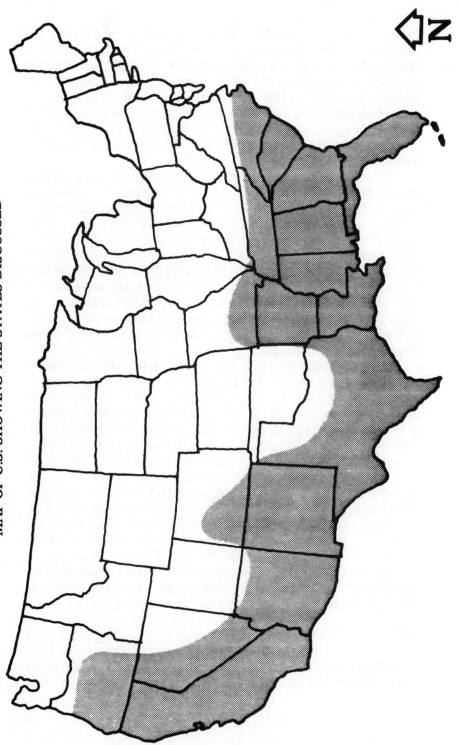

MAP OF U.S. SHOWING THE STATES DISCUSSED

the ocean. Next stop was the Oregon coast, where the summers are delightfully cool. They liked it so well there that they bought a double-wide home in a mobile home park and sold their house in the Midwest. But then came winter, with its days of drizzling rain. Back to the desert, this time to Phoenix and Tucson. So now, they're convinced that they have the best of all possible worlds: A home base by the ocean, and a portable base which they can use for trips anywhere from Florida to California. We'll talk about this mode of living in a later chapter.

Another variation on the theme of travel-retirement is *foreign country* living. Many people have discovered that Mexico, Costa Rica, Argentina and other Latin American countries (see Chapter 16) offer an ideal retirement situation. Because of the low cost of living (for those with dollars in their pockets) and friendly people, a couple can live graciously there--even hire servants--for far less than most people receive in Social Security! The key to success here is finding a place where there are other North Americans living, so you can break into the culture without having to immediately learn Spanish. What better way to pass a winter than on the beach in Acapulco while the icy winds blow up a storm up north? More about this in a later chapter.

Later on in the book, we will discuss still another alternative for temporary living, and that is retirement hotels. An example of this is the Casa del Rey, in Santa Cruz, Calif., or any one of hundreds of similar facilities around the country. For $560 a month, at the Casa del Rey, a couple can have a room, with maid service, plus two meals a day. For a single, a room starts at $420, everything included. Once a popular beach hotel, this establishment specializes in catering to senior citizens. Only a block from the boardwalk and beautiful beaches, the Casa del Rey provides organized activities, transportation to shopping and many other services. One lady I interviewed says, "I make my reservations a year in advance, and usually get my same room. I come here immediately after the Christmas holidays, and stay until the first of April--just in time to return home to Indianapolis for the spring." Another couple does the opposite; they make their reservations for the summer months to escape the shimmering heat of their Phoenix retirement home.

## MOVING PERMANENTLY

Many people find that when they retire, there is not really much to keep them around. Their children have moved away, their friends are all work-connected acquaintances and they are tired of battling winter--winter always wins. So the temptation is to move to a warm climate and start over again with new friends, new sights and a new home. My only word of caution here is to make certain that buying your home is what you *really* want to do. The country is full of "senior citizen" developments, who send out slick brochures full of enticing photos. There are lots of benefits in a development, particularly if you are the type of person who can enjoy that kind of life.

The problem is, you have to look very carefully, beyond the slick brochures and salesman's pitch. A picture is cleverly painted for you, where suddenly, upon paying the down payment, you will become part of a glamorous social whirl, with terribly interesting neighbors, golf partners, tea dances, stimulating cocktail parties and the like. The model homes are decorated with elegantly designed furniture that often cost as much as the entire housing unit that you are considering. Decorator use of mirrors and specially designed furniture makes the rooms seem enormously large and luxuriant. Sometimes in addition to being costly, the furniture is deliberately made smaller, which gives an impression of the rooms being larger than they really are.

Insist on seeing one of the unfurnished units. Then imagine your furniture crammed into the rooms. Or, if you will be buying new furniture, imagine furniture that you can *afford* being placed in the rooms. Unless you are exceptionally good at making friends and "networking," don't assume that your social life is going to become instantly stimulating and glamorous just because you pay a lot of money for a condo. Look past the glitter and consider what life will really be like. Most of the people who bought in are just like you, and it behooves you to talk to some of them and find out their opinions. Will you really use that swimming pool, or that exercise room, or the golf putting green enough to make the high payments worth while? Are you sinking so much capital into your housing that you won't have money left for emergencies or minor luxuries? If after looking at all of these items (and as many more negative aspects as you can think of), you are still sure you can afford it, then go ahead.

People in our age brackets seem to have a fixation about "owning" their own places. The idea of owning a piece of land and a house and a lawn, all have a symbolic meaning of stability and safety to many people. But it turns out that many people just *think* they own their houses. The fact is, their house and yard own them!

Having spent most of my life in the West--California mostly--in places where yards are designed for easy care, it always amazes me when I travel through the eastern parts of the country. Everywhere I look, I see enormous stretches of lush green lawn. And everywhere I look, I see someone out mowing the lawn. (I was 15 when I mowed my last lawn, and I swore it would be my last.)

I have a friend who lives in Missouri; she has a gorgeous lawn surrounding her home--a couple of acres. To keep the lawn in shape, she has to spend about four hours every other week riding around on a mower, and another couple of hours trimming, edging and whatever else is involved. This isn't even mentioning all of the other chores that are involved in taking care of a large house and yard. When I ask people why they spend so much of their life cutting grass, the defensive answer is: "I *enjoy* working around the yard." If it's all that much fun, how come rich people *hire* someone to mow their lawns, while they go out and play golf? The fact is, my friends *have* to cut that damned grass whether they enjoy it or not-- otherwise they end up with an ugly lawn, and sneering neighbors. Myself, I would rather spend that time doing something with a little more quality than following a lawnmower.

Unless you are one of those strange people who derive some perverted pleasure out of doing chores which unskilled, low-paid laborers can do better than you, you might think about whether you *really* want to own a house. There is one saving grace about owning in a senior citizens development: They are generally maintenance-free. Maybe "free" isn't the word, because you are paying for it in your monthly fees. At least you don't have to sweat and strain your-self.

Why not rent? If you find that you don't *have* to own something, you might find that renting solves a lot of problems. One benefit is that the landlord is responsible for repairing that leaky roof, or unstopping the toilet, not you or your spouse. Another benefit is the knowledge that you don't *have* to live there. When your lease is up, you are perfectly free to look for a better place.

What do you lose by renting? "It's like pouring money down a rathole," is the answer I often receive. Maybe there was a time in your life when that might have been true, when you were earning a large salary and huge interest payments brought you a tidy income tax refund at the end of the year. And, during the time when housing was appreciating at a high yearly rate, and when capital gains were taxed at a maximum of 20 percent--you might have had a point. But today, the situation is different. The real estate market has leveled off, and dropped in some areas, and many financial experts are pronouncing the end of the real estate boom. New tax laws have stripped away many of the advantages of property ownership, and I suspect there are even worse laws to come.

Remember when you bought your first home? Chances are the down payment was minimal and the payments were much less than you could rent a house for back in those days. It's a different story today. Many homes need a substantial down payment, and in many areas, you can rent *cheaper* than you can own. This is particularly true when you consider the loss of potential equity income on your down payment.

## HIGH FINANCE

Recently, I interviewed a couple in Santa Barbara who had been paying $720 a month rent for an apartment--a nice place with a swimming pool and an exercise room, plus organized activities in the clubhouse. Santa Barbara isn't the cheapest place in the country to live; you've probably guessed this by now. They decided to buy a house in a new development. The price was $145,000. Because of their age, the lender required $33,000 down and their payments were over $1,200 a month. The first year's interest came to $13,392, about $1,116 a month. "Well, with the house," they told me, "we get a tax break on the interest, but with the apartment we got nothing back at the end of the year. It was like pouring money down a rathole." True, but they had to sell some utility stocks to make the down payment, stocks which paid about $230 a month in dividends. If you add the loss of income to the $1,200 payments, we find that it costs $1,430 a month to live in a house with a large yard which demands many hours a month of upkeep.

Suddenly, they find that they have to budget carefully to make the payments, and have to forgo some luxuries to which they'd become accustomed. Did they benefit? They received a refund of all the taxes they had paid that year (a tax refund of $2,448) because of the $13,392 interest they paid that first year. Had they been in a higher income bracket, it would have been much more, granted. But no matter how you look at it, it cost them $10,944 *more* to live in the house as opposed to an apartment. That is not counting the $2,760 income they would have received on the down payment had it remained in utility stocks. "Oh, but they are building equity by paying off the loan," I hear a real estate salesman argue. Sure they did; they paid off $420! Had they stayed in an apartment, they would have had an extra $13,284 in their pockets to spend that year. Where's this rathole I've been hearing about?

All of this might make good sense for a young couple whose earning power will probably grow over the years. As time goes by, they pay off the loan with larger paychecks and with dollars that will inevitably be shrunken by inflation. They are building for the future, just as you did at their age. But before you take on any long-term commitments to build for another future, you might want to consider whether it wouldn't be better to invest your money in your retirement rather than in some nebulous future 30 years down the line. Will you be able to enjoy your money as much 30 years from now as you can today? How old will you be then? In short, don't automatically fall for the *down the rathole* line. Figure out the tax advantages for yourself realistically, with an eye on today.

## WHERE TO RETIRE?

The areas recommended for retirement by this book are divided into *West Coast, Southwest Desert, Texas and the Rio Grande, Gulf Coast, Florida, East Coast* and *Ozarks*. The biggest handicap in doing this kind of study is the lack of space. In each of the areas covered here, there are hundreds of suitable places for retirement. Somewhere along the line, there had to be some choices made as to which towns to cover. The choices are arbitrary, selected because they are representative of a larger area. No attempt is made to list all possible retirement locations. From these presentations, you should gather an idea of the sections of the country which will fit your needs.

## WEST COAST

Some of the best retirement country is in the western part of the United States, between the shores of the Pacific Ocean and the Rocky Mountains, several hundred miles inland. The climate there is even, mild and predictable. The key to the climate is the prevailing westerly winds which constantly come in off thousands of miles of ocean. On the ocean coast this means cool summers and mild winters. Because of the rainfall patterns--it only rains in the winter time--it sometimes feels like springtime is misplaced. The countryside doesn't really become green until November, when the rains come, and by June, the grasses start to turn golden, as if it were autumn back East.

Oregon, Washington and the northern coast of California, are sparsely settled, with land and housing costs relatively low. There the rains fall more profusely in the winter (and occasionally in the summer), making the countryside greener. Much of the land is covered with conifer and hardwood forests, with abundant wildlife and nearby wilderness the rule. Inland, once you cross the spine of the coastal ranges, the climate becomes warmer and dryer. Temperatures hitting the 100s are possible in summer, but low humidity makes the days quite pleasant. Although the inland section of the West Coast supports more people than the northern coastal areas, it still is basically rural in tone, with most cities under 50,000 population.

Southern California is the largest metropolitan area of the West Coast. Between Los Angeles and San Diego stretches a loose collection of towns and communities that sometimes seem to be one huge metropolitan area. Nevertheless, these are separate towns, despite the lack of much open space between them. Los Angeles itself is unlike any other large city I've ever seen (except for Buenos Aires), in that it consists of a group of neighborhoods, each quite individualistic, with its own special character. Fifty years ago someone coined what has become a cliché, to the effect that Los Angeles is "70 suburbs in search of a city." Maybe this is a cliché, but I feel that it holds true today. Residents there identify with their neighborhoods, not the legal and statutory city.

Another condition that keeps the Los Angeles area from feeling like a "city" is that once you reach the northern and eastern edges you are suddenly out in the "country." Open land with no fences (much of it empty desert) complete with coyotes, rabbits and mountain lions, gold prospectors working placer claims, all these things are within an hour's drive from City Hall. And of course, the beaches are there for everyone to enjoy, with strict enforcement of the "open beach" laws--access to the ocean cannot be blocked by some luxury motel or someone's mansion. Once away from the coastal cities, many pleasant small-town locations are popular with retirees who want California's climate but not the freeway bustle.

## SOUTHWEST DESERT

An enormous percentage of our country is in desert lands. Some deserts are in high country, where winter snow and cold winds make them unlikely spots for retirement. In the low deserts, the winters are great, but summer heat can melt the wax in your ears. Some people compromise by living in both types of deserts only seasonally, while others choose to live there year around and ignore the bothersome season. Folks who retire in the low desert have made one basic choice: "It's easier to live with summer heat than with winter's cold."

Some towns, like Palm Springs, Calif., or Sun City, Ariz., rely almost totally on retirees for their existence. Others, like Phoenix, have a mixture of industries as well, or Las Vegas with its gambling and tourist industries. Mobile home parks are big in desert country, and of course, travel trailers, motor homes and campers make their presence known in the wintertime as "snowbirds" make their seasonal migration.

In addition to the typical warm desert climates, we'll also take a look at some of the "high desert" locations. These have several advantages, not only as seasonal retirement spots for glorious summer living, but for year around living by more and more people.

## GULF COAST

With winters warmed by the Gulf of Mexico and summers tempered by constant breezes, the Gulf Coast from Florida to the southern tip of Texas offers both inexpensive and pleasant living. Some stretches of the coast are quite touristy and crowded with summer visitors, while other places, quite as nice, are all but ignored. While tourists fill the beaches for summer, it's the traveling retiree who typically moves here for the winter. They close up their homes "up north" and take advantage of low, off-season rates to spend an economical winter retirement at the seashore. The disadvantage is that the water is too cold to swim in comfortably, but the compensation is a quiet, economical and tourist-free environment. The Gulf Coast is particularly popular with Canadians.

## FLORIDA

Almost synonymous with the word *retirement*, Florida seems to be the goal of the majority of East Coast folks when they talk about retirement. Certainly the state is conscious of retirees and provides a lot of services for senior citizens. And wherever you go, you are likely to find people from your home state, people with similar interests and members of your age group.

Even though Florida is mostly flat and bordered on three sides by water, the climate varies widely, sometimes within a few miles. The northern part is similar culturally and climatically to Georgia. Sometimes heavily wooded, with lakes and farms, this northern section has a "down-home" atmosphere. The beach areas, such as Jacksonville and St. Augustine on the east, and Panama City and Pensacola on the Gulf, tend to be summer resorts, going into a state of light hibernation during the winter months.

Florida's central section reminds me of a collection of suburbs, not much different from those you find anywhere in the country. Some of these towns, like Orlando, Gainesville and Ocala, seem to be growing very fast, with more than their share of retirees. I rather like the town of Kississmee, and a few other small towns in central Florida. An advantage to locating here is the nearness of either the Atlantic or the Gulf--either being about a 90-minute drive. You can have your quiet suburban life and then on weekends boogie on into Daytona Beach or St. Pete and romp with the college students, should that be your thing.

Florida's east coast--or as it's popularly known, the Gold Coast--is the glittering glamour star of the state. West Palm Beach, Boca Raton, Pompano Beach, Fort Lauderdale, Miami and Coral Gables all connect into one enormous beach metropolis. Tall buildings and condominiums form forests of steel and concrete, while a few blocks away small bungalows face quiet palm-lined streets. This is truly a land of contrasts.

The big attraction about the Gold Coast is the weather. Miami, for example, has very few days over 90 degrees and very few when the temperature fails to top 75 degrees. The 75 percent humidity makes up for these nice statistics, making an 85-degree day seem sweltering. But this is where Florida retirement began, and here is where the majority come today. A drawback is the crowded highways and streets. Here is where some of the most expensive homes can be found, as well as some of the more inexpensive.

Last but not least, as they say, we come to West Coast Florida. Because the Gulf Stream runs up the other side of Florida, the West Coast doesn't receive the blessings of steady, ocean-controlled weather. Winters here tend to be cooler, while summers are warmer. Fewer people retire here year around, preferring to winter in the pleasant months of November through April and then return to their home base for a summer at home. Prices of housing reflect this lowered popularity of all-year retirement. Traffic is somewhat less, and people seem a bit more friendly, at least in my experience.

## SOUTH AND EAST COAST

Many people from New England, Michigan and Wisconsin, when driving to Florida for their annual vacations, had to pass through North and South Carolina on their way to Florida. As years went by they became more interested in these states and began to think of them as potential retirement locations. Myrtle Beach and Columbia, S.C., have trapped their share of retirees, as have most other popular locations. "The winters here are often cool," admitted a retired college professor who chose Augusta, Ga., "but they beat Ann Arbor, Michigan by a mile!" Many deluxe apartment complexes at reasonable rents can be found in the South and along the Atlantic Coast, and housing in general can be ridiculously cheap in some towns.

## THE OZARKS

One of the fastest growing areas for retirees is in the Ozark Mountains of Missouri and Arkansas, as well as the similar type country in Tennessee and Kentucky. Arkansas, for example, is second only to Florida in the number of senior citizens moving in. Several reasons account for this. First of all, here is a place where land can be had at almost giveaway prices. A small farm or acreage for horses can be a reality for people who could never afford them elsewhere. Another attraction is a very low crime rate, and the absence of urban stress. Life is slow-paced in the Ozarks, sometimes too slow-paced for some. With more people moving there from northern and midwestern states, the chances of folks finding their own kind of people to hobnob with increases all the time. The drawback to the Ozarks is that winter is definitely represented among the seasons. Still, it isn't that bitter cold and below-zero kind that some states have. Maybe it will snow one day, and the next day it will be in the 70s.

In the next chapter, we will start looking at these sections of the country.

CHAPTER FIVE

# *West Coast Retirement*

From the Canadian border down to Mexico, there are many delightful beach towns and coastal cities on the Pacific Ocean, and farther inland, varied climates and topographies make for great retirement locales. Some places, like Beverly Hills or Pebble Beach, and most large cities can be dreadfully expensive, way out of range of this book. Others can be real bargains, places many retirees have chosen for their new life-styles. Still other locales are relatively expensive, but possibly worth sacrificing or scrimping to live there.

## CALIFORNIA

When you mention the *West Coast,* many people immediately think about California, often negatively. A word about California: It's a badly maligned place, with many people believing it is full of kooks, fruits and nuts. Where do they get these impressions? From movies and television series, where California is presented as a state inhabited by criminals, victims and serial killers. The truth is that California is a young state, a continually growing state. It's populated with many newcomers just like yourselves.

Chances are that one or more of your neighbors have made the trek out west to settle in a better climate, where ocean and mountains, plus beautiful cities, make life just a little better. Do you really think that moving to California would make your ex-neighbors somehow different? They've settled into neighborhoods much like the ones they left behind, among new neighbors who have come from various other parts of the country, not much different from "back home." If it weren't for palm trees in some neighborhoods, the suburbs wouldn't look different from where you probably live now.

California isn't all palm trees and swimming pools, either. Except for areas in Southern California, and a few places here and there where newcomers from the East have stubbornly planted palms, most California folks prefer prettier and easier-to-care-for trees. (If you ever try to trim a palm tree, you'll know why.) Much of the state looks little different from your home town, although possibly a little better kept up than average. It's a newer state, so you don't see as many old houses, rundown neighborhoods, and slums as you would notice in many areas "back East."

## WHAT ABOUT CRIME?

Another common myth is that California is plagued with juveniles who carry switchblades and wear black leather jackets, or that cops and robbers routinely chase each other around city streets, shooting at each other as their autos careen around corners. Even people who live in Europe or South America are convinced of this after years of watching TV re-runs of "Streets of San Francisco" and other guns-and-violence movies. It's next to impossible to convince them that this is make-believe, and that California communities are just as law-abiding, if not more so, as most other similar-sized places in the country. Crime statistics compiled by the FBI show this to be true.

I personally feel very secure in California. This is particularly true in the smaller towns and cities, but I feel the same way about Los Angeles or San Francisco. In 30 years of living there, I've never been robbed or mugged, nor do I know anyone personally who has. Things like this happen, of course. They happen anywhere in the country, probably in your neighborhood, as well.

Yes, it's true that California has been the source of some far-out ideas that have garnered sensational publicity. Some religious cults from the 1920s and 1930s, for example. But the center of these movements seems to have slipped away into the depths of the southern states in the past few years. Beatniks (who were mostly poets and intellectuals) began here, and the "hippie" movement is said to have started in California. But these fads, like most fads, have blurred into dim memories. Actually, the state is remarkably slow in accepting some modern trends. One of the more refreshing things about California is that most people aren't totally committed to keeping up with the neighbors.

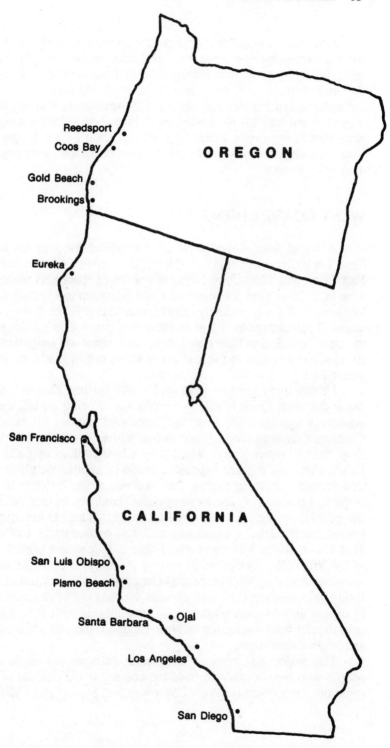

Reedsport

Coos Bay

OREGON

Gold Beach

Brookings

Eureka

San Francisco

CALIFORNIA

San Luis Obispo

Pismo Beach

Santa Barbara • Ojai

Los Angeles

San Diego

N

Few Californians feel compelled to rush out and buy new clothes simply because some magazine dictates that this year's fashion is different from last year's. Seldom does a restaurant request that their patrons wear ties, because most California men can't see the point of tying a piece of silk around their necks. A sport coat or a sweater suffices for all but the most formal occasions. I keep one good suit in my closet which I wear only when I have to "go back East" to visit somebody important. If sport coats feel more practical than suits, so be it.

## WEST COAST LIVING

A friend who moved west after spending most of his life in New York City, once told me, "A big difference I can see between East Coast and West Coast living is a sense of space and belonging. That is, in New York I always felt that I *belonged* to a certain neighborhood, and I felt perfectly comfortable there. When I went elsewhere, I felt almost as if I were intruding, that I didn't *belong*. But in the West, I don't feel this restricted sense of neighborhood. *Everywhere* belongs to me and I don't feel out of place, no matter where I am."

I think there are two reasons for this feeling. One is that because the West Coast is still in the process of being settled, there is no deeply ingrained sense of "neighborhood" among the residents. California families tend to live in one house for shorter periods of time than in other states; when they can afford to upgrade their living, they buy a more expensive home in another neighborhood. The second reason for feeling that so much space "belongs to you" is the fact that most of the western states' lands do, in fact, belong to the people. A huge percentage of all western states is in nationally owned forests, deserts, mountains and state-owned tracts. Unlike the East Coast, where just about every acre is fenced and posted, most of the West Coast (even much private property) is open for anyone to enjoy. Actually, 49.7 percent of Oregon and 47.8 percent of California belong to the U.S. Government. Nevada is 85 percent federally owned and Arizona 44 percent. Compare this with only 3.8 percent federal land ownership in New England, the Eastern Seaboard and Midwestern states.

The major and obvious difference between Westerners and people who live in other parts of the country is the amount of time spent outdoors. Because West Coast weather, particularly California weather, is pleasant year-round, people tend to find "outdoor" things to do. Most live within a few hours' drive to excellent ski country or uncrowded beaches. You can enjoy snow sports in the afternoon, then drive back down the mountain to swim in your pool or relax in the hot tub that same evening. And because most of the West enjoys low humidity, it is also relatively bug-free. You don't need screened "Florida rooms" for protection against bloodthirsty mosquitoes and other insects. If a backyard barbeque is in order, people simply drag out the patio furniture and enjoy. The West is outdoors country.

## EAST VERSUS WEST

The West Coast has a deserved reputation for being "laid back." But what's wrong with kicking back and enjoying life? I'm convinced you'll live longer, and you'll enjoy life much more. Where people from Connecticut think nothing of commuting an hour and a half each way to work, the average Westerner complains bitterly if the drive to work is over 15 or 20 minutes. Much more time than that, and he or she will buy a house closer to work. People in New York seem to *run* everywhere they go. But pedestrians in San Francisco stroll leisurely, pausing from time to time to window-shop or to take in the azure-blue view of San Francisco Bay. San Diego, Santa Barbara, Seattle--no matter where you travel in the West--you get a feeling of unhurried peacefulness. What's so kookie about that? People from the East Coast could learn some valuable lessons from Californians.

Another remarkable difference between East and West is the attitude toward education. Universities, community colleges and adult education programs on the West Coast are virtually free, and liberally patronized by senior citizens. Many universities waive fees for anyone over 65, and welcome senior citizens, recognizing their potential contributions to the school. But Eastern universities are not only prohibitive in their tuition costs, but are focused on youth, particularly youth from wealthy families. Western education is for everybody, young and old, rich and poor. If you decide to pursue a new academic career, you will find classmates of your own age group; you won't feel like the proverbial sore thumb among a roomful of college freshmen. In the West, education is looked upon as a life-long process. Can you see anything kookie about that idea?

To sum up, I feel it's extremely unfair for people to judge California and the West by sensational movies, books and trite TV series, so many of which depict West Coast living as either glamorous or debased. It's neither; mostly ordinary people living in ordinary neighborhoods, living slightly more interesting lives than they did before they moved there. Go out there and see for yourself, and keep an open mind. Where to go? Let's take a look.

## PACIFIC COAST RETIREMENT

Along the Pacific ocean, temperatures vary little between summer and winter, from San Diego to Vancouver. The farther north you go, however, the cooler the average temperatures. Winter freezes are something that makes headlines in coastal towns and cities. Because a chain of low mountains runs down the coast, from Puget Sound to San Diego, separating the beach towns from the inland valleys, there is an interesting "air conditioning" effect. When the inland valleys heat up, the air rises. This causes a low pressure area, which draws cool air inland from the Pacific to keep things pleasant. In the winter, when the sun doesn't burn as hot, the air doesn't rise, and the breezes are stable, thus allowing the beaches to keep warm. The "hot and sunny" coastal weather occurs in late September, sometimes on through November. It is November 11 as I write this and the weather is almost 80 degrees, with beautiful, clear sunshine.

## BEACHES AND REDWOODS

I regret there isn't enough space in this book or hours in my lifetime to present in any detail *all* the desirable retirement locations on the West Coast, because there are so many lovely places. Instead of aiming for a brief listing of hundreds of towns and cities, I'll discuss a few places in detail. These will be locations typical of an entire area. Some will match your needs, others won't. By getting a feeling for these towns, you'll be in a better position to make intelligent decisions as to whether the rest of the area deserves further investigation. Let me emphasize further that these descriptions and recommendations come from personally visiting each place, careful research and interviews with retirees. These impressions are mine--not taken from some atlas or guide book--and as opinions and gut feelings, they cannot be accurately measured. Nevertheless, I've done my best to keep the descriptions accurate and reasonably unbiased. I hope you will agree.

Let's begin with a look at some of the California coastal locations that attract many retirees.

**SANTA CRUZ**--About a 90-minute drive south of San Francisco, Santa Cruz has all of the advantages of being on the ocean, yet close to metropolitan areas and all the conveniences and luxuries found there. Beautiful and fashionable Monterey, Carmel and Pebble Beach are less than an hour's drive south around the Monterey Bay. San Jose is little over a half an hour away. Santa Cruz, about 44,000 people, spreads out along the beach, and is backed up by the gentle Coast Range mountains. The mountains are cloaked with impressive redwood groves, interspersed with oak and pine forests, all very pretty and quite accessible. Typical of the West Coast, much of this forest is open land, not fenced off and private like most eastern woodlands.

Santa Cruz and other smaller towns along the Monterey Bay have long been popular with retirees. Several older hotels, both in the smartly landscaped downtown mall area and by the beach boardwalk, cater exclusively to retired folks. Many people come here just for the season. They make reservations for a month or so at a time, for a pleasant escape from weather "back home." Others stay year-round.

The exceptionally mild climate and relatively low cost of living are two commonly given reasons for going to Santa Cruz. Like many beach areas on the Pacific Ocean, summer days are often overcast until afternoon, thus shielding the beaches from the onslaught of the sun. Summer rain is all but unknown. Then, from September on, the sun makes its presence known, beaming warmth to keep the chill off the air, making Santa Cruz a truly 12-month resort.

There are four golf courses, 20 parks and many beaches, both public and semi-private. (In California, property owners cannot keep the public from the beach, and are often required to provide access paths.) A favorite activity for those who can afford it is boating, with a municipal yacht harbor for small craft. Another favorite pastime is fishing from the long pier that extends into the ocean. If you don't catch anything, you can always have a fish dinner at one of the several restaurants on the pier.

Not only are there many pleasant ocean communities nearby, from Moss Landing and Castroville on the south to Half Moon Bay on the north, but the mountains behind Santa Cruz provide the answer to retirement dreams for many people. Narrow blacktop roads unobtrusively wind through the low mountains, often giving no clue to the homes hidden back in the canyons or screened by groves of trees. Property costs there vary from affordable to expensive, depending on the usability of the land and its location. Because the cloud cover usually stops at the mountain slopes, there is almost perpetual summer sunshine when you change altitudes by only a few hundred feet. There, the sun's rays are tempered by tall red-woods, tan oaks and other shade trees. So, when people at the beach feel like more sunshine, they simply drive 10 or 15 minutes and they find all they want! Winter rains in the mountains tend to be quite heavy, however, with twice as much falling there than elsewhere. Like most of the West Coast, there are practically never thunder or lightning storms. When thunderstorms do strike, they make front page headlines in all the papers.

The Santa Cruz part of Monterey Bay isn't cheap as far as rents go, with some areas approaching the high end of the scale. After all, it is close to Monterey-Carmel and San Francisco, two of the most expensive places in the nation. But there are many older homes and apartments, often jammed together as they tend to be in beach towns, and often renting for $350 on up. At present, a one- to two-bedroom apartment normally starts at $450 a month on up, and small houses for $500 up. Many mobile home parks dot the area, some with gorgeous views of the ocean. However, you'll pay plenty for this panorama. If you are on a limited budget, you might prefer one of the parks away from the beach.

The more affluent areas near Santa Cruz seem to be in towns like Aptos or Soquel, which are newer and farther away from "downtown" Santa Cruz. Property prices in Santa Cruz have been slow in catching up with the California real estate boom, and many homes can still be found for what might seem to be bargain prices to those used to real estate markets in San Francisco, New York or Los Angeles.

**PISMO BEACH**--Once the butt of many Jack Benny jokes, Pismo Beach is today having the last laugh. People are discovering that it's a very pleasant place to spend a vacation, plus, it's a very popular place to retire. Located about 200 miles north of Los Angeles, Pismo beach has a population of around 5,500. It's just one of five adjoining towns spread along the beach which gives the town its name. The word *pismo* comes from the famous pismo clams that at one time seemed to almost pave the long stretches of sandy shoreline. I include Pismo Beach as an example of smaller beach-retirement towns on the California coast.

At one time people flocked from all over the West to slip their clam forks into the sand at low tide in search of the large, succulent clams. They still do, but today's clam diggers aren't like the crowds of a few years ago. The feisty sea otter and too many clam forks have thinned the mollusk population considerably. But clams are still there for the persistent, and fishing is still great from the long pier that juts out past the surf (no license required). Bottom fish, such as ling cod, red snapper and sand dabs, are favorite catches. Fishing and clamming are year-round sports here. Boat launching facilities are available at Avila Beach, at the sheltered northern section.

Pismo Beach is one of the few places along the California coast where it is permissible to drive a motor vehicle onto the sand, and there are several ramps that give access to the beach. Huge, undulating sand dunes are meccas for four-wheel-drive vehicles and dune buggies. Converted Volkswagens, Jeeps and other souped-up contraptions zip up and down the dunes like motorized roller coasters (away from the more quiet beach crowd, of course). Another favorite beach activity is horseback riding. A couple of stables rent horses for leisurely rides along the surf line. Golf is popular, with several courses in the area.

The beach area is made up of several small towns that connect loosely to form a sprawling, lightly populated "city." The communities that comprise the Pismo Beach area are: Shell Beach, Oceano, Grover City, Avila Beach and Pismo Beach itself. Arroyo Grande is away from the beach, but is considered part of the "metropolitan" area (pop. 30,000) of Pismo Beach. Housing is naturally more expensive along the cliffs, or anywhere an ocean view fills your picture window. Still, for a California beach area, Pismo Beach is surprisingly affordable. Brand new two-bedroom condos can be had for $68,000 up. Nice two- or three-bedroom homes range from $75,000 on up. While these prices may not seem "affordable" to people moving from some areas of the country, for the West Coast, they are cheap. Some very expensive homes sit on the cliffs of Shell Beach, homes with gorgeous views and walled privacy. Yet just a block or two back from the ocean are many modest homes with low-maintenance yards, along neat, comfortable-looking streets. Numerous mobile home parks dot the area, with low monthly rents.

One reason for the reasonable housing market here is the exodus of the workers who labored on the nearby Diablo Canyon nuclear power project. Once the electric generating plant was completed, the housing market dropped considerably. At the moment, it's a renter's and buyer's market when it comes to choosing your new residence. Typically, a two-bedroom apartment rents for as low as $400 a month with one-bedroom units going for $350. Houses are going for $500 and up, with the median about $600 for three bedrooms. If you look around you may find a small house for as low as $375. Condos are plentiful, some with excellent views of the ocean. But you don't have to live in town; much of the five-city area is rural. There are farms for sale, and acreage for rent, sometimes with mobile home hookups available.

As you might expect, where there are large numbers of retired folks, you will find active senior citizens organizations. There are many organizations, ranging from grandmothers' clubs to a singles club for members over 60. There is an active Retired Senior Volunteers Program (R.S.V.P.), Meals on Wheels and a senior citizen ride program. You will find plenty of opportunities to get involved in volunteer projects. Several retirement facilities and nursing homes are available.

**SAN LUIS OBISPO**--Although Pismo Beach is quiet and seems isolated, it's only about a 15-minute drive north to San Luis Obispo, a city of about 38,000 people. There you will find many cultural events at the local state university, such as plays, lectures and concerts, many of which are free to senior citizens. San Luis Obispo itself is a viable retirement location for those who don't *have* to have daily access to the beach. The summer climate there is a bit warmer than in Pismo Beach, because the town is 13 miles inland from the ocean. Evenings can be shirt-sleeve weather rather than the typically cool beach after-dark sweater affairs. About a two-hour drive south is posh and fashionable Santa Barbara, with its prestigious university and abundant cultural offerings, as well as first-rate shopping.

San Luis Obispo, being a much larger community than the Pismo Beach area, naturally has a lot of senior citizen activities going. From bowling leagues to golf tournaments, the sports sector is covered. Woodcarving, folk and square dancing, lectures and all sorts of social activities are there for your participation.

Two excellent senior citizen's newspapers serve the San Luis Obispo-Santa Barbara areas, full of relevant news, activity calendars, travel bargains, health tips and advertisements directed toward retired folks. Reading these newspapers gives a clue that retirees are important to the economy and business of the mid-coastal area.

SANTA BARBARA--One of the prettiest places on the West Coast, Santa Barbara was "discovered" early in the century. Back in the heyday of Hollywood, when cinema stars were loaded with riches, matched only by the money of Los Angeles real estate developers and promoters, the wealthy wanted someplace for weekend getaways. They wanted a beautiful, peaceful and exclusive Southern California spot where they could escape the burgeoning monster they were creating in Los Angeles. They discovered Santa Barbara. Set on a narrow coastal plain, bounded on the north by the San Rafael Mountains, Santa Barbara faces miles of lovely beaches. It was perfect.

The newly wealthy set about building mansions and lavish homes with typical Southern California flair. Stuccoed Spanish and Moorish palaces with red tiled roofs and swimming pools competed to show the most opulence along landscaped boulevards. Even the downtown municipal buildings look like something out of a Hollywood version of the Arabian Nights. Don't misunderstand, construction wasn't done cheaply--these people had real money to spend, and spend it they did. Although the architecture may have seemed garish at the time, the years have mellowed it into a charming, nostalgic place. The extensive landscaping has matured--with decorative trees and plants from all parts of the world--turning Santa Barbara into a virtual arboretum.

This is one of my favorite West Coast beach cities. It isn't too large (less than 100,000), it has a major university that is a source for cultural and intellectual stimulation, its climate equals or excels any other place in California and it's an absolutely gorgeous place. Unfortunately, like any place with all of these attributes, it is also expensive. It was established as an enclave for the wealthy, and it remains so today. Low-cost housing here begins around $140,000, and apartment rentals seldom dip under $650 a month. But, if you can afford it, it might be worth your while to investigate. Because of the affluence of the area, there are plenty of tax dollars to be spent on senior citizen services. Libraries are top-notch, and there's a local symphony orchestra and a great adult education program.

There are several smaller towns near Santa Barbara where prices are a bit more affordable, and within an easy driving distance. The largest is Ventura, a city of 75,000 about 30 miles south of Santa Barbara. Here you'll find housing much more affordable, with houses costing almost half as much as in Santa Barbara. Rentals and mobile home parks are plentiful and competitive. Ventura is a working-man's town. On the extreme northern fringe of metropolitan Los Angeles, Ventura has several manufacturing industries. But these industries don't affect the air because Ventura, like nearby Santa Barbara, is smog-free.

OJAI--The Ojai Valley and the town of Ojai (about 8,000 population) are something of a well-kept secret in Southern California. This is probably because the valley is off the freeway--a pleasant, winding, half-hour drive away from the ocean. Few uninformed tourists bother to take this detour off fast-paced Highway 101. If they did, they would find a beautiful valley with orange groves, avocado orchards and homes on large, tree-shaded lots (many with horse stables). In this valley of rolling hills and sometimes steep slopes are several attractive communities, comfortably rural-looking, such as Oak View and Ojai.

Ojai is particularly interesting. It has acquired the reputation as an artist colony, with several world-famous artists, writers, painters, potters and sculptors electing to make their home here. There are numerous galleries, museums and studios that display the works of Ojai's artisans. The Ojai Art Center presents many events throughout the year, such as concerts, exhibits and theater. The town itself has an artistic flavor, as if yesteryear's planners were determined to incorporate the natural beauty of the valley into the town. The main street has a long, arched promenade designed to look like the Spanish mission that had originally been there. Across the street is a lovely park with huge trees, fountains, walks and a place in one corner known as the "Bowl," which is formed in part by a uniquely shaped oak tree. Here is where the well-regarded Ojai Music Festival has been held for the last 40 years.

Because of its location in the coastal mountains, and because of its lakes, streams and beautiful mountain terrain, Ojai Valley is very popular with campers. Lake Casitas, with over 100 miles of shoreline, and scores of hidden coves and inlets, is a great place for family camping, fishing and sailboating. Others choose to camp farther back in the mountains. The fishing streams are reputed to be well stocked with rainbow trout. More than 400 miles of hiking and horseback riding trails crisscross the valley and climb to nearby mountain passes. For those who like their outdoor recreation more civilized, there are two golf courses, one a county fairway.

The weather is typical of Southern California, with 90-degree summers and mild winters. The humidity is low enough to make the warmest summer days feel pleasant. Most of the rain falls between December and March, leaving the rest of the year bright and clear for outdoor activities.

As you might suspect, Ojai is *not* one of the bargain paradises of the world. Housing costs push it toward the upper limit of this book. But I was so impressed with the area that I felt it should be included here. The very low end of rentals start at $450, with most two-bedroom units closer to $600-$700 or above. Mobile homes are available in the many parks that are nicely landscaped, selling for about $20,000 and up. But residential real estate is as high as any you might find anywhere in California. Many homes list for $450,000 and up, with building lots going for as much as most people in the country would pay for a house. However, when you take a look at the setting and the architecture, prices don't seem to be out of line. If you can afford it. The lowest prices I found listed were a three-bedroom, two-bath (eight-year-old) house for $129,900, and an older two-bedroom place on a large lot for $117,500. Part of the real estate prices are reflected in the quality of life that you are also buying. As an alternative, there are some retirement complexes with country club atmospheres, complete with putting greens and social directors.

Ojai has a hospital with intensive care and coronary units, and Los Angeles medical care is less than two hours away.

**LOS ANGELES**--This is the place most people think of when they hear the word "California." Images of Hollywood, surfboards, swimming pools and starlets in Cadillac convertibles come to mind. This imaginary Los Angeles is the sort of place people fantasize about but never expect to *live* there. A book on retirement alternatives wouldn't be complete without some lines on this fantasyland. Many will be surprised to learn that retiring there is not impractical at all. Many thousands do it every year, and wouldn't dream of going anywhere else. Don't misunderstand, Los Angeles isn't a cheap place to live, but there are benefits and facets to its style of "California living" that are worth a few sacrifices and corner-cutting.

Before the original retirement boom, which started around the 1880s, Los Angeles was a sleepy town with not a whole lot going for it except a gorgeous climate. Then the word got out that this was a great place for retirement. Before long, whenever anyone talked of "retiring in California," you could assume they meant Los Angeles.

I don't care for large cities. I've seen few I would care to retire in, so why would I recommend Los Angeles? After all, doesn't Los Angeles County have about 8 million people living within its boundaries? And the surrounding counties have towns and cities that are for all practical purposes considered part of the Los Angeles metropolitan sprawl. I admit that Los Angeles is big, but I deny that it is a *city*, at least not in spirit. To my way of thinking it is simply a collection of neighborhoods loosely gathered together to make up that vague entity we call "Los Angeles," but basically they are neighborhoods.

There is a sort of downtown area--tall buildings and all--but it isn't the same as in other cities. Instead of a central focus, like New York's Fifth Avenue or San Francisco's Union Square, Los Angeles commerce is spread throughout the county among several regional "downtowns," hundreds of shopping malls and business parks.

Each neighborhood has its own character, its own kinds of restaurants and style of living. It's easy to forget that you are living in enormous Los Angeles County as you begin to think of your neighborhood as just another small town. Some neighborhoods have less style than others, just as some towns are nicer than others. Still, there are few neighborhoods that residents can't find something to brag about.

Even though there is a small-town character about Los Angeles, many cultural advantages, usually found only in big cities, abound. Museums, art galleries, symphonies, theaters, adult education, plus all kinds of senior citizen activities, are there for your enjoyment. Senior citizen groups are very active, and have been unusually successful in obtaining discount privileges for theaters, restaurants, drugs and other consumer goods. And, unlike many large cities, outdoor recreation is plentiful, with wilderness areas within one or two hour's drive from City Hall. Gold panning in the San Gabriel Mountains, skiing and trout fishing at Lake Arrowhead and Big Bear, golf at Palm Springs, or rockhounding in the desert-- all this and more are available.

People in Los Angeles share one characteristic that's extremely rare in large cities. They are *friendly*. This friendliness is partly because of a sense of neighborhood and partly because the residents come overwhelmingly from outside the state. The average person your age that you meet on the street moved here from a small town, maybe in the Midwest, or the South. When they came, they were strangers, but they brought that hometown sense of neighborliness with them. They weren't strangers for long. Moving to California doesn't change anyone. If the custom "back home" was for people to smile at strangers and make friends with the neighbors, then that's the way they'll behave in their new homes.

Yes, a lot of people live here, but they're not concentrated in high-rise apartment buildings as in many other large cities. People are spread out over an immense extent of land, mostly living in single-family dwellings that cluster around a neighborhood center. The biggest drawback to Los Angeles area, however, is that with things so spread out, and public transportation system is all but non-existent, an auto is essential. The freeway system at first seems confusing, but most people catch on pretty fast. The amount of people the freeways move is surprising, and unless you make the mistake of getting on one during rush hour, you can move rather quickly and smoothly.

You hear a lot about Los Angeles smog. It's there, and will always be there, due to the way the mountains are positioned around the area. The mountains trap cool Pacific air, causing an inversion layer of cooler air which holds the warmer air close to the ground. This warm air contains water vapor and impurities which we call smog. This isn't anything new; the first Spanish explorers made note of the water vapor haze and Indian campfire smoke that hovered over the basin. In fact, the Indians called the Los Angeles Basin the "Bay of Smokes," because campfire smoke would rise, hit the inversion layer, and linger all day. When automobiles and industry moved into the basin, problems began in earnest. Air quality grew worse until some days you couldn't step outside the house without your eyes watering. Residents used to joke about it, saying, "We don't trust air that we can't see." This didn't stop people from moving there.

Then about 20 years ago the state decided to do something about it. Strict emission controls on automobiles and industry did the trick. The change in air quality has been dramatic. Often, when I visit Los Angeles nowadays, I am surprised that I can actually see the mountains, which years ago were only visible after a heavy rain cleared the air. On those days, I remember understanding why early settlers felt that the Los Angeles basin was such a paradise. Although there are still plenty of days when the brownish haze returns, it is rarely like the eye-smarting cloudiness of 20 years ago. The worst days I've seen recently aren't any worse than those I've experienced in many midwestern cities.

With so many neighborhoods from which to choose, it's difficult to list favorites. But generally, it's agreed that the closer to the ocean, the better. Miles and miles of excellent beaches stretch all along the coast. Remember, almost all beaches are public in California. L.A.'s near-perfect climate permits plenty of sunning on the beaches, even on many days in December and January. As a rule, the closer you get to the beach, the cleaner the air, which makes beachside neighborhoods most desirable. There are few places here where something nice can't be said about living there. The foothills of the mountains have marvelous views of the basin's major valleys, while towns to the east enjoy desert scenery. There's something for everybody.

You have your choice of housing, ranging from plush Beverly Hills to inexpensive Carson. Near the center of Los Angeles, west of downtown, you find more apartments and condos. Away from the center, the more mobile home parks you'll find. The variety of neighborhoods and the ethnic mixture are among the strengths of Los Angeles. Chinese, Japanese, Mexican, Korean, Samoan, Filipino and Vietnamese neighborhoods lend a cosmopolitan and exotic flavor to Los Angeles, as well as providing some excellent restaurants. Among the biggest attractions for me are these restaurants. I'm convinced that the best Asian food in the country is served here. (My next book may well be titled, "Ethnic Restaurants of Los Angeles.")

The only way to discover which part of L.A. might suit you is to spend a few weeks driving around the area. It will take a few weeks, because the area is so large and spread out. Above all, don't allow yourself to be influenced by box-office sensationalism about Los Angeles. Go and see for yourself if it isn't very much like your home town, only with near-perfect weather.

SAN DIEGO--All along the Southern California coast you'll find some beautiful beach cities, places where retirement would be wonderful. The problem is that most of them are like Santa Barbara, priced out of sight for most retirees, and in some cases over-priced. Laguna Beach, Costa Mesa, San Clemente, La Jolla, to name a few, are worth looking at if you have the money to settle there, and if living within walking distance to the beach is on your list of "must haves."

Property values are sky-high and single-family houses tend to be squeezed together, with as much construction as possible crammed onto each lot. Only the most expensive real estate affords a sense of spaciousness. I personally find these beach towns to have a cramped, touristy feeling, with a propensity for fast-food restaurants and teen-age-oriented attractions. I think that if I could afford to live in a Southern California beach city I would choose living in Santa Barbara rather than some of the more southern cities.

On the other hand, at the bottom of California, and at the top of the scale of good climates, is the city of San Diego. It's a large place, with around a million people living there, but it's one large city where I wouldn't mind living. Compared with high-priced La Jolla or Coronado, housing in San Diego isn't expensive, but compared with other places in the state, it's high. Like Santa Barbara, this is a place where the extra expense of living is worth it. According to National Weather Bureau statistics, San Diego has the best climate in the continental United States. It never freezes or snows, and it rains a scant 11 inches a year--just enough to keep the flowers blooming all year.

Most large cities seem to have a grungy, deteriorated look about them, probably due to industrial pollution, smoke and harsh weather conditions. Not so San Diego. Because of the constant breeze off the ocean, there is no smoke, no air pollution and the weather is very benign. Commercial buildings, as well as houses, tend to be pastel colored, beige and buff predominating, with red-tile roofs. Native shrubs and foreign decoratives that gaily compete around residences and the city's many parks give San Diego a delightful landscaped look. The sum of these is a city that looks pleasantly happy instead of grim.

With such good weather and pleasant living, it's no surprise that San Diego has attracted more than its share of senior citizens. I get the impression there is a higher percentage of retirees here than in any other large city in the West. There are more than 100 senior citizen organizations in San Diego, and they claim to have memberships totaling more than 100,000. With this many active organizations, you can be confident that assistance will be at hand should the need arise.

It probably also comes as no surprise that such a delightful place to live is expensive. According to the local chamber of commerce, it is one of the most expensive cities in the United States. Out of 230 cities surveyed by the government, San Diego ranks in the top 10. The culprit in this high cost of living is housing. Typical housing here runs around $120,000, more than double that of most retirement places around the country. For many people, retiring here would mean a tight budget and looking for ways to economize. Many feel it's worth it.

The other side of the coin is that heating and cooling costs are negligible. This brings down the utility bills, that second factor in the cost of living that is so variable. Many households don't bother with air conditioning; the few hot days in the summer don't justify buying a unit. Houses rarely sell for under $100,000, and low apartment rents start around $500. Many senior citizen developments, some with meals and health care, are available, at correspondingly higher prices than in other areas. Mobile home parks are top-notch in San Diego, most of them beautifully landscaped, but they're not cheap and they're not plentiful. More than 10 have recently been replaced by commercial developments, with tenants forced to move their homes. Rents of $350 a month are common, but they sometimes can top $550.

Another point the chamber of commerce makes is that seasonal changes of clothing aren't necessary, and home vegetable gardens can be productive all year. There are free fishing piers where no license is needed to supplement your diet with fresh fish. And the city gives out senior citizen ID cards that qualify retirees for special discounts on transit buses and trolleys, the San Diego Symphony, the zoo, theaters, movies, beauty shops, restaurants, sporting events and much more.

SAN DIEGO SUBURBS--For more reasonable housing in the San Diego area, you must travel east or north. Within easy shopping distance from San Diego are the towns of El Cajon, Alpine, Lakeside, Ramona, Julian and other smaller communities. Although only 18 miles from the ocean, El Cajon (pop. 85,000), east of San Diego, is in a totally different climatic zone. This is desert country, with beautiful rock formations, cactus gardens and frequent adobe houses. Land is much cheaper here than in San Diego, and people tend to have large lots. Many keep horses, since there are lots of riding trails that wander through the adjacent mountainous country. Housing is less costly than in San Diego, but the tradeoff is that it gets much hotter in the summer and cooler in the winter. Your utility bills will go up correspondingly.

Thirty miles northeast is Escondido (pop. 79,000), which enjoys an inland climate similar to El Cajon. The country around here is rolling, grassy valley country with low mountains in the background. It's ideal for small ranches, perhaps with a horse or two. Many people buy acreage and place a mobile home on it for instant housing. The commercial center of town looks rural and comfortable. Still, Escondido has many amenities retirees might want, such as a hospital, an excellent senior service center, a community college and adult education programs that are free to those over 60 years of age. Add to this the fact that rents average at least $100 a month less than in San Diego, and you can understand why Escondido is popular with retirees.

As you travel farther from San Diego, southeast toward the Mexican border, you'll find a delightfully rural area of low mountain and semi-desert landscapes. Tiny communities like Jamul and Dulzura offer necessary shopping, and also the border town of Tecate is nearby for bargain shopping. The vast Anza-Borrego Desert State Park and the Cleveland National Forest are also nearby for outdoor recreation.

## NORTHERN CALIFORNIA/OREGON COASTS

From San Francisco north to the Columbia River, the Pacific Coast is totally different from Southern California. This country is much cooler, enjoys more rain, and suffers less from tourism. The coast is lush and green all year, with stately redwood groves along some highways, and pine forests or rolling hills in the rest of the area. The coast alternates between rugged cliffs where waves crash and toss picturesque sprays of surf into the air--and tranquil, deserted beaches that invite beachcombing or surfcasting.

A short distance inland, the coastal range parallels the ocean, separating the coastal lowlands from the inland valleys with mar-velous wilderness areas. Millions of acres are accessible only by horseback or on foot. These mountains are low and gentle, without the altitude of the Sierra Nevada and are warmed by Pacific wester-lies, so they aren't plagued with winter snows except at their highest elevations. Many people choose to retire back in the wooded valleys and canyons, or on hilltops. Some find their idyllic homesteads in tiny crossroads communities, others on small farms that have been carved from the forest. Few of these farms are really serious, how-ever. Vegetable gardens and maybe a few chickens or ducks are among the more ambitious farming activities. However, the warm, dry summers make for excellent outdoor recreation, particularly trout fishing in mountains streams, or patrolling beaches for driftwood or Japanese glass fishing floats.

Once you cross the Golden Gate Bridge going north, Highway 1 winds around through some of the most peaceful and rural landscapes to be found anywhere. The towns are all small, neigh-borly and uncrowded. The only large town on the California stretch of coast is Eureka the next "metropolitan" area being the Coos Bay-North Bend area in Oregon. Quite a few villages sit along the coast, interspersed with forest and grazing land, sleepy and laid-back just as they should be. If you are looking for discos, beach parties and tourist traps, you are much too far north.

The major industry along the coast is lumber, but that seems to be in a permanent state of depression all over the West. The second industry is fishing, much of which is done by amateurs or people just out for fun. Since neither of these industries are hiring, jobs are scarce, housing is affordable, and younger people are leaving for the cities. The moral of this story is: If you need to work part-time to make ends meet, forget about Northern California and Oregon. If you can satisfy your need for meaningful work through volunteer jobs, you will do just fine.

SAN FRANCISCO--Since we did a section on Los Angeles, it is incumbent upon us to give equal time to Los Angeles's northern rival, that fabulous city of cities located on beautiful San Francisco Bay. If you suggest that I sound biased toward San Francisco, then I accept your suggestion. No other city I've seen compares with it for breathtaking scenic vistas, restaurants, architecture, cultural ambiance and excitement. If you haven't guessed it by now, I'll admit that this is my favorite city in all the United States. At least, it's my favorite city to *visit*. By the way, most natives refer to it as *San Francisco* (or affectionately, *the City*) and will wrinkle their noses disdainfully if anyone calls it *Frisco*. Newcomers who have adopted *the City* as their own personal property, will occasionally hold their breath in indignation until they turn blue when they hear someone say *Frisco*. Well, the oldtimers (those who can remember the days before Pearl Harbor) tell me that it was always *Frisco* until after World War II, when lots of snooty people from back East started coming here and decided that *Frisco* didn't sound classy. I derive a perverse satisfaction at the sight of snobs turning blue. So! *Frisco, Frisco, Frisco!* There!

As I say, it's a great place to visit. I tried to live there once, and rented a great apartment in the posh Pacific Heights District. To my dismay, my camper was too tall to enter the garage. For the next six months, I spent my life running down to the street to attend to the parking meter every two hours, or having to move the vehicle before the street sweepers came by. I'll try it again someday, but next time I'll make sure I have a parking spot. Until then, I'll do as many retirees choose to do: Live close enough so that I can drive in, sample a new restaurant, absorb the special ambiance that is "the City," and then go home where I can park in front of my home without having to worry about getting a ticket. But, many people who live there don't have to worry about things like that because they don't own cars; public transportation is terrific. Between buses, cable cars, reasonable taxi fares and the BART underground system, you don't really need private transportation. Maybe, but I need a car wherever I am.

Like Los Angeles, San Francisco is a collection of neighborhoods. But there is a difference: Whereas Los Angeles neighbor-
hoods are often similar in appearance and composition, San Francisco's neighborhoods are startlingly different from one another. Cow
Hollow is so different from nearby Marina District that you can tell
where you are just by looking at the kind of restaurants. Chinatown,
Japantown, the Fillmore, the Financial District, the Mission District,
Fisherman's Wharf, Potrero Hill, Twin Peaks, the Tenderloin,
Castro Street, Pacific Heights, the Western Addition, the Sunset
District--all of these names mean something special to San Francis-
cans. Each neighborhood or ("district" as it is called) has its distinctive flavor and coloring, from restaurants to languages. There is
even an Irishtown where you'll hear strong brogue spoken in pubs
over glasses of Guinness stout.

Every ethnic group seems to have its own neighborhood. One
of my favorite neighborhoods is the Mission district. This is the center for emigres from Central America, Mexico, and all of South
America. Restaurants offer delicacies from just about every Latin
American country you can think of. You can order *papusas, en-
chiladas, empanadas, gallo pinto* and even a hamburger or pizza. I
suppose you have detected my use of restaurants as a basis for
evaluating a neighborhood? Chinatown is my second favorite: *Dim
sum* breakfasts, with shrimp rolls, steamed dumplings with quail
eggs poached over the tops, *char siu, hoc gau, siu mai,* and on, and
on. Whereas Los Angeles was settled by Midwesterners and
Southerners, people who feel at home in sport shirts and sneakers--
San Francisco attracted the more formal East Coast types, people
who adore Manhattan and wouldn't wear sneakers, not even to the
beach. Indeed, the old-time San Francisco native (now a rare,
endangered species) speaks with a distinct accent which sounds to
me exactly like a New York City accent. And, as in Manhattan,
people here tend to dress more formally. Three-piece suits, ties and
cocktail dresses are much more common here than in Southern California.

Actually, San Francisco is a surprisingly small city in area. It's
limited to a small piece of the peninsula that separates the bay from
the ocean. The population is likewise limited and small, with about
745,000 residents listed in 1986 estimates. This is quite small for a
major city. But it's the financial and cultural center for a large population in adjoining counties. Millbrae, San Bruno, Pacifica, San
Mateo, Palo Alto, Mill Valley, San Jose, Hayward, Oakland,
Berkeley, San Rafael, Vallejo--and on and on--all of these suburbs

are where the population of "San Francisco" actually lives. Some aren't really suburbs, either; for example, San Jose, is almost as large as San Francisco, and Oakland has almost 400,000. So, San Francisco is the hub and the central attraction around which the rest of the Bay Area revolves.

Some suburbs are exceptionally beautiful, others rather ordinary, but all have one thing in common: Absurdly high housing costs. Land is at a premium, and high construction costs tend to boost prices of homes and rents way up. For what you might pay for an apartment, you could live well in other parts of the country.

The climates of the suburbs vary with the locations: Places near the ocean are often overcast and cool while five miles away the bright sunlight can make it uncomfortably warm. So you have your choice of climates from hot in Contra Costa County to cool in San Mateo County. My favorite place in the Bay Area happens to be Los Gatos, a town of about 25,000 set between San Jose and the Santa Cruz Mountains.

EUREKA--Going north along the coast, there are numerous small towns along the ocean, places like Marshall, Inverness, Bodega Bay, Mendocino and Fort Bragg. Farther north are Eureka, Arcata, Fortuna, Crescent City and some other small towns that are attracting retirees. Eureka is the largest of the towns along the North Coast and is the center, culturally and commercially, of a 100-mile area. The other coastal towns are similar to Eureka, only on a smaller scale.

Eureka is a wonderfully Victorian city, graced with a profusion of such wooden architectural gems as rounded towers, scalloped siding and carvings. The old homes here are showcases for now-forgotten arts of carpentry. The builders worked with redwood, an interesting and as indestructible a wood as you can find; termites eat it reluctantly, it's rot-resistant, and relatively fire-resistant. Since many of the early settlers were lumber barons, you can imagine the care and attention to detail with which the artisans constructed the homes. The famous "Redwood Empire" forests begin near the edge of town and climb the mountains beyond and out of sight. Eighty percent of the county is forested.

The weather here is typical of beach towns along the coast north to Washington; it's a place for retirees who hate the thought of hot, steamy summers, or icy, frigid winters. Except for heavier winter rains, there seems to be little difference in the weather year around. A sweater feels comfortable almost every evening of the year, and noonday weather is seldom, if ever, hot enough to make you sweat. Air conditioning is something people read about; they don't need it. And for winter heat, many homes burn local wood in their fireplaces or wood stoves. The older houses often have fireplaces in every room. Contractors there know the secret of building fireplaces that actually heat a house instead of smoking it up like a barbecue.

This is fishing country, with salmon, shrimp, albacore and dungeness crab the favorite targets. With the generally benign weather, some kind of fishing, crabbing or clamming is usually possible all year. And for those who get seasick, the country immediately behind the town, for 100 miles or so, is full of great trout streams. Deer, river otter, herons and other wildlife are plentiful, for much of the Coast Range and inland Klamath Mountains are jealously preserved as wildlife areas. Needless to say game hunting is great, and hunters have only to drive a few miles up the highway to be into extensive national forests.

Since there is little industry in any of the beach cities, wages are low. Fishing and lumbering are the major sources of income, and both industries are chronically depressed. As a result, housing is quite reasonable--probably as low as you might expect to find anywhere on the West Coast. Typically, a small two-bedroom home will sell for $35,000 on up. For $65,000 you can buy a large, fairly new two-story home. I saw an enormous Victorian, with high ceilings, a formal dining room, bookcased library, four or five bedrooms, with a great view from a cupola on the roof, going for $99,000. Mobile homes are likewise selling cheaply, with prices starting as low as $5,600 for a one-bedroom unit. Rents range from $240-$425 for a two-bedroom apartment or duplex, and from $375-$750 for two- or three-bedroom homes.

A particularly attractive town for Victorians is Ferndale, a short drive south of Eureka. Started in the late 1800s as a prosperous dairy center, the early settlers built some splendidly ornate homes that became known as "Butterfat Palaces." Even though the town is a tourist attraction, it's mostly a "stop-for-lunch, look around and get-going-again" sort of tourism. Ferndale, like the other towns around Eureka, has managed to preserve a small-town atmosphere of neighborliness. Bed and breakfast places are popular here.

Humboldt State University in nearby Arcata is the economic mainstay of the area today. It's the largest non-manufacturing employer in the region. With a good reputation as a serious school, the university is also the source of many cultural and intellectual events. In addition, there is the College of the Redwoods, a two-year school and Eureka Adult School, with many community locations. The Eureka area is far from being a backwoods, culturally deprived section of the country.

## OREGON COAST

Going north on Highway 101, are the towns of Crescent City (pop. 3,100) and Smith River (pop. 1,000). These have pretty much the same thing to offer as the towns around Eureka, inexpensive housing, cool summers and mild winters, plus friendly small-town attitudes. Crossing the Oregon-California border takes you to the small towns of Brookings, Gold Beach and Reedsport. They're quite popular with retirees, each with a healthy percentage of its population over 60, sometimes as much as one-third.

Gold Beach has an interesting history. It derived its name from an incident that started a frantic gold rush back in the '49er days. A prospector passing through the area discovered a small quantity of gold mixed in with beach sands. He panned some color and mentioned the fact to some other miners. The word spread, and the story grew until gold mining camps all over California and Oregon were buzzing with the news that the Pacific Ocean was placering out huge nuggets of gold, and the beach was covered with riches, there for the gathering. Many camps in California's Mother Lode all but emptied as miners frantically rushed to the "Gold Beach." Actually, gold is rather common on Oregon and California beaches, usually found in black streaks of magnetite sand mixed in with beach terraces. The problem is that it is very fine and difficult to separate from the coarser sand. Back during depression days, when many people had nothing else to do, a lot of gold was gleaned from the beaches, but it was tedious work. Several miners, discouraged with unprofitable mines, decided to retire from gold panning and settled at Gold Beach, thus starting the first retirement community on the Oregon coast.

Today, Gold Beach, like other towns along the Oregon coast, is mining the wealth of the sea and harvesting forest products rather than gold. These towns make great retirement places, and in some ways, retirement is becoming a significant industry. Brookings, Reedsport, Coos Bay, Florence and Newport; each have adequate shopping, downright cheap housing and organized senior citizen groups. Single family homes, cottages and mobile homes are the general rule, with people living in multi-generational communities, although there are some adult developments. One of the larger ones, a place called Sandpiper, is located just across the state line from California.

For economical living, I cannot imagine anywhere in the country that can beat the Oregon Coast. Mobile home park spaces commonly rent for $75 a month, and two-bedroom mobile homes can be found for under $10,000. From an issue of the *Reedsport Courier* (Nov. 26, 1986) comes the following examples of rentals: One-bedroom apartments, clean and freshly painted, $140-$160 a month. Two-bedroom townhouse, free TV cable, $210 per month. Three-bedroom house, carport and storage shed, $275 per month. Two-bedroom, two-bath apartments, $200. One-bedroom house in Gardner, carport, $115. Rents like this are available all along the coast. Real estate sales are "soft" as well, this being a renters' and buyers' market. About 37 percent of the homes for sale are listed for under $45,000, with many in the $19,000-$35,000 range, and 67 percent are under $55,000.

The only population center of any size on the Oregon coast is Coos Bay-North Bend. Although each has its own municipal government, police department and such, the two towns for all practical purposes merge into one, with a combined population of 25,000. It's difficult to determine where one ends and the other begins. Since the municipality of Coos Bay is the larger, folks usually refer to both towns as Coos Bay (probably to the chagrin of the North Bend City Council). The town seems larger than 25,000 though, probably because it's a trading center for an area extending 50 miles north to Florence and 100 miles south to Brookings.

Coos Bay-North Bend is situated on the blunt end of a peninsula, with Pacific beaches on one side and the waters of Coos Bay on the other. The Coast Range, heavily timbered and colored a shadowy blue-green, makes a pretty background for the town. The mouth of the bay is crossed by graceful McCullough Bridge where a third town, Charleston, makes up another integral part of Coos Bay, although it, too, has its own city council, mayor and city staff. Fishing and lumber are the major industries, with fine harvests of Salmon, tuna, crab, shrimp, oysters and clams. Because the well-protected harbor is navigable by ocean-going vessels, Coos Bay claims to be the world's largest forest products shipping port. But since lumber isn't the hottest item going nowadays, things are rather slow.

The Oregon coast is big on parks. Within a six-mile drive are four exceptional ones, including Cape Arago, the site where, according to the local chamber of commerce, Sir Francis Drake first set foot on the North American continent. Deep sea fishing, crabbing and clamming are favorite pastimes. Just north of here is the lower entrance to famous Oregon Dunes National Recreation Area, with 50 miles of unspoiled beaches, woods and marvelous sand dunes. This is a great place for picnics, camping and beachcombing. A current sweeps ashore, bringing all sorts of treasures, some from as far away as Japan. Among the prizes are weathered redwood burls, which make marvelous natural sculptures. The smaller ones are made into lamps, while the larger ones cut into slabs, polished and turned into cocktail tables. One retiree I spoke with, a man from Parma, Idaho, turned his woodworking hobby into a rather lucrative business by creating artistic lamps, clocks and furniture from redwood burls. "I sell all I can make," he said. "Problem is, I keep too busy to go out and look for burls--have to buy 'em nowadays."

In addition to ocean and bay fishing, there are numerous streams flowing through the Coast Range mountains, from large rivers that are navigable for several miles inland, to mountain brooks with native rainbow and brown trout. Salmon invade the streams at spawning time, and travel amazing distances, sometimes up creeks so small and shallow that it's hard to imagine how they manage it. I've seen salmon skeletons almost three feet long on the banks of a stream near Roseburg, about 50 miles from the ocean! Little more than a creek, the stream is dry in summer and not more than a foot and a half deep in the winter. Once the salmon arrive at the spawning grounds and accomplish their mission, they die. They just buy one-way tickets, I suppose.

Like most of the coast, the climate is mild. Summer temperatures are around 60 to 70, with an occasional "heat wave" into the 80s. Winters are cool, with 45- to 50-degree highs, but not a whole lot colder at night. Freezes and snows are unlikely. It rains a lot on the Oregon coast, but 75 percent of the annual rainfall comes during November through March.

Apartments and condos are more plentiful in Coos Bay because of its more urban character. Studios range from $130, with an average of $144; one-bedrooms range from $103 to $378 with an average of $204; two-bedrooms average about $270. Houses range from $219 to $601 a month, with an average three-bedroom rental at $310.

Being from a high-rent area, I find these low rents along the Oregon coast simply amazing. With $270 a month for an apartment or $75 a month for space in a mobile home park, and low utility needs, I would give the Oregon coast top honors in inexpensive, yet quality living. My major complaint would be the cool summers: I like 'em *hot*. But for the people who live there, cool summers and offshore breezes are major attractions.

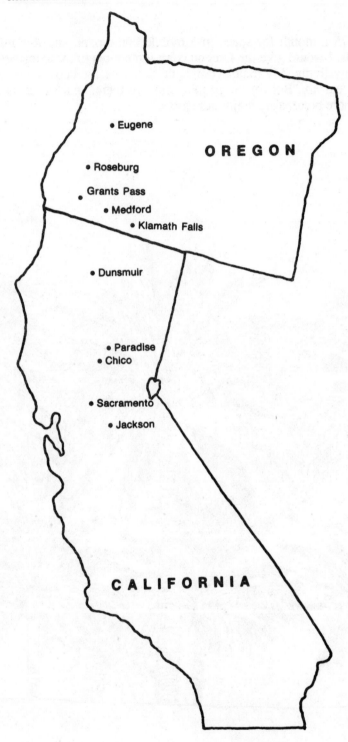

CHAPTER SIX

# *Mountains and Inland Valleys*

The best known parts of the West Coast are along the Pacific Ocean. But there is another world just a few miles inland, eastward across the Coastal Range of mountains. There's a series of valleys which run the length of the country, interspersed and crossed by mountain ranges. The valleys are wide and fertile, patched with farms that help feed the nation. Along the eastern edges loom the Sierra Nevada, with their snow-capped peaks. This country is about as far from the ordinary perception of Southern California and palm trees as you can get.

This land was settled primarily by folks from the Midwest, so it is no coincidence that the inland towns, both valley and mountain, remind one of the Midwest. As the topography rises from flat farmland to rolling hill country, and finally to mountain grandeur, the retiree is presented with an astounding range of choices. I don't know of any place in the Northern Hemisphere where there are so many different climates within such a limited area. Those who think of California as Hollywood have some surprises coming!

Within a few hours' drive you can go from the below-sea-level deserts of the south to wheat and cattle country in the center of California. Then, another couple of hours and you can be skiing or panning for gold in the Sierra. Housing ranges from practical desert adobes to mountain chalets. Scenery varies from flat rice paddies to snow-covered granite peaks. The good news is that housing costs haven't joined the coastal madness. There are places where ordinary people with ordinary incomes can live about as inexpensively as they lived back home.

**THE MOTHER LODE COUNTRY**--If California has a "historical heartland," it would have to be in the picturesque *Mother*

*Lode* country. This is where the intrepid *'49ers* discovered and worked the fabulously rich mines in the wild days of 1849. There are a multitude of reminders of those times in the small towns of the Mother Lode. Gold mining country stretches for about 300 miles, from Downieville on the north down to Coarsegold in the south. The Mother Lode itself takes in nine counties--Madera, Mariposa, Tuolumne, Calaveras, El Dorado, Placer, Nevada, Sierra and Amador. Then, 100 miles to the northwest, another area of historic gold mining towns covers several more counties--Butte, Siskiyou, Tehama, Shasta, Trinity and Lassen--from where even more gold flowed to enrich the country.

Where did all this gold come from? Along this north-south ridge of foothills and mountains, runs a 120-mile-long series of gold-bearing quartz veins. They originated deep within the earth, sending stringers of gold to the surface in ledges and veins of glass-like quartz rock. Over several millions of years, this quartz eroded and weathered to release its gold which eventually washed down the western slopes of the Sierra Nevada to concentrate in streams and gullies. The gold concentrates were unbelievably rich, causing fevers of excitement when a worker at Sutter's Mill, near Sacramento, found the shining metal in the creeks in 1848.

News of the discovery leaked out, and the rush was on. People came by covered wagon, or on horseback, some sailed around Cape Horn in a frenzy of prospecting seldom seen before in history. Eager miners attacked these streams with gold pan and sluice box to fill buckets and chests with gold nuggets. The city of San Francisco, 150 miles away, was built because of and with this bonanza of precious mineral.

The '49ers didn't get *all* of the gold. There's enough left to keep hundreds of weekend prospectors and amateur miners working at their dredges and sluice boxes. With much of the countryside still public land and national forest, there is plenty of room to try your luck. A favorite family outing is to take a picnic lunch and a couple of gold pans and while away the afternoon working one of the many creeks and streams that traverse the oak-and-pine covered hills. Some people do quite well, but you can expect them to be very close-mouthed about *where* they find their private bonanza.

But the biggest resource today isn't gold. The attraction is pleasant living in one of California's most beautifully endowed sections. From rolling hills studded with black oaks and manzanita, to the majestic peaks of the Sierra Nevada, the Mother Lode encompasses a unique scenic wonderland. Here you find not only a true four-season climate, but variation on the seasons, depending on the altitude you choose. From mild winters and warm summers in Jackson and Angels Camp to deep snow-pack and cool summers in Lake Tahoe, you have a smorgasbord of climates and seasonal colors. Trout streams offer some of the finest fishing imaginable, with even the rare golden trout waiting to be hooked in high, remote lakes. This is about as far from the media's "California image" as you are likely to find.

Perhaps the most famous scenic resource of the Mother Lode is its collection of old mining towns. Narrow streets, with buildings of native stone and brick, harmonize perfectly with the green-clad mountain backdrops. These towns are jealously preserved as a charming part of California's past. You'll find such towns as Jamestown, Angels Camp, San Andreas, Enterprise, Placerville and Mokelumne Hill, to name only a few. A visit to any of them is a step back into the past. This was the country of Bret Harte and Mark Twain. Some towns survived through the years intact, while others are today nothing more than historic location markers along the roads and highways of the Mother Lode.

Often called "ghost" towns, the survivors are anything but that, since plenty of people have discovered how pleasant it can be to live there. Far from being abandoned, the Mother Lode is booming. A good deal of the boom comes from people seeking quiet, but interesting and picturesque, places for retirement. And, unlike many popular retiree areas, there is no danger of it becoming overcrowded. The area is too vast and the towns too small to ever feel crowded. Because there is very little basic industry, there aren't a lot of highly paid workers to bid up the price of housing. That, plus the gentle climate make the Mother Lode country a prime candidate as a retirement choice.

**AMADOR COUNTY**--As an example of the Mother Lode country, let's look in detail at one location, Amador County. In the center of the Mother Lode, Amador County straddles historic Highway 49, which runs along the route of the trail that once connected the busiest of the mining towns from north to south. One of the richest gold mining districts of all, Amador County accounted for more than half of all the gold harvested from the Mother Lode. Here we find such fascinating towns as Jackson, Sutter Creek, Volcano, Fiddletown and Plymouth. Drytown, now a little wide spot on Highway 49, was once not so small or so dry. At its prime, Drytown boasted 27 saloons. That was before it attracted the notice of some enthusiastic prohibitionists, after which it acquired its current name.

Loaded with relics of the past, each of these towns takes pride in maintaining and restoring the historic old buildings. Jackson, the largest town in the county, is an intriguing mixture of old and new, with the downtown perfectly preserved in the tradition of the gold rush days. Brick and stone buildings line narrow streets, adorned with iron shutters and wrought iron balconies in the style of the mid-1800s. Yet the newer outskirts have modern ranch-style homes, as suburban-looking as you might expect to find anywhere. Like most Gold Country towns, Jackson has plenty of old brick and Victorian frame houses that have been restored, with all modern conveniences added, and plenty which are awaiting someone's loving care, imagination and restoration. Rentals are reasonable, with two-bedroom apartments and duplexes ranging from $200 to $650 per month. Two- and three-bedroom houses rent from $235 to $750 per month. There are five mobile home parks in the county.

Highway 88, the trans-Sierra route, cuts through Jackson on its way east across the mountains at Carson Pass and down into Nevada. Highway 88 was designated as the country's most scenic highway by *Parade Magazine*. The highway passes through Pine Grove and Volcano, past Inspiration Point, Maiden's Grave and Tragedy Springs, just to name a few of the historical sights along the way. This route was once called the "Carson Emigrant Trail" because of its popularity with gold-seeking settlers.

In western mountain areas, climate varies with altitude, and the altitude varies wildly in Amador County. The lower elevations start at 200 feet and range all the way to more than 9,000 feet. Magnificent views of snow-covered peaks, mountain lakes and meadows are everywhere. With summer humidity of about 33 percent, even the warmest days are not uncomfortable. The yearly mean temperature is about 61 degrees. The winters are short and mild (January maximums are at 56 degrees) and summers are long and pleasant.

When I asked Marcia Oxford of the Amador County Chamber of Commerce why she thinks retirees are moving there she replied: "It *must* be attractive here; almost 50 percent of our population consists of retirees. Because of the geographical diversity, people can live in the rolling foothills, in the pines and evergreens or higher in the snow country. We enjoy four distinct seasons, the air is clean, and there is a wonderful, warm small-town care and friendliness that we all enjoy." I don't know what else to add.

PARADISE--There are hundreds of great retirement locations in the California and Oregon foothills. It would be impossible to list or describe all of them, and that's a shame, because some of these towns are favorites.

A particularly nice retirement California mecca is the town of Paradise. Perched atop a wide, forested flat spot called Nimshew Ridge, Paradise is a particularly scenic place. At an altitude of around 2,000 feet, it is below the snow belt, yet above the smog level of the Sacramento Valley. (There isn't really that much smog there, but occasionally, when farmers burn the rice fields down below, there will be a trace.) This altitude also means about 10-degree lower summer temperatures than the valley floor below.

This is an area of crystalline trout streams and picturesque canyons, with towering pine trees set against a mountain background. The 34,000 people who live here take great care to build their homes without disturbing the trees any more than necessary. Building lots are large, usually a quarter- to half-an-acre, sometimes several acres, and the houses are scattered so that it's hard to believe there could be that many people there. Because of the low housing density, with lots of forest, Paradise is a sanctuary for wild game, since hunting is prohibited in town. Deer and raccoons saunter about town insolently, as if they were taxpayers. Instead of regular city streets, Paradise has roads that wander off in random directions, seemingly in no particular order, and unencumbered by sidewalks. This adds immeasurably to the rural feeling and belies the fact that it's a city of 34,000.

The Paradise area was originally a collection of scattered little villages and gold mining camps with picturesque names such as Dogtown, Toadtown, Poverty Ridge and Whiskey Flats. It was at Dogtown (now Magalia) that a 59-pound gold nugget was discovered by a couple of happy prospectors back in 1859. Several nuggets weighing up to nine pounds were found, but after that biggie, nobody paid much attention. I assume that nine-pounders were still considered "keepers."

Gradually space filled in between the settlements until today you just have Paradise and adjoining Magalia. Although basically residential and rural in nature, the area has enough population to offer the amenities of a small city. There are adequate shopping facilities, with several tastefully done shopping complexes. Cable TV is available, and even home delivery of pizza, that ultimate mark of civilization. Yet, because things are so spread out, Paradise manages to retain the atmosphere and flavor of a village. The "downtown" part is just a few blocks long, and with very few buildings more than one story high.

About a ten-minute drive from Paradise is the development of Paradise Pines. Homes and mobile homes are scattered throughout the area on large lots, with plenty of trees and shrubs. A golf course, restaurant and shopping center keep the "Pines" from being too isolated. The altitude here is only a little higher than Paradise or Magalia, but high enough to catch a lot more snow in the winter. People don't seem to mind, though, since snowplows keep the streets and driveways clear, and there are no sidewalks to shovel. Health care is unusually good for an area this size. There's a 109-bed hospital, two convalescent hospitals, three medical care centers, plus several residential care and guest homes. One reason for this is the large number of retired people living in Paradise. Forty-nine percent of the population is over 55 years old. This large population of retirees means lots of organized activities and clubs. In addition to the usual AARP organization, there is a Golden Fifties Club, a Retired Teachers Association, a senior singles club and a couple of senior citizen political action coalitions.

As a residential and retirement community, Paradise offers few job opportunities; most employment is in construction, building homes or remodeling. This means wages are low. Retirement is the industry here. Because almost half of the population is living on fixed retirement incomes, there is little pressure on housing and related expenses. Therefore, housing costs and rents haven't been pushed to the ridiculous highs of some other parts of California. Home prices start at around $40,000 for a modest place to over $200,000 for something with a spectacular view of the Feather River Canyon down below Nimshew Ridge. Rentals for two- to four-bedroom homes range from $310 to $650 a month, with mobile homes renting for $150 to $375. Mobile home parks are plentiful and space rents quite affordable. As an example of prices, I have a three-bedroom rental in Paradise, on a three-quarter-acre lot, with loads of trees and landscaping, which has been on the market for $39,000 with still no takers. Hopefully, it will be sold by the time this book is published. If not, maybe...

An interesting housing alternative in the Paradise area is placing a mobile home on an individual lot. Most California towns frown on this, but because the lots in Paradise are so large and have so many trees, the mobile homes seem to fit in well. Although lots are becoming scarce within the city limits, there are many available within a 10-minute drive from a shopping center. Typically, a couple will buy a two- to 10-acre parcel, then clear away enough trees to park an older mobile home. Once they dig a septic tank, they hook the mobile home up and have instant plumbing, plus a kitchen. Then they convert the rest of the mobile home into one large bedroom, and build on a large, spacious living room and extra bedroom. Because they are outside the jurisdiction of building inspectors, they can do much of the work themselves with the assistance of whatever hired help they need. Since they don't have to worry about doing plumbing and extensive electrical work (they're built into the mobile home), they have little need for high-priced, high-skilled workers. Once they attach a garage and a workshop, they end up with a spacious home for a minimum investment. Then, the good part: When it comes to property taxes, they only pay at the rate of an unimproved lot with a mobile home and attachments.

Farther up the highway, in true snow country, is a town built by the Diamond Match Company back in 1903: Stirling City. For years the town prospered as a lumbering center. A narrow-gauge railroad carried pine boards and timbers down the mountains to Chico. But a few years ago Diamond Match phased out its operations, tore up the railroad tracks and sold its houses and buildings. Today, the depressed real estate market offers some rather attractive buys. Bank financing is difficult on some homes, however, since many are built on pilings rather than cement foundations. As far as I can tell this doesn't affect livability, but lending banks usually insist on foundations.

**CHICO**--About 20 minutes away by automobile is the typical Sacramento Valley town of Chico. While its population is about the same as Paradise (around 30,000 inhabitants), it is quite different in many respects. For one thing, the topography there is as flat as a table, and the predominant kind of trees are oaks rather than pines. But most of all, Chico is a conventional small city, with streets arranged in blocks, running at right angles to each other, with buildings and houses lined up in orderly fashion. The streets are neatly bordered with sidewalks and mature shade trees. In short, Chico is small college town, U.S.A., with a Central Valley climate.

The state university there is preferred by many California parents when choosing a school for their children. Regardless of what *Playboy* might have hinted, Chico State has the reputation of being quiet and serious. It's far away from the temptations of big cities and beaches, and is renowned for turning out well-educated graduates. Like all of the state universities, Chico State is inexpensive (for California residents) and prides itself on hiring good, dedicated professors. And, like the other schools in the state university system, it encourages senior citizen participation. Cultural events, such as concerts, plays, lectures and foreign films are plentiful and more often than not, free.

Most homes in Chico are older, in rather comfortable neighborhoods. Most are of frame construction, often with stucco finishes. Throughout California this kind of construction is favored because of its resilience in earthquakes. A brick building tends to crack and suffer damage, while a frame house simply twists and rolls with the punches. Some newer, more costly housing inevitably crops up as the city expands, but even these aren't particularly expensive, at least not by California standards. Some new three-bedroom homes can be purchased for $70,000.

An advantage of living somewhere like Chico is that it is not only a nice place to live, but that a short drive into the mountains will bring you to the natural beauty and the recreational opportunities of the Feather River Canyon wilderness country. Skiing is available at Inskip, about 40 minutes away, and some of the best striped bass in the West are caught in the nearby Sacramento River. Incidentally, I've seen some monster sturgeon hauled in from that river, many tipping the scale at over 200 pounds! Since sturgeon is a game fish and seldom sold commercially, few people have ever tasted a succulent steak from one of these large fish. It's like no other fish you've ever tasted--as firm as lobster, and as juicy as a filet mignon, yet with a flavor that is closer to frog legs than to fish.

The weather in Chico, as in all Central Valley towns, is both a blessing and a drawback, depending on your opinion of how hot summers should be. Here, you can find days on end with temperatures approaching 100 degrees. Balance that against the warm, seldom frosty winter days, and I believe that Chico's weather comes out a winner. After all, when the summer gets going, that's the time for you to get going for the nearby mountains for a picnic beside a cool stream, or a day's prospecting and panning for gold in the Feather River. Maybe open a cold beer while you're at it.

Other comfortable Sacramento Valley locations that seem attractive to me are Oroville, Marysville-Yuba City and Redding. The climates are about the same, with mild winters and hot summers. Fortunately, the humidity is fairly low, so the summers aren't totally unbearable. Redding, by the way, is the farthest point north where palm trees can grow. They don't seem to like altitude or freezing weather.

LINDSAY--As an example of a San Joaquin Valley town, I picked Lindsay, partly because I know it well and partly because it is typical of most towns in the valley. Like the other valley settlements, Lindsay is full of small-town charm. Quiet residential streets are anchored with large, white-painted homes, shaded by mature sycamore and ash trees. Trimmed lawns and hedges demonstrate a definite pride of ownership, even though most houses are quite modest in appearance and in price. The original inhabitants here were midwestern and southern farmers. They built replicas of the homes they left in Illinois, Kansas or Oklahoma. With a population of only 7,000, Lindsay maintains this quiet midwestern dignity. It's as different from Southern California as Oklahoma City is from Los Angeles.

Back in depression days, streams of "dust bowl" refugees made their way toward the Sacramento and San Joaquin valleys in search of employment and a new life. John Steinbeck dramatized their plight in his famous book, *The Grapes of Wrath*. He did much of his research in this area, talking to the refugees and observing what went on. One of the most poignant settings of the book took place at a labor camp near Lindsay. The scene was an experimental government camp, a clean, well-managed place where the unfortunate Joad family received its first decent treatment on the journey. The camp is still there, although long abandoned as a labor camp. It really deserves a historical marker, but to date it has been ignored.

Many of these migrant workers found work here and stayed on. They toiled hard, saved what they could, and survived. Times got better and they managed to buy a little land to farm for themselves. Then they bought some more. They grew cotton and corn, as they did back home, but also planted oranges, olives and plums. Then they bought more land and irrigated and planted even more acreage. According to the county chamber of commerce, there are over 400 different crops grown in Tulare County. (I just threw that in for your amazement as well as mine. I'm trying to imagine what 400 legal crops they are raising.)

Today's prosperity obscures the tragedy which drove them from their homes in places like Oklahoma, Arkansas, Nebraska or Texas. The grinding poverty of 50 years ago is but a dim memory. Families who arrived in bailing-wired Model T's, today drive new Buicks and have air-conditioned pickups to work around the orchards. They live in neat stuccoed houses with swimming pools and barbecues in the backyard. Instead of laboring for others, most own or lease land and depend upon Mexican migrant workers to do what they used to do. Times have changed. Although some families are quite wealthy today, they don't flaunt it by ostentatious living; that wouldn't be Lindsay's style. If a family feels the need to drive flashy cars and live in fancy hillside homes, they move to Los Angeles where hillside mansions are admired. Besides, Lindsay is flat--there aren't any hillsides to build mansions on.

Like most of central California, Lindsay has the look and texture of a midwestern farming town, little different from ones you would find in Iowa or Indiana. Were it not for orange groves and an occasional palm tree, you would have a hard time remembering you were in California. As in the Midwest, agriculture is the major industry, providing a stable economy. The quality of life is quite high, combining with a low cost of living, a low crime rate and small-town charm to make the Central Valley a good bet for retirement living.

Lindsay boasts a multitude of recreational activities. Besides the usual golf, tennis and bowling of small-town America, the people of the San Joaquin Valley have the rugged Sierra Nevada for outdoor sports. The foothills begin just a few miles east of city limits and quickly turn into abrupt serrated granite--a scenic marvel. Hunting, fishing, backpacking and water and snow skiing are just minutes away. Yet the valley floor is warm enough, year-round, to permit outdoor activity whenever you feel you need it. A three-hour drive brings you to Los Angeles, and San Francisco is four hours north. The Pacific beaches are three hours to the west.

Twenty or thirty similar towns are scattered throughout the valley, virtual clones of Lindsay. Some located in the same county are: Porterville, Exeter, Dinuba, Farmersville, Tulare, Visalia and Woodlake. But just 30 minutes' drive from Lindsay, up into the Sierra, are some other good places for retirement that have been attracting more attention lately. Lake Success and Lake Kaweah provide boating, fishing and water skiing and have more of a view and picturesque qualities than the Central Valley towns. Three Rivers, a little higher into the mountains is another scenic place for retirement.

Weather on the valley floor is typical of central California: Hot summers and mild winters. Occasionally it freezes in the winter, an event that calls for frantic, sometimes heroic efforts on the part of the farmers to protect the orchards. Smudge pots, windmills, water sprays and other frost-fighting machinery are mobilized in an anxious effort to keep the crops from damage. I used to own a five-acre plot of valencia oranges near Lindsay, and although I paid someone else to take care of them, I lost a few nights' sleep worry-ing that a freeze might strike my precious crop. However, in the five years that I owned the orchard, I only had one minor freeze damage, and Federal Crop Insurance paid for that. Even though it might drop below 32 degrees in the night, the sun's first rays in the morning usually evaporate the frost, and by noon the farmers are usually working in their shirt-sleeves. On the other end of the scale, when

summer temperatures become uncomfortable, it's a simple matter to hop in the car and drive to higher ground and enjoy a picnic beside a lake or a dip in a cool mountain stream.

   **DUNSMUIR**--Farther north, past Redding and beautiful Lake Shasta, straddling the Sacramento River (not far from its source), is the mountain town of Dunsmuir. Dunsmuir sits in a canyon, overlooked by ridges covered with Christmas tree pines and segmented by streets that climb steeply from river bottom to the interstate highway above town. Year-round, the town enjoys a spectacular view of snow-covered Mt. Shasta in the distance. This ancient volcano, 14,110 feet high, is one of the highest peaks on the continent, and offers some pretty fair skiing at a place called Snowman's Hill.

   Dunsmuir is an old town, with very few homes younger than 50 years. A sense of history permeates the old-fashioned downtown section, with its one main street, where the Greyhound station is still called the "stage stop" by local people. The town began as a roundhouse and station to service passing trains, providing fuel and water for the locomotives and food for the dining cars. With the decline of steam engines, the original purpose of the town evaporated. With declining employment opportunities, the bottom dropped out of the real estate market, which didn't have far to fall, since property was always quite reasonable. Retirees found this an ideal location--great fishing, economical living, a gorgeous view from the front porch every morning and unforgettable sunsets.

   Schools of trout, sometimes large native ones, tempt the fisherman to the shores of the Sacramento River. Wild blackberry bushes on the banks yield delicious makings for cobblers should the fish not be biting that day. The river, springing from a rocky gorge a few miles north, makes its way south, picking up clear waters from brooks and creeks on its way to the Sacramento Valley far below. By the time it reaches the city of Sacramento, it is wide, sluggish and coffee-colored with sediment.

   Like Paradise, one of Dunsmuir's major sources of income is pension and Social Security checks. Summer tourism helps, as people come for a few days of fly fishing. Because Interstate 5 bypasses the town nowadays, the pace along the one main street is leisurely and unhurried.

   Dunsmuir's northern location and 2,300-foot elevation provide for some awesome winter snowstorms. But it's a special kind of snow, seldom seen elsewhere, that falls here. Snowflakes, sometimes looking as big as your fist, come drifting down, piling up one atop another, adding inches in depth as you watch. It's an amazing sight. Two or three feet of snow can build up overnight, turning the canyon into a billowy white winter fantasyland. Oldtimers claim they've seen it snow six feet in one day. But the temperatures are usually too warm for snow to last. Almost as quickly as it comes, the snow disappears, usually melting the next day or the following day at most. At higher elevations, the snowflakes are much smaller, and the snow is less frivolous about its business, sticking around for longer periods. At really high elevations, snow sticks around all winter long, and sometimes through the summer as well.

Here are some classified ads taken from the Nov. 26, 1986 issue of the *Dunsmuir News*. They are typical of those in the classified ads from that day. Rentals: --2 bdrm. apt--garbage, water, refrig. & stove. Adults, $285 mo. --1 bdrm. furn. or unfurn. $175 to $250. --Cozy 1 bdrm home, stove & refrig. $200. --3 bdrm house on river, double garage, fenced yard $350 mo. For Sale: --1,500 sq. ft. 2 bdrm., large beam construction, solar & wood heat, quiet with good view. $47,500. --2 bdrm, 1 bath custom log home, lg. wood stove, 2/3 acre-plus, fenced rear yard, outbldgs, corral. $68,000. --3 bdrm, 2,800 sq. ft. with guest house, $75,000.

# OREGON

It used to be that when you crossed from California into Oregon you were greeted with signs that said, "Welcome to Oregon, We Hope You Enjoy Your Visit." As if that weren't plain enough, someone usually added beneath the sign, "And Then Go Back to California!" You used to see bumper stickers that pleaded, "Don't Californicate Oregon!" The concern was that so many outsiders--not only Californians, although these were the main offenders--were descending on Oregon, buying up property and bringing disturbing new ways into this conservative, old-fashioned state.

Their fears were well founded. Outsiders with money were discovering that Oregon had a lot to offer. A near-perfect climate, inexpensive land, fantastic fishing and scenic wonders at every turn of the head. The word leaked out, and the natives grew restless as foreigners arrived with their Jaguar convertibles, hot tubs and sushi-sashimi California culture.

Oregon was, and is, a pickup truck and chicken-fried steak state. The natives weren't eager for change. Besides, they weren't sure whether sushi was something to eat or to rub on your belly after a hot tub.

But two things happened to change the Oregonians' minds. First of all, the lumber industry collapsed, and with it, the job market. Many of those who bitterly complained about the "Californication" of Oregon were forced to move to California to seek employment. The second thing was the discovery that when Californians moved to Oregon, they shed their exploitive ways and became true-blue Oregonians. Convertibles were traded in for four-wheel-drive International pickups and log cabins came into demand (maybe with four bedrooms and three baths, but still log cabins). Hot tubs were discarded in favor of wood-fired saunas. The new residents immediately joined in the campaign to discourage "outsiders" from spoiling their paradise. They became instant Oregonians.

Things certainly have changed. To show you how different things are today, Medford, 30 miles north of the California border, has developed a symbol of welcome called the "Huggy Bear." A furry, cuddly creature, the Huggy Bear's slogan is, "We Hug Visitors in Medford!" According to the Medford Chamber of Commerce, this is not an idle promise, "Come and see for yourself that *we HUG visitors in Medford!"* I think they're serious, that "Medford is fast becoming the hugging capital of the world," as the Chamber claims. Nevertheless, I'm not sure I care to be hugged by some furry, cuddly creature--not unless I was quite sure of its intentions.

You might not get hugged in other parts of Oregon, but you can be sure that you will be welcomed when you go there to retire. In fact, in many communities, the money retirees pump into the economy makes the difference between business as usual and stagnation. Local people *love* retirees!

Some Oregon communities have attracted so many retirees (both Oregonians and outsiders) that the political balance is in the hands of the over-60 crowd. This is an important development to consider, a development that is happening in towns and cities all over the country. Senior citizens living in this kind of situation have a chance (often for the first time in their lives) to actually have a say politically. Your voice means something when you vote. When you attend a senior citizen political meeting, your opinion can be heard. Don't misunderstand, the tax base isn't terribly large in a state where there is high unemployment, low property values and low incomes. There isn't a whole lot of tax money to be thrown around. But when senior citizens become active politically, you can be sure that their needs won't be totally ignored in favor of some other special interest group.

Oregon is basically a rural state. There is only one city of any size, Portland. The rest of the state consists of small cities or towns with lots of farming and generous areas of forest and wilderness. Far from being overcrowded, Oregon is quite sparsely settled, with room for many, many newcomers. In fact, 49.7 percent of the state is in public hands, either belonging to the state of Oregon or to the U.S. government. We've already talked about the Oregon coast, so let's look at inland Oregon.

**MEDFORD-ASHLAND**--Since Medford is so heavily into welcoming visitors, let's start with a brief description of this town and its neighbor, Ashland. The country around here, the Rogue River Valley, is gently rolling hills, with sizable remnants of the thick forests that once covered the area. Early pioneers recognized the agricultural potential and cleared the forest to build their farms. Mild winters and a long growing season make for profitable farming. Summers see a few 90-plus days, but evenings always cool off to the point that a sweater feels comfortable.

Off in the distance, about 30 miles to the east, run the forest-covered mountains of the Cascade Range. About 80 miles from Medford, up on the spine of the Cascades, is spectacular Crater Lake. An eye-popping sapphire gem, Crater Lake is the deepest lake in the United States and is the centerpiece of a national park of the same name. Boundary Springs, just inside the park, is where the Rogue River originates for its 215 mile journey to the Pacific Ocean. The scenic beauty of the river is legendary as it falls through gorges and canyons. It widens as it passes through the Rogue River Valley, then narrows sharply on the other side of Grants Pass as it cuts through the hard igneous rocks of Klamath Mountains on the way to the Pacific.

On the south, another 30 miles distant, is Mt. Ashland, which dominates the Siskiyou Mountain Range. Skiing is usually available from Thanksgiving through April, with up to 22 runs operating. The summer months, filled with wildflowers and sunshine, make picnics memorable events.

Medford (pop. 43,000) and Ashland (pop. 15,000) are quickly becoming retirement meccas for several reasons, not the least of which is bargain real estate. Here are a couple of newspaper examples of Medford house offerings as of spring 1987: 2-story, 1900s era home, 6 bedrooms, 2 baths, $49,900. Duplex, owner will finance, $37,500. A 10-acre hay farm was advertised for $75,000 which includes a 3-bedroom, 1-1/2 bath home, outbuildings, a pond and 8 to 10 head of cattle.

Homes in Ashland are priced a bit higher, but there are many rock-bottom priced cottages along the river, some going for under $30,000. Rents are also affordable, and mobile home parks are plentiful.

Another often-cited reason for choosing this part of Oregon for retirement is its unusually rich cultural atmosphere. Ashland is the site of a nationally celebrated Shakespearian festival. The outdoor theater was patterned after the Globe Theatre of Shakespeare's time in 16th century London. Contemporary theater is also produced here. The presence of Southern Oregon State University contributes a lot to the climate of abundant culture and fine arts.

Seventeen miles away from Ashland's Shakespearian Festival is the historic town of Jacksonville, where the Britt Festivals are held. They are the oldest outdoor music and performing arts festivals in the Northwest, numbering five festivals each summer, featuring world-class artists. Concert-goers combine theater with picnics, sipping wine and sampling cheeses while they relax and listen to classical music, jazz, bluegrass, or watch ballet and musical theater.

Once the site of a major gold strike, Jacksonville lost its chance at becoming the largest town in southern Oregon back in 1883 when the Oregon & California Railroad pushed its tracks northward. When the railroad requested a $25,000 "bonus" to place a station in Jacksonville, the city fathers unwisely refused to pay. Instead, the station was built at a crossroads called Middle Ford. "Middle Ford" shortened its name to Medford and grew while Jacksonville languished. In some ways this was fortunate, because "progress" passed the town by, saving its historic old buildings from the wrecking ball. Its shady, tree-lined streets and restored Victorian homes are a delight to behold. In 1966 it was designated a National Historic Landmark Town.

The climate in southern Oregon is the other major interest of people looking for a place to retire. Here is a four-season climate, but a *gentle* four seasons. Summers are very mild, with warm, sunny days prevailing. Winters are mild with some snow expected, but mostly rain. A word about rain: People talk about Oregon as if it rained all the time, claiming that Oregonians have webbed feet. Statistics show that Medford-Ashland gets between 17 to 21 inches of rain a year, about half that expected in most areas of the Midwest.

**GRANTS PASS**--River-rafting enthusiasts, some who have braved white-water rapids all over the world, will tell you that Oregon's Rogue River is about the prettiest white-water experience they've ever seen. Because of its incredibly gorgeous pathway to the ocean, Congress designated it as the first of the nation's protected rivers under the Wild and Scenic Rivers Act of 1968. Here is where Zane Grey chose to build his home and to write many of his famous western novels. Many of the scenic descriptions in his books were inspired by the picturesque Rogue River country. Moviemakers have found inspiration as well, with Hollywood crews making the trek to Grants Pass to take advantage of the scenery. I've rafted the river three times, and will make it four if anyone suggests doing it.

The town of Grants Pass guards the north bank of the Rogue-- its name closely connected with the river and all of its attractions. For river rafters, fishermen, hunters, backpackers--all of those interested in the outdoor activities--Grants Pass is the starting point. Not a very large town, with about 17,000 people living within the city limits, it is nevertheless the commercial center for people living for miles around. And because of its scenic beauty plus inexpensive housing, the area around Grants Pass has become a retirement goal of more and more retirees. Even though people may live several miles outside of town, they consider themselves residents of Grants Pass. This community spirit is one of the retirees' major benefits, because there is a commonality of purpose and goals it gives them. Senior citizen organizations are take-charge here, with wonderful participation in R.S.V.P. and other volunteer activities.

Volunteer groups are most important here, because the state of Oregon has little money to spare. If things are to be done, they will be done with volunteer labor. Another good thing about volunteering here is that there are very few part-time jobs available for retired people, so those who need meaningful work to feel personal fulfillment will have plenty of opportunities. This is a good thing, because jobs of *any kind* are scarce in Oregon's stagnant economy. Since the bottom dropped out of the lumber market, the younger people have been leaving southern Oregon, taking jobs elsewhere. This means that retirees moving into the area take up the slack. Again, the merchants and business people appreciate the money put into circulation by senior citizens. They're recognized as a vital, dynamic part of the community. Isn't it a good feeling to know that at least *somewhere* people still consider you vital and dynamic?

Downtown Grants Pass is adequate, with plenty of shopping and merchants with a small-town attitude of wanting to please the customers. Don't expect spiffy shopping malls or exclusive fashion boutiques. JC Penney is about as fancy as you get, but then, who needs fashion in Oregon? Denims and plaids are the order of the day.

Houses in town are predominantly older, frame buildings, mostly single-family, neat, well-cared-for and affordable. Newer houses tend to be away from downtown, built on an acre or so, with trees and natural shrubbery planted as low-maintenance landscaping devices. A perusal through the classified section of the local newspaper, the *Daily Courier*, gives you an idea of prices. Here are a few random ads from the Nov. 16, 1986, issue: Two-bedroom home with new carpet, skylight. Fenced, irrigated pasture, two barns with training ring and shop. Mature fruit and walnut trees: $65,000. Or, newly painted 3 bdr. house in quiet area. 7 yrs old, $49,900. Many houses were offered below $40,000. Example: 2 units, $39,900--1 2-bdr home plus a separate studio apt. Or: Remodeled 3-br, covered patio, detach. garage, .78 acre, $39,900. Mobile homes and park spaces are heavily advertised, which tells you that competition is fierce, prices reasonable. Spaces are advertised as low as $95 a month. Please don't get the impression that Grants Pass is all low-cost housing. I saw several rather impressive homes on the market for as much as $400,000.

Dense conifer, maple, oak and dogwood forests begin at the western edge of town and spread over hills and low mountains all the way to the Pacific ocean, some 60 miles away. Many small farms have been carved from the woods, and many a retired couple engages in hobby-farming, with chickens, gardens and maybe a horse. I have a friend who bought a marvelous five-acre tract on the Rogue for less than $60,000. Her house sits high on the bank, giving her a beautiful panoramic view of the river from her living room. This piece of property, complete with a three-bedroom house and a barn, is a 20-minute drive from downtown Grants Pass and five minutes from a country grocery store. Not only couldn't she have found anything like it for the price in California, she couldn't have found the scenic beauty anywhere in the country.

At first I worried about her "fitting in" with the local people. After all, she was not a country person, having been born and raised on the Monterey Peninsula in California. What would she have in common with her neighbors, so far from town, and so isolated? It turns out that she has plenty in common. Her immediate next door neighbor is a widow from Los Angeles. On the other side of the property is another couple from California, who moved there so they could try their hand at raising horses. It seems to me that the majority of the people living around southern Oregon moved there from a city environment to "get away from it all." My friend felt perfectly comfortable and soon acquired an interesting circle of pals. She bought a kayak and learned how to maneuver it, and to my amazement, took it down the Rogue River, through all of the scary rapids and falls--by herself!

Incidentally, the river trip is not really all that bad, provided you go with an experienced boatman. None of the rapids are past "class three," which means even cowards like me can have fun. But I'd like to recommend an extremely interesting way to see the Rogue River Canyon: By backpack. Many senior citizens make this 39-mile hike to the pickup point at Panther Run. It starts at Grave Creek, about 10 miles west of Grants Pass, and follows the north bank as it twists its way west. The trail is quite easy, with a continual downhill slant, and crosses creeks and brooks on well-maintained bridges, courtesy of the state of Oregon. It's strictly a hiking trail and is closed even to horses and pack animals. By making proper reservations, you can stay at delightfully rustic lodges tucked away behind the trees. By day you can leisurely enjoy the beauty of the Rogue River, and at night sleep in the comfort of a real bed after enjoying a gourmet meal. Along the way you can explore abandoned mining claims, old pioneer ranches, and enjoy the unfrightened wildlife--deer, river otter, great blue heron and osprey.

**ROSEBURG**--I know a lot about Roseburg, because my older brother moved there over 20 years ago. Actually he lives on a 110-acre farm a few miles away from Roseburg. Why this part of the country? After all, my brother first retired to Whittier, Calif., after his 20 years in the Navy. Why would he pull up stakes and head north for an Oregon farm? His story is the usual one given by Oregonian immigrants: "I had to get away from the rat race, noise, smog," he says, "and, besides, where could I have found 110 acres with a house and barn for only $21,000?"

Of course, the $21,000 purchase price is about 20 years out of date, but bargains can still be found. Today a piece of property like that would go for well over $100,000--still a bargain! He raises about 60 to 75 head of cattle, mostly letting them shift for themselves, and sells a few critters whenever he feels the need to supplement his retirement income. He does quite nicely for a Los Angeles native.

The country surrounding Roseburg is full of small farms like my brother's place. Actually, few of the farmers are truly serious about making a living on their farms, particularly those who have small acreage. Much of their acreage is in woods, and the rest is often valued more for its scenic value than for economic potential.

Growing one's own food is relatively easy, but making a killing in farming is a little more ambitious than most retirees care to think about.

The city of Roseburg somehow looks more like a city than Grants Pass, although it isn't much larger (pop. 18,000). Buildings in the downtown section tend to be taller, and businesses look much more commercial. Despite this, the people living in and around Roseburg can't help but be small-town, friendly folks.

The climate here is mild, with four distinct seasons. It rains more here than in the south, with an average of 35 inches a year. This accounts for the lush, open farming country in the area as opposed to forest in the more southern parts of Oregon. Early settlers didn't bother clearing land when there wasn't enough rain to sustain profitable crops. As along most of the West Coast, the rain comes in the winter, with only 5 percent of the rain occurring in the summer. This translates into very pleasant spring, summer and fall, with over-90-degree days few and far between. This also means that there are many "snowbird" retirees who try to squeeze the very best out of the weather by flocking to Tucson or the Salton Sea to escape the rainy Oregon winters. Yes, it snows here occasionally, but often only enough to make things pretty for one day before disappearing. To people who come from the Midwest or from the East Coast, there really isn't any winter at all. The temperature never drops to zero, and the lakes never freeze over!

Housing in Roseburg, as in most of Oregon, is a real bargain these days. With the lumber industry in a slump (my guess is a permanent slump), real estate is also down. Only the most reasonably priced homes or farms are selling. Mobile home parks and apartments are also fighting the competition, and you know what that does to rents. All of Oregon is bargain country for people on limited, fixed incomes.

## NORTHERN OREGON

**EUGENE**--Located halfway up the state, Eugene has more rainfall, about 42 inches a year, about twice as much as in the southern part of the state. This ensures that the Eugene-Springfield area stays green all year. The biggest "industry" there is the University of Oregon, with an enrollment of nearly 16,000 students. There is a definite college town air here, as the University of Oregon and Lane Community College contribute immeasurably to the cultural life of the city with ongoing schedules of lectures, concerts, plays and sports offerings, many of which are free. I once attended a segment of a Bach Festival given at the Hult Center for the Performing Arts, at which some of Bach's music was explained and analyzed in a most understandable and enjoyable way.

The most popular sport is trout fishing in the Willamette River, which runs through the heart of the city. Dozens of parks and recreation facilities provide plenty of open space for outdoor recreation. There are miles of jogging and hiking trails, bike paths and river walks. The weather is mild enough that senior citizens can enjoy the outdoors. A 90-minute drive west, through some beautiful low mountain country and the Siuslaw National Forest brings you to the ocean town of Florence. Fishing, picnicking, clamming or beachcombing for Japanese glass fishing floats and driftwood makes an interesting day, and you can return in time for a late supper. Going the other direction is the Deschutes National Forest, crowned by the Mt. Washington and Three Sisters wilderness areas.

To the north are the towns of Corvallis, Salem and finally, Oregon's big city, Portland. All of these towns have great potential as retirement spots. As in most of northwest Oregon, the climate is benign, with cool winters and mild summers. Because property is inexpensive, many retirees choose to own a second home here, and use this part of Oregon for their snowbird escape from summer heat in Arizona. In Eugene, on the average, there are only 15 summer days a year that reach or exceed 90 degrees. Average July and August high temperatures barely top 80 degrees, with 50 degrees at night quite common. Portland enjoys even cooler summers, with high temperatures rarely climbing into the 80s.

**BEND, KLAMATH FALLS**--About 125 miles southeast of Portland, on the other side of the Cascades, is another retirement area that is popular with many retirees, particularly those from California. This is Bend, a city of 19,000. I suspect that its popularity stems partly from the inexpensive cost of land here. This is high desert country, a place where winter is known to visit and leave several inches of white stuff at a time. It's also fishing country, with some landlocked salmon and rainbow trout of marvelous size coming out of the rivers and lakes. To the south and west is national forest land, but in any other direction, for hundreds of miles, the country is very sparsely settled.

Klamath Falls is farther south, near the California border. This is also a fisherman's paradise and great for outdoor sports. One thing about eastern Oregon, you had better be able to take winters, because they have a full four season climate. While not nearly as severe as most of the East and Midwest, it does snow and lakes do freeze. The good news is that, like the other dry, semi-desert climates in the West, the day warms up as soon as the sun comes out.

CHAPTER SEVEN

# *Southwest Desert Retirement*

The American Southwest is enormously popular with retirees. A great deal of this area is desert, but anywhere enough water is found for irrigation, the land becomes lushly green and productive. For the purposes of this book, I define the Southwest as including West Texas, New Mexico, Arizona, parts of Colorado, southeast California and Nevada.

Warm or mild winter is generally the attraction for Southwest and desert retirement, although some places can get downright cold during January and February. Likewise, summers can be baking hot. Summer highs and winter lows vary, depending on such accidents of geography as altitude or the fortuitous location of mountains that shield against winter winds.

Two things you can count on in the desert: Summer heat and lots of sunshine. Phoenix, for example, averages 295 days a year of sunny or partly sunny days. The winters are usually delightfully warm, but daily summer high temperatures average *over* 100 degrees. We can't have everything. Of course relative humidity there averages a low 36 percent, so summer temperatures don't seem nearly as warm as they would in a high-humidity location.

Humidity is an important variable that can affect temperature by making it *appear* to be warmer or colder than it really is. A look at the chart in Chapter Three, illustrating the relationship between temperature, humidity and *perceived temperature* will show that a 95-degree day in Las Vegas (at 20 percent humidity) would be perceived by the body as being 93 degrees. Yet a 95-degree day in Florida (at 75 percent humidity) would be *perceived* as 130 degrees!

No wonder people sit in front of their air conditioners in Florida summers.

So we're faced with a dilemma: Except for the Pacific Northwest, either we enjoy a warm winter and a hot summer, or live elsewhere and have a warm summer and a chilly winter. Many people gladly opt for escaping the cold winters and feel that a little summer heat is worth it. After all, in areas of low humidity, evening temperatures often drop 25 to 30 degrees, into the low 70s. Mornings are cool enough to get outdoors and play a little golf or perhaps take a brisk walk before the sun begins its work in earnest. On the other hand, cold winters can keep you a virtual prisoner indoors.

## MIGRATING PATTERNS OF THE SNOWBIRD

Some people, however, refuse to consider year around retirement in a place where summers are harsh, yet at the same time, they reject frigid winters. These people find the ideal solution in becoming "snowbirds." When the first days of fall begin to turn frosty, they pack up their golf clubs, tennis racquets and suntan oil and then head south, in this case to some warm dry desert town. There, they spread out their chaise lounges to enjoy a sunny winter. When April showers bring spring flowers "back home," they reverse the process. The snowbirds have the best of both worlds, and they have the opportunity to enjoy an active, year-round life with good weather.

Many desert spots cater to the snowbirds in their yearly migration from the frigid northlands. Some mobile home parks in Yuma, Arizona, for example report that 90 percent of their residents arrive in October or November and are gone by the end of April. Mobile homes are perfect for snowbird retirement. They are inexpensive to buy and park space rent is cheap. They don't require a lot of yardwork. With low-maintenance desert landscaping, the homes can be shut up for several months at a time without worrying about the yard becoming shaggy. Cactus seldom requires mowing, so you won't get stuck with that job.

Motor homes, travel trailers and campers are another alternative for many people. Instead of leaving their winter quarters in the desert, they drag them back home come springtime. Some recreational vehicle parks report that 100 percent of their tenants commonly haul or drive their traveling homes to cooler climes in Colorado, Oregon, Massachusetts or other places "back East" to their home towns.

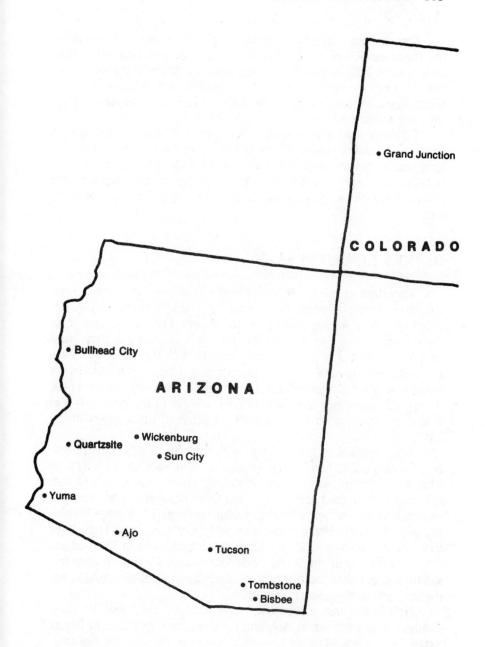

One couple I interviewed, who were wintering in Arizona on the Colorado River, said, "Our utility bills in Michigan were running almost $250 a month, and we couldn't do anything all winter but sit around waiting for spring. So, we decided to become snowbirds. Here, it costs $120 for rent and electricity, and we have a fishing dock at our front door."

Of the people who have bought substantial homes, only about 5 percent regularly "snowbird" north for the summer. This is particularly true in larger towns, like Phoenix or Las Vegas. In many cases, because the larger towns have more employment opportunities, the retirees have part-time jobs and don't care to quit them for the summer.

## DESERT LIFE-STYLES

There are as many life-styles in the Southwest as there are imaginative people. One couple I interviewed, a big-city couple, decided that they would like to try the desert. During the course of their investigation, they discovered a town in Arizona they liked very much, where it seemed that about half of the residents had a few acres and owned a riding horse or two. This couple had always loved animals, but their pets had been limited to a dog and two cats. At age 62, were they too old to learn the ways of the country? Was it too late to become horseback riders after all those years in the city?

They decided to give it a try. With the help of a friendly neighbor, they set out to buy horses and tack, and to learn as much as possible by listening, reading and imitating. Before the year was out, the wife was elected secretary of the local horsemen's association, and both were busily involved in various volunteer activities involving both the horsemen's association and the community. Their lives took on new meaning. They found new friends, and in the process, they became rather proficient horseback riders. Having to care for, saddle and exercise their horses regularly gave them pleasurable activities and healthy exercise for themselves.

"It's been three years now," says Sandy, "and I feel 10 years younger than I did when Bob and I moved here. We can do things today that we would never have dreamed of when we were working. The confidence we've gained is worth any inconvenience of being caretakers to our horses."

# SOME LIKELY PLACES TO RETIRE

Again I point out that it would be impossible to cover *all* the possible retirement locations in this book. This is particularly true of the Southwest. The Southwest is too big, too varied for every town to be listed and covered in any important detail. So, rather than give a list of facts about 500 towns--facts which you can quickly find for yourself in an almanac or atlas, I will concentrate on a few towns I find representative of different sections of the American Southwest, towns I might consider for my own retirement. The first three locations aren't exactly typical, but they are good locations because of some special circumstances.

**BISBEE, Ariz.**--Tucked away in a canyon in the southeastern part of Arizona, only a few miles from the Mexican border, historic Bisbee is one of the newer retirement "discoveries." The town isn't new, in fact it's quite old, and loaded with charm. The streets are narrow and winding, in the classic style of old mining towns. The buildings are authentic Victorian and western mining camp, with brick and clapboard construction dating from the 1890s and earlier. Because of its steep hills and ornate Victorian construction, people often describe the town as having a certain San Francisco aura--sans cable cars, however.

A stroll through the streets of Bisbee is like stepping into the past. The pace is slow and quiet. Since the town is off the standard tourist track, relatively few visitors disturb the ghosts of yesteryear. Night sounds are muted, and after midnight the streets are all but deserted. Still, there are several excellent restaurants, set in authentic period decor.

Bisbee Canyon first attracted attention when U.S. cavalry troops, chasing an Apache war party, chanced upon some outcroppings of silver and copper. Naturally, claims were staked, and the rush was on. Before long the canyon filled with homes, stores and businesses--a bustling town of 20,000. Bisbee at its peak boasted several first-class hotels, prosperous commercial enterprises, plus the usual rash of saloons and shady ladies found in any mining town. Homes of brick and of painted wood terraced themselves into the slopes of the canyon and climbed toward the rim, sometimes precariously, but always picturesquely. It all remains there today, little changed from generations past, giving Bisbee a special flavor difficult to match anywhere else in the world. The shady ladies, however, have moved on, presumably to catch a suntan in Las Vegas.

This was a bustling, thriving little city. But suddenly, in 1975, financial disaster struck. Phelps-Dodge, the mining company that had always been the sustenance of Bisbee, ceased operations. Panic struck the hearts of the canyon's households. Families began leaving in droves--sometimes abandoning their houses, furniture and all. If it hadn't been for the fact that Bisbee was the county seat, disaster might have been total. Today's population has stabilized at just over 8,000.

This collapse happened around the tail end of the "flower child" movement of the '60s-'70s. Word circulated through the underground that Bisbee was a great place to "be," so many young adventurers, intellectuals, artists and just plain bums floated into town on a wave of fading idealism. Some bought houses for a song, others squatted in vacant houses. In those days you could buy a *furnished* home for $4,000, or $2,500, sometimes even as low as $500.

Naturally, retirees and potential retirees heard about these bargains, and found the climate ideal. Thus began a new wave of emigration to Bisbee: Senior citizens. Gradually, retirees bought out most of the "flower children" while other members of the Love Generation, with no means of financial support, opted to join the new "Yuppie" generation and move on to places where they could earn enough money to afford the now obligatory Mercedes or BMW. In case you haven't noticed, among the younger crowd, *money* is "where it's at" today. Thus began the second exodus from Bisbee. But some didn't want to leave. A few representatives of the "now generation" stayed behind, convinced that Bisbee is a great place to live. These "kids" are now in their 40s, some pushing 50, with graying hair, moving inevitably toward senior citizen status. Fortunately for Bisbee, most who stayed on were loaded with talent: Artists, writers, intellectuals and such. Enough quality people stayed to give Bisbee the reputation and flavor of an artist colony.

But be aware that the days of the $500 homes are long gone. Some "fixer-uppers" can still be found for as low as $10,000, but asking prices for a two-bedroom, one-bath place start at about $15,000 and up. The most expensive two-bedroom listing in town (Jan. 1987) was $38,000, which included a garage (a valuable item in a town of narrow streets and scarce parking spots). The building that houses the town's movie theater and two stores was on sale that week--$79,500.

Of course, we are talking *old* houses. Most probably require a lot of work to bring them up to acceptable standards. Yet, for many people, renovating and rejuvenating an old house is enjoyable, a chance to allow artistic and creative abilities to run rampant. And, at the price you pay for an old home, you can afford to be creative! If you aren't into old homes, there are new, two bedroom townhouses selling for $51,600--which includes a community building and swimming pool. In some cities I've visited, $51,500 wouldn't buy a slum apartment. It would just barely purchase that Mercedes Benz for which the ex-Bisbee Yuppie is sweating out payments.

Bisbee is no longer in danger of becoming a ghost town. Far from it. Permits for building and renovations are up about 300 percent over 1984, and many homes are being readied for occupancy. The new rush is on, but this time it's retirees instead of miners. A community college located a few miles east of town offers lots of activities for senior citizens. Several excellent restaurants do good business, and there is even a 9-hole golf course. I didn't see the golf course in person, and I often wish I had. I just can't imagine where they would find enough level ground for it!

Medical facilities are impressive for a small town. It boasts a 49-bed hospital, eight full-time doctors, five dentists, two optometrists, a chiropractor, an osteopath and an ambulance service. The town has a daily newspaper to keep up with local and national happenings.

The climate is excellent, with enough altitude to keep the summers pleasant, plus low humidity to make the winters brisk, but not bitter. During my January visit, the thermometer dropped into the 40s one night, yet I walked around town in a light sweater, feeling perfectly comfortable. Many summer residents come here from Phoenix and Tucson, fleeing the baking, 100+ degree July-August season. One reason for the cooler summer temperatures is that the steep canyon walls cast early afternoon shadows across the town to block the searing heat of the desert sun. A sign painted prominently on one of the downtown business buildings proclaims Bisbee to have the "best climate in the world." I wouldn't go that far, but I have to admit that I've felt few better.

**AJO, Ariz., another busted boom**--The rock-bottom prices in Bisbee are over, but if the idea of living in a ghost town appeals to you, it might not be too late to get in on another bonanza of low-priced real estate. Ajo, about 100 miles west of Tucson, is going through a similar trauma of collapse. Also once sustained by Phelps-Dodge mining interests, the rug was pulled out from under the town in 1983. With the closing of mining and smelting operations, Ajo went from being a bustling town with a peak population of 10,000 down to a being a ghost of its former self, with a skeleton crew of 2,800. Where 1,100 people were once employed at Phelps-Dodge, there are 23 today! Plans are to phase out the remaining 23. Most workers who could take early retirement did so, and remained in Ajo. The rest pulled up stakes and went to seek employment elsewhere.

Since most of the houses belonged to the mining company and were rented out to the employees, there wasn't the mass abandonment of dwellings as happened in Bisbee. The tenants simply vacated the premises, leaving them in the hands of the company. In May 1987, I asked the manager of the Copper Crown Realty Co. about prices of homes. "We have 600 for sale at the moment," he replied, "one-, two- and three-bedroom homes, some with two baths." The price? "From $13,000 to $42,500!" He pointed out that almost all sales have been made to retirees, and this has brought the population back up to around 3,500.

An oasis in the Sonora Desert, Ajo has a pleasant town center which is clustered around a park. Two churches, the library and the post office are located on this plaza, built in the old Spanish mission style, although they weren't actually constructed until 1917. The mining company built the plaza and relocated the town around it when it was discovered the original town sat squarely on top of a rich ore body. Shady palm trees and tall organ pipe cactuses underline the oasis feeling.  Not far away is the 300,000 acre Organ Pipe Cactus National Monument, which was designated to preserve these green, spiny plants whose tall clusters of pipelike arms dominate the landscape through much of the Sonora Desert. About 100 miles west, over a pleasant, lightly traveled road--a little over two hours of easy driving time--brings you to the Mexican town of Puerto Penasco on the shore of the Sea of Cortez. The warm waters there offer some great saltwater fishing.

All in all, the town of Ajo isn't as picturesque as Victorian Bisbee, but then, few places are. Still, there's a small-town desert charm that's likely to captivate someone who really wants to settle in a desert environment. Besides, the prices are right, especially at $13,000 for a house!

Weather is typical Arizona desert, although the local chamber of commerce describes Ajo as the place where "summer breezes, warm winters and friendly smiles await you," and claims that it's "noted for having the best climate in the country, with warm winters and continuous sunshine that other parts of Arizona cannot equal."

Understand, I'm quoting from the Chamber of Commerce. The truth is, I've never been there in the summer, but if Ajo is like the rest of Arizona, the summer breezes are, uh, warm.

I doubt if the town will ever regain its boom-time peak population, but for retirees, this is an obvious benefit. Today it's a calm, quiet place with no crime or vandalism. One of the newcomers stressed this when he said, "One of the best parts about living here, is how safe I feel. Lots of times I forget to lock the house, and it's been a long, long time since I've done that!"

The town has its civic and social organizations, with Elks, Moose, VFW and even a country club left over from more affluent days. The senior citizens have organized, as you might expect, and have a lot of things going, including a lunch program. Apparently, the most active group has adopted the title of "Recycled Teenagers." All in all, this might be a good choice if your personality fits desert living.

**GRAND JUNCTION, Colo.**--We've discussed towns like Bisbee and Ajo, Ariz., where the unexpected collapse of the main industry threw the towns and real estate markets into tizzies and turned these areas to once-in-a-lifetime opportunities for retirees. Get ready for another disaster story. This time it's in western Colorado. I hope I don't sound gleeful about these tragedies, because the workers who lost their jobs suffered plenty, both financially and from their shattered dreams and plans for the future. The damage in mental anguish and material losses can never be accurately measured. But these aren't situations of our making, and no one can be blamed for moving in to fill the gap made by those who left.

Grand Junction, the largest city in western Colorado, is located in a valley of the spectacular high plateau country west of the Rocky Mountains. Its name came from its location near the junction of the mighty Colorado and Gunnison rivers (the Colorado was originally called the Grand River). Grand Junction is the center of an urban area of some 82,000 people, although the town itself has a comfortable 33,000 inhabitants. It also has an abundance of sunshine and a mild winter that permits golf and tennis to be year-round sports.

What's the sad story here? Well, this is the typical rags-to-riches, back-to-rags scenario. During the late 1970s, encouraged and subsidized by the government, several oil companies began exploration of and experimentation with the enormous oil shale deposits of Colorado and Wyoming. Thousands of workers came here to help develop this potentially valuable natural resource. With foreign oil selling at extortionate rates, shale petroleum seemed a sure bet; the future of western Colorado looked rosy, indeed.

These newcomers put pressure on available housing. Single family homes, apartments, condominiums and mobile home parks began springing up. Construction workers and their families added to the boom, moving into Grand Junction and the surrounding town, confident that work would be steady, their futures assured. All this new building still wasn't enough, so Exxon, one of the larger companies, was forced to enter the construction business to provide housing for its employees. Among other things, Exxon developed a flat mountain top, a place called Battlement Mesa, into a spiffy housing development. The company constructed 684 residences, complete with a multi-million dollar recreation center. Other companies involved in this shale operation were Union Oil, Occidental and Chevron. All were hiring at a time when the rest of the nation was suffering through a recession in the early 1980s. New businesses opened, motels and restaurants thrived. An estimated 13,000 people moved into the county.

Suddenly, it collapsed. On Sunday, May 2, 1982, Exxon Corp. announced it was closing its $5 billion Colony Oil Shale Project. Slumping oil prices had made it too expensive to squeeze petroleum from the shale. Grand Junction remembers this date as "Black Sunday."

By the end of a year, almost 8,000 workers had lost their jobs. Most wanted to sell their homes and move on to look for another job, but the real estate market had not only reached rock-bottom, but had fallen even lower. Everybody was selling, nobody was buying. Almost as quickly as they came, the workers began leaving. Knowing they hadn't even a prayer to make payments, many simply walked away from their homes. They couldn't even *give* the properties away because they owed more money on the mortgages than the market value of the houses. The few buyers who were in the market waited for foreclosure and then bought from the mortgage holders.

Battlement Mesa was all but abandoned, its tennis courts and recreation center silent. Many merchants lost everything when they tried to hold on in a hopeless situation. The business people who survived realized that the solution to the problem lay in attracting industry with a stable financial base, something not subject to boom or bust like petroleum. Economic incentives for new and expanding industries such as free land were offered.

At the same time, they began concentrating on an industry that is clean, doesn't pollute the air, and which brings in an obvious source of steady income: Retirement industry! Exxon began marketing the $100-million Battlement Mesa as a retirement community. Other nearby towns, such as Parachute, Palisade, Fruita and Clifton joined the efforts.

Real estate is beginning to move again, with over 50 percent of the sales going to retirees. Battlement Mesa and Parachute are returning to prosperity as they appeal to the new boom of senior citizens who are looking for a great place to retire. These new residents bring stability and steady income into the area and contribute immensely to the community by becoming involved. By June 1987, over 600 retirees had moved into Battlement Mesa. At least that many settled in Grand Junction, while others were buying property in other parts of the rock-rimmed valley. Around 2,300 retirees were expected to settle in all of Mesa County in 1987.

Although property is finally beginning to move, it is still going at bargain-basement prices. A three-bedroom home on a spacious lot can sometimes be purchased for under $25,000. According to one real estate broker, a fourplex can be found for as little as $50,000, and duplexes for $30,000. The foreclosed homes are being handled by the U.S. Department of Housing and Urban Development (HUD), which reports that the average selling price is $39,500. Prices range from $22,500 to over $50,000. The oil companies, under pressure from state and local officials, had installed water and sewer lines and built wide streets in anticipation of new single-family homes. These lots are now being offered as mobile home sites.

Farming is an alternative that some retirees are looking into here. Family fruit ranches are important contributors to the local economy. Palisades, just 12 miles east of Grand Junction, calls itself the "Peach Capital of Colorado" because of the numerous small orchards. The first peaches were planted there in 1884, and today there are over 1,700 acres under cultivation. In addition, there are 375 acres of pears, 1,000 acres of apples and 550 acres devoted to cherries, apricots, plums and grapes.

## CHEAP PROPERTY? SO?

Cheap housing alone is a foolish reason to choose a retirement location. There has to be more than that. It turns out that Grand Junction and Mesa County have plenty to offer.

At an elevation of 4,500 feet, this area is high enough to escape the searing heat of summer that plagues many of the retirement places to the southwest, in Arizona. Average summer high temperatures are in the 80s to low 90s, with cool evenings. Yet winters are surprisingly mild. Unlike Denver, to the east, which catches several blizzards every winter, Mesa County receives just a few inches of snow, and it melts away a few days after it falls. Other Colorado places that are popular with retirees, such as Crested Butte or Aspen, get plenty of snow and cold weather. Still, an hour's drive away are the skiing resorts of Powderhorn and Sunlight, and famous Aspen and Vail are less than two hours.

This mild weather and the beautiful Colorado countryside presents residents with a wide range of outdoor activities. There's golf, tennis, bicycling, horseback riding and hiking from early spring to late fall. Catfish and bass are available in the Colorado River and fabulous trout fishing awaits your lure in such streams as Rifle Creek, Roaring Fork, Frying Pan and White rivers.

Less than an hour's drive takes you to more than 200 well-stocked lakes up on 10,000-foot-high Grand Mesa, the world's largest flat-topped mountain. Camping, backpacking and four-wheel driving are idyllic in this country. The mesa is also the home of deer, elk, bear, pheasant, quail and ducks, even an occasional mountain lion.

Situated about halfway between Denver and Salt Lake City, Grand Junction is the "health care center" of this part of Colorado and Utah. There are three hospitals (one a veterans' hospital) with around 450 beds, plus five nursing rooms with accommodations for 779. I've been told that some doctors in Mesa still make house calls. If this is true, it's a decided plus in Grand Junction's favor.

**TOMBSTONE, Ariz.**--Not too far from Bisbee is the town of Tombstone (pop. 1,700), the town made famous by Wyatt Earp and the "Gunfight at the O.K. Corral." This is where the Earp brothers, Doc Holiday, Johnny Ringo and Bat Masterson gained much of their reputation. Bat Masterson went on to become a sports writer for the *New York World*, so I've always wondered if some of his reputation wasn't due to his skill at getting into the newspapers. I think the reason I want to include Tombstone is the wealth of old-west history that happened here. If it weren't for this glamour, the town would probably have crumbled into the landscape long ago.

Tombstone at one time sat atop rich silver mines that burrowed beneath the streets and homes. But they "played out" long ago.

Were it not for the money that awed tourists spend to gawk at Wyatt Earp's town, there would be precious little of Tombstone today. The surrounding countryside is flat and uninteresting, with dusty brush providing the main vegetation. After looking at Bisbee, Tombstone comes up very short as a retiree's paradise, although many of its residents are retired.

This might be a place for someone wanting to start a retirement business. Property is cheap, and many "downtown" businesses are boarded up. A storefront should be easy to rent. Someone who is into antiques, jewelry making or crafts could start an antique store, a rock-shop and jewelry emporium, or just about any kind of business that might attract tourists. I wouldn't imagine too many Tombstone businessmen become wealthy in a hurry, but if you'd like a business-connected hobby, and if your needs are modest, this might be fun.

**TUCSON, Ariz.**--You may have noticed that most towns given as examples in this book are relatively small. There are several reasons for this, not the least of which are lower crime rates and lower housing costs. Another factor in choosing smaller towns is that senior citizens can carry more political weight by becoming proportionally larger than other age groups in number. One notable exception to this generalization is the city of Tucson.

With almost 400,000 inhabitants, Tucson is no small town, and it is still growing. Interestingly, the fastest increasing age group is over 55, way up from the official 1980 census of 20 percent. Remember, the age group of 55 and above is the one most likely to vote. The well-appointed Tucson Senior Citizens Center clearly shows the attention that city politicians show retired people.

Another favorable aspect to the Tucson area is inexpensive housing. It's unusual for a city of this size and high quality of life to have so many rental units going for as low as $250 a month. A thick rental magazine comes out every few weeks with the latest selection of apartments and houses for rent. One apartment complex offers one-bedroom units, with a pool and exercise facilities for $198 per month for senior citizens. Another two-bedroom furnished apartment lists for $295, including color TV! Many adult apartments commonly go for $250, complete with the obligatory swimming pool and other amenities to lure in renters. Recent overbuilding is a key factor in the glut of housing on the market.

The housing market is also poor from the seller's standpoint, but great for the buyer. In January, 1987, there was a 53 percent increase in the number of unsold houses on the market over the previous year, as well as a 17 percent drop in sales. Asking prices are low, and selling prices even lower. Your dollars can buy more housing in Tucson for the dollar than about anywhere you go. But, with rentals so cheap, does a person need to buy? Unless you feel like you *must* own your home, you might be better keeping that down payment in your pocket.

## MOBILE HOME LIVING IN TUCSON

The housing glut apparently extends to mobile home parks. The newspapers listed 17 parks advertising spaces available. This is extremely rare for a metropolitan area. The problem with most urban areas is that mobile home spaces are so scarce (or non-existent) that park space rents are high, and prices for mobile homes are sky-high.

As we've discussed in another section of this book, when there is no place to move a mobile home in an area, you end up paying a premium for a space on someone else's land. A two-bedroom, double-wide mobile home that might sell for $9,000 without a place to put it, can go for $29,000 to $39,000 in a town where spaces are at a premium. Thus, you end up paying $20,000 to $30,000 for the privilege of using land that doesn't even belong to you. When parks are scarce, and if for some reason you don't like your neighbors, you have no choice but to sell. You can't move, because there's no place to move to. So the situation in Tucson is a happy one for mobile home owners.

A space in one of Tucson's adult mobile home parks can be found for as low as $95 a month, sometimes less. The nicer ones charge more, with $150 considered a fairly high rent. Compare this with $350 to $400 in some cities, and you'll understand what a bargain mobile home living is in Tucson. Prices of the units are similarly cheap when you buy one already set up (my recommendation). Or, you can purchase one new, if that's your preference, and you have the luxury of picking and choosing a park to suit your personality.

Prices in the local newspaper for mobile homes: 1980 14-wide, $9000, $900 down.--1985 double-wide 2 bdr. $13,900.--3 Bdr with expando, $9000.--1967 12x55 2 br., $4995.--10x45 1 br., $3850.--12x50 2br, adult park, $4500. These prices were picked at random from a January 7, 1987, newspaper. At these rates, you can understand why many retirees choose to buy a mobile home and leave it vacant for the summer.

With so many parks to choose from, you would be well advised to do some shopping. Some parks are strictly living conveniences for the residents. Most of the people work, and their interests and social lives are intertwined with friends who live somewhere else. These parks will seem cold--not that people are unfriendly, but they prefer their lives to be more private. Other parks have mostly retired folks, where you can find lots of activities that might interest you, and lots of people from which to choose friends. Visiting a park residents' meeting, or attending one of the bingo sessions can tell you worlds about who your new neighbors might be.

## ADULT COMMUNITIES

Tucson is also famous for its organized retirement and adults-only complexes. With beautifully designed homes, extensive sports centers, shopping and medical facilities, these complexes are small cities in themselves. The developers of Sun City and Sun City West near Phoenix are building a new retirement town in Tucson. Green Valley, another complex outside of town, has long been attracting retirees. A newer adult community, Saddle Brooke, calls itself the "youngest adult community" because it sets its lower age limit at 45 years of age instead of the usual 55. Housing prices in these adult communities range from $60,000 to $150,000. Typically, these complexes feature 18-hole golf courses, shuffleboard, bocci and tennis courts, cardrooms, jogging tracks, exercise rooms and, of course, the ubiquitous swimming pools.

Smaller, apartment-type quarters are available in Tucson itself. They range from places where you must be active to "Senior Care Concepts," a euphemism for "nursing home." There is also the concept of "Life Care Center," in which apartments are provided for ambulatory retirees, and then rooms, and finally nursing care.

## CITIZENS CENTER

The Armory Park Senior Citizens Recreation Center, in Tucson's downtown, area is quite large and very active. Senior citizens seem to take an energetic part in running the center, and have no trouble getting all the volunteer help they need. At any one time there are several hundred volunteers on call. They try to use every-one's special skills. For example: Retired accountants and tax prac-titioners give free income tax assistance. Others teach handicrafts such as jewelry making, crochet and painting. A senior citizens housing authority high rise is across the street from the center, and another is planned, making it convenient for everyone to participate. Medical care seems to be adequate; Tucson is served by 12 hospitals with a total of 2,914 beds.

So, if you like desert, you might think about Tucson. Its 2,400-foot altitude saves it from the searing summer heat of places like Yuma, even though it gets warm enough, with 100 degrees normal for June and July, and 84 degrees the year-round average. Winters are pleasant, with little rainfall. The climate is similar to places like Phoenix and Sun City, but prices are much lower, and traffic is less hectic.

**SUN CITY, Ariz.**--I have to admit that I have always looked with some perplexity at large commercial developments like Sun City (pop. 50,000), near Phoenix. Why would anyone want to join a closed community, where the presence of children and young people are discouraged? However, a visit and tour to one of these large Arizona developments persuaded me there might well be some attractive points to the idea. Like most retirement plans, this isn't for everyone. It's important that retirees know themselves well, and are confident they understand all of the pros and cons of such a com-munity before plunking down their savings. Oh, yes, it's possible to rent or lease in large developments like this, so you can "try before you buy."

But many people, after just one tour through the model homes, are sorely tempted to buy immediately. The architecture is bold and imaginative, (to match the payments), the furniture is top-quality and luxurious. It's terribly easy to stand in the middle of one of these well-lighted and superbly furnished units and imagine how happy you might feel living there. That's exactly how I found myself while walking through the model homes. The luxury is there, but some prices seemed affordable, at least compared with what similar homes could cost elsewhere.

The homes in this particular development started at about $70,000 and went on up to top $200,000. A look at the prospective buyers and at their automobiles in the parking lot told me that I was seeing some of the more affluent types, people who might think that $70,000 or $90,000 is a steal. And for those who live in areas where a two-bedroom home or condo might cost $150,000 to $175,000, the prices here seem reasonable, indeed. Many of the buyers are from California, although other parts of the country are well represented. According to a salesman, many buyers come from Florida, having given up on retirement where there are so many insects and rainy days. However, I didn't know whether to accept his word on this, because almost everywhere in the country I went, salesmen kept telling me that a big percentage of their clients came from Florida--except in Florida, where they claimed it was California that retirees were fleeing.

One of the advantages to buying into a planned community, rather than an ordinary neighborhood, is that you know everyone in the development is about your age, and you have a good chance to meet many others of your own age group, people who need to make friends as badly as you do. Here, you are assured that you won't be bothered by children or teenagers, because there are restrictions against them. You must be over 50, with no dependent children, in order to buy into the development. To further ensure against children, the residents have voted against any of their property taxes going for schools. The result is no children and no schools--only adults. I was told that this has cut teenage vandalism and crime to almost nothing. (This leaves only the problem of senior-citizen vandalism. However, I was assured that local senior-citizens vandalism is pretty much under control.)

One couple I interviewed pointed out that they feel exceptionally secure in Sun City, and that it suits their interests in golf, bridge and swimming. As members of the homeowners association, they could play tennis. "We are transferring our equity from our Indiana home to this one, with a little left over to make the move and buy new furniture," said the husband. "And with the community rec centers, we will have a chance to learn tennis, use the exercise equipment and maybe even join a bowling team." A yearly fee of $89 is charged for use of the recreation facilities. Everything from archery to woodworking is offered at seven recreation centers.

Sun City is not the place for everyone. Some will find it very sterile, living with others of the same age, seldom having contact with younger people, having everything planned for you, even to the landscaping of your house. On the other hand, there are those who feel very comfortable with the security of such a development, the absence of racial minorities and children. Developments like Sun City--there are many around the country--offer a regulated, safe lifestyle, with all the conveniences a person could ask for. But it comes at a price--not only in property costs, but in loss of some individuality and contact with other age groups. A lot depends on how much you prize security, regulation and the appearance of elegance.

Although this development is probably the largest in the country, it's typical of many being built from Florida to California. More and more are being developed as more retirees opt for complete-package retirements.

The major facilities at Sun City and Sun City West are: Eleven golf courses (four of them 18-hole layouts) a 40-acre recreation center, 7,169-seat Sundome Center, a library, seven medical complexes, restaurants, banks, seven other local recreation centers,


**WICKENBURG, Ariz.**--About an hour's drive northwest from Phoenix, the town of Wickenburg is attracting retirees who don't want to accept the neatly arranged, orderly and secure life of Sun City or the bustle of traffic-bound Phoenix. In small-town Wickenburg, they savor the flavor of the Old West. The town has been famous for years for its guest ranches (they used to call 'em "dude" ranches) which go way beyond being simply ranches. They come complete with a lot of amenities, including tennis courts, and sometimes even a golf course. Today, while the guest ranches are still popular with tourists, the emphasis is on small-acreage places where you can keep riding horses and live year-round.

In Wickenburg, land is relatively cheap and building lots are typically sold by the acre. You can keep horses in your yard if you care to; the local horse population is considerable. You can saddle up and go for a ride through open desert and brush country, in almost any direction you care to. You don't know how to ride horseback? No problem, there are saddle clubs with friendly members who will help you get started. The clubs organize numerous social activities centered around horseback riding, from participation in parades and afternoon rides for beginners to the grueling Desert Caballeros Ride for seasoned horsemen, who come from all over the country to participate.

This area is highly mineralized, and was the site of a considerable gold rush back in the late 1800s. Several rich mines encircled the town, with millions of dollars worth of the glittering mineral taken from the ground. Although most of the richest locations have been worked out over the years, enough remains to keep the local people busy prospecting and panning for the gold that the old-timers may have missed. And not only gold: Other valuable minerals, such as silver, copper, turquoise, mercury, nickel, tungsten and other ores have been found within a 25-mile radius of Wickenburg. Don't expect to become rich panning for gold, because yesteryear's miners were pretty busy. The fun of prospecting, besides the outdoors activity it entails, is that long chance that you just might make a "big strike" and find something that everyone else has overlooked.

The town's Wild West past is celebrated in February with "Gold Rush Days," a weekend of rodeos, gold panning and dressing up in Old West costumes.

There are several mobile home parks in town, with many units used only in the winter since their owners choose to live elsewhere during the hot summer months. Don't worry about your horses; there are several boarding stables where your animals will be well cared for while you are enjoying your "other place" at the beach or in the cool mountains. At one time, it was possible to buy a lot and install a mobile home, but nowadays this is frowned upon by the city council.

Housing isn't exactly cheap in Wickenburg, but there are places to had for $50,000 and under. Examples from classified ads of January, 1987: $49,500--3-bedroom, 2 bath 1800 sq. ft. on most of an acre. $39,900--2 bedroom stucco, large trees, easy landscaping. Apartments average about $300 a month, and houses -$400 and up. One rental ad read: "Adult complex starting from $65 per week, $240 per month, furnished, utilities paid."

It does get hot there in the summertime, with July and August averaging highs of 100 degrees. But like most of the Arizona desert country, low humidity takes much of the sting from the high temperatures. Year-round, the average highs are 83 degrees. Winter nights can be cold, with frost common, but day temperatures are quite pleasant, with shirt-sleeve weather being the noonday norm.

Health care is pretty good for a small town (about 6,000), with a 34-bed hospital and doctors available. Wickenburg is only 50 minutes from excellent Sun City hospitals which specialize in and cater to problems of the elderly.

**COLORADO RIVER AREA**--All along the Colorado River, from the Mexican border north to a town called Bullhead City, you'll find a string of small towns, marinas and clusters of mobile homes and RV facilities. Innumerable boat docks jut out into the Colorado River with boats tied up waiting for an excuse to go angling for catfish, striped bass and panfish. Because of the rather large population of campers, fishermen and tourists, there is no shortage of bait shops, stores and other recreational facilities.

One of the largest, and probably better developed, of the Colorado River resorts is Lake Havasu City (pop. 18,000), about midway along this north-south stretch of the river. Lake Havasu started in 1963 as a development of McCulloch Corporation--a new town created in the desert. McCulloch bought up huge tracts of land, established a factory and encouraged other manufacturing entities to move there.

As a part of the hoopla surrounding the development of Lake Havasu City, McCulloch bought and imported, stone by stone, the London Bridge. The bridge had been declared obsolete in the early 1970s by the London City Council. The reconstruction of the London Bridge across a narrow bypass of the Colorado river garnered the desired international publicity. Lake Havasu City basked in this promotion and prospered. As tourists and retirees came to town to see the bridge, they noticed the other small towns along the river, and one thing became apparent: The Colorado River is a great place for retirement. Land sales, homes and condos, trailers and mobile homes, all began to boom along the river, a boom that continues to this day.

The interesting thing about this development is that, by far, most purchasers are from nearby California. Typically, they buy a house, condo or mobile home for vacationing. Then as an investment, they rent their property during the winter months--the rent covering the year's payments--and then use the property during the hot summer months themselves when tenants are scarce. This means there are plenty of rentals available year-round.

So, there are basically two ways to enjoy the fishing and retirement attractions of the river communities. One way is to follow the example of the enterprising Californians and buy recreational property for investment. The other way is to simply become "snowbirds" and rent a place for the mild winters, delightful springs or the warm but tolerable falls. Another alternative is to stay there year-round, but few retirees opt for that. Most are "snowbirds," heading for Pacific Ocean breezes or cool redwood groves when the sun starts getting up early and hanging around until late. The sun is serious about its work along the Colorado River, putting in an average of *350* days a year, and no charge for overtime.

During the summer months, you must be ready for some really hot spells. In the months of June through September, you can expect daily highs of over 100 degrees. With less than five inches of rain a year, don't expect much in the way of relief from that quarter. On the other hand, the low humidity keeps things bearable and promotes the efficiency of evaporative air coolers. An interesting arrangement in cooling, by the way, is to "piggyback" a regular air conditioner by first cooling the air with a "swamp cooler" before running it through the conventional unit. This creates an efficient and economical cooling system, since the conventional unit doesn't have to work so hard to remove heat from the air.

Even though Lake Havasu City boomed from a small desert outpost into a town of almost 20,000 (with another 6,000 to 8,000 winter residents), rentals and sales prices aren't out of range at all. For example, a well-designed one-bedroom condo was selling for under $39,900 during my visit. A similar condo in a metropolitan California area, 200 miles west, would probably go for over $100,000. Homes begin at $45,000 and range upwards toward $200,000, with many new models averaging around $60,000. Air conditioning is taken for granted as part of the package.

Mobile home and RV parks dot the river banks, each with its own boat loading ramp and nearby bait shop. By the way, fishing isn't the only sport to be found here. There are three golf courses and a bowling alley. There is an active senior center, as you might imagine, with the usual nutrition facilities, bridge games and arts and crafts. There are also some activities coordinated with Arizona State University, including drama performances, concerts and lectures.

There is a small hospital in Lake Havasu, used by 32 doctors in the area. Another 36-bed hospital is available in Bullhead City 50 miles north. For serious cases local doctors aren't able to handle, patients are sent to nearby Phoenix by Air Evac service. There is also a community college in Lake Havasu City, with a new 280-acre campus in the works.

## OTHER RIVER TOWNS

At the end of 40-mile-long Lake Havasu, south of Lake Havasu City, are the towns of Parker, Blythe and Lake Martinez, as well as many small marinas, and hunting and fishing facilities. This being true desert country, with most land belonging to the government and open to the public, there are many places for RVs to "boondock," that is, to park for free along the river or back in a canyon. The river's rugged backdrop of cliffs and jagged mountains make this a particularly beautiful spot in which to pass a winter. Sunsets are incredibly beautiful, with colors of red and orange forming blazing backdrops to ink-dark rock formations.

The northern sector of the river has similar gatherings of houses, mobile homes and RVs, with lots of empty land in between. North of here, past Davis Dam, begins Lake Mohave, which is considerably larger and wider than Lake Havasu, which in turn, ends at Hoover Dam and the start of Lake Mead. Obviously, water recreation is a central attraction in this driest of desert landscapes.

**BULLHEAD CITY, Ariz.**--Bullhead City (pop. 17,000) is the largest of these towns and is the same size as Lake Havasu City, offering much the same retirement attraction. It is growing by hops and skips (as opposed to leaps and bounds) and appears to be a rather progressive little city. There is a new extended-care facility for senior citizens, which operates in conjunction with Bullhead Community Hospital, and is located across the street from the hospital.

Bullhead City, in addition to having a funny name, has a promising future as a senior citizen mecca. Part of its popularity is no doubt due to the rapidly growing gambling resort across the river, Laughlin, Nev. This is the southernmost point in Nevada where you can gamble, and it appears that better than 90 percent of the patrons are retirees. They come on with canes, wheelchairs and even walkers, all determined to make a "killing." The casinos long ago discovered that they can make lot of money by putting slot machines and senior citizens together. They've put a lot of money into building first-class places with everything you'd expect from Las Vegas, but without having to drive over 100 miles to get there.

Four large casinos perch on the riverbank just below Hoover Dam's spillway. One place is built in the shape of an enormous Mississippi riverboat. It has 200 hotel rooms in addition to the casinos, lounges and restaurants that go with a typical Nevada gambling establishment. The other hotel-casinos have about 400 rooms each, and 900 more are on the drawing boards, because business is so brisk that rooms are often sold out by early afternoon.

One unique feature of these riverfront casinos is the way you visit them. You don't have to trudge along in the hot sun from one to another. Instead, you go down to a river dock right in front of the casino, step onto a waiting boat, and zip up or down the river to the next casino. These shaded pontoon boats are fun, they run frequently, and get you where you're going in a hurry. The casinos are concerned that you won't waste precious time away from the slot machines. Suppose you don't care to drive the 10 miles up river and over the dam to Laughlin? No problem. You park your car in Bullhead City and catch one of the speedy launches across the river to your favorite casino. Like many things connected with gambling casinos, this is all free.

The truly interesting thing about Laughlin is the number of RVs it attracts. I'm sure it's the recreational vehicle gambling center of the nation. The casinos permit trailers, motor homes and campers to set up in their parking lots and to stay overnight. They *encourage* RVs to use their parking lots for as long as the people want to stay, or until their money runs out, whichever comes first. There are no electrical or sewer hookups, of course, but this is no problem for self-contained RVs. Most can last a week on their holding tanks and judicious conservation of water and their 12-volt battery system handles lights and TV for a long time. Many have generators, and enjoy air conditioning as well.

My observation is that almost all of the RVs belong to senior citizens. Talking to them, I discovered that they are almost all snow-birds. One man, a widower from Los Angeles said, "If I had to stay in one of those hotel rooms, I'd be out of money in one big hurry. But I've been here a week, sleeping for free in my own bed, cooking my own dinner. It hasn't cost me a penny, and I've been staying almost even playing the poker machines." He admitted that he did eat breakfast in the casino restaurant because of the specials offered. "At $1.50 for eggs, hashbrowns and toast," he said, "I can't afford *not* to eat there." His trailer sat in the middle of a virtual sea of RVs, blocks and blocks of them, everything from humble camper-pickups to sleek and expensive diesel models. And, as far as I could tell, they were all owned by senior citizens.

South of the casinos, on the road toward the tip of Nevada is a rapidly growing residential section. Condos, apartments and single-family dwellings, plus plenty of building sites are for sale. A shopping center and some stores serve the residents, but a new, more elaborate Town Center Mall is under construction. A new library opened recently, a branch of the Las Vegas-Clark County library system. A movement to incorporate is growing, and I'm sure Laughlin will formally become a town before long. Because there are so many employees needed for the growing casino, restaurant and entertainment industry in Laughlin, this might be a place to earn money with an interesting job in a casino. Working, not gambling.

It's my guess that the twin cities of Laughlin and Bullhead City are going to become the dominant center both for gambling and retirement along the Colorado River. If you go there, just be sure you can control your gambling.

**QUARTZITE, Ariz.**--Although not on the river, a very interesting town lies about 80 miles north of Yuma, a magnetic attraction for RV enthusiasts and hobbyists from all over the country. The town--perhaps "crossroads" is a better description--is called Quartzite. It's located at the intersection of Interstate 10 and Arizona state highway 95, which goes toward Lake Havasu in one direction and Las Vegas to the north. If you don't believe that the RV craze has been taken over by retirees, just go to Quartzite. South of town is a place called La Posa Recreation Area. It's a government supervised, long-term camping area. Approximately 11,000 acres of public land have been made available for RVs. Campsites are undeveloped and unmarked; you pick your own location among the sagebrush and mesquite. The only facilities provided are holding tank disposals, and you must go into Quartzite to replenish your water supplies. The setting is beautiful, quiet and the fees are right: $25 for the entire eight-month season from October 1 until May 31. Outside of the season, camping is free.

From the highway it seems that as far as the eye can see, motor homes, trailers, vans and tents are spaced through the desert. The residents form loosely organized social groups among neighbors, watching out for each other's campsites when someone is in town for supplies. RV clubs such as LoW (Loners on Wheels) and S.K.P. (Escapees) usually have a temporary headquarters and organize activities such as "happy hours" and other get-togethers.

This is truly a winter mecca for RVs. For a while I kept track of the traffic passing by on highway 95, and better than half, closer to two-thirds, of the vehicles driving along the road were motor homes, campers, trailers or vans. Almost without exception, the drivers appeared to be over 60 years old.

But the real RV concentration is in "downtown" Quartzite. The downtown consists of a crossroads with a few stores and gas stations, surrounded by thousands of RVs. It appears that anyone interested in jewelry making, rock collecting, or gem polishing, who owns an RV, heads for Quartzite at some time or another. There, in a special, fenced-off area of many acres, hundreds of RVs sit, each with a stand set up with something on display, for sale or trade. By day they set up shop, displaying their wares or manufacturing them on-site, and by night they have their home right there for socializing and sleeping. Electricity, water and sewer hookups are provided, so this becomes a miniature city of hobbiests.

The emphasis is on gems and minerals, jewelry and antiques, but in effect it's a permanent winter flea market. You can buy anything from homemade jams and breads to western shirts. Guitars, antique bottles, dinosaur bones, wood carvings, coins, acrylic earrings, shotguns, wind chimes, paintings and gold nuggets are among the goods for sale in bewildering rows of displays. Almost without exception, the vendors are retirees. And they seem to be having a marvelous time. I suspect that most "business" conducted is by bartering and trading among themselves, and that the same items move about from collection to collection with little money changing hands. "So, we don't make any money on each transaction," jokes one vendor, "but we make it up in volume."

"Main Event," as they call it, starts the last of January and lasts a couple of weeks, when thousands of hobbyists load up their equipment, finished jewelry and gems, and head for that desert crossroad. Some of the finest craftsmen in the West make the trek to display and offer their artwork for sale. If you have a set of wheels and are in the area at that time, it's well worth a visit.

**YUMA, Ariz.**--Yuma (pop. 50,000) is a "snowbird" paradise. The retiree population is the most mobile of any town I've surveyed. Every fall, people descend upon Yuma in motor homes, trailers, vans and autos--filled with summer clothes, suntan oil and other necessities for a winter's stay. So many come here to escape miserable weather at home that the population just about doubles during the winter. The season is delightful, with daily temperatures hovering in the low 70s, and climbing occasionally into the 80s, or even the 90s. Sunshine is almost guaranteed. There is a 93-percent chance of sun on any winter day, according to the National Weather Service. You don't have to worry about your golf game being rained out.

Summers in Yuma are another story. Daytime temperatures climb into the 100s day after day. So, around the first of May, when thermometers begin rising, the snowbirds pack up and begin their exodus to cooler climes. Many people, of course, live here year-round, generally choosing to live in conventional homes. Real estate is reasonable, with most houses selling in the $60,000 range with some dropping as low as $45,000 for a three-bedroom, two-bath home. But it seems to me that unless you intend to become a permanent, year-round resident, Yuma is one place where it makes more sense to have a mobile home. Most people have compelling reasons for staying year-round, such as owning a business or having a job there.

Rents drop during the summer, particularly park rent for mobile homes. For example, monthly rent in a typical park might be $250 a month, but if you rent on a yearly basis it drops to $1,200 a year, or $100 a month. Another park charges $125 a month, but on a yearly basis, only $62 a month. Consequently, many people drive their RVs to Yuma and simply leave them in a park permanently. They figure it's cheaper to fly there every winter than to pay for the gasoline and take the trouble of driving back and forth.

Retirees here have developed mobile home and RV living into a highly organized, fun way of life. Most parks hold elections every fall to select officers for the coming snowbird season. An important elective post is that of entertainment and activity chairman. The beginning of each new winter season is a happy, exhilarating time, as old friends reunite, and newcomers are welcomed into the social group. Many of the parks recruit residents with musical ability and form bands to perform for dances, not only in their own parks, but exchanging with other parks for a change of repertoire. Most are quite professional-sounding, which should be no surprise, because many of the musicians were once professionals. Card games, bingo, lectures, arts and crafts, almost any activity you can imagine, are part of mobile living in Yuma.

Unlike many places in the country where older, single-wide trailers are discouraged and forced to move out of a park when the owners sell, there are many parks--nice parks--where older mobile homes are common. As long as they are kept looking nice, with approved landscaping, there is no problem. Some are advertised for low as $4,000. At this price a person can afford to let one sit vacant during the summer season, waiting as a winter escape. Since there are few rainstorms, and no ice and snow to deteriorate the trailers, they last a long, long time in the Yuma desert.

"I'm always sorry to see the season end," said one couple. "We feel sad having to say goodbye to all the new friends we've made." But they were quick to add, "Once we are on the way home, we get excited again, anxious to see our grandkids and our friends we left back in Oregon. We have the best of all worlds and it's great to get home again!"

Yuma is large enough to have the big city amenities, yet small enough to escape the drawbacks of big-city life. It's located about halfway between San Diego and Phoenix (180 miles either way), so big cities aren't too far away. There are public golf courses, and water sports on the famous Colorado River which runs along the edge of the town, and Mexico is just a few miles away. About 50 miles south of the border, on the Sea of Cortez, you will find long stretches of empty beach exclusively yours for clam digging, swimming or surf casting. Some of the best duck hunting in the West is in the marshy tules of the Colorado that extend clear down to the mouth of the river where it empties into the Sea of Cortez.

Home for the majority of the snowbirds is someplace in the West: Washington, Oregon, Montana, Alberta or other places where winters can be damp or snowy but summers are delightful. But people come from all over. We met retirees from Maine, Vermont, Michigan and Illinois. They journey here, stay the winter and fly home with the ease of the migrating snowbirds they are named after. If you are an Easterner and are considering becoming a Florida snowbird, I would encourage you to check out the advantages and friendliness of Yuma, Tucson or some other Southwest Desert location first.

The downtown Senior Citizens Center is one of the more dynamic I've seen. Although not physically large, it has enthusiastic and imaginative people running it. Every day, at lunch ($1.75 for a tasty, nutritious meal), one of the mobile home parks furnishes a band for dancing. The music is great, and it is heartwarming to see senior citizens having such a marvelous time for such a small outlay of cash. Incidentally, these afternoon dances are ideal for singles and widowed to meet. They tell me that many romances have blossomed from these afternoon get-togethers.

Medical facilities seem to be adequate, with a 283-bed hospital in town. There are over 100 physicians, surgeons and specialists offering assistance. With such an enormous population of retirees in the area, my guess is that they have plenty of experience in geriatrics. Incidentally, many people go to nearby Algodones, Mexico, for unorthodox medical treatment. There is an RV park within a few hundred yards of the border, and many people stay there while crossing into the little border town to have dental work done at cut-rate prices, or to have laetrile or other treatments for cancer, arthritis, or whatever. These medications and treatments are usually ones that are prohibited in the United States. Do they work? Some say yes, some say no. Medical authorities claim that the treatments are generally harmless, worthless vegetable substances. My question has always been, if they are harmless, why do we make it a penitentiary offense to administer them? Like Mexicali to the west, there are some dentists here with generally good reputations.

Algodones, incidentally, happens to be one of the grungiest-looking of all border towns. For Mexico bargain shopping, Yuma residents prefer to drive about 25 miles south to San Luis. It is much cleaner and has more to offer, including a couple of fair restaurants. But for "real Mexico," the snowbirds drive another 60 miles south to the fishing village of El Golfo de Santa Clara. The Colorado River empties into the Sea of Cortez near here and the fishing is legendary. The warm, nutrient-rich water of the Sea of Cortez encourages fish to grow to prize class in great numbers. Local fishermen haul in catches of unbelievably large shrimp, almost the size of lobsters. These are difficult to purchase in the United States because Japanese wholesalers contract for most of these monster crustaceans. How wonderful they are barbecued with garlic butter! On the plateau above the town is the *Gran Desierto*, a huge wasteland of sand dunes and desert shrubbery. In ancient times this had been a flood plain of the Colorado river, and today is a favorite place to look for petrified cypress and pine logs that washed down the river ages ago.

Reno

Lake Tahoe

**NEVADA**

**CALIFORNIA**

Las Vegas

Yucaipa

Desert Hot Springs

Palm Springs

Indio

Brawley

Imperial Valley

N

CHAPTER EIGHT

# *California and Nevada Deserts*

If there's one place in the California desert that spells "class," it would be Palm Springs. Sheltered in the lee of the rugged San Jacinto Mountains, watered with abundant irrigation, Palm Springs is the "miracle mile" of the low desert. Golfers with famous names: Bob Hope, Bing Crosby, Jerry Ford and a host of others have drawn attention to the great, year-round tee sports available there. You'll find more golf courses in Palm Springs than most towns have super-markets. The claim is that there are 65 golf courses within the area.

A drive through the Palm Springs area can be overwhelming, with one street after another competing for the title of the fanciest, most expensive and most opulent. Shopping centers that look as if they were built for sultans or nobility offer any kind of luxury item you can afford (and many that you can't afford). The clean desert air and the astonishingly rugged mountain backdrop give Palm Springs an aura of pristine beauty combined with regal affluence. It isn't dif-ficult to see why the rich, who can live anywhere they please, choose to have at least one of their homes in Palm Springs.

Actually, when people refer to "Palm Springs," they really mean the area *around* the city of Palm Springs. Over the boom years, building spread away from the town itself, where much of the construction is older, with many ordinary condos and apartments. Movie stars and millionaires built their lavish spreads way out in the desert to be away from the plebeians. But before long, "ordinary rich people" moved in. They soon surrounded the desert showplaces with even more expensive layouts. The fanciest places are found in nearby towns like Cathedral City, Rancho Mirage, Palm Desert or Indian Wells. So many houses, apartments, restaurants and businesses have popped up that it's impossible to tell when you leave one town and enter the next, except for signs telling you so.

This is a retirement place for people who insist on urbane, spiffy living, in an atmosphere of luxury, fine restaurants and beautifully landscaped surroundings. Problem is, these things are expensive. Fortunately, there are alternatives available. First of all, there are hundreds of mobile home and RV parks in the Palm Springs area. Some are elegant, costing as much as an expensive apartment. Others are reasonable. Some are run-down and cheap.

And, surprisingly, house prices are not out of sight, provided you don't insist on living next to a movie star. There are some rather ordinary neighborhoods there. A two-bedroom house can be found in the Palm Springs area for as low as $90,000, with some selling for under $80,000. One reason for these lower-than-expected housing costs is recent overbuilding. Another reason is that people who can afford to have a second home here can also afford something in the $250,000 range and over; they shun "low-cost" housing. But, most Palm Springs residents work for wages; they can't possibly pay that much money. With little industry outside of support services--working in restaurants or hotels, or gardening for wealthy families--wages are low. Low wages always force rents and housing prices down. So the housing market is an "either-or" thing: Either you can't afford to pay high housing costs, or you're rich and you don't give a damn!

Some condos go for a lot of money, while others--not bad at all--are advertised at $55,000. I haven't looked at them, but I can hazard a guess that at that price they won't be luxurious. Many are advertised at prices up to $300,000. Rents for apartments seem reasonable to me, considering the tone of the area. Many are advertised at $350 for a one or two-bedroom unit. Of course, many list for over $1,000. If you can't find anything reasonable in Palm Springs, there are other nearby towns to investigate.

**DESERT HOT SPRINGS**--Sort of a "workingman's Palm Springs," the little town of Desert Hot Springs lies across Interstate Highway 10, about 15 minutes' drive away. Hot springs flow under the town from nearby mountain slopes and are commonly tapped by residents who then enjoy the water in their backyard hot pools and Jacuzzis. Much smaller than Palm Springs or any of the ritzy sections on the other side of the interstate, Desert Hot Springs has a lot to offer in pleasant, economical desert retirement location.

Here, you have most of the advantages of Palm Springs without the higher prices. With a slightly higher elevation, the summer temperatures are a smidgen lower, and there is more of a breeze than you'll find in Palm Springs. I have to admit that this is somewhat offset by more winds in the winter, winds which can bring some chilly air, if they come from the north. The fabled restaurants, golf courses, shopping and social life of Palm Springs are just a few minutes away, but then so are the traffic jams and crowds. Desert Hot Springs attracts a following of Europeans who come here every winter to enjoy the hot baths, the warm, sunny weather and the low prices.

Like Palm Springs, a large percentage of the residents live here year-round. Many are retired, but there's also a large balance of younger people who work in Palm Springs but can't afford the prices there. The downtown area is low-keyed, as is the rest of the town. For fine restaurants and night life, most people drive across the interstate where they find unlimited selections. But for family restaurants, shopping and services, Desert Hot Springs certainly offers anything you need.

Being used to large-city California prices, the rentals and property prices in Desert Hot Springs looked like giveaways to me. Here, you can buy a brand-new, three-bedroom home, with its own hot pool, for as low as $80,000. An acceptable three-bedroom, two-bath home typically sells for $62,000. Real estate brokers estimate that you can subtract about $10,000 from Palm Springs prices for similar property in Desert Hot Springs.

Most people live in single-family bungalows or mobile homes. However, several new apartment buildings have added to the number of units available--and because the builders were slightly over-optimistic about filling their rentals, rents were quite competitive. New units are going for $350, or $250 for furnished studios. Swimming pools and hot springs spas are typically included for these prices.

As you might expect, mobile homes and RV parks are plentiful, with few parks even approaching the elegance of the "other side of the tracks." This abundance of manufactured housing means that monthly space rentals are reasonable and that used mobile homes are priced competitively.

**INDIO**--Indio, the last town that can be considered part of the Palm Springs area, used to be miles and miles from anywhere, sitting by itself out in the desert. It was a town that specialized in citrus and date palms, with a handful of RV parks and motels to handle travelers on their way to or from Palm Springs. Today, the overflow from Palm Springs has worked its way southeast until it has almost joined with Indio. The result has been a surging interest in Indio as a retirement community. Mobile home and RV parks are springing up almost daily.

Indio doesn't have the class of Palm Springs, or quite the charm of Desert Hot Springs, but it's drawing retirees at an amazing rate. The attraction here is the comfortable desert atmosphere, with tall date palms, older and inexpensive homes and plenty of mobile home and trailer parks for economical full- or part-time living. I've been through Indio many times in the winter, and I've always found it to feel as close to summer as you could dare hope for so early in the year.

IMPERIAL VALLEY--At the bottom end of California, south of the Salton Sea and west of Yuma, the Imperial Valley sometimes dips below sea level. For those who like desert living, but without the formality of Palm Springs, there are several places here worth investigating. Brawley, El Centro and Calexico sit in a straight 25-mile line north from the Mexican border. There is a relaxed style of living here, with a touch of old Mexico's Spanish heritage. You'll hear a lot of Spanish spoken here especially in the border town of Calexico, and you'll have an opportunity to learn the language if you care to.

But make no mistake, this is desert country. With less than two inches of rain a year, this area probably has more sunshine than anywhere in the United States. Were it not for irrigation from the Colorado River and from wells, this place would look as barren as Death Valley. But when you add water, the desert suddenly blooms into some of the richest farm country imaginable. Winter daytime temperatures average 70 degrees, giving the Imperial Valley a 12-month growing season. *Seven* cuttings of alfalfa a year are common! Summers are quite hot, with early afternoons best spent in the shade or in an air-cooled shelter somewhere with a cold drink grasped in your hand.

There are other towns nearby, places like Calipatria, Holtville and Westmoreland. But they are not much more than little crossroad-farming communities, places with small grocery stores and hardware supplies for those too busy to run into El Centro or Brawley. The more attractive retirement communities would be in those two towns or in Calexico. Calexico is distinguished by broad streets, many lined with stately date palms, neatly maintained homes and green lawns that mock the desert's stingy natural water supply. Mobile home and RV parks abound. This is one of the more popular snowbird destinations, with warm winters and inexpensive living.

When I asked retirees here what they liked best about Imperial Valley living, almost all indicated warm winters as the biggest draw. Those who like to hunt pointed out the abundance of ducks, geese and pheasant during the season. Others mentioned the nearby Anza-Borrego Desert State Park, rock and mineral collecting and four-wheel driving through open lands.

Some people, particularly in Calexico, live there because of the availability of medical treatments across the U.S.-Mexican border that are prohibited in the United States. Many swear by Mexican arthritis medications, acupuncture treatments, or laetrile injections. Others disagree. But all agree that the dental work, bridges and dentures available in Mexicali are top quality, and at prices long forgotten on the U.S. side of the line. Caution is urged, however, to patronize only dentists whose work is recommended by other retirees. Eyeglasses are also a bargain there, with identical frames costing a fraction of those in the United States.

Mexicali, on the Mexican side of the line, is a large place, growing constantly and in a constant state of change. A few years ago it was a rather grim place, with cabarets, hookers and rampant vice among its major attractions. But the city has done a fairly good job of cleaning up its act. The downtown area is closely monitored to make sure no hanky-panky goes on. Police are conspicuous by their presence. The city encourages merchants and property owners to keep things neat and clean, and to make things attractive for tourists and residents alike. The problem is that changing the face of a city requires tax money, something in short supply in Mexico. Still, I have to give Mexicali good marks for doing so much on a limited budget.

YUCAIPA--About midway between Palm Springs and Los Angeles is another interesting retirement area, one that is neither desert nor temperate. The Yucaipa Valley actually sits on the borderline of three climatic zones. To the south, the desert stretches to Palm Springs and on to Mexico. On the eastern and northern edges of the valley the mountains rise to over a mile high, up to the ski country of Big Bear and Lake Arrowhead. Finally, to the west, the lower portions of the valley are orchard country, with plums, peaches and grapes growing in a profusion of well-tended orchards. The higher altitudes of the valley are ideal for apples, which love a touch of frost in the fall and winter, and nice, warm summers.

With 25 inches of rain a year, the countryside is considerably greener than much of the nearby country discussed here. In fact, the word *Yucaipa* is supposed to have come from a Serrano Indian word meaning "wet, green place." The altitude varies from 2,000 to 5,000 feet, with most people living at around 2,600 feet. This a country of small homes on large acreage, usually with a generous amount of the land in orchard or pasture for riding horses.

Despite a population of about 37,000 in Yucaipa and nearby Calimesa, the valley is unincorporated. This means several things which may or may not be beneficial, depending on your point of view. One advantage is that there aren't any city taxes, many of which would normally go for duplicating services already provided by county and state governments. For example, there is no Yucaipa city police force to duplicate the services of the county sheriff's office who already patrol there. There aren't separate city and county library systems, or road building and maintenance departments operated by both city and county. The county or state provide these services, at a considerable saving of taxpayers' money. There are several parks, a community center, tennis courts, swimming pool and services of that nature, all county funded. Probably more would be available were there a city government as well as county.

A disadvantage might be the distance of local government, and the lack of some personal services that a low tax base can't provide. With a smaller, more accessible city government, senior citizens carry much more weight than when their voices and votes are diluted among an entire county. When the elderly complain about lacking services, the county or state finds it convenient to plead insufficient tax funds, or to simply ignore the requests.

Yucaipa's central focus shows a clear emphasis on mobile homes. Almost 60 parks dot the valley, some elegant, some plain. As usual, proliferation of mobile homes and parks means lower prices and reasonable rents. The local newspaper lists more than twice as many ads for mobile homes for sale than for houses. Asking prices are exceptionally low, with two-bedroom units starting around $7,000. This wouldn't be in a luxury park, however. With so many choices, you should have no problem finding a mobile home park that suits your personality and needs.

Housing is also inexpensive, despite being so close to Los Angeles. Here, $70,000 to $80,000 buys a traditional three-bedroom home, and $59,000 fetches a new, two-bedroom place. "Fixer-uppers" can be found for as low as $35,000. The more expensive houses are found higher in the mountains, where many ranch-type places are set on a couple of acres, complete with a horse or two and a small stable. This may be one of the most inexpensive places in the Greater Los Angeles area where you can buy a spread like this. One place was advertised as: Ranch-style, two-bedroom, horse property, over an acre, including corral, barn, hay storage and tack room, for $93,500.

Yucaipa isn't the fanciest retirement area around. It's an earthy, folksy kind of place. Don't expect to find many gourmet restaurants or much in the way of nightlife. But, since it's less than an hour's drive from Los Angeles and 45 minutes from Palm Springs, you can have the amenities of sophisticated city life when you choose.

## NEVADA

LAS VEGAS--Although you might think it's out of the question to retire in Las Vegas, many people find it a great place to hang up their shields. Unlike Yuma, Lake Havasu City and other parts of the desert, people tend to live in "Vegas" year-round. For some reason, the temperatures don't climb into the 100s quite as often, and during the winter there aren't as many of the windstorms that affect some other desert locations. As a matter of fact, the people who've retired in Las Vegas absolutely rave about their year-round climate. Of course, some seldom leave the air-conditioned casinos, so what do they know?

"Sure, it gets hot in the summer," reported one of my correspondents, "But, 100 degrees here seems like 85 back where I come from. The difference here is when the air is dry you can breathe it."

True, Las Vegas isn't an inexpensive town, but you really didn't expect it to be, did you? Rents for a two-bedroom apartment begin around $400 a month, and selling prices for new three-bedroom homes start in the low 80s. Older houses selling in the low 50s are considered bargains. As in most desert locations, mobile homes and trailers are popular, but probably higher priced because of Las Vegas's popularity. To find something truly cheap, you'd have to get away from the city. The winter population of snow refugees fills the RV parks during the winter months, but when they leave, their spots are taken by those who breeze in and out of town during the summer.

Las Vegas has several active senior citizens groups, as well as the usual volunteer organizations like R.S.V.P.. The *Las Vegas Sun* runs regular features on activities directed toward retirees.

Medical care there is adequate, although *Places Rated Almanac* gives the town a rather poor rating. There are a couple of good sized hospitals there, but some people I've talked to say they would travel to Los Angeles or Phoenix if anything serious happened to them.

## GAMBLING FEVER

A word of caution about gambling and Las Vegas: Don't go there if you have even the slightest tendency to go overboard in gambling. The difficult thing about this is that many people don't suspect they have a problem until they are exposed to the lure of bouncing dice and whirling slot machines. They tell me that banks and finance companies are reluctant to grant newcomers credit until they've been through at least six months under "Las Vegas conditions." Some people fall apart when the gambling bug hits them.

On the other hand, there are plenty of Las Vegas residents who love to gamble and know how to keep things under control. One couple I interviewed explained how they put aside $20 apiece for a once-a-week gambling spree. "When the money is gone," said Sue, "we go to a lounge show, have a few drinks while watching the free entertainment, and then go home happy. Once in a while, we get lucky and we rake in enough to enjoy a dinner show where the big-name entertainment is; we can afford to shoot the works." Her husband added, "The problem with many people is they don't know when to quit. When and if we reach our goal for the evening, we stop and celebrate. If you keep on, you know the house is going to end up with it all. That's how it works."

They told me the story of a Presbyterian minister who was on his way to California to accept an important position in a new parish. He stopped off in Las Vegas and decided to see what gambling casinos were all about. He tried a bet or two and discovered, too late, that he was a compulsive gambler. He lost everything he had, then borrowed all he could on his credit cards. When he began calling friends to borrow more money, he realized his danger. Fortunately he made it to California, and hopefully, never returned to Las Vegas.

**RENO-LAKE TAHOE**--Reno's atmosphere is as different from Las Vegas as San Francisco is from Los Angeles. Las Vegas is new, touristy and tries to be trendy and fresh. Its landscape is table-flat desert and high-rise hotels. But Reno is an old town, with an air of the Old West, proud of its rowdy gold and silver mining past. Its backdrop is snow-fringed peaks of the nearby Sierra Nevada. Back in the early part of this century, the town's biggest business was supplying the mines. When the mines started to play out, a new industry arose in the form of "quickie" divorces, for which the state soon became famous. Ironically, today it's become a *marriage* center with 10 times as many marriages performed than divorces.

Las Vegas construction is Southern California-style stucco and imitation tile roofs. Reno is built of honest bricks and has an air of stability. In the old days, contractors used a deep red brick, building slowly and solidly. The older homes and buildings add greatly to the impression of a settled, mature city. Las Vegas's image is that of an eastern glamour girl, visiting out West in her minks and diamond bracelets. But Reno is pure West--a cowboy in a Stetson hat and a string tie. Reno is forever; Las Vegas is for one-night stands.

That's not to say that Reno doesn't have its share of Nevada glitter and razzmatazz, or 'round-the-clock nightlife. Actually, it's proud of its self-bestowed title of "The Biggest Little City in the World." Gambling and entertainment are big businesses today. The town was one of the pioneers in the gambling industry. But there is something "hometown" about Reno gaming tables that few other gambling resorts enjoy.

This hometown feeling was deliberately cultivated when gambling was legalized in 1931, during depression days. Harold Smith, founder of *Harold's Club*, decided that his future business would be best built on *local* money and loyal customers rather than depending on tourists. He instituted the practice of giving free drinks to customers and allowed gamblers to take "double odds" at the crap table. He cashed paychecks for free, and made local people feel especially welcome. He hired only local residents to work in the club, so that dealers and players were often also one's next-door neighbors. Other clubs in the state hired glamorous-looking youngsters, but at Harold's Club older people got breaks, something appreciated in depression days. The other Reno gambling halls didn't necessarily like this, but to keep Harold's from getting all the business, they had to follow suit. Today you find the legacy of these policies: An unusually friendly class of employees and customers in Reno casinos; places where senior citizens feel welcome and comfortable.

## UNUSUAL WEATHER

At a 2,400-foot higher altitude than Las Vegas (4,400 feet), and 300 miles farther north, Reno enjoys much cooler summers than Las Vegas. Air conditioning is an option that isn't necessary here. The hottest month of the year, August, has an average high in the 80s, but the interesting thing about Reno's weather is that no matter how hot it gets in the daytime, you can be sure you will feel comfortable in a sweater that evening, even in August. The temperature typically drops to around 65 in the evening and down to 50 degrees by early morning. With these kinds of cool summer nights, you would expect winters to be fierce, but surprise, they are quite mild. Even in December, January and February, the coldest months of the year, midday temperatures are warmer than August morning low temperatures! Furthermore, the low humidity fools you into thinking that 50 degree days are shirtsleeve days. Unless the wind is blowing, a sweater or light jacket is all you'd ever want to wear in Reno. Thus, both heating and air conditioning costs are minimal in Reno.

Snowfall is very sparse, about the same as Raleigh, N.C., or Portland, Ore. Seven inches is the average. Compare that with 10 times that (70 inches) in Albany, N.Y., or Portland, Maine. But if it's snow you want, you can drive less than 45 minutes and see it packed six-feet-deep in some of the most famous ski country in the world. Nearby Squaw Valley was the site of the 1960 Winter Olympics. There are 22 ski areas within a 90-minute drive from town, with 15 of them around beautiful Lake Tahoe. The snow sports season lasts from November until late spring. Ski lifts usually operate until long after Easter.

Reno's overall cost of living is above-average for everything but utilities. One reason for this is the boom in casino building, which has attracted many construction workers into the area, thus pushing up housing costs. Still, much of Reno is older, and there are many sections of more-or-less inexpensive homes that can't compete with the newer apartment and condo housing that's been going up simultaneously with the casinos. The nice thing about these older neighborhoods is they are just that--older neighborhoods, not slums. So housing for senior citizens isn't as bad as it might seem.

One of the benefits of living in Reno, according to some retirees I interviewed, is the services provided by the senior citizen center. There is a nutrition section with Meals on Wheels, Care & Share and a kitchen serving meals at the center. There is a retired volunteer program, a foster grandparent program and home aid for those who can't get out. There's also a legal service that offers free assistance with wills, Social Security, leases, etc. Because there are so many retired residents, they've managed to organize and work through the center to gain more control over their lives. A bonus is that there is a municipal bus service that seems to cover the area adequately.

Reno is the only large city (pop. 116,000) in the 700-mile stretch between Sacramento and Salt Lake City, so it serves as the principal medical center for northern Nevada, plus parts of California. Emergency cases from as far away as Fall River Mills, Calif., 135 miles distant, are often transferred here. There are four hospitals with 1,255 beds, complete with emergency and trauma centers. Because of the large area served, emergency helicopter ambulances are utilized to get patients there quickly. The University of Nevada has a four-year medical school, as well as a school of nursing. The retirees I interviewed are satisfied with medical care in the Reno area, although some claim it is expensive.

## GREEN FELT JUNGLES

Why senior citizens seem to love gambling so much is a subject that some social scientist somewhere must have studied. My own theory is that most of them couldn't afford to gamble when they were young adults with kids to raise and bills to pay, so now they are living it up. A tour through Reno's gambling casinos will convince you that slot machines and crap tables in the "green felt jungles" hold a definite fascination for the over-60 crowd. Senior citizens are in the large majority here, particularly on nickel slot machines, quarter crap tables or small-bet roulette wheels. "I wouldn't gamble in any other town in Nevada," said one elderly man as he placed a quarter chip on the crap table's *pass line*. "Not unless they gave me double odds like they do here."

Don't get the idea that Reno is all gambling. I'll guarantee you that if that's why you go there, you won't last very long. An old story they tell about Reno concerns the couple who arrived there driving a $5,000 Ford and left in a $200,000 Greyhound bus. Most residents quickly learn to control their urges, restricting their gambling to no more than they can afford to lose. Quarter crap tables and plenty of nickel slots make Reno gambling a bit easier on the budget. For most retirees, gambling is simply an infrequent diversion. There are too many other things to do in the Reno area.

Retirees have access to a surprising number of cultural events, such as the Nevada Opera Association, the Philharmonic Orchestra and Community Concert Series and a municipal band. Four theater groups are active, as well as theatrical and musical performances presented by the University of Nevada. Art galleries, museums and expositions by the historical society and the Sierra Arts Foundation add to the cultural variety of Reno. And for those who like the outdoors, there are the Sierra and the high desert to play in.

The Sierra Nevada starts almost at the edge of town. Local highways climb through forests, alongside sparkling streams, through steep canyons and past placid glacial lakes, clear to within reach of snowclad summits. Wildlife, fishing, hiking or just plain driving an auto, are all special here. Winter snowfall is quite heavy in the mountains, accounting for the great skiing. The highway department clears the roads immediately so skiers and tourists can get through. If you should feel nostalgia for snow, it's a simple matter to hop in your car, drive half an hour and look at from six to 16 feet of it piled alongside the road. Then, feeling thankful you don't have to shovel any of the damned stuff, you can return to Reno and climb into your hot tub.

With 250 to 300 days of sunshine each year, you have plenty of opportunity to enjoy the Sierra wildernesses, but if you go any direction but west, you will find the desert waiting for your investigation. One of my favorite pastimes in Nevada is exploring the ghost towns which abound in almost all parts of the state. Some are nothing but abandoned mines, houses and cabins, where the wind whistles through empty windows and roofless shells. These are fun places to search for old purple-glass bottles and artifacts discarded or lost by the residents of years past. It doesn't hurt to keep the eyes open for gold, while you're at it.

Many retirees go a little further than exploration; they study mineralogy at the University of Nevada or adult education classes, then get into serious rock hunting and prospecting. Don't get the idea prospecting is a waste of time. First of all, it's great outdoor recreation, and there's always a chance you'll find something valuable. It's also a form of gambling. Here's why: Many western silver mines were abandoned back in the 1930s when silver dropped to 25 cents an ounce, and all gold mines were closed during World War II on orders of the federal government. After the war, most mines were considered unprofitable because silver was around 90 cents and the government kept gold at $35 an ounce. If you poke around mineralized country long enough you might stumble onto a location that has become valuable at today's high prices.

# GHOST TOWNS

But not all ghost towns are abandoned. A particularly interesting one in the Reno-Lake Tahoe area is **Virginia City**. Located atop the world-famous Comstock Lode, the old town perches at an altitude of 6,700 feet. This city was once fabulously rich in silver. At its peak, in the 1860s and 1870s, 30,000 miners, businessmen, storekeepers, gunfighters and shady women lived here. Many miners toiled in the mines, going deep into the bowels of the earth to send up silver ore. My grandfather was one of these miners, working here around the turn of the century; he died in a mining accident and is buried in a cemetery in town. The fortunes of many famous families got their start here. Hearst, McKay, Flood, Stanford and others who went on to influence the country and the world. Mark Twain worked as a printer and reporter for the *Territorial Enterprise*, beginning his career as a one of America's most famous authors.

Many substantial buildings of brick and wrought iron were constructed, their builders confident of the inexhaustibility of the Comstock Lode and Virginia City's permanence. But after several collapses of the silver market, work ceased in the mines. Water filled the shafts and tunnels, and Virginia City became a ghost town. From 30,000, the population dropped to almost nothing.

For a while, Virginia City was a retirement dream. Abandoned, boarded up buildings were all over town, available almost for the asking. Retirees renovated the old homes and businessmen took over the main street, restoring such attractions as the *Territorial Enterprise* newspaper plant, the Red Dog and Bucket of Blood Saloons and across the street, the Silver Queen. By the way, my daughter was married in the Silver Queen Saloon's wedding chapel; the entrance is on the other side of the baccarat table. That may sound like a strange place to hold a marriage ceremony, but my daughter explained it perfectly: "The reason is, that the Bucket of Blood doesn't have a wedding chapel. Can you can believe that? So we *had* to hold the ceremony in the Silver Queen Saloon."

The population of Virginia City has grown to 700, with many of them retirees. There are enough retirees to support their own senior citizens' center; for a town of only 700, that's doing pretty good. Although there are a few buildings that have been converted to apartments, the predominant mode of housing is single-family dwellings. There are always a few rentals available, but most people own their own places. The altitude here makes for much colder winters than in Reno, with occasional deep snows, so it isn't exactly an idyllic retirement place. But for someone who is into history, who loves to walk in the footsteps of the famous, the brave and the intrepid, a ghost town can be fun. Particularly if you enjoy nosing around old mines and looking for outcroppings of some new bonanza.

Here are some other ghost towns where retirement might be an interesting alternative. Before you go packing your gold pan and go charging out to Nevada, remember that most of these places are isolated. Otherwise they wouldn't be ghost towns.

**AUSTIN** (170 mi. E. of Reno)--A silver boomtown of the 1860s, contemporary with Virginia City, has 350 inhabitants. **Dayton** (pop. 300, 10 mi. E. of Carson City)--One of the oldest towns in Nevada. It was used as a film location when "The Misfits" (Clark Gable, Marilyn Monroe) was filmed there in 1960. It claims to be in the Comstock's "banana belt." **Eureka** (pop. 1,400, 77 mi. W. of Ely and 115 mi. S. of Elko)--Lead and silver mines, looks like a stage setting for a western movie; has little tourism. **Goldfield** (pop. 300, 25 mi. S. of Tonopah). This was a roaring gold camp around the turn of the century. It grew to a solid-looking city, but a series of labor problems, which resulted in calling out the army to put down the workers, ended in abandonment of the mines and the town. Lots of fine buildings and are homes still standing. **Rhyolite-Beatty** (pop. 900, near Death Valley)--Classic examples of southern Nevada ghost towns. With almost no industry, land and housing is affordable.

**LAKE TAHOE (Nevada and California)**--Straddling the state line between Nevada and California, Lake Tahoe is one of the prettiest lakes in the world. The only lake country I've ever seen that surpasses Tahoe is in Bariloche, Argentina. After a while you become numb, trying to take in all the beauty here. Mark Twain had this to say about Lake Tahoe, in his book *Roughing It*:

"Three months of camp life on Lake Tahoe would restore an Egyptian mummy to his pristine vigor and give him an appetite like an alligator. I do not mean the oldest and driest mummies, of course, but the fresher ones. The air up there in the clouds is very pure and fine, bracing and delicious. And why shouldn't it be?--it is the same the angels breathe . . . [Lake Tahoe] must surely be the fairest picture the whole earth affords."

This is an all-year resort, with heavy-duty skiing in the winter, seven golf courses, hiking, boating and fishing in the summer and serious gambling and partying in all four seasons. Many people choose to retire here, to take advantage of the crisp air and the positively gorgeous scenery. But it isn't inexpensive. Most people I know who have retired here bought their homes long ago in anticipation of retirement, and then rented them out to make the payments until retirement time came along. The fortunate ones have their places paid for before they move there full-time. Rentals can be a quite lucrative business, since many people from California and from the East are willing to pay premium rents for a week or two at a time. But be prepared to pay plenty if you intend to buy, and if you plan on renting, don't think about short-term. Long-term rentals or leases aren't much different than you would expect to pay in California, and occasionally you may uncover a bargain in a smaller cottage.

The lake is enormous, almost 200 square miles, and is both deep and wide. Ringed by snowy mountain peaks, the lake is always a deep blue. You can barely see across to the other side. On the Nevada side, both north and south shore, there are gambling casinos. On the California side are housing developments, villages and lots of state-owned land with stunning views. Much of the shoreline is protected from development in order to preserve the scenic value of the lake. Once you leave the lake, you are in almost unpopulated Tahoe and Eldorado National Forest. There are more than 20 campgrounds in the area, some with tents already in place, which you can rent day by day. Places like Emerald Bay, Incline Village and Crystal Bay are interspersed with unspoiled stretches of forested, rocky shore, and numerous public beaches offer swimming and boat launching. "Living here is like being on permanent vacation," says an acquaintance of mine who owns a lakefront cottage near North Shore.

If you decide that you can't afford to live here, you can always visit if you choose to live in Reno; it's just a 50-minute drive. It's just 15 miles from another retirement possibility: **Carson City**. This is the state capital, but it doesn't look like one; it's too small, with only 36,000 people living there. Even more than Reno, Carson City gives the impression of being old and proud of it. Intimately connected with nearby Virginia City's history, the town is clearly a product of the Comstock Lode's silver bonanza. Today, it verges on being a touristy, casino city, but manages to maintain its individuality with a charming blend of its colorful, oldtime architecture and the zesty air of political prominence. Just two moderate-size casinos and a few small ones try to stir action, but somehow don't generate the enthusiasm of Reno or Las Vegas.

The pace is slower here; most streets are lined with mature, large cottonwood trees and old frame or brick homes. Real estate prices are lower than in Reno, and again, the older sections of town aren't slums, simply low cost housing, with comfortable neighbors. Outside of town, there's some new construction going up, but somehow, I like the older, in-town streets best--they're like wearing old shoes.

CHAPTER NINE

# *The Southeast Coast*

For many people, particularly those who live in the East, the idea of a West Coast retirement is a pleasant thought, but a little too distant. If the family lives in Toledo, let's say, or Indianapolis, the odds are that you'll get to see them much more often if you find a location on the Southeast Coast. Driving home from South Carolina to see the grandkids is a much less terrifying event than driving all of the way from San Diego. Besides, so many eastern people vacation in Florida every year that you might find plenty of family and friends who would appreciate a place to visit, or even stay the night as a pleasant break on a vacation trip.

Several conditions combine to make the Southeast Coast an ideal retirement locale besides its convenient location. These are: A low cost of living, affordable housing and mild, four-season climates. From Virginia down to Georgia, people are discovering retirement alternatives that fit their needs. Many who are choosing to move here previously had Florida or the Gulf Coast on their minds. Yet when they get a hankering for some beach action, it's not that far away. When asked why the change in plans, they cite the non-touristy atmosphere of most of the Southeast Coast.

Southeastern landscape varies from rich agricultural lands with neat farms and white fences, to rugged mountain scenery, where bears and herds of deer roam almost unmolested by mankind. Ocean beaches yield harvests of shellfish, and fishing of all kinds abounds both in the surf and inland streams and rivers, where trout lurk in pools, awaiting a lure.

All of these ecologies are within easy driving distance from almost anywhere in the Southeast. This gives a wide latitude in making choices. The areas that impress me most are parts of Vir-

ginia, North Carolina, South Carolina and the Georgia coast. I tried
to visit towns that are representative of each area. My criteria were
quality living, friendly neighbors, cultural stimulation and recreational opportunities.

Almost everywhere in the Southeast has something to recommend it as a retirement choice, if nothing else, low living costs. At
the same time, there are some areas where I personally wouldn't
feel particularly comfortable. On paper, these places look great--
incredibly inexpensive towns where you can rent a house for $150 a
month or buy one for under $20,000. But a good retirement area is
more than just cheap housing. Quality surroundings, neighbors with
whom you have something in common, cultural stimulation and
recreational activities--all of these factors enter into choices. How
far do you have to drive to shop for major appliances, or get them
repaired? To a theater or a movie? A tablecloth restaurant or a department store? Most people need regular access to these kinds of
things. For this reason, I've not gone into any great detail about
small-town living in the Southeast except in cases where I found the
necessary amenities. This isn't to say that I've covered all or even a
major fraction of the acceptable places. Furthermore, some people
don't require much in the way of amenities. Suffice to say that if
your life-style can fit into one of these small Southeast towns, you
might find one of the best retirement bargains in the country. Un-
questionably, this area enjoys the country's lowest cost of living.

## SOUTHERN HOSPITALITY

"Southern hospitality" is an oft-tossed-about phrase, but there's
a lot of truth to it. It's always been interesting to me to notice how
Southerners interact with one another and with strangers. There is
an openness and sharing that is quite different from the custom in
other parts of the country. For example, when visiting friends or relatives in the South, I notice people drop in at all times of the day.
Sometimes it seems like a procession, coming and going all day
long. They arrive unannounced, and if they are really close friends,
they sometimes don't bother to knock. They might open the door
and call out, "Anybody home?" They know they're always welcome
for a chat and a coffee. "Just passing' by," they say, "so I thought
I'd stop in to say hello." A cup of coffee is usually on the table before they can pull the chair out. In other parts of the country, this
would be unheard of. Before you make a visit, you telephone first

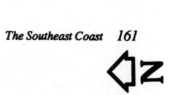

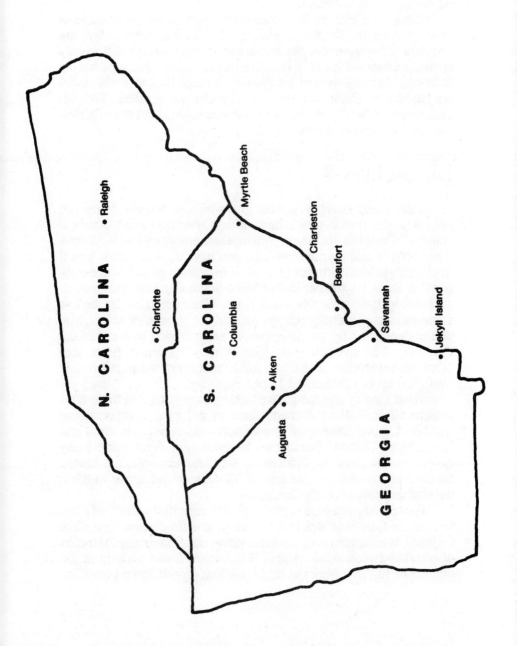

and receive an invitation. In still other parts of the country, even this is unheard of. You either wait for an invitation or you suggest meeting for coffee at a nearby restaurant. I think the Southern style would take some getting used to. Some people can feel quite imposed upon if someone comes by and expects them to drop what they are doing to entertain.

What's the climate like? Summer temperatures are bearable in most parts of the Southeast, although humid and muggy days are common along the coast. Winters are mild and short-lived. The only appreciable snows come in the Appalachian ridges that separate the Southeast from the rest of the country. Except for those who insist on Florida or California weather, the climate is ideal. The advantages over Florida are more tolerable summers, and over California, the four-season climate.

## THE CAROLINAS

Take sandy beaches, rolling green hills, mountain ridges and rugged peaks, then combine them with a genuinely mild "southern climate." Complete the scene with azaleas, mountain laurel, flowering magnolia and myrtle trees--and you have the Carolinas. You'll find a delightful assortment of outdoor recreation mixed with exceptional cultural advantages in North and South Carolina, plus moderate housing and reasonable living costs. When you consider the low crime rates and friendly people, particularly in smaller towns, you will understand why so many people are choosing to retire in the Carolinas. The over-60 population is growing much faster than other age categories, accounting for 10 percent of the population in 1980, and up to an estimated 15 percent today.

What kind of climate are we talking about? It's a definite four-seasons affair, with a five-month summer and a short winter, spring and fall. Despite these lengthy summers--which begin in April and last through October (sometimes beyond)--you don't catch many extremely hot days. In Charleston, S.C., for example, the hottest summer afternoons average around 90 degrees and closer to 85 in the northern part of North Carolina.

Winters are likewise benevolent and mercifully short. My last visit to the Carolinas was in a February, at a time when New York City and Washington, D.C., were digging out from under 20 inches of blizzard-driven snow. Aiken, S.C.,(where I was visiting at the time), also suffered from the cold wave that dipped down from Canada. The town buzzed with excitement because of a half-inch of snowfall that made everything "right pretty," as they say in South Carolina. We stood outside admiring the scene, wearing light sweaters and lamenting that there wasn't enough snow to crunch together a decent snowball. Within a few hours, the "right pretty" stuff melted away into memory. But farther north, shivering New Yorkers were shoveling snow and chipping ice from their windshields for days afterward. Why are weather conditions so different just a few hundred miles away? Here is the explanation from the publication, *Retiring in South Carolina* (South Carolina Commission on Aging, 1984):

"Several major factors combine to give South Carolina a pleasant, mild and humid climate. It is located at a relatively low latitude, and most of the state is under 1,000 feet in elevation. It has a long coastline along which the warm Gulf Stream current moves. The mountains to the north and west block or delay many cold air masses approaching from those directions. Even the deep cold masses, which cross the mountains rapidly, are warmed somewhat as the air is heated by compression when it descends on the southeastern side."

The same description applies to North Carolina, although the elevation is a bit higher, and the latitude is farther north. This means slightly cooler winters and even more pleasant summers. And, of course, as you move into the Piedmont and Blue Ridge Mountains, the winters will be longer and more snowy. I think if I had my choice of anywhere in the country where I would be forced to look at snow on a daily basis, I'd choose either the Blue Ridge Mountains or the Sierra Nevada at Lake Tahoe. I hope I never have to make a choice, however, because I much prefer to *visit* snow, make the appropriate remarks about snow making things look "right pretty," and then go someplace where I can lounge beside a swimming pool.

## WHAT DOES IT LOOK LIKE?

The geography of the Carolinas is divided into three distinct regions. The first is a broad coastal plain that rises from the Atlantic, often stretches of low, marshy land studded with palmetto palms and scrub oak. Several hundred miles of beautiful white-sand beaches draw retirees who need to include the seashore in their plans. Farther inland, fertile fields and comfortable small towns offer a quieter, usually more intellectual, life-style.

The flat lowlands end at a place known as the "Fall Line" where the foothills of the Blue Ridge Mountains begin. This is the Piedmont or foothill region. Rivers, creeks and streams flowing down from the mountains suddenly change into rapids and low waterfalls at this point, hence the name "Fall Line." This is a country of rolling hills, covered with hardwood forests and dotted with more than 400,000 acres of lakes. Peach orchards, horse farms, intimate small-town squares and country lanes characterize the Piedmont country.

The third region is the Blue Ridge highlands, where the Appalachians lift the elevation to nearly 3,000 feet. The mountains run in a northeastern-southwesterly direction from near the Canadian border down to just north of Atlanta, Ga. Ancient, eroded mountains, sometimes scarcely touched by civilization, they are richly cloaked with hardwoods and flowering trees, pines, beeches, poplars and birch. Crystal-clear rivers and streams cascade through canyons and tumble over waterfalls into deep pools. This is a nature-lover's treat. There are over 250 miles of trout streams in South Carolina, and probably at least that many in North Carolina. But the elevation isn't so high that it creates a harsh winter scene. Yes, there is snow, and yes, it may stick around more than a day or two. But compare it with New York weather, and even the coldest parts of the Carolinas come off looking mighty mild in the winter time.

## HOUSING IN THE CAROLINAS

Small cities and towns characterize the Carolinas, with most people living in single-family dwellings in "intergenerational" communities. This means you won't be segregated from younger people and growing families should you decide to retire here. This is one healthy aspect of living in non-urban atmospheres. Another is that prices for housing are bargain-basement. Naturally, you can expect to pay more for a place on the beach, or in one of the ritzy sections of Charleston, Greensboro or Chapel Hill. And, you can expect to pay a little more in Virginia than in North or South Carolina, but not significantly.

Many retirees, particularly those from urban backgrounds, feel more at home in condos, apartments or retirement "villages." Responding to this demand, more and more developments are sprouting up, places that appeal to the needs of senior citizens.

Along the ocean, you'll find many rather nice mobile home parks that cater to retirees from other states. Some parks look quite livable. But inland, as in many other places in the South, mobile home parks tend to be rather grim-looking affairs, with little or no landscaping or charm. Many communities look upon them as the country equivalent of city slums.

## ROCKS AND MINERALS

This is a great place for the "rockhound" and jewelry maker. Particularly in the Piedmont and the mountain areas, many interesting minerals and gemstones are there for the finding. This might be a hobby you should consider. In addition to getting you outdoors to search for gemstones, you come into contact with many others who are into polishing gems and creating jewelry masterpieces. This is a hobby many couples find highly satisfying. A major attraction is that it's an activity that can be shared equally--from the finding of the stones, to polishing and mounting the finished gems into a beautiful setting. Then the social interaction of displaying your jewelry at shows makes for many new friendships.

Always wanted to try your hand at panning for gold? Well, you don't have to go to California to test your luck. All along the Piedmont, the streams commonly yield small amounts of gold. A good place to look is where the creeks start downward toward the plain. According to state geologists, especially productive gold locations in South Carolina are in McCormick County near the town of McCormick, in Kershaw and Lancaster counties, in Chesterfield County near Jefferson, in Union County near West Spring, and in the Cherokee and York counties near Kings Creek and Smyrna. In North Carolina, gold counties include Union, near West Spring, and Cherokee.

Don't expect to get rich, but on the other hand, keep in mind that the first gold rush in North America started here back in 1799, when a 13-year-old North Carolina boy dug up a *17-pound* nugget. Not knowing the value of his discovery, the boy sold it for $3.50. That came to a little over 10 cents an ounce! In those days, the population was very light, so there wasn't really much of a gold rush. I doubt that the boy bothered looking around much after that; after all, at 10 cents an ounce for gold, why should he? Still, it occurs to me, that if there was one nugget that size laying around to be discovered, there should be more, and there should be a source. If you find the source, you can call me (collect), and I'll be right there. I'll even consider paying more than 10 cents an ounce.

Let's take a look at some locations in the Carolinas that seem to be feasible retirement locations:

## NORTH CAROLINA'S MIDLANDS

Between North Carolina's coastal regions and the mountains is a stretch of forested and gently rolling hills. Here, you'll find a unique combination of Americana. From Beethoven to Bluegrass, from stock car racing to scholarly research, just about any kind of intellectual and recreational pursuit imaginable is available. People from all over the U.S.A., from all walks of life are well-represented. Unlike some sections of the South, where outsiders are rare curiosities, the area known as the *Triangle* particularly attracts folks with academic interests and technical skills. It is claimed that there are more Ph.Ds and scientists per population group here than in any other part of the country.

The Triangle consists of the cities of Chapel Hill, Durham and Raleigh. Within these three cities there are three major universities, plus several other academic institutions which account for the accumulation of intellectuals and technicians from all over the nation. The world-renowned Research Triangle Park draws the best scientists, and is located within easy driving distance from any of the Triangle cities. The University of North Carolina was chartered in 1789 at Chapel Hill, and was the nation's first state university. This began the tradition of education in the Midlands of North Carolina. From one building, 100 students and two professors the University has grown to 22,000 students and more than 1,800 professors teaching in more than 100 fields. Durham is the home of Duke University, well-known as a center of higher learning, and famous for its hospital. The Raleigh-Cary area lists five institutions of higher learning: N.C. State University, St. Augustine's College, Peace College, St. Mary's College and Wake Technical College. Between Raleigh and Durham, there are eight two-year colleges and eight four-year colleges and universities, with 64,000 students. You can see that education is big business here.

Because of the schools, research and related industries, wages in the Triangle are higher than in most of the Carolinas. This means higher standards of living and of course, higher costs of living. Homes tend to be more expensive and more luxurious than in places where lower incomes are the rule. Many homes in the $200,000 plus price range have no trouble finding buyers.

Still, this is North Carolina, and lower wages for non-academic or technical workers are the rule. This creates a two-tiered standard of living. On the one hand we have homes for over $100,000 attracting their buyers, but at the same time, plenty of homes for sale under $60,000, and even some below $40,000. While some condos sell for well over $100,00, there are others, perfectly livable, in the $35,000 range.

## SOUTH CAROLINA

COLUMBIA--As an example of the coastal plain province, let's take Columbia, the capital of South Carolina. Columbia is situated at the point where the coastal plain meets the beginning of the Piedmont. At the western edge of the city, the rolling foothill country begins, and at the opposite edge, the country is flat all the way to the ocean. This is a very comfortable town, with modest-looking housing, neither poor nor rich. The vast majority of the housing here is owner-occupied. The streets are shaded with tall trees, and there's a quiet charm that comes with ordinary people living in ordinary neighborhoods. Yet, Columbia has its sophisticated side as well, with the cosmopolitan feeling that goes with being a university town (University of South Carolina).

Established in 1686, Columbia is different from many southern cities that simply grew out of colonial crossroads settlements. Columbia was one of the first planned cities in the country. From the beginning, the centrally located town was intended to be the capital of the British colony of South Carolina. The city's broad boulevards and colonial-style architectural gems attest to its early beauty. Robert Mills, one of the pioneers of U.S. architecture, designed several buildings here, as well as many in Washington, D.C. (One of his more famous works is the Washington Monument.) Unfortunately, Columbia suffered terribly during the Civil War when General Sherman's troops, in their infamous "March to the Sea," burned the city and destroyed as much as of it as they could. It's a credit to early architects and builders that anything survived the holocaust.

Today, with a population of 110,000, Columbia vies with Charleston as the "cultural center" of South Carolina. The University of South Carolina, with 28,000 students, is a major reason for this ambiance. It and a nearby two-year college, attract academics from around the nation, many of whom later decide to join the ranks of the retired in Columbia. By the way, you'll find the highest percentage of retirees living here than anywhere else in the state.

One nice thing about South Carolina is that for residents over 60, tuition is waived (on a space-available basis) at state colleges and technical colleges. Every school district in the state offers adult education programs, and you can pursue just about any educational goal you care to, at affordable costs. This is not only true in Columbia, but also at regional campuses in Beaufort, Lancaster, Allendale, Sumter, Union, Aiken, Conway and Spartanburg. Spring and summer residential academic programs are available exclusively for senior citizens at low cost.

Not only academics, but military retirees are attracted to Columbia. This is partly because of the town's proximity to Fort Jackson and the obvious advantages of retiring near a military installation. Thousands of GIs who were stationed here during World War II recall the mild weather and friendly people. At retirement age, these fond memories draw them back to Columbia. These two groups, academic and military (mostly non-southern), contribute a lot to making the Columbia area heterogeneous, with open, accepting feelings toward newcomers.

When I interviewed retirees here, I found several who had started out intending to retire elsewhere, but wound up happily retiring to the Carolinas. For example, retiree Warren Coulton, a pharmacist from Jackson, Mich., admitted that he and his wife had always planned on retirement in Florida. This was something they took for granted for years. But each year, on their way to their Florida vacation, they had to pass through the Carolinas. They made it a point to stay over in Columbia on their way to Florida, and again on their way home.

"Then, one day, just before we were to finalize our retirement plans," Warren explained, "we realized that we really liked Columbia better than Orlando, which we had originally figured on." They decided to rent an apartment, just to "see how Columbia feels." They found low living costs and friendly, cultured neighbors. "We never made it to Florida," he said with a satisfied smile. "Maybe we'll go there some day for a vacation, though."

I asked him how he felt as a "Yankee" moving into a "Deep South" town. Did he find any prejudices? "To tell you the truth, I haven't noticed anything like that," he said. "My neighbors are just as nice as the ones we had back home, but they're definitely more friendly. Other Northerners tell me, 'They'll be neighborly, yes, but they'll never invite you to their daughter's debutante party unless you were born in Columbia'." Warren shrugged his shoulders and said, "That's a relief to me, because the last place I'd want to be invited would be to some teenager's debutante party! I'd have to invent some kind of excuse why I couldn't go."

Another advantage Warren pointed out about Columbia retirement--aside from the low cost of quality housing--is the excellent medical care available. As a pharmacist, he was aware of such things. It seems there are 13 hospitals in the area with over 500 doctors.

Labor costs here, as in all of the Carolinas, are relatively low. This is reflected in housing costs. New homes, with two or three bedrooms, can be bought for as low as $50,000. "Fixer-uppers" go for even less. I've seen advertisements for two-bedroom houses renting for less than $350.

## PIEDMONT COUNTRY

AIKEN--As an example of a Piedmont retirement location, let's look at a town in the western corner of the state. Aiken (pop. 17,000) looks to be larger than it actually is, because it's the shopping and employment center for much of Aiken County. The county has about 115,000 people. The only large industry there, the Savannah River Atomic Project, employs a huge number of workers, some of whom drive from Augusta, Ga., every day to work. That's only 17 miles away.

I choose Aiken as a good example of a Piedmont town for a number of reasons, not the least of which is its beautiful, "Old South" setting. Streets shaded by enormous trees, graced with marvelous antebellum mansions, and people ingrained with notions of politeness and southern chivalry, all add immeasurable charm to the setting. Unlike many southern cities that suffered damage during the Civil War, Aiken escaped the torch of vengeful Union soldiers. General Sherman dispatched a detachment of cavalry with orders to burn the cotton mill and the town, but General Wheeler's rebel troops took up position and bluffed the Federal forces into thinking there were more Confederates than there really were. The Yankees retreated to rejoin their main force, and went on to ravage other towns like Savannah, Charleston and Columbia. So today, Aiken is a showcase of homes that survived the war, some dating back 150 years.

From its inception, Aiken was known as a health resort. Wealthy people from Charleston and the coastal plantations came here to escape the sultry, lowland summer heat and malaria-bearing mosquitoes. The Civil War and its aftermath of poverty put a temporary halt to Aiken's role as a summer health resort. But by the 1890s, Aiken began enjoying a golden age when some wealthy Northerners, looking for a pleasant, quiet location for winter homes, "discovered" the town. At an altitude of only 527 feet, the climate is mild enough to permit year-round grazing for livestock. It's a perfect place to raise thoroughbred horses. Soon the ordinary rich, the filthy rich and the disgustingly filthy rich began buying up the old mansions and building new ones of their own. They bought farms for their race horses, and enclosed pastures with lovely, white fences. They established the Palmetto Golf Club in 1893, and were slicing drives into the lake by the time the first thoroughbred colts were frisking in the meadows. The Northerners became known as the "winter residents" because the term *snowbird* hadn't been invented yet.

This quickly established Aiken as a rich man's playground, mostly a haven for wealthy Yankees from New York and Connecticut. These newcomers brought prosperity to Aiken and, with it, a genteel life-style that had disappeared with the Civil War. Aiken's old, aristocratic families gladly accepted the newcomers and their different customs, and assimilated them into local society. This established a tradition of openness and hospitality that has characterized Aiken ever since. Today, the super-rich have gone elsewhere, yet the legacy of hospitality and friendliness remains.

This isn't to say that there isn't a tightly knit social world of Aiken's "old families." Like many, if not most southern small towns, either you were born here, or you remain a permanent outsider as far as the town's "high society" is concerned. To me, this is one of the drawbacks of many small towns, but it's an attitude that is not restricted to the South. Sometimes, if you're greatly outnumbered, it just isn't comfortable to be the only stranger in town. But a unique thing about Aiken is that so many "outsiders" have moved there that the differences blur between natives and newcomers. Townspeople are so used to hearing other accents and seeing other life-styles, that few things strange or outlandish to them any more.

This brings us to another reason why I am discussing Aiken: Like other towns in the Carolinas, such as Charleston, Columbia, Chapel Hill and Durham, people from all over the country have broken through social barriers here. People from widely different backgrounds, social and economic strata, have made themselves at home and have been accepted for who they are, not necessarily who their *families* are. Society is much more open in places like this. True, like the retiree I interviewed in Columbia, you may not receive invitations to debutante parties. Fortunately for you, occasions like this are reserved for family and old-line family friends. But there are plenty of opportunities for making close friends with people from your own part of the country, or perhaps from your own hometown, just as you would do at "home."

Where did all these outsiders come from? Well, when du Pont Corp. was building the atomic installation, people from all walks of life, from all parts of the country, came to work on the project. Engineers, physicists, technicians, bricklayers, you name it. At one time, the payroll was in excess of 13,000. This many people and their families put a severe strain on the housing situation in Aiken, so du Pont built a lot of single-family dwellings and rented them to employees.

Suddenly the plant was finished. No more construction jobs. Most workers went elsewhere to work on another project, but others, nearing retirement anyway, elected to stay right here. Du Pont was stuck with hundreds of homes, so the corporation began selling them at fire-sale prices. For a time, $10,000 was the going price for a house. Naturally, this knocked a hole in the local real estate market, from which it has never quite recovered.

Many homes were bought by new workers coming in to operate the nuclear plant, among them technicians, engineers and academicians with different skills. But the word slipped out that here was a beautiful little town, with mild winters, friendly people and cheap housing. Retirees started looking very closely, and many are moving in.

Aiken isn't all single family homes, antebellum mansions and honeysuckle. There are condominiums and apartments with rents sometimes dipping to the low $200s per month. There are mobile home parks plus many properties outside of town where you can place a mobile home and have an instant farm. A newly constructed retirement community, Kalmia Landing, offers luxury retirement accommodations and an atmosphere of studied elegance. It's as posh as any I've seen, even those in Florida.

Aiken boasts a campus of the University of South Carolina and Aiken Technical College. This means free, or nearly free, courses for senior citizens and entry into the academic community of the town. There's a 190-bed medical facility which, I'm told, has an excellent reputation. For military retirees and their dependents, there are VA hospitals in both Columbia and Augusta.

Recreational choices abound for those who wish to use leisure time outdoors. The weather is generally mild, so year-round outdoor activities can be a reality. There are 19 golf courses within a 20-mile radius of Aiken, many with organized senior citizen clubs. In nearby Augusta, the famous Masters Tournament plays every year. Each autumn on the shores of Lake Hartwell, Clemson University conducts a camping program for senior citizens. Fishing, swimming, even water skiing for all of those oldtimers who go for that sort of nonsense, are available at any number of nearby ponds or lakes. Hunting and fishing permits are free for residents over 65 years of age. The city of Aiken has a full-time staff in its recreational center, which offers such activities as sewing, square dancing, bridge, horseback riding and numerous craft classes.

Harness racing is big here at the Aiken mile track and is known nationally as a training center for harness horses. This is a tradition that started back at the turn of the century and, along with polo, has given Aiken prominence in the world of horse breeding.

Included among cultural activities are the civic ballet, a winter concert series, a community playhouse, an arts and humanities festival and many events sponsored by the University of South Carolina. With plenty of intellectual stimulation, and with the city of Augusta (pop. 48,000) only a 20-minute drive away, Aiken is far from being a small-town, redneck community. This is the type of "Deep South" living situation that I can recommend.

## BLUE RIDGE MOUNTAINS

If you've ever driven the Blue Ridge Parkway, you'll have some idea of the beauty of the Appalachians. The parkway starts at the small town of Front Royal in northern Virginia and wends its way southwest until it ends at Great Smoky Mountains National Park, which is partly in Tennessee and partly in North Carolina. Much of North Carolina's western parts are in these Appalachian highlands, some of the prettiest scenery in the eastern United States.

Scenic roads wind through beautiful mountain terrain, past wild rivers and thick forests. In the spring, blooming mountain laurel and dogwood light up the woods, and in the fall, leaves glow orange and red in the crisp, cool air. Hikers and river rafters love this country. The Chattooga National Wild and Scenic River originates in North Carolina and sends its sparkling mountain water along the South Carolina and Georgia border for more than 40 miles through rapids, flumes, and an occasional tranquil stretch where paddlers can relax and enjoy magnificent Sumter National Forest. The best part is that it's no more than a day's drive from anywhere in the Southeast you might choose to live.

This is definitely a retirement place for outdoors-type people. From Front Royal to northern Georgia, you'll find pleasant living conditions: Inexpensive housing, friendly people and a fairly mild climate with brisk winters and cool summers. You can expect about 100 days a year below freezing, about 18 inches of snow (total, not at one time), so, Miami it isn't. But summers are delightful, with only about five or six days a year when it gets into the 90s.

Unless you are country-bred and raised, you'll probably think about getting within striking distance of a city. Once in a while you'll get a hankering for a supermarket or a department store, and even the larger towns aren't all that large: Asheville (53,000), Greenville (59,000) and Hendersonville (44,000) in the southern parts; and Bristol (24,000) and Johnson City (41,000) near the Tennessee border.

I've traveled through this country and I love it; I can see myself spending some time there soaking up the ambiance and enjoying the outdoors. But I'm not so sure I'd be comfortable in some of the more isolated little communities in the Blue Ridge Mountains. A popular retirement guide awards this part of the country top honors, naming some rather small towns here as the top-rated retirement places in the country. Among other things, the authors point out the abundance of outdoor recreation, with which I agree. But, unless you're used to small-town living, you could find yourself stifled in a restricted social environment.

Before I made any commitment, I'd want to make sure I wasn't going to be an "outsider," a stranger in a place where there are few or no other "outsiders" with whom I might have interests in common, and with whom I might make friends. I once found myself in such a position, in a small town with a closed society that was an hour's drive from the nearest real library or decent hardware store. It just didn't fit my life-style. Any relocation move entails a great deal of self-examination of your personal needs and individual personality. There's more to retirement than pretty scenery and cheap housing. If you and your spouse are those outgoing kinds of people who require lots of social interaction, you might quickly grow tired of "just sitting."

## ON THE OCEAN

CHARLESTON--Long known as the "cultural center of the South," Charleston, S.C. has scrupulously--almost jealously--maintained this tradition for over three centuries. Like an aristocratic southern belle who has been brought up to appreciate and worship the finer points of chivalry and good manners, Charleston rejected the unspeakably common intrusion of steel and colored-glass buildings and towering condominiums. She has refused to replace tradition and history with glitter and quick profits.

Like many other aristocratic southern belles, Charleston suffered her share of tragedies: Fire, earthquake, hurricanes, attack by enemy cannons, occupation by hostile troops, urban blight and assault by profit-hungry developers. But Charleston stood firm, protected her chastity when she could, repaired the damage and healed the wounds when she couldn't. The result is a treasury of historical architecture and purity that can't be found anywhere else in the country. The city is not simply a collection of historical buildings, but a living museum of the Old South; its traditions, cuisine, architecture and gracious manners. Charleston is a way of life.

After its settlement in 1670, Charleston quickly became one of the most prosperous cities in Britain's new colonies. It became the standard against which people measured other cities in terms of beauty, culture and riches. Planters, acquiring wealth from fantastically productive rice plantations, began designing mansions as lavish as they could afford. They built with such loving attention to detail, and such devotion to quality and style, that future generations of Charlestonians resisted all temptations to exchange these prizes for new fashions. Today you can find 246 homes known to have been built before 1840, 76 of which are pre-Revolutionary, with some dating from as far back as the 1720s. Hundreds more date from the time of the Civil War and the Reconstruction era. Charleston is so steeped in history that a walk through its downtown streets seems like an adventure in a time warp. It doesn't take much to imagine fine carriages perking along the narrow cobblestone streets, or finely dressed women and nattily attired men strolling along the sidewalks. I get a powerful feeling of humility when I look at a home that was built in 1720, and try to mentally recreate the atmosphere of that time, wondering how many families have lived there, how many generations of children were born and raised, and maybe died, in the same house. In California, where I live, any building over 100 years old is considered a priceless antique, so you

can see why I am overwhelmed. A house built in 1840? Amazing!
1820? Wow! 1720? !!!

The downtown section of Charleston isn't very large. It's built
on a narrow peninsula, almost an island between two rivers that
empty into the ocean at this point. About 15 blocks wide and 20
blocks long, the downtown has relatively few businesses. And the
ones that are there are rather unobtrusive. Most space is devoted to
private homes. But there are a few restaurants in this downtown section, most of them places I can highly recommend. The particular

culinary delight in Charleston is *She-Crab Soup.* It's creamy, made with the roe and meat from the female blue crab, and laced with a spot of sherry and some subtle spices.

As far as I am concerned, it's worth a trip to Charleston just to have a bowl of this soup and to savor the air of history about the city.

Living there probably isn't for everyone. It can be a formal place, with emphasis placed on a tempo of southern society, intellectual pursuits and traditional manners. But even if you aren't into buying an historic mansion and entering the social whirl of Charleston, there are some alternatives which might be an adventure for a part-time living arrangement. You can do as the old-time planters did, live in Charleston for the season, and somewhere else the rest of the year.

It turns out that many of the old mansions have long ago converted to apartments. Rents are uncommonly reasonable, considering the enthralling atmosphere. I looked at a one-bedroom apartment with a nice kitchen in a historic house on Bull Street, which rented for $375 a month. Also, the carriage houses behind the mansions have often been converted into rental units for supplementary income to the owners. Many of these have been fixed up into charming cottages, with one or two bedrooms upstairs--they afford private, quiet and gracious living. They're usually in the midst of the gorgeous flowered landscaping for which Charleston is so famous. I've seen carriage houses advertised from $360 to $700. I'm sure you can pay a lot more.

Should you become ambitious, and want to own your own historic mansion, you might be surprised at some of the prices. I expected prices starting at $500,000 and up. But several were priced at under $200,000. I can't vouch for the condition of the amount of restoration needed. Certainly you would have to be prepared to invest a lot of money in items whose importance wouldn't become apparent until too late, but there is a certain satisfaction in restoration. If you can afford it.

When you leave downtown Charleston, the houses are still old, but not well maintained. The result is heavy urban blight, and places you would not likely want to live. But these areas are fascinating bits of history, and some old houses were undoubtedly as beautiful in the old days as their restored cousins downtown. Antique houses are still antiques, even if they do lack paint. Ornate side balconies and tall pillars hint at past glory, but sagging roofs and unpainted walls hint at a questionable future.

## IT TAKES IMAGINATION

There are many pleasant areas on the fringes of Charleston where you will find mobile home parks, reasonably-priced houses and rentals. But the most interesting retirement alternative I found was that of a couple who decided to purchase an eight-acre island for their home. The husband retired from the Air Force, and the couple, remembering Charleston from his military travels, decided on retiring there.

At first they considered buying a conventional home. Then they came across an interesting idea: Why not *build* a house, and what better place to build a house than on their own island! A network of rivers meet at Charleston: The Stono, Ashley, Cooper and Wando rivers, make Charleston Harbor and the surrounding coast a virtual conclave of islands. Most are uninhabited, overgrown with thick brush, and only a few feet above high-tide level. The price was right, so John and Michelle decided on a thickly wooded island that already had a causeway leading out to it.

They hired a bulldozer to clear an acre or two for their homesite, and they set about learning how to build a house. Because they were out of the city, and away from stiff building restrictions, they had considerable latitude in making plans and doing the work themselves. John learned plumbing and electrical work by reading a book. Michelle, who had never done anything more mechanical than operate a sewing machine, learned how to use a table saw and a riveting gun. Their children came to help, and they enjoyed the project so well that one son and daughter-in-law decided to move to Charleston and build their own place on the other end of the island.

"But, what about high tides?" I asked. "What happens when a hurricane sends in a lot of water?"

"That's why be built the house high," John replied. "The first level is a garage and things that won't be hurt by water. And we made sure all our landscaping was plants that won't be destroyed by a little extra water."

Michelle added, "It only happened to us once in the 10 years we've been there. A hurricane backed the river up about three feet over our property. But nothing was hurt except a vegetable garden I had planted that summer." Fortunately, the Isle of Palms runs east along John and Michelle's island, cutting off the brunt of wind-driven tides.

Other possibilities, perhaps less imaginative, can be found in the proliferation of new condos and houses, many of them built near

Charleston Air Force base. Of course, many retirees are ex-military, not only Air Force but also Marines. Farther south are the islands of Laurel Bay, site of Beaufort Marine Corps Air Station, and Parris Island, a Marine training facility. The town of Beaufort (pop. 8,800) is the largest center for retirees, with several small towns scattered around the islands. Although many ex-Marines may have negative feelings about their boot camp experiences on Parris Island, many also remember the climate and sub-tropical vegetation of this area with some positive feelings.

# GEORGIA

SAVANNAH--Farther down the coast from Charleston is Savannah, Ga. Much larger (about 150,000) than Charleston, Savannah is also filled with old homes. Although it promotes the image of gracious, old southern charm, the city falls short of possessing the magical aura of history that makes Charleston so special. One section of Savannah, down by the waterfront, has been restored, with antique stores, restaurants and bars, and many of the mansions in the center of town look rather nice. Many of the old, Civil War homes are for sale at reasonable prices, should anyone have the urge to try a hand at restoration.

Still, as far as I'm concerned, Savannah cannot be compared to Charleston; in fact no city anywhere compares with Charleston. The main difference is that most of the "old" homes here are post-Civil War. General Sherman's destructive "March to the Sea" exacted a heavy toll on the beautiful old antebellum homes. And today, Savannah's crime rate is higher than I think acceptable. Still, this rate is influenced by inner city social conditions, and may not be as bad overall as they might seem at first glance. As long as you choose the right neighborhood to live in, crime statistics can be almost academic. As you get into the suburbs, and away from the city, everything becomes rather peaceful no matter where you go.

There are several islands near Savannah that are said to be popular with retirees. These are Wilmington, Skidaway and Tybee islands, plus the area around Richmond Hill State Park. About 40 miles north of Savannah is Hilton Head Island, a rather expensive resort for Savannah's wealthy. This is reputed to be a good place for retirement, but its reputation for exclusiveness and higher-priced living prevented me from visiting there.

## BRUNSWICK AREA

Another traditional retirement area, one that is attracting more and more retirees, is Brunswick and the islands of St. Simons and Jekyll on the south Georgia coast. Brunswick is on the mainland and is quite modest in comparison with its island neighbors. It is a rather ordinary place of about 20,000 people.

The town was founded before the Revolution. Its streets and squares honor members of English nobility of that time, with names like Prince, Gloucester, Norwich and Newcastle still in use. The town itself was named for Brunswick, Germany, ancestral home of the Hanover kings of England.

Property here is reasonable (if not downright cheap), and the homes are well kept. Streets are sheltered by overhanging oak trees, hung with Spanish moss--quiet and peaceful. Some antebellum homes, with columns and balconies, grace the side streets, mixed in with more modern cottages. Because Union troops destroyed much of the town during Sherman's "March to the Sea," many of the homes were rebuilt at the end of the Civil War in the same architectural style as before. You will find some mobile home parks, but from what I can tell, they are much the same as other such facilities throughout much of the South--uninteresting, without landscaping or organized amenities.

Brunswick is the place to live for those who want to enjoy the fishing, beaches and ambiance of nearby Jekyll and St. Simons islands without paying the higher cost of actually living on the islands.

**THE GOLDEN ISLES**--The main contenders for retirement here are the islands, popularly known as "the Golden Isles." The story is that this name was given them by the Spanish during their explorations of the Georgia coast in the early 1500s. Not because they found gold, but because of the glorious beaches and the great weather. Maybe, but it seems more likely to me that the name came from the number of millionaires who early on claimed the islands as their private discovery. This area's biggest endorsement, as far as I am concerned, is this millionaires' connection; if super-rich people, who can live anywhere they jolly well please, chose the Golden Isles, then there must be something here worth choosing.

It all started in the 1880s when world-famous and wealthy families like the J.P. Morgans, Rockefellers and Goulds began moving onto Jekyll Island. They founded the Jekyll Island Club, one of the most exclusive in the world. Only club members were permitted to live on the island. It's estimated that Jekyll Island Club members once represented one-sixth of the world's wealth. World War II brought this to an end, and the state of Georgia bought the island in 1947. The fabulous mansions are still there, but most of the "old money" families moved away when "ordinary" people began taking over.

Today Jekyll Island is still expensive, but somewhat more affordable and much more accessible. The average three-bedroom home sold last year went for $127,000. A real estate broker told me that he has sold duplexes (two three-bedroom units) for as low as $70,000 and as high as $110,000. This is on the western side of the island, away from the beach. The Atlantic side, with its lovely beaches, commands higher prices, as you might well imagine. An average house on the beach sells for $250,000, a mere trifle compared to what it would be were the Jeykll Island Club still in charge.

The extra cost of beach properties is of dubious benefit for many people because the entire island is beautiful and wooded, and homes are set on spacious grounds. Most try to use natural landscaping. There is but one place on Jekyll Island that accommodates RVs and camping (in an isolated section of the western side). There are no mobile home parks, and I doubt if they will ever be permitted. The tone of Jekyll Island is strictly high-class. Some apartments and duplexes are available for rent, from $450 a month for a 3-bedroom apartment on the lee side of the island to $1,200 a week on the beach side. Since there are so may weekly rentals during the summer season, average rents can go quite high.

To discourage use of the beaches and facilities by outsiders, there is a charge to cross the causeway. It isn't called a bridge toll, but rather a $1.00 parking fee, collected in advance.

**ST. SIMONS ISLAND**--St. Simons Island is reached by driving across a long causeway (toll) to the live-oak-and-pine-forested island. Once there, a sharp right turn takes you to the town of St. Simons. You drive past golf courses and sprawling homes on large lots with magnificent trees and landscaping. If it weren't for the Spanish moss hanging from the tree limbs, typical of the Deep South, this part of St. Simons Island would look like Del Monte Forest at Pebble Beach in California. Originally, the island was the site of several plantations, and it isn't hard to imagine what it was like back in the days of Southern aristocracy and slavery. A couple of slave houses still stand and are open to the public for inspection.

About 12 miles long and four miles wide, the island is bounded on the east by the Atlantic Ocean, and on the west by the Intracoastal Waterway. Blessed by mild winters, tempered by the Gulf Stream and relatively cool summers, St. Simons and its neighbor, Jekyll Island, draw hundreds of thousands of visitors every year. These visitors and vacationers are the ones who eventually decide to retire here. As they collect fond memories of idyllic days of frolic on the many miles of beaches, and balmy evening walks through the town, many of the islands' devotees begin thinking thoughts of eventual retirement to the Golden Isles. The result is a pleasant blend of people from all over the country making up the retiree population.

An interesting retirement community, the only one of its kind in the area, is found on St. Simons. There are many like it around the country, and the concept is growing: Long-range, total care facilities.

The complex on St. Simon Island offers three stages of retirement. First, there are the Villas, which are either cottages or apartments for those who want to be totally independent and cook meals for themselves. Next is the Heritage House, for those who aren't quite up to doing their own cooking (or are fed up with it), or who might have trouble taking care of themselves. Here the guests live in their own studio apartment, but have three meals a day provided in the dining room. Finally there is The Inn, for those who need skilled care. A traditional nursing home environment, The Inn differs from other places in that a patient doesn't have to leave his or her friends and go somewhere new. Thus, the one complex takes care of all possible life-style changes.

Costs are rather high, with apartments starting at $875 a month for a single and $1,075 for a couple, and the Heritage House at $900 and $1,100. But in both cases this fee includes housekeeping services and complete maintenance.

The advantage in this kind of arrangement is that you can make friends when you start out, and keep them all through your stay there. The friends you knew as golfing or bridge partners will probably be the ones who are also in the other two facilities as you advance from one stage to another.

The important thing to realize is that when you enter a complex like this, you must be completely satisfied with not only the living arrangements, but also with the people who will be your potential friends. If they turn out to be of a different social class, people with whom you have nothing in common, or people who are boring, you will be wasting your time. I can picture myself in a long-range retirement program, but only if I were totally convinced that there is nowhere else in the world where I could possibly be satisfied living. So far, I've never found that "one place." But that's just me. Many people can't understand why anyone would want to move away to retire in the first place. My only recommendation on one of these three-step retirement places is to first live in that area on a temporary basis, and be solidly convinced that you would be miserable if you had to live anywhere else, and that you can't imagine making any better friends than you find in the complex.

St. Simons has a very pleasant, small-town atmosphere, although a rather upper-class small town. An attractive pier and public park are at the center of a low-key "downtown " if you can call it that. Actually, it's more of a collection of tasteful shops by the park. The pier was once the dock for a ferry boat, before the bridge was built. A quiet shopping center hides behind shrubbery on the main road that curves along the beach side of the island. There are several miles of fine public beach and excellent places for picnics. Good restaurants aren't scarce, with seafood the most popular fare.

Housing costs are about the same as on Jekyll Island, with perhaps more apartments and condo rentals available. Nothing is cheap here, but everything looks first-class. There are no mobile home parks, and probably no plans for any.

A few miles' drive east from St. Simons and crossing a short causeway brings you to Sea Island. Here is one of the wealthiest residential districts I've ever seen. It isn't simply a few flashy mansions among a base of ordinary houses; it's a solid congregation of appallingly expensive homes. I didn't bother to check prices, but my guess would be that most homes come closer to being worth a million dollars apiece than they do to a half-million. The shocking item is that most are simply "summer cottages" for their owners. I don't think I care to see their winter homes. My envious heart couldn't stand the pain.

CHAPTER TEN

# *Florida, a State of Mind*

When most people consider retirement, one of the first things that pops into their minds is *Florida*: Soft, sandy beaches with swaying palm trees and balmy days for the rest of your life. Sounds great, and for many, many people Florida has become their dream fulfillment. But most people who retire there don't suddenly decide one fine day to pop on down to Miami and buy a home. They've been coming to Florida for years, spending almost all of their vacations there. They know pretty much what they like, and when the time comes, they are well prepared. For those of you who aren't familiar with Florida, this chapter should be helpful.

What is Florida? Certainly, parts of Florida match the picture of beaches, palms, sunglasses and glamorous hotels. But there is a lot more. True, Florida has some of the most heavily populated places you can imagine, with clusters of high-rise apartments and condominiums set closer together than even Manhattan might dare. But Florida also has some of the most sparsely populated land in the world. Thousands of square miles of land scarcely know the sound of anything but wildlife. Heron, egret, ducks, storks--wildfowl of all description share vast tracts of land with animals that range from from panthers to rabbits, and alligator to turtles. Deer abound in the open countryside and in the state's large system of national forests. Other parts are flat to rolling farm country with towns that look little different from similar-sized places in Iowa or Illinois.

People tend to choose a few of the nicer locations and squeeze together there, largely ignoring the rest of the state. Of course, a lot of Florida's land simply isn't suitable for development. Everglades swamp, much in wildlife sanctuary, makes living difficult for humans. Torrential summer rains turn much of the land into impassable swamp. Because a substantial part of the state is flat, with a very high water table, swampy land with picturesque cypress trees make many parts of Florida pretty, but uninhabitable. Once you leave the tourist-encrusted coast, you will discover many areas of rich farm land, pleasant small towns, and even some pretty rolling hill country that looks nothing at all like your tourist-and-boardwalk Florida.

The climate also varies widely. In the lower part of the state, from the Florida Keys up along the west coast to Vero Beach, the climate is about as close to tropical as you can expect. Actually, Miami is only a couple of hundred miles north of the Tropic of Cancer, the imaginary line where the tropics officially begin. Combine that with the benevolently warm Gulf Stream that sweeps along the east coast, and you have one of the best climates imaginable for winter-haters. But in the northern parts of the state, particularly inland, where the ocean's waters cannot temper the weather, you'll catch a short but definite winter season, and not infrequently, cold and frosty winter mornings. Snow isn't unknown in the north, but it visits rarely.

The west coast of Florida and the Panhandle in the north aren't quite as lucky as far as the Gulf Stream goes. The flowing warm water heads for western Florida, but suddenly veers south to hook around the Florida Keys on its way north. This makes the Gulf of Mexico side cooler in the winter and warmer in the summer. Not by very much--summer temperatures are only a couple of degrees higher in Fort Myers or Tampa than in Miami--but with Florida's high humidity that's enough to make a big difference if you are sensitive to heat. Winter days can be quite chilly on the west coast, but overall, winters from Tampa south are quite pleasant, averaging only about one degree lower than the "Gold Coast" part of the Atlantic side. But to those who are escaping northern winters, even the briskest Florida winter morning is like a gentle breath of spring compared to home.

The Gulf Stream flows close to shore, bestowing its warm blessings on the Atlantic coast until a point near Vero Beach. Then it begins to swerve out to sea. This leaves the northern part of the Atlantic side with even cooler winters than the Gulf of Mexico side, although summers are about the same. Jacksonville, for example, sees highs in the mid-60s and lows in the mid-40s during December through February.

Again, this is balmy weather for those who think in terms of below-zero chill factors all winter long. Often I've heard residents

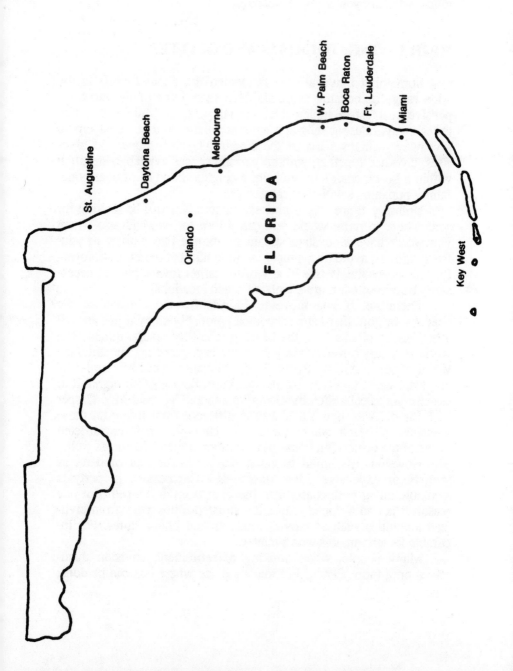

of Minnesota or Michigan defend their state by saying, "Why, we've had an unusually mild winter this year. It hasn't gotten much below zero all season." I often feel like asking, "If it's so mild there, why are you here in Acapulco?" But that would be unkind, and would invite the obvious return question, "If you like California so much, what are *you* doing in Acapulco?"

## HIGH LIVING, TOURISTS AND GLITTER

Something that's always fascinated me about Florida is the wide range of housing available. I've seen some of the most expensive real estate imaginable, virtual palaces, while just a few miles away, housing sells and rents at what would be considered a giveaway in many parts of the country. Densely populated high-rises, crowded together, with no parking spaces available, are often within a beach chair's throw from a neighborhood of ordinary one-family bungalows with two-car garages.

Unless you are a very unusual person, you will be looking for somewhere to retire where you can afford to live, and also where you won't have a constant stream of zombie-like tourists in your front yard. To avoid this, simply avoid looking at beachfront property. This is absolutely true in any of the larger towns, but not necessarily true in smaller, more isolated beach locations.

Therefore, if you move to Florida for the climate, or the beaches, or golf, or whatever, you can probably enjoy it just as well a half-dozen blocks from the beach (preferably several miles). The world is totally different away from the beer-guzzling, suntan-crazy world of the beach. By living close, you can do your beer-and-sun-crazy act when you feel like it, and return home before nightfall to assume your secret identity of mild-mannered Mr. and Mrs. Casper T. Retiree. True, living this way is different from living on those stretches of beach where the super-rich enjoy their unrestricted vistas of the ocean. But house payments are quite different, as well.

However, it's unfair to categorize all beachfront property as touristy or expensive. More uncrowded, inexpensive property is available along both coasts than has ever been developed. But one reason it is undeveloped is that it's situated miles away from civilized amenities such as movies, markets and liquor stores. For incurable fishermen, this won't matter.

Many people, when thinking of retirement, envision themselves on a farm. Central Florida is a place where this can be done, and at not too great an expense. From south of Orlando on north, you'll find plenty of good farming land. Some may have patches of boggy land and cypress trees or perhaps some acreage in pine forest. I don't claim to know anything about farming, but the farm country I've seen in Florida looks pretty good to me.

## LIVING CONDITIONS

Although I'd been in Florida before and had worked there at one time, I made a special trip in early 1987, spending a month and driving almost 2,000 miles throughout the state. I wanted to get a special feel for how it would be for me to live there. My overall impression was favorable. Many towns appealed to me, places where I could be comfortable making a choice.

By and large, people are friendly, although the larger the town, the less cordial strangers seem to be. That comes as no surprise, since that seems to be the rule in most parts of the country. But in doing this research, I discovered that Florida real estate people, instead of being happy to provide information (as their colleagues were happy to do, without exception, in other states) seemed reluctant to spend their time with me. After one lady in Pompano Beach was particularly rude, I began pretending I was a potential customer, interested in buying. I dislike taking a salesman's time under false pretenses, but it did change attitudes and supplied all-important information.

A plus for Florida retirement is the special services the state and communities provide for senior citizens. Because of the enormous retired population (and because of its vote) extensive programs are provided at all levels, from volunteer opportunities for the active to in-home service for the frail and elderly.

One disquieting aspect about some parts of Florida is crime statistics. Miami, for example, has an appallingly high rate of crime. Murder is three times the national rate. Robbery, assault and burglary are more than double the norm. Much of this is attributable to drugs; Miami has the dubious honor of being the drug importation capital of the country. Since few retirees reading this book are apt to become heavily involved in drug dealing, some of the statistics can be discounted. The people who are involved in the crime statistics are counted repeatedly. Still, the burglary rate in some of the Gold Coast towns bothers me.

Yet, despite the high crime climate, Rand McNally's *Places Rated Almanac* ranks Miami among the top places to live in the

United States, ranking it 52nd. On the other hand, Fort Myers, with an exceptionally low crime rate, ranks 179th as a desirable place, according to the same source. The reason for this discrepancy is that the authors of *Places Rated Almanac* place emphasis on such items as job opportunities, the arts (opera, concerts, museums, etc.), education and health care (which includes availability of teaching hospitals and medical schools).

Some of these factors are important for people retiring, others probably aren't. In *my* retirement plans, job opportunities in an area don't demand top-drawer priority. How can I retire, if I am going to need a job? My children are already educated and working on educating my grandchildren, so I don't require excellence in education in my retirement plans. And finally, I think I can forego a concert or access to museums in return for a little more security in my life. After you've been to the museums in your area, how many times a year do you go back?

Another item that bothers me about Florida is the traffic in some areas. Traffic is particularly heavy the farther south you go. I become highly annoyed at having to wait several minutes for a break in traffic in order to make a right turn out of a shopping center parking lot (I long ago gave up even hoping for a left turn break). And, the scarcity of traffic lights that change on demand makes me furious while I'm waiting in line at a red light while we give right of way to an empty street. It's only fair to point out that Florida drivers seem to be orderly and polite. Of course, the streets are so filled with autos that there's no room to speed. I suspect that part of the problem is a lack of funds for roads. Since Florida voters are reluctant to institute a state income tax or to raise property taxes, the road crews should be commended for doing as well as they have.

## RECREATION

When I first began collecting data on Florida, I was struck by the number of localities that advertised themselves as a "golfer's paradise." It turns out that just about anywhere you go you find plenty of courses. Many retirement complexes are built around golf courses, and in addition to having a green near your back yard, you usually won't have long to wait for a starting time. Tennis and racquetball courts are also plentiful, with most municipalities building them as part of the public park system. Fishing is an obvious sport that can be engaged in almost anywhere in the state, if not in the ocean or gulf, then in the ever present rivers, lakes or canals.

Let's take a look at a few communities I feel are representative of others in the state. As always, understand that this is not an exhaustive list, but merely a guide to the kinds of communities that might be suitable for your retirement consideration. We'll start at the top of the Atlantic coast and work down and around to the Panhandle.

**ST. AUGUSTINE**--Take a touch of old Spain, mix it with northern Florida's beaches, add a dash of Disneyland--and you have St. Augustine (pop. 12,000). It's the oldest permanent European settlement in North America, founded in 1565, two generations before the Pilgrims made their trek across the ocean. Most of the colonial Spanish architecture has long since disappeared, the victim of fire, hurricane, pirate raids and modern-day "progress." The Disneyesque touch enters the equation with stucco reproductions of ancient Spanish buildings, wax museums, alligator wrestling, plaster pirate cannons and other marvels designed to separate awed tourists from their dollars.

Downtown St. Augustine sports a Victorian era complex of imitation Moorish designs on municipal buildings and a downtown college campus. They might look attractive were it not for the incongruity of the ancient-looking towers and sculptures--done in red tile--sitting atop ordinary looking, poured-concrete walls. A little beige stucco would do wonders for downtown St. Augustine. Nevertheless, you'll find a comfortable, small-town atmosphere, not nearly as hectic as some Florida locations.

There seems to be two levels of awareness in the town: One tourist, one resident. These two groups exist side by side, neither totally aware of the other's existence. While tourists ride tour buses, slack-jawed and wide-eyed, gawking at real, artificial and imaginary marvels, the local people go about their business of living, as oblivious of tourists as the tourists are tuned-out to anything but their tour guide. While tourists may pay $85 a night for a small room, local people are paying $325 a month for a nice, two-bedroom apartment, or buying a three-bedroom home for under $65,000, and occasionally as low as $50,000. Duplexes are advertised for $45,000. To my surprise, these prices seem to be available in most parts of Florida (once you get away from the beaches, of course).

There are many mobile home parks around this part of Florida, and unlike most in Georgia and the Carolinas, you'll find landscaped and orderly looking parks the rule rather than the exception. Since mobile homes are the residences of more-or-less permanent people, the rents are priced according to local economy and don't fluctuate with the season.

All in all, St. Augustine is at heart a small town, rather pleasant, if you can be like the other residents and ignore the flocks of tourists. The town isn't too large, and in the off-season, traffic isn't bad. From September to February, rates drop on seasonal rentals, and you can find some moderately inexpensive rentals as a base from which to try out the area before making any hard decisions.

The weather here is typical north Florida east coast. Winter highs are in the mid-60s and lows in the mid-40s. Summer high temperatures average in the 90s, but don't go much higher. The record high for July is only 99 degrees; that happened back in 1978. Like most of north Florida, St. Augustine is a summer town, catering to vacationers who crowd the beaches when school is out, then leave the city to local residents in the winter season.

Across from St. Augustine is Anastasia Island. To get there, you cross an ornate bridge with cast-iron sculptures on its approaches. Fishing is obviously the central focus of people living here. Boat yards, bait shops, fishing supply dealers and other similar businesses seem to be everywhere. Anastasia Island is long and narrow, with sandy beach on the ocean side. It stretches all the way to Daytona Beach, some 65 miles to the south. The island is liberally sprinkled with luxury condos, both fancy and ordinary homes, and occasionally a shack or two. Fishing and beach lounging are the popular pastimes here. There isn't much else to do on this long, often rural-looking island. As I drove along the lightly traveled highway, I thought how nice a peaceful place like this would be for an artist or a writer who wanted a quiet place to work, and the tranquility of an ocean beach.

**DAYTONA BEACH**--About 65 miles south of St. Augustine, we come across Daytona Beach (pop. 57,000). The temperature is about the same as St. Augustine, although there are those who claim Daytona is warmer in the winter. The beach here is 23 miles long and at low tide, 500 feet wide. This is one of the few places in Florida where automobiles may journey along the beach. The hard-packed sand can be driven at low or out-going tide. At other times it isn't so hard-packed. Overnight parking or camping isn't allowed. In the center of the tourist area is a wide promenade, an amusement park and a fishing pier. The city of Daytona Beach is partly on the island, partly on the mainland.

To keep tourism alive during the slower months, automobile and motorcycle racing is promoted. These events draw race enthusiasts from all over the nation, and bring revenue into the surrounding communities. During racing events, the race fans are said

to outnumber the residents. So local people pay close attention to when the traffic jams are about to occur and avoid going near the island at that time.

Daytona Beach is one of the nicer-looking beach cities, with graceful buildings on both the island side and on the mainland. A drive across the causeway, which is tastefully lined with tropical trees, gives a feel for Florida, one that is not tinged with tourist gewgaws. The Indian River, which is the inland waterway, is perfect for learning how to sail, and for harboring boats. (The Indian River, by the way, is not really a river, but a long, long stretch of water that runs between the mainland and the narrow island strips, such as the one Daytona Beach is on.) Ships, yachts, power boats and fishing dinghies cruise up and down this waterway all the way down to the Florida Keys. Besides being a place for tourists and racing fans to go and raise hell, the island serves another important purpose: It buffers the mainland from the occasional hurricane-class winds.

In contrast to St. Augustine, Daytona Beach's tourist section is on the island rather than the mainland. Rents fluctuate wildly here, depending on the season, and some of the condominiums are priced according to the view rather than the facilities. The rational, affordable places to live are on the mainland. There you'll encounter many older, comfortable rentals that are quite affordable. As you get away from town, newer units are more frequently available. But even on the beach side, prices aren't outrageous.

Beachside condos are commonly advertised at $45,000, and under, for two-bedroom units. But when buying on the island, always make sure you aren't buying into a party pad. Any place where most of the units are rentals to tourists by the week is sure to be trouble. Particularly if your neighboring condo is rented to a nice-looking college student who immediately invites the whole fraternity house to an around-the-clock party. Single-family homes are also available from $50,000 off the island, some of them looking like real bargains.

Nearby communities that might be worth looking at would be Ormond Beach and Port Orange. As you go down the coast, there are many likely retirement communities, such as New Smyrna beach, Cocoa Beach and Indian Harbour Beach. Ormand Beach (pop. 22,000) was the original beach race course where daredevils like Barney Oldfield tried to break the 60-mph speed barrier. There's an interesting museum there dedicated to automobile speed. Races were held on the beach until the 1960s. South of Daytona, below New Smyrna Beach (pop. 14,000) is as far as autos can be driven on the sand, for this is where Canaveral National Seashore wildlife preserve begins. Among the wildlife here are alligators, turtles, the mysterious manatees and all sorts of birds. Where the wildlife ends, the Canaveral Peninsula begins. This is where the John F. Kennedy Space Center is located. Cocoa Beach, (pop. 11,000) is at the southern terminus of the space center, halfway between there and Patrick Air Force Base. Cocoa Beach and the nearby towns have attracted their share of military retirees.

**MELBOURNE**--One town that looks particularly attractive as a retirement spot is Melbourne. It's a relatively quiet place, seemingly more for residents than tourists. Melbourne (pop. 46,000) is on the mainland, and because of the nearby space complex has developed an electronics industry to supplant tourism. A causeway takes you to the island part of the area and the dual towns of Melbourne Beach and Indialantic. Melbourne itself reminds me of small-town Midwest, but with stucco and palms instead of brick and oak trees. The large number of retirees means active senior citizen clubs and service groups. This area, including Cocoa Beach, is sprinkled with very attractive apartments, complete with swimming pools, tennis courts and social directors, going from $249 to $575 a month. Single-family housing and condos are comparatively priced. I saw two nice little condos offered for just under $40,000. Mobile home parks are plentiful and well maintained.

Below Melbourne, all the way to West Palm Beach, town after town straddles U.S. Highway 1 like loosely strung pearls. Sometimes the highway branches out into side roads that run along the Inland Waterway or on the long, narrow islands that run along almost all of Florida's Atlantic coast. A few miles west of the water, the country is almost uninhabited; it seems as if everyone tries to crowd as near the ocean as possible. This stretch of the coast is still quite sparsely settled. Most of the towns are small. Vero Beach, Fort Pierce and Jensen Beach, among others, offer some of the better east coast retirement spots, in my opinion. Housing costs are reasonable, the towns are relatively uncrowded, beach access is liberal, and most importantly, the Gulf Stream runs close to the shore. North of here, Gold Coast climate disappears as the Gulf Stream waters head out to sea. Vero Beach is the largest of these communities with about 17,000 people, and is the winter home of the Los Angeles Dodgers. This might interest some baseball fans who would enjoy watching winter exhibition games.

## THE FLORIDA GOLD COAST

Stretching from just north of Palm Beach south to Key Biscayne is Florida's famous "Gold Coast." A drive along the coastal highway will explain how it received its name. It certainly took a lot of gold to build it, and more to maintain it. This strip of coast was the first in Florida to build up as a winter retreat and retirement haven. The gold came from the wealthy of the United States and Canada. Owners of industry and commerce, "robber barons," inventors, bootleggers and gangsters invested their money in lavish mansions overlooking the ocean. Large expanses of lawn and palm trees, and surf rolling across private beaches, served as constant reminders of success in this world.

Why here, and not farther north, or on the western side? Because at a point around Vero Beach, the Gulf Stream swerves away from shore a bit, thus allowing winters to be cooler and summers a smidgen hotter in the rest of Florida. For example, in West Palm Beach, the average high temperatures in December, January and February are right at 76 degrees, while June, July and August see highs of around 88.5 degrees. So, the Gold Coast became a place to spend the winter, to enjoy the social whirl of Palm Beach or Key Biscayne. Anyone who was anybody *had* to have a beach house. To spend the winter freezing in New York or Boston would have been a humiliating admission of failure.

Those who could afford the best naturally clustered together in places like Palm Beach, Boca Raton or Miami Beach. Employees, servants, and support personnel moved there, too, and built houses on the mainland, away from the beach. Businesses of all descriptions sprang up to service the new residents. You'll find everything from hardware stores to tree farms (raising all imaginable varieties of palms to supply the demand for tropical landscaping). Before long, everyone who could afford it, and many who could not, joined the boom. For those who could afford the best, mansions and highrise apartments began crowding the beach islands.

Those who wanted Florida winters, but couldn't pay for oceanfront property, accepted less pretentious, more modest housing on the mainland. Many houses were, and still are, rather modest; after all, the working folks must live somewhere. Here is where you find the bargains in Florida housing. By living a mile or two from the ocean, you can enjoy the weather and beaches; you only sacrifice the very expensive view.

The 1920s saw a tremendous surge of building. Some great collections of opulent art deco hotels and mansions sprang up along the beaches. After World War II, the boom regained strength and is still on, although from time to time the glamour falls from new construction, only to regain momentum later on. From Vero Beach, south to the outskirts of Palm Beach, things haven't built up as densely as in Miami. The Miami area, after its vigorous growth in the '50s, has been somewhat dormant, although lately there are signs of rejuvenation, especially commercial, because of its role as a Caribbean banking center.

Individually, the cities from West Palm Beach down to Coral Gables don't appear to be particularly large in population. Miami only has 350,000 people, and Miami Beach about 97,000; West Palm Beach only about 67,000. But, together, the more than 40 towns there comprise one long, enormous metropolitan area (about 2.8 million people). You can barely tell where one town ends and another begins. Although I dislike large cities, I have to admit that the balmy, tropical winter weather makes the Gold Coast somewhat worthwhile.

Another point where the Gold Coast differs from other large metropolitan areas is that it is strung out along the beach with no chance of having a central focus, or a common "downtown" area. Broken up into a string of suburbs without an urban area to be suburban to, it's a string of neighborhoods, each with its own shopping center, stores, businesses, and sometimes its own small political entity.

Except for the classy sections along the beaches, most of the housing is single-family bungalows or low-profile condominiums and apartments. Florida retirement living looks like a real option here. Because some of the lesser developed areas aren't tightly packed, it's easy to get the feeling that you aren't part of the urban sprawl, but rather that you are living in your own small town. People commonly don't go shopping or visiting in other parts of the area; they have no need to. This is true of both the seasonal residents as well as the permanent folks.

Along the Gold Coast, you'll find the biggest contrasts in all of Florida. From tall forests of condominiums and apartments that remind you of New York's Park Avenue, to rows of tract houses reminiscent of Los Angeles, you'll find almost every imaginable type of housing and neighborhood. All within miles, or sometimes yards of each other. Then, just 10 to 20 miles to the west, the land is uninhabited, totally the domain of wildlife. Contrary to what many think, southern Florida offers any kind of choice you might care to make--or can afford to make.

It doesn't have to be expensive. Remember that the main differences in living costs from one part of the country to another are housing and utility bills. Here, you can keep your winter heating costs to a bare minimum (if not zero) and, with only about 30 days a year over 90 degrees, your summer cooling bills should be low. Well, they won't be if you insist on keeping the temperature at 68 degrees. The other major expenditure, housing, can be as inexpensive as you care to make it. Housing bargains are available.

## A GOLD COAST RETIREMENT EXAMPLE

Many condominium developments have been taken over almost totally by retirees along the Gold Coast. Often the residents choose their condos because they know others from their home towns or neighborhoods have congregated in a particular development. One example is a condo development in Deerfield Beach, a place called Century Village East. This seems to be almost exclusively New York City people, many of whom knew one another "back home." Century Village is not only large, but well organized, so much so that they put out an impressive 48-page newspaper every month to carry news of the development's activities.

There are over 8,000 living units in Century Village. Residents have their own shopping center, golf course, even buses and trolleys. They elect residents to serve in positions analogous to mayor, city council, etc.

In addition to the strict security that this sort of co-operative offers, there's some great entertainment available. The clubhouse entertainment schedule reads like a Las Vegas nightclub theater, with top-notch performers on the bill, from opera singers to comedians. An ongoing fine arts series offers musical ensembles ranging from string quartets to symphony orchestras. Full-time entertainment and activities personnel make sure the schedules are full. I have no idea what all of this costs, but I noticed in the village newspaper that the entertainment budget overspent by $100,000 last year, so you can imagine that the cost is substantial. They've created in Century Village East an atmosphere of Manhattan that's so dear to the hearts of New Yorkers, in a Floridian climate of Florida--also important to New Yorkers.

Still, living in Century Village is, if not inexpensive, certainly affordable.  A two-bedroom condo here can be had for $55,000. Rentals can be had for as low as $500 per month. Others, outside the development are advertised for under $35,000. Deerfield is adjacent to Boca Raton, one of the more exclusive areas, but even in Boca Raton itself, reasonable property can be found. Beachfront condos (two-bedroom, two-bath) are selling from $80,000 on up. On a golf course, you might buy one for under $60,000, or under $40,000 further inland. One was advertised for $45,000 when I was there. If you insist on having a place for your yacht, you could probably find a place with a dock in Pompano Beach for as low as $150,000. Farther away from the beach, in Coral Springs, rentals start at $450 a month. Many areas will have condos selling for less than $35,000, and three-bedroom homes for $45,000, but at the same time will have some on the market for 10 times that amount. It all depends on what you can afford.

To make a decision about living along the Gold Coast requires some testing. If prime weather is a major consideration with you, you might find that the extra traffic, the higher crime rates and the crowding are minor inconveniences. Almost 3 million people feel that way, so there must be something commendable about living there.

## KEY WEST, A SUMMER WITHOUT END

At the southern tip of Florida, a paved highway boldly starts out across the ocean. Skipping from one coral atoll to another, each festooned with palm trees, hibiscus and bougainvillaea, the highway stretches by bridge and causeway for over a 100 miles. It finally ends at Key West, the most southern part of the continental United States. Although technically labeled *semitropical*, the islands are truly more tropical than many places you would find farther south, in the actual tropics. The Tropic of Cancer lies only about 150 miles or so to the south. The true secret to the Keys' perpetual summer is the Gulf Stream, which bathes the narrow chain of islands on all sides with its benevolent warmth.

The island was discovered early on as an perfect retirement spot by writers and artists. Wallace Stevens fell in love with Key West back in 1922, and in his poem "The Idea of Order in Key West," he praised "a summer without end." Having let the cat out of the bag, Stevens soon found company in other intellectuals who wanted to participate in this "summer without end." Ernest Hemingway, John Dos Passos and Tennessee Williams all maintained houses in Key West. Some of their homes are now major tourist attractions.

The tradition of an artist colony continues. Today, over 50 published writers and poets--among them several Pulitzer Prize winners--live in the Keys, some full-time, some during winters only. They refer to their haven as "the end of the world." When asked why so many writers and artists are drawn there, a travel specialist says that they come "to work out their fantasies and to look for surprises."

The end town, Key West (pop. 25,000) is the jewel at the end of the gold chain. It's a mixture of New England, the Caribbean and the South Seas, all flavored by nearby Cuba. Some of the older, sun-weathered homes were built by ship carpenters, who used wooden pegs instead of nails. Other houses are Bermuda, Conch and Cuban-styled, as well as Florida stucco, and there's a sprinkling of mobile homes. Yachts are "in" here, large ones and small ones. Many amateur sailors insist on cutting berths into the coral and limestone backyards of their homes. Other houses are set back against networks of canals, where their occupants can tie up after a day's adventure of fishing or treasure hunting in the warm winds of the Gulf Stream. I've even seen mobile homes with their own docks.

One problem that appears to me, and one that is perpetually present, is the threat of hurricane-driven tides. Many homes and businesses are raised off the ground some 10 or 12 feet, and insurance companies are insisting that new construction be built on pilings in that manner. This solves the problem of waves threatening to sweep over the low-lying lands. But it doesn't answer my questions about what to do in the event of a hurricane warning. It's a 110-mile drive back to the mainland. People there laugh off my worry, much as we Californians laugh off an Easterner's worry about earthquakes.

Real estate on the Keys is more expensive than on the mainland, but I was surprised to find it isn't sky-high (maybe because too many other people worry about that 110-mile drive with about 30,000 other cars in front of them). Compared to some parts of the country, housing is downright reasonable. Newly constructed three-bedroom places can be found for $90,000; make it $110,000 if you want your own boat dock. I saw a two-bedroom, two-bath mobile home with a dock and huge screened porch that sits out over the water for $83,000. Other mobile homes can be bought for under $30,000, and older conventional "fixer-uppers" can be located for $50,000. Needless to say, the Keys sport their share of homes in the $350,000-and-up category. Well, if you can afford that $150,000 yacht, why not?

Key West is the most expensive, and is set on a large island, but all along the chain there are excellent locations, sometimes with a view of the Atlantic on one side of the house, and the Gulf of Mexico on the other. Key Largo (pop. 7,400) is the first town you come to, and it had a lot of older homes for sale when I visited there. It's the largest of the Keys, 30-miles long, and has lots of narrow side-roads lined with small houses in quiet, tropical settings. Also, the smaller towns--villages, actually--of Plantation, Islamorada, Marathon and Big Pine are worth looking at as you drive through the "summer without end."

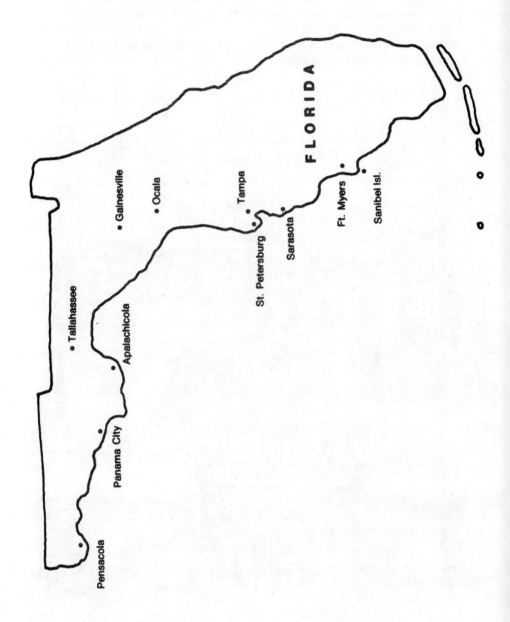

# CHAPTER ELEVEN

## *Gulf Coast Florida*

As mentioned in the last chapter, the Atlantic side of Florida, particularly the Gold Coast, is heavily populated with people from the northeastern United States. From its earliest boom days, the Miami side of Florida has been the traditional playground for rich New Yorkers and "old money" wealthy from New England. Miami's forest of tall hotels and condos seems like an effort to recreate crowded Manhattan in a semitropical setting. Boca Raton's breathtaking estates appear to duplicate the plush mansions of the New England society in a tropical, and lavish Spanish-stucco motif.

But the Gulf of Mexico side of Florida is different. Its boom years came later, and are still underway. Because of lower land costs, west-coast construction favors fewer skyscrapers and less crowding. There's an informal feeling here. Generous lawn areas and lots of single-family homes make the Gulf side a re-creation of Middle-America with an unmistakable Florida flourish. Here, instead of New York and New England expatriates, the predominant visitor and resident comes from the Midwest or the South. Canadians can be found everywhere, of course, but my impression is that they favor the Gulf coast over the Atlantic side.

The climate is different, too. The Gulf Stream, which stabilizes temperatures, misses the west coast. It heads that way, but at the last minute the current changes course and turns south to caress the Florida Keys, then sweeps up the Atlantic coast to keep temperatures warm in the winter and moderate in the summer. This means summers along the Gulf of Mexico stay a couple of degrees warmer and winters a couple of degrees cooler than along the opposite shore. Rainfall is slightly less on the Gulf side than on the Atlantic coast.

The small average temperature difference in summer temperature is more significant that it would appear at first glance. For example, on the average, Miami has 30 days a year over 90 degrees, whereas on the other side of Florida, Fort Myers has 100 days over 90 degrees--more than three times as many. This is enough to encourage many more west coast retirees to return north for the summer. Winter is the season here on the west coast.

If you are a person who loves warm weather, 90-degree days aren't bad at all, even with the 75-percent humidity you find in most of Florida. As one person from Rochester, N.Y., pointed out, coping with hot weather is simply a matter of changing your living arrangements. "Back home, I stayed indoors all winter. I only went outside to go to work or to shovel snow. Here, I stay indoors during the summer, but mornings and evenings I can spend outdoors."

It's obvious that Gulf Coast Florida was settled later than the Atlantic side, and by different people than those who poured millions into the mansions of the Gold Coast. Most Gulf Coast towns seem much more casual. Dense clusters of condos and apartments are comparatively rare. Here, single-family homes and mobile home parks are more common. Condos tend to be just two-story affairs, usually with generous allotments of land, often built around a common golf course. Some of them are astonishingly affordable.

That isn't to say that the multi-millionaires don't have their favorite spots on the Gulf of Mexico, because they certainly do. Yet, interspersed with the luxurious villas of the rich and famous, you will find beach homes in the moderate-to-expensive range. And, of course, like the east coast, once you withdraw from the saltwater and sandy beaches, you find the ordinary houses, condos and mobile home parks of us non-millionaires. The important thing is that, on the Gulf Coast, the person of average means has the opportunity to enjoy some prime real estate, should he decide to put his retirement investments there.

SANIBEL ISLAND--An example of a west-coast discovery, but by no means the only one--just a place I happened to stumble onto--is Sanibel Island, near Fort Myers. This is my favorite place in all of Florida, and looks more like what I always imagined that Florida should. Sanibel Island is reached via a causeway that hops across some tiny islands of sand, which in themselves are favorite places for locals who take advantage of the long stretches of sandy beach on either side of the highway to sunbathe and fish.

Sanibel Island is long and narrow, often no more than a few hundred yards wide, just enough room for a couple of blocks of private homes looking toward the Gulf side of the island. On the San Carlos Bay side of the island, facing the mainland, is a marvelous wildlife preserve, covered with mangrove swamp and pine and cypress forest. A jungle-like tangle of trees, vines and palmettos constantly reminds visitors of the semitropical location. There is a special, exotic ambiance to the island.

When people speak of Sanibel Island, they usually include the sister island of Captiva. Sanibel is about 11 miles long, ending in a bridge that spans a *blind pass* to connect with Captiva Island. (A blind pass is a flow of water, like a small river that flows between islands at the whim of the ocean--sometimes a sandy beach builds up and closes off the pass, and other times it runs as clear and free as a river.) The road continues on another few miles along a wondrously tropical road that winds through thick stands of cypress and overhanging oak. The island is usually just wide enough for homes on either side of the road, homes that are obscured from sight by gnarled oak trees, stands of bamboo and tall grasses. You wouldn't know anyone lives there were it not for mailboxes alongside the road. Sometimes the island is just wide enough to accommodate one house, with a palm-tree-lined beach on the other side of the road. The narrow pavement finally ends at a jealously protected section of the island. This is an exclusive resort where celebrities and super-wealthy come to spend their Florida vacations, away from the curious stares of us plebeians.

But Captiva Island is rather small. Most people live on Sanibel. At one time, the state of Florida had complete control over Sanibel Island, devising a plan whereby the maximum population would reach 20,000 residents. But established property-owners felt that this would be disastrous for their paradise. With 20,000 people trying to use the one main road on the island, you would have seen the most humongous traffic jam this side of New Jersey Turnpike at rush hour. The island residents organized and formed a city government. With a measure of control now, they set the maximum number of residents at just under 9,000. This number includes the people expected to stay in the few motels on the island, and counts the number of sites in the island's only RV park. This cap effectively limits the number of people on the road at any one time, and it's possible to drive around without too much hassle.

Some other things limit tourism. For one thing, a $3.00 bridge toll discourages many ordinary tourists. Another item is limited public beach parking. Although all of the beaches are open to the public, non-residents have just four or five places where they can park and walk to the beach. The residents don't have to drive to the beach; almost everyone has a bicycle. They use the many bike paths or lightly traveled side roads to get to their favorite strand. This is one place in Florida where it appears that bicycles outnumber automobiles. If you are visiting to see how you like the islands, you can rent a bike and enjoy miles of winding trails that sometimes loop into the wildlife reserve.

For those who can afford a yacht or a sailboat, some homes sit on a network of canals. Boats can tie up in their owners' backyards, after sailing up a water passage that leads from the sheltered Florida side of the island. And for those who prefer an unrestricted view of the open ocean, there are homes and condos on the other side. By local law, buildings can't be over three stories, so the island is in no danger of becoming another Miami Beach or Fort Lauderdale. True, there are many restrictions self-imposed on the island, but most of them are essential if the ecology and delightful tropical atmosphere are to be preserved.

As you might suspect, these places aren't cheap, at least not by my pocketbook. But compared to prices of similar properties on the other side of the state, they are almost modest. A two-bedroom home on one of the canals can be had for as low as $130,000, and a condo with an ocean view might be found at $170,000. Although these prices are probably out of reach for many readers of this book, they're not as bad as they seem. That is, rentals are very scarce, and a person can conceivably make up much of his investment by renting the place out when he isn't there. Some real estate firms specialize in handling rental properties for absentee owners. This isn't a place for mobile homes, because they are strictly prohibited. Locals permit a single RV park as a sole concession to tourism.

Another consideration is that property values don't appear to be going anywhere but up, especially with the restrictions the residents have placed upon themselves limiting new construction. Government restrictions against any development of the present wilderness area and wildlife preserve further ensures that the islands will remain pretty much as they are today. Very little new construction can be undertaken because most of the available property has already been developed.

Other nice, but expensive, areas in southwest Florida are Marco Island and Naples, both of which share the high-class image and higher property costs of Sanibel Island. Naples offers 41 miles of public beaches, and is said to be one of the faster-growing resort communities in Florida. It's also the western terminus of the Tamiami Trail, a two-lane highway that crosses right through the Everglades. In addition to golf and the usual Florida pastimes, swampbuggy racing is popular in the Marco Island-Naples area. Hopped-up swamp machines run special events in October to mark the beginning of the Everglades hunting season.

Naples has a reputation for being super-expensive, but a few condos and houses still go for slightly under $70,000, and mobile homes can be found from $40,000 up. Certainly, this area is one of the quality living places in Florida. Overall, you can expect to pay for it.

**FORT MYERS**--On the mainland, in and around Fort Myers, are very comfortable and rather inexpensive places for retirement. Fort Myers itself (pop. 37,000) is one of my favorites on the west coast. I particularly admire the landscaping throughout the town. Palm trees dominate the town's flora, and their variety is bewildering. Residents claim that over 70 varieties of palms grace the streets of Fort Myers, some tall and stately, some short with bottle-like trunks, others with astonishing leaf patterns that look as if they were created by fashion designers. The profusion of palms, mixed with outrageous displays of flowers, constantly reminds you that you are in Florida.

The overall theme of this area is one of prosperity, with few sections of town looking seedy. Well-manicured lawns, flowering bushes and magnolia trees give the town a quiet, homey look. This isn't to say that there aren't plenty of expensive places, even mansions, in Fort Myers and the surrounding countryside. But reasonable homes, condos and mobile home parks are abundant and affordable.

Whereas northern Florida is a summer target for tourists, Fort Myers is more a winter place. The population is said to double during the season, in this case between November 1 and Easter week. Then, when summer's humidity and over-90-degree weather sets in, the snowbirds leave for home. Obviously, many believe this area to be a part-time retirement center--great for the winter but quick to be abandoned during the summer. The year-round residents protest when I suggest that summer might be harsh. "Check it out; it's just a little bit warmer than Miami Beach," they point out, "and it's a lot safer living around here!"

Downtown Fort Myers is unusual in that it is purely a business center. Shopping malls have drawn so many people away from the center of town that after 6:00 in the evening, downtown Fort Myers is a ghost town. I couldn't find a restaurant open, or any shops. But once you leave the town's center, you will find many restaurants, shopping centers and lively retail commerce. By the way, traffic in Fort Myers is far easier to negotiate than almost any city I found on the state's east coast.

Of particular interest are the condos, many of which are located around private golf courses. This means no long waiting for a starting time, and the first tee is near your front door. Generally, these condos are not high-rise construction, but instead are two-story buildings with the bedrooms upstairs, so there's not another family living overhead or underfoot. Condominium developers have been magnanimous in providing lawn areas between the condos, so you don't get the cramped, hemmed-in feeling that comes with east Florida multi-story skyscrapers and concrete parking lot complexes.

Mobile home parks are plentiful. Most are beautifully landscaped, and offer organized activities in their clubhouses and recreational facilities. Some are downright luxurious and some are super-expensive. An example is discussed later in the book.

**PUNTA GORDA AND SARASOTA**--As you travel north from Fort Myers, you will find several other towns worthwhile considering, if you have your heart set on Florida. Two of them are Punta Gorda and Port Charlotte. Here there is a real emphasis on retirement, as opposed to seasonal tourism. I was told that almost half of the residents in these towns are retired. As you might expect, there are plenty of programs for senior citizens.

From here along the 30 miles south to Fort Myers are some of the most impressive mobile home developments I've ever seen. In utter contrast to mobile home living in many southern states (where "trailers" are considered a kind of trashy way of living), mobile homes here carry a stamp of elegance. Some parks are country clubs in every sense of the word. They aren't cheap, but well worth a visit even if you can't afford them--just to see how the "other half" lives. In some developments you purchase the lot your home sits on, in other places you lease, and in still others you rent. Each system has its own advantages and drawbacks.

Let's look at a typical luxury development and see what you get for your money. The one I'm using as an example is called Del Tura Country Club. There are 870 homesites located on approximately 300 acres. Because there are 10 lakes and an 18-hole golf course, a lot of this land has been taken out of residential use, but the population density is still quite low. The clubhouse is deluxe, with everything from exercise rooms to a library.

What's the cost for all of this? First of all, a mobile home--or as they prefer to call it, a *manufactured home*--will begin at $39,000 and go to well over $100,000, depending upon your pocketbook and the salesman's skill. In truth, the way the units are manufactured, the housing looks like ordinary homes in an upper-class suburb, and it's all but impossible to discern that they are not of traditional construction. Every unit has a two-car garage and professional landscaping.

The land here is leased rather than sold, so you aren't paying for land, but for long-term rights to live there. There are advantages and disadvantages to this arrangement, I suppose, but I would suggest that you make sure of several things: One, that the lease is renewable in perpetuity; two, that monthly payments cannot go up more than the Consumer Price Index adjustment for inflation; and three, that the lease is transferable, just as a piece of property is transferable.

The price for the average nice-looking three-bedroom mobile home at Del Tura is $65,700. This includes the base price of $52,400 plus a furniture and housewares package of $8,500, plus 5 percent sales tax and county fees of $1,700. Ten percent down would equal $6,570. A 30-year mortgage of $59,130 at 8 percent makes the payments $494.59 per month.

To this you add lot rent ($2,820 per year), taxes, insurance, water and sewer fees, etc. to come up with another $3,395 a year in fixed expenses. Then figure in utilities and maintenance. Add this all together, and the fixed costs of living in this luxury development are around $900 a month. Understand, these are the figures supplied by the salesman; they could be the kind of optimistic figures salesmen are fond of supplying. I would urge you to investigate such calculations, and to do so before you sign any papers. This $900 figure plus about $50-a-month lost interest on the down payment, is about twice what you would pay to rent an apartment or a small house around here. The price of the mobile home is about what you would pay for a nice condo.Some people obviously believe the price tag is worth it.

Included in the maintenance fee are services, some that might make a difference in your life-style. For example, these costs include lawn mowing, 24-hour security, use of the activities center, swimming pool, tennis courts, spas and shuffleboard. Social activities are arranged by a professional, and it looks like there is plenty going on to keep your mind occupied. Golf is extra, but greens fees are reasonable.

Del Tura is just one of at least a dozen similar developments in this part of Florida. Some people might decide that all of the services available, plus living in a spiffy, country club atmosphere is worth it. I can't quite make up my mind, but I have to admit that these developments are attractive. The drawback I see is that there might be lots of services I'd never use, and I'd have a lot of money tied up. But don't take my word for it, just because I'm a lousy golfer.

Farther north are the rather pleasant towns of Sarasota and Bradenton. Sarasota is famous for being the winter headquarters of the Ringling Bros., Barnum & Bailey Circus. Apparently, John Ringling spent a lot of money making the town look well, and it shows clearly to this day. Sarasota is also known as an art colony. Painters, musicians and writers populate the town, and among the cultural attributes are an opera and a symphony orchestra.

Bradenton is a baseball city. It's the winter training camp for the Pittsburgh Pirates, and hosts two minor-league teams during the regular season.

**ST. PETERSBURG-TAMPA**--Separated by Tampa Bay, the twin cities of St. Petersburg and Tampa are connected by three causeways. Interstate 275, the area's main link to southern Florida, crosses the wide mouth of Tampa Bay on yet another long causeway as it heads south to Bradenton. Together, the cities and their suburbs have about 1.6 million people, making it the second largest metropolitan area in Florida.

St. Petersburg (pop. 250,000) promises year-round sunshine, and the local newspaper is famous for its pledge to give away a newspaper every day the sun doesn't peek out at least some. I wouldn't know. I've been there twice, and it was overcast almost every day that I was there. I never did get my free newspapers. According to the U.S. Weather Bureau, the Tampa-St. Petersburg area can expect an average of 127 cloudy days a year, and 107 days of rain. This surprised me, especially when I compared these figures to San Francisco, which I always thought had a lot of overcast days. Turns out that San Francisco only expects 100 cloudy days and only 67 days with rain. And, according to the statistics, even Fort Myers has fewer cloudy days than Tampa-St. Petersburg. However, this is nitpicking, because the weather there is typical Florida retirement weather, and lots of retirees have made the choice to live there.

St. Petersburg entered into the retirement business long ago by stressing its great climate and emphasizing the pleasant retirement possibilities there. It worked so well that the city fathers became worried that the town would soon become overrun with senior citizens. They reversed their advertising to try to attract industry and younger people. The story goes that the city even took up park benches in an effort to discourage senior citizens from "hanging out." I suppose they were worried about gangs of geriatric delinquents or something. That didn't discourage retirees; they kept on coming, presumably bringing their own park benches. But the effort to attract industry worked.

Obviously the balance between retirees and industry worked out well, because both St. Petersburg and Tampa are exceptionally prosperous looking. Few highrises score the landscape; most buildings are pastel-colored and low to the ground. I saw little evidence of slums or shabby looking parts in either city, although maybe I wasn't looking in the right places. A large percentage of the area is in neat, owner-occupied bungalows or ranch-type homes. The freeway network makes traveling about fairly stress-free (I avoided the rush hours).

Saltwater fishing is one of the attractions here, both for tourists and residents. Early summer sees fishermen out after the "silver king" tarpon, and then after kingfish in early fall. By the way, no licenses are needed in Florida for saltwater fishing. Baseball fans might be interested to know that this is the winter home for both the St. Louis Cardinals and the New York Mets. And for a change of pace there is greyhound racing in "St. Pete." Gate fees are around 50 cents. (Rabbits get in free.) At the very tip of the peninsula is St. Petersburg Beach, a good place for beach picnics and fishing from the piers. As you might expect almost anywhere in Florida, there are golf courses galore, over 60 of 'em.

If living in a metropolitan area bothers you, a short drive from the city limits puts you into some very comfortable rural settings. Lutz, Land O'Lakes, Lake Fern and other towns north of Tampa are small places, with affordable acreages. Small homes on large lots are the rule here. The highway and interstate system makes it a snap to run into Tampa for "heavy shopping," or a night on the town. North of St. Petersburg are places like Indian Shores, Clearwater and Tarpon Springs. About 15 small towns are within a 30-mile drive of St. Pete. Clearwater (pop. 85,000) isn't so very small. It's famous for its stretch of pure white sand beach.

**OCALA AND GAINESVILLE**--The north-central part of Florida is a different world. While most of Florida is about as hilly as a billiard table, this country is rolling and wooded, and specializes in farming rather than tourists. The countryside is checkered with horse farms. The area around Ocala (pop. 37,000) is one of the most important thoroughbred areas in the country. Some areas feature "farm subdivisions" where you can buy a few acres, a barn and a house, and become hobby farmers, maybe even raise a couple of horses if you like. I looked at one place, 20 acres with a three-bedroom home and a horse barn, for $129,000.

Around Ocala you find real mobile home country. One of the nicer parks I've seen anywhere is about eight minutes by car from Ocala. Shaded by large, spreading oaks, the housing units are placed back on nice-sized lots along winding roads. A radio-operated gate keeps high-pressure salesmen and religious pushers out. An ample clubhouse hosts the senior citizens' activities, and it turns out that all but a handful of residents are senior citizens. When I was there, in spring 1987, the monthly park rent was $110. Several units were for sale for between $14,000 and $32,000.

Not only are there plenty of mobile home parks, ranging from deluxe to quite ordinary, but it's possible to buy a few acres, or just a lot, and install your own mobile home. Many small farms of five to 50 acres dot the countryside, with nothing but a mobile home and a barn on the property.

The business district or downtown of Ocala is rather ordinary, looking like a town from the Midwest, set in farming country that also looks very much like the Midwest. One retiree told us that he chooses to live here because Ocala reminds him of the countryside he grew up in northern Illinois. "The only thing it lacks is the ice and snow in the winter time," he added. When asked about northern Florida summers, he replied, "I don't believe they are any hotter than they were back home. Anyway, whenever we get the notion, the wife and I drive an hour and twenty minutes to Daytona Beach and cool off in the Atlantic ocean. We can get there by nine in the morning and be home with sunburns by supper time!"

A few miles farther north is Gainesville (pop. 81,000), home of the University of Florida. It's surprising how much one university town can resemble another, with the same kinds of businesses, services, students, even similar street names. I spent some of my younger years in a university town (Ann Arbor, Mich.), and I was impressed by the similarity between Gainesville and Ann Arbor. Were it not for an occasional palm tree, I could have easily imagined that I was wandering along University Avenue or State Street back in the old days in Ann Arbor. Large old homes on tree-shaded streets, some converted to fraternity houses, plus tasteful, unobtrusive university construction bring back pleasant memories.

Some obvious cultural and social advantages are always available in a college town, and Gainesville is no exception. Lectures, concerts and cultural events are frequent, and often free. Nearby are some wildlife areas which should provide great pleasure to birdwatchers and those interested in ecology. Besides the 35,000-student university, there is also a two-year college with a student body of about 7,500. Add to this the number of employees of the various public and private schools, and you will find a large commitment to education in Gainesville. If you are looking for Florida retirement in an intellectual climate, this might be a place to investigate.

ORLANDO--Billed as "one of the world's major tourist destinations," Orlando is also one of the fastest-growing cities in the country. The state's largest inland city, Orlando will before long top one million population. Local people take great pride in these figures, and they have a lot to be proud of, for the area has managed to grow with a certain measure of dignity. Palms, oaks and citrus trees beautify the streets and boulevards of Orlando and the city's lush landscaping is striking. But again, my bias against large cities interferes with my judgment. Combine this with my hatred of traffic jams, and you will see why I like Orlando mostly as a place to be near, a place to visit, rather than as a place to live.

The countryside around Orlando is rolling, with groves of oranges to blossom-sweeten the air. Over 50 lakes dot the landscape, many with gorgeous, tropical shores edged with cypress, pines and tall palm trees. Fish abound, and there is an occasional alligator. I had just been swimming in one lake near Kissimmee, when a local resident mentioned with pride that one of the 'gators in the lake was 14 feet long. When the color on my face changed to that of a fish's underside, he said, "Oh, don't worry--those 'gators are timid. When they see you coming, they slip away." Then he thought a moment, and added, "Well, not unless you get between the 'gator and her nest of eggs." I never learned how to determine where the alligator's nest might be, and it's entirely academic, because I lost all enthusiasm for swimming in that lake, anyway.

There are at least 10 smaller towns around Orlando, any one of which would make a good Florida retirement choice. Here you have the advantages of inexpensive housing, excellent health care centers in Orlando, and being only an hour's drive from Cocoa Beach. Plus, it's just a short drive to either the east or west coast beaches for a day's outing any time you feel like it.

There are numerous smaller towns scattered throughout the center of Florida. Depending on your personality, you might find one to suit you and your needs. But most of them seem pretty ordinary to me, not much different from similar-sized towns in Georgia or Texas.

## FLORIDA'S PANHANDLE

Lightly populated, much of Florida's Panhandle is either heavily forested or dotted with farms and small towns not much different from those in nearby Georgia and Alabama. There are but two cities of any size, Pensacola and Tallahassee. Except for the stretch of beach from Pensacola to Panama City, the Panhandle attracts neither tourists nor retirees in the same numbers as do other parts of Florida.

This isn't to say that this part of Florida wouldn't be suited for people who don't "need" the companionship of other retirees or special services for senior citizens. If you'd rather live in a multi-generational community, or if you are interested in inexpensive farm land in a place where it doesn't snow in the winter, then the Florida Panhandle may be your ticket. Land prices are as low as you will find in Florida. And, since a large percentage of the Panhandle is wilderness, the hunting and fishing is superb.

Tallahassee displays a certain amount of sophistication that naturally goes with being the state capital, yet it reminds me of a small college town rather than a bustling center of political intrigue. Its population of 81,500 is small enough that a person won't feel lost in the crowd, yet it's large enough to have most of the amenities of big-city living. The out-of-state retirement population here isn't too large. Most people, when thinking of Florida retirement, picture the Gold Coast or other fancier places.

However, the other Panhandle city, Pensacola, is quite popular with retirees, particularly those in the military. Eglin Air Force Base, Whiting Field Naval Air Station and the Pensacola Naval Air Academy ring the town. Upon retirement, pilots who've served here naturally recall the attraction of the Panhandle's "Riviera" beaches and the convenience of military hospitals and PX privileges.

The name "panhandle" comes from the narrow strip of land that juts westward from the Florida peninsula, under the states of Georgia and Alabama. When you get away from the beach and closer to Georgia and Alabama, you find that culturally, you are no longer in Florida. The accents are pure Deep-South, the thinking is pure country. The main tourist and retiree attraction is the 100-mile length of beach which begins at the little town of Mexico Beach and runs westward to the Alabama border, just past Pensacola. This is the mecca for summer vacationers from all over the Midwest. Winter months are too cold for swimming, and the beaches would be deserted, except for Canadians, for whom no month is too cold for swimming.

Knowing that Panhandle winters are pleasant, but sometimes cool, I asked some local residents about summer temperatures. The reply was, "Whoo-ee! It sure gets *hot!*" Then I asked why the tourist season around there is in the summer, since winters aren't bad at all. The reply was unanimously, "Tourists love hot weather. It flat can't get too hot for tourists!"

Being hot is always a personal thing that varies from person to person. For me, anything under 100 degrees is tolerable, whereas others run for air conditioning at 80 degrees. According to weather records, the Panhandle can expect around 80 days a year when the temperature climbs to 90; that doesn't seem unreasonable to me. And clearly, it isn't unreasonable for the summer vacationers.

A particularly interesting part of Florida--a part that's very sparsely settled--is the stretch east along Highway 98/319 from Port St. Joe to Lighthouse Point. This 60 mile stretch of two-lane road traverses beaches and forests, and passes through some rather interesting and historical towns.

With empty beach on one side of the road and thickly forested tracts on the other, you can drive for mile after mile seeing nothing but a few cabins or an occasional mobile home set back into a clearing in the pines and moss-draped oaks. Occasionally you'll have to pause for loggers hauling out pine and cypress from the woods.

Most of the villages along the way are fishing centers. Fishermen unload their catches and sell them to wholesale and retail outlets. Tiny restaurants offer steamed crab, fresh oysters, fried mullet and other seafood delicacies--to eat there or to take with you. Trucks line up at a multitude of fish wholesalers to rush the produce of the sea to restaurants all over the South. And, of course, there are numerous bait shops and boat rentals for the amateur fisherman's convenience. Ninety percent of Florida's oysters come from this area, particularly around Apalachicola, where 10,000 acres of oyster beds are maintained.

**APALACHICOLA**--The only settlement along this stretch of beach that might be considered large enough to be called a town is Apalachicola. While most of Florida is new, with buildings from the 1920s considered antiques, Apalachicola is a fascinating treasure trove of pre-Civil War memorabilia, a quiet town steeped in the past. Homes built in the 1830s are commonplace. There are stately, two-story frame or brick mansions, churches imported from New England, and a business district that looks as if it had been transported from a Mississippi River levee of a hundred years ago. There's nary a blemish of flashy Florida stucco here.

The downtown section, made of old brick, slopes gently down to abandoned docks by the Apalachicola River. One gets the feeling that this could be Natchez, Vicksburg or some other Deep South river town. Before the Civil War, this was one of the largest shipping ports on the Gulf, competing with Mobile and New Orleans. When war broke out between North and South, the port was used to smuggle in supplies for the Confederate armies.

Particularly interesting is the Orman House, an unrestored mansion which was used as a signal for Confederate ships trying to run the Federal blockade. The widow Orman would place a nail keg on the roof of the house if Federal troops were in the vicinity. Today, the house is in horrible disrepair, badly in need of paint, and the expansive grounds overgrown with brush and tangled vines. The city of Apalachicola was debating whether to purchase it as a city museum when I was there in 1987. The town is loaded with historic buildings that are sold at the market price of ordinary old houses. For anyone who is into restoring old homes, this would be a great place to pick up a piece of history at a bargain price tag.

Whether Apalachicola or any of the other places along this stretch of Gulf would be plausible candidates as retirement havens would depend a lot on your personality. If you like quiet, not too many tourists messing in your life, and if fishing and seafood are important, you might take a look here.

## PANAMA CITY TO PENSACOLA

About 20 miles west of Apalachicola the land ends abruptly at Cape San Blas. It makes a right-angle turn north toward Port St. Joe. From here, all the way to the Alabama state line, two main features characterize this part of Florida's Panhandle. These are: Military bases and powder-white beaches.

First comes Tyndall Air Force Base, with 6,300 people working there. It's property line starts just west of Mexico Beach and extends to Panama City. There's also a Naval Coastal Systems center in Panama City, with about 2,300 personnel. Next is Eglin Air Force

Base and finally, next to Pensacola, is the famous Pensacola Naval Air Station. The military presence is huge indeed, with large payrolls supporting the economy, and many civilians working on the bases.

From Port St. Joe to Pensacola there are more than a dozen little towns that cater to tourists and retirees. Often no more than a few blocks wide, the towns string along the highway and beach in a very laid-back manner. Many single-family homes, duplexes and small apartments are available for either seasonal or year-round rentals. However, there are stretches of high-rise construction that would do justice to places on the Gold Coast.

**PANAMA CITY**--The largest center is Panama City (pop. 34,000). Like many towns along here, Panama City has a dual personality. One side is that of a happy summer resort, the other a peaceful winter retreat. From November until March, the beaches are uncrowded and quiet. Practically the only tourists in sight are those speaking French. As you drive by the motels, it seems as if all of the cars have license plates. There are so many French Canadians visiting here in the winter that I wonder who is minding the store back home. Those French Canadians who aren't in Florida seem to be in Acapulco. Who takes care of Quebec in January? But with warmer weather, French Canadians leave and Midwesterners arrive.

An offshoot of the Gulf Stream, called the *Yucatan Current*, comes close to Panama City's beaches. This tends to warm the water in the winter, just a tad. This flow also brings nutrient-rich waters from the Caribbean, and with it, lots of sport-fish. Fishermen haul in marlin, sailfish, tuna, dolphin, as well as lots of panfish. A fishing pier extends about 1,600 feet into the Gulf for convenience of anglers. The Yucatan Current may temper the summer weather, but I suspect that it isn't all effective. Summers are hot here. This doesn't deter the tourists, because as my correspondent in Apalachicola pointed out, "It flat can't get too hot for tourists!"

Part of the dual personality is the question of housing costs. Of course, rentals drop in the off season (winter months), just as you would expect. During this period, or for year-round rentals, a two-bedroom house rents for around $400 a month. Apartments start at $300. Many condos are rentals and some are time-shares. Prices for these rentals vary wildly, depending on the season and the demand. Real estate seems to be normal for most of Florida, with condos selling from the low $50s and houses from the low $60s.

Between Panama City and Pensacola, you have a selection of towns, ranging from ordinary to luxurious (on a small scale of luxury). Many places look very comfortable, and living isn't too expensive. Other towns, like Fort Waldon Beach, look as if they coddle tourists to the nth degree. The skyscraper-type condo towers would fit in nicely in Boca Raton.

**PENSACOLA**--One of the oldest settlements on the Gulf Coast, Pensacola was early-on recognized as an excellent seaport. With both an offshore island and a peninsula barrier against hurricane-driven tides, the town is quite secure. The Spanish settled there first in 1559, and since 1698 it has been growing and attracting people who hate winters.

Pensacola has had a checkered history, with its political allegiance changing 13 times--from Spain to France, England, the Confederacy and United States, the flags were probably mounted on a revolving flagpole. It's grown amazingly since I first worked there back in 1952, changing from a rather small town into a city of over 60,000.

The beaches are extensive here, with pretty white sand. But they're becoming covered with condos. Summer sees more influx of younger people than other parts of the Panhandle coast. You'll find an emphasis on things like discos and bars that might be underplayed elsewhere. That shouldn't deter retirees, since they'll be living away from the hustle and bustle of the beach scene.

This is the tip of the Panhandle. A few miles west is the Alabama state line.

CHAPTER TWELVE

# *The Gulf, from Florida to Mexico*

From the tip of Florida's Panhandle west, around the Gulf of Mexico to the Rio Grande in Texas, stretches a thousand miles of coastline. There are long strands of sparkling beaches with gracious old southern mansions, moss-draped bayous, modern cities, small towns, fishing villages and wildlife sanctuaries. Much of the coast is saltwater marsh, the home of egrets, herons, roseate spoonbills and dozens of other shorebird species. You'll find sheltered bays, natural harbors and offshore islands. You'll find miles and miles of beaches almost untracked by human footprints. The water teems with life: Shrimp, pompano, flounder, speckled trout, plus weird specimens like blowfish, rays and robbinfish. No telling what might be tugging on your fishing line. Seafood offerings are legendary along the coast.

Some parts of the Gulf Coast can be seen from your automobile window as you drive along only a few yards from the beach. Other places are accessible only by boat or swamp buggy. Some towns are tourist-oriented, with large throngs of summer vacationers crowding the beaches. You'll find boulevards lined with palm trees and three-star restaurants. Other towns are quiet, perfect for pleasant, inexpensive retirement. The southern tip of the Gulf Coast, where Texas ends and Mexico begins, is at about the same latitude as Miami, so local people like to call this "the new Florida." But anywhere you go along this part of the Gulf, you will find mild winters and tolerable summers.

**ALABAMA GULF COAST**--Just a few miles west of Pensacola is Alabama. Alabama claims only a small stretch of the Gulf Coast, with less than 50 miles of beach facing the open water.

This part can hardly be considered a major retirement area, since most of it is narrow spits of beach with very few people living there. Only a couple of sites can be considered beach towns. One is Dauphin Island; the other is Gulf Shores. Between them, they are lucky to scare up 3,000 people, but like all incipient resort towns, the people bubble with optimism, expecting a boom any minute.

The more populated part of Gulf Coast Alabama is Mobile and its suburbs. It's the only large town in the southern part of the state.

Mobile Bay is all but closed in by the islands and long peninsula at the bay's mouth. This makes the bay quite placid and a nice place for quiet boating and fishing during calm weather. The city of Mobile sits on the northwest corner of the bay, and has an attractive, Old-South feeling. The climate is much the same as the rest of the Gulf Coast, with warm to somewhat muggy summers and mild winters.

Years ago I spent a winter in Mobile working on the local newspaper. I remember the huge live oak trees that arched over many residential streets, giving an impression of driving through green tunnels, and I recall many enormous antebellum homes with tall, fluted columns, like something out of a movie set. To my delight, some of that scenery is still there. But to tell the truth, I wasn't very impressed with Alabama as a place to live for long periods (I also worked in Birmingham). Please don't accept my bias on this, because I understand that there are many happy retirees living there, some of them congregating along the shores of Mobile Bay. Perhaps my negative impressions have something to do with the exceptionally rainy winter that year, or the restrictive liquor laws that were in effect in those days. They may still be in effect, for all I know.

My last visit was a little more favorable. The city has kept pace with time, and parts of it seem appropriately modern. Like most non-tourist centers along the Gulf Coast, rents and housing are reasonable. Yet I suspect that most retirees around Mobile Bay are originally from Alabama or Mississippi. Mobile isn't a particularly well-known city for tourists and visitors to the South; the Gulf beaches are a 35-mile drive away. Most people drive on through Mobile on their way to Florida beaches or towards Gulfport-Biloxi in Mississippi. They seldom stop to sample the charms of Mobile. This pretty much leaves the area to those who know it well and find good reasons for retirement here.

While Mobile might be an appropriate retirement spot for someone who knows the area, some smaller towns in the Deep

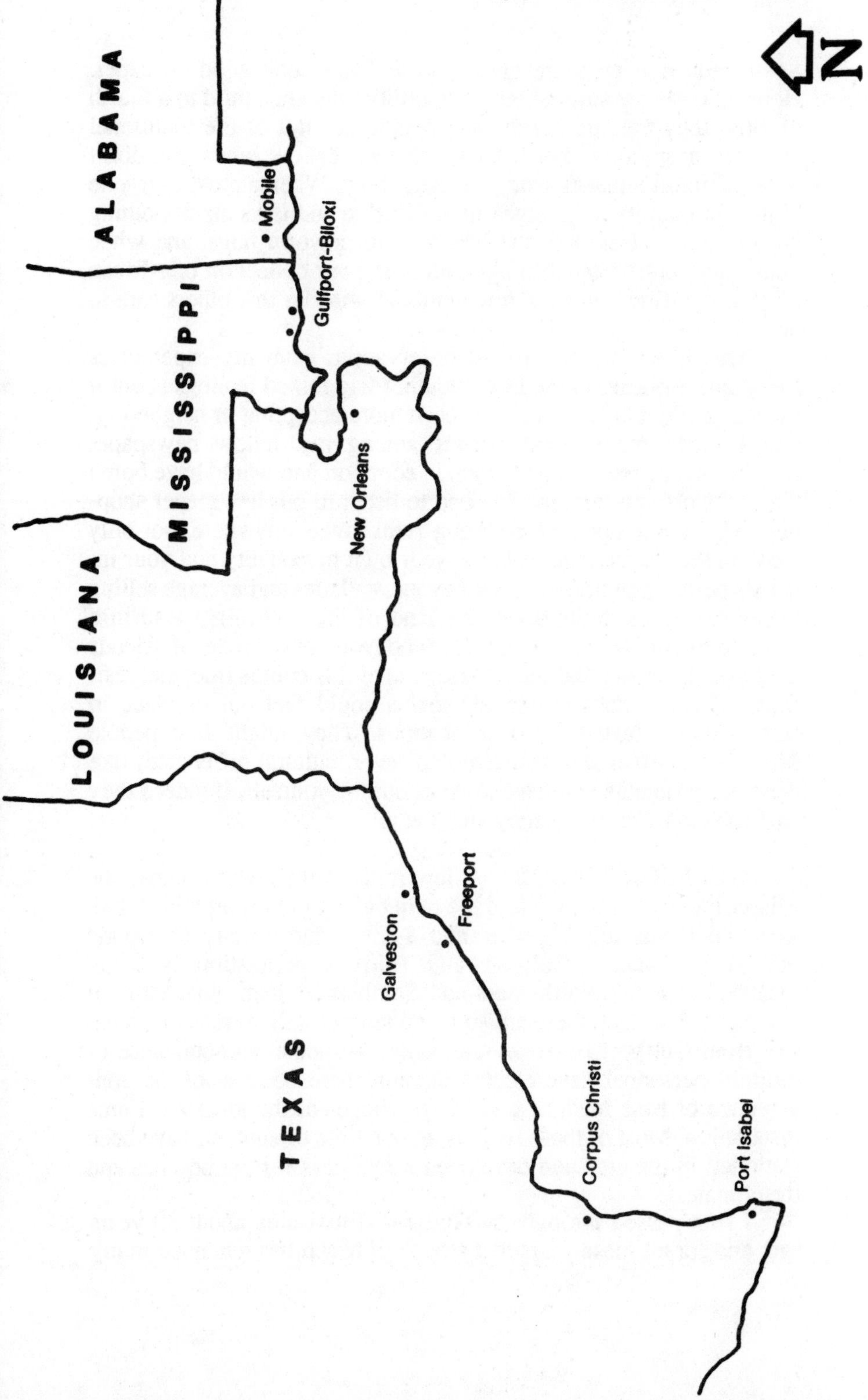

N

ALABAMA

MISSISSIPPI

LOUISIANA

TEXAS

• Mobile

Gulfport–Biloxi

New Orleans

Freeport

Galveston

Corpus Christi

Port Isabel

South require even more investigation. They look good on paper. Housing costs are surprisingly low, utility bills are a third to a fourth of what they are "up North" and people are full of the traditional southern hospitality. Yet it's easy to feel left out when you don't have common interests with your neighbors. When almost everyone in the community is involved in agriculture and talks about nothing but the price of corn or the best way to deworm hogs, and when your only connection with agriculture is your collection of African violets, you find you have few words of wisdom that others care to hear.

This is strictly a personal observation, from my experiences living and working in the Deep South. I had mixed feelings about it even then. People couldn't have been more accepting or neighborly, and I made many good friends among my fellow newspaper workers. Of course, we had much in common and would have bored the socks off any farmers who had to listen to our newspaper shoptalk. My advice about considering rural towns anywhere, not only those in the South, is to examine your own personality and your interests before jumping in. Look beyond statistics and average selling prices of homes; think about the kind of life you might lead in a rural southern location. Consider who your new circle of friends might be. I suspect that the reverse side of this coin is true, that residents of some rural crossroads towns could feel out of place in certain sophisticated big-city locations. They might find people stuffy, standoffish and insincere. However, cultural differences like these are problems you have to work out for yourself, if indeed they are problems. For many, they aren't at all.

GULFPORT-BILOXI--A few miles farther west, across the Mississippi state line, we find the twin cities of Gulfport and Biloxi. The two towns join together into a long, narrow city of around 90,000 inhabitants. Gulfport and Biloxi's population is better balanced between Northerners and Southerners than other parts of Mississippi. In fact, there are so many retirees and tourists that a native from Gulfport-Biloxi is rare. Like Pensacola, an abundance of military personnel have elected to retire here because of the convenience of base medical and PX privileges at the local Air Force installation. Most of these retirees, at one time or another, have been stationed in the area and developed a fondness for the beaches and the climate.

I first passed through the Gulfport-Biloxi area about 30 years ago, and for all these years that stretch of beach has remained in my memory as one of the prettiest seascapes I've ever seen. I could never forget the vast stretches of sugary beach with gentle waves pawing at the sand. A lovely street, arched over with majestic oak and magnolia trees, proceeded leisurely near the water, while large, formal estates surveyed the scene with southern majesty. Here was-- and is--the mansion where Jefferson Davis chose to live out his days, writing memoirs of his days of glory as president of the Confederacy.

Today, some of this beauty has worn thin. The street has been widened into a four-lane boulevard with a divider strip down the center, and one line of the oaks has disappeared. Some of the beachfront vistas are now obscured by restaurants, boutiques and souvenir shops, which further takes the edge off yesteryear's magical aura. Still, the charm of the Old South and Gulf of Mexico is hard to negate. Besides, only those who remember back 30 years will feel some disappointment, because others have no memories with which to make comparisons. To be honest, there are few places in the country that haven't changed for the worse, according to my eyes, and I tend to take "improvements" for granted. Nevertheless, for my money, Gulfport-Biloxi is still a great place for a visit, a regular winter sojourn, or a permanent retirement choice.

Here, as along most of the upper Gulf Coast, the tourist season begins around April or May. This means that winter offers exceptional rental bargains for those who want to make a temporary stay and test the waters for possible full-time retirement. Many people regularly take advantage of this low-cost housing to escape winters at home.

One man I interviewed has been coming here for eight years, arriving at the end of the tourist season, and leaving as soon as snow and ice are out of the question back in his native Iowa. "I used to say I didn't want to spend a summer here," he said, "but it seems that I'm arriving earlier and leaving later every year. I imagine that I'll be looking to buy a place next season." He told us that one of the attractions of snowbirding in Biloxi is the fact that he can rent an apartment for $250 a month in the off-season. "I get by on my Social Security check," he said happily, "and I don't have to touch my pension or my investment income to live here."

Along Ocean Boulevard, Biloxi's main drag, most of the lavish mansions I remembered from the past are still there. Large, manicured lawns and tasteful landscaping grace these jewels of southern architecture, epitomes of opulence and formality. But once you get a block or so away from the beach, the homes become rather ordinary, mostly single-family of stucco, brick or shingle. All of them are well kept. Some look expensive, but next door might be a rather modest home. This mixture gives a pleasant, comfortable feeling to these older neighborhoods. The trees are mature and gardening is obviously a popular hobby. Homes in these older sections of town can be found for under $50,000, sometimes just a few blocks from the beach. In the newer sections of Gulfport-Biloxi there are some excellent choices of new brick homes starting in the mid-to-high 50s.

There are plenty of apartments, condominiums and tourist accommodations, to be sure, but not nearly as many per capita as you will find at Fort Walton, or Pensacola, in Florida. Off-season apartments ought to be available for $250 to $350. You'll have to sign a lease to hold onto a place during summer. The emphasis is on smaller-scale construction. This results in somewhat lower density population, therefore automobile traffic is lighter than it would be if multistory apartment buildings were the rule. However, nothing can eliminate crowding and traffic during the summer tourist season. An additional perk is that, for the most part, the beach is observable from the road and not totally fenced away from view by cement high rises, as is the case in most of Florida.

As I pointed out earlier, military bases and retirees are plentiful all along the Gulf Coast, from Florida to New Orleans. Many retirees have spent some of their service careers at one of the many Gulf Coast military installations, and upon retirement, find themselves thinking of these pleasant places. Military retirees are quick to indicate the advantages of PX privileges and excellent base hospital facilities. With officers and enlisted retirees drawn from all over the country, from all social and educational backgrounds, the population is fairly cosmopolitan.

Gulfport and Biloxi seem to be one city. It's difficult to tell where they separate. The Biloxi end is the more elegant, although both places seem rather "down-home" and comfortable once you get away from Ocean Boulevard. The people hereabouts have a deserved reputation for friendliness, and because there are so many northern residents and tourists, a "Damn Yankee" won't feel out of place. As a matter of fact, this seems to me the biggest change in Gulfport-Biloxi of the past 30 years--residents from anywhere in the world won't feel like a rarity nowadays.

## LOUISIANA

The happiest part of my research for this book was spent in Louisiana. I gained five pounds and renewed my conviction that I could not get enough crawfish if I were to stay there for the rest of my life. I visited a couple of days with friends in Simmesport, a small town 60 miles northwest of Baton Rouge. They were highly amused when I requested leftover gumbo for breakfast every morning. I raided restaurants from obscure Cajun villages to the New Orleans French Quarter for generous helpings of shrimp estoufe, jambalaya, oyster-artichoke soup, cajun popcorn (deep fried crawfish tails), boudin and as many other delights as I could pass along to my astonished stomach. While eating one meal, I was plotting the next one. I brought home some of the hard-to-get ingredients, plus a recipe for gumbo, and I intend to have it for breakfast whenever I like, despite the hilarity the idea seems to raise in Cajun country.

NEW ORLEANS--New Orleans has always been one of my favorite towns. (By the way, I was born in New Orleans on Canal Street near Jefferson Davis Parkway. To my chagrin, there are no historical markers at the site to record the important event.) I would enthusiastically endorse New Orleans as a retirement area except for one problem: A high crime rate. Its murder rate surpasses New York City's, as does its rape rate. Much of these statistics are due to problems that arise during the wild Mardi Gras season. Tourists, sometimes of an unsavory character, converge upon New Orleans with the idea of an orgy of total abandon. So, during the weeks around Mardi Gras, arrest figures shoot sky-high. They bend the city's crime statistics out of shape for the entire year. Although the figures are a bit misleading, New Orleans, like most other metropolitan centers in North America, does have its problems.

Yet I interviewed several people who choose to live there despite its reputation as a crime-plagued town. "We haven't noticed any crime," said a woman who lives in a nice section of town near Lake Pontchartrain. "But, of course, we take plenty of precautions. And we stay away from the French Quarter during Mardi Gras when they are playing looneytoons." Her husband added, "We love living in the city, and there is no way we could afford a house this nice in any other interesting town in the country."

In a way, New Orleans residents are like those who adore living in New York City. They ignore statistics and wouldn't dream of moving to some place that is more secure, but boring. New Orleans' atmosphere, exotic, steeped in history and mystery, is anything but boring.

## LOW COST OF LIVING

Rents astonished me when I did a survey there in spring of 1987. Apartment rentals are lower than in any large town I've seen, with many offered for under $250. Of course, an apartment for that price could be in a neighborhood where you might want to be extremely careful, but there are others, more secure, for $350 and up.

The prices on houses seem more like some small town in Arkansas, rather than in one of the most dynamic and exciting cities in the country. Going through the Sunday classified ads, I found most houses listed in the $40-$50,000 range, with rare ones listed over $80,000. These newspaper ads might be somewhat misleading since many areas of New Orleans aren't suitable for retirement living. It would require a lot of on-the-spot investigation to separate the bargains from the disasters. Still, I was quite impressed when I visited one couple who paid what I considered a giveaway price for a four-level home in a fancy neighborhood near the lake and the university. I drove through areas on the edge of town where houses were advertised for sale, and looked at a couple. They were certainly affordable, and I wouldn't feel at all out of step living there. Incidentally, almost anything you buy or rent includes air conditioning. New Orleans summers demand it.

One reason for low-cost housing in New Orleans, and in most of Louisiana for that matter, is a depression in the oil industry. When foreign oil prices dropped through the floor, domestic oil became too expensive to produce. Petroleum companies capped their wells and laid off their workers. The situation is much worse in other parts of the state, since New Orleans has more diversified industry, but as the financial capital of the state, it clearly feels the effect. When money is tight, prices of everything, including housing, drop.

**SMALL-TOWN LOUISIANA**--While crime in New Orleans is admittedly high, once you leave the city, the crime rates drop dramatically. In towns like Houma or Thibodaux, less than 75 miles to the southwest, the FBI reports some of the lowest incidences of crime to be found anywhere in the country. According to *Places Rated Almanac*, this area is ranked 10th in the nation in safety. The Louisiana countryside is not only quiet and peaceful, but it enjoys one of the lowest costs of living in the United States. Apartments and houses can be rented for as low as $175 a month. Towns like Houma, Thibodaux and Lafayette are given high marks by people who have retired there. These are small towns, though, with agriculture by far the biggest topic of conversation.

I wanted to see this town of Houma, the place with such a low crime rate. It's about a 60-mile drive from New Orleans along a wide road flanked much of the way by a bayou. Roadside stands sell barbecue and crawfish dishes, so by the time I arrived in Houma, I felt a strong hankering for seafood. The first stop in researching a town is usually the chamber of commerce office. After conducting business there I asked for a recommendation for a restaurant. "Well sir, there are half a dozen restaurants in Houma, but I'm afraid they are mostly all seafood restaurants." Perfect! Which one is the best? "Sir, there just aren't any bad seafood restaurants in Houma!"

She was correct. I selected a restaurant at random; the fried catfish and and crawfish bisque were marvelous, better than at any high-priced New Orleans restaurant. A plate of cold steamed crabs was thrown in because they were left over from last night's dinner special. The bill for two, including wine, was around $12. I could like Houma even if there were muggers on every street corner, provided they didn't block the restaurant doors. But the truth is, Houma is an ordinary place, much like thousands of other small towns throughout the country. The streets of residential homes are comfortable looking, with neatly mowed lawns, children rollerskating on sidewalks and neighbors talking over backyard fences. It's just like small towns anywhere.

I suspect that the reason for so little crime is that young people growing up here have lots of relatives observing their behavior; aunts, uncles, grandmothers, etc. When this happens, juvenile delinquency is rarely a problem. As you know, juveniles can quickly send a crime report out of kilter with malicious mischief, thefts, thrill burglaries and gang fights. People around here don't seem to be the type to put up with that kind of nonsense from their kids. Like most Louisianians, the people of Houma seem to be down-to-earth, common-sense people.

Houma isn't unique in the property bargains to be found there. You'll encounter distress sales just about anywhere in the oil-dependent parts of Louisiana or Texas. Since the demise of petroleum markets came quickly and unexpectedly, there are many partially completed homes available which banks would love to get rid of at any price to protect their repossessed investments. Families who moved here and bought or built new homes suffered when the bottom dropped out. Many had to abandon everything to the lenders and move on to new jobs elsewhere. The result is rock-bottom prices, perhaps a once-in-a-decade opportunity for buyers. This could just as quickly change, however, should some unforeseen change in the oil market explode.

BATON ROUGE--The state capital, Baton Rouge (pop. 225,000), is reported to have the country's lowest cost of living for any metropolitan area. Yet Baton Rouge is definitely not a cheap-looking town. It has neat, prosperous-looking neighborhoods, attractive subdivisions, and one of the prettiest university campuses I've ever seen. I visited friends who live in a gorgeous two-story brick home, set back on an enormous tree-shaded lot. It's brand new and just a mile from the Louisiana State University campus. Their house is the kind of place most of us dream of owning but can never afford. Even though I knew home prices are low in Louisiana, I was shocked to learn the price they paid for it. I can't mention the price because it might embarrass them, but suffice to say that where I live, you could buy just an average-looking tract home for what they paid.

Baton Rouge has a lot going for it in the way of retirement. Location is one thing. It's just 70 miles by fast interstate to New Orleans for those extra special "nights on the town" or for the hilarity of Mardi Gras. Fifty miles to the north is historic Natchez, Mississippi, where there are more *antebellum* homes on display than anywhere in the country. And the famous Cajun and Bayou country starts just west of Baton Rouge. The city is quite proud of its historic past and is taking vigorous steps to preserve and restore two downtown neighborhoods, historic Beauregard Town and Spanish Town.

The countryside around Baton Rouge is among the prettiest and most historic in the state. Gracious old plantation homes, with huge porticoes, wrought iron balconies and lead-sheathed roofs, sit half-hidden by enormous trees, just as they have for almost two centuries. Plaquemine, a delightful little town about 20 minutes south, dates from the 1700s. With winding streets and shuttered houses, ancient trees and camelia bushes, it's not surprising that it is a nationally designated historic site. A ferry boat carries passengers across the Mississippi to visit the town.

In Baton Rouge there are a number of old, historic neighborhoods, suitable for retirement, where spacious homes retain the elegance of years ago. Of course, there are plenty of new neighborhoods, with some developments still under construction. The number of new housing starts isn't high, since the petroleum disaster affects the whole of the state, and Baton Rouge hasn't escaped its share of misery. Rents and real estate prices are quite low. This is a shame for many people who are affected by the slumping market, but it's a definite advantage for retirees on fixed budgets.

Another advantage for retirement living is the presence of Louisiana State University (LSU). This highly rated school attracts people from all over the country. Students, faculty, support personnel and families of all these people bring outside views and ways of living to the community. Like New Orleans, Baton Rouge is cosmopolitan. I haven't taken a survey, but my impression is that most residents do not have a southern accent in their speech patterns. This isn't surprising, because so many people come here from places where midwestern accents are the norm. I attribute the presence of the university for part of this leveling of accents. And, among the natives, if anything, there may be a touch of a Cajun accent, which is different, but clearly not southern.

The university touches the people's lives in other ways, culturally as well as educationally. A saying here is that "art is the heart of Baton Rouge." Using the talent in theater, music and fine arts that LSU attracts, the community has organized some commendable programs. Every year a 10-block stretch of downtown is blocked off so people can see potters at their wheels, musicians making music and artists at their easels. Mimes entertain the crowds and craftsmen of all kinds sell their wares. Two ballet groups bring stars from major companies to work with local students, and the Baton Rouge Opera is in its fifth season. Two light opera companies, a symphony orchestra and a professional theater company round out the cultural offerings of Baton Rouge. The university itself presents a continual program of jazz artists, classical concerts and theater.

Of interest to retirees is the wide variety of services for senior citizens. Many of the services are coordinated by the Baton Rouge Council on Aging, an organization formed 15 years ago. They coordinate the Retired Senior Volunteer Program (R.S.V.P.), three senior centers, a Meals on Wheels program and a free, short-term home care for elderly persons who are temporarily disabled, or recently home from the hospital. Other services are legal aid, health services, consumer information and a foster grandparent program. Although only about 10 percent of the population in Baton Rouge is over 60, the community obviously intends to take care of the retired.

CAJUN COUNTRY--West and north from Baton Rouge is the famous "Cajun Country" which occupies about a third of the state's land area. The Cajuns were once notorious for their insularity. They jealously maintained their French language and their private ways from outsiders. Descendants of the French Acadian refugees who were exiled from Nova Scotia in 1755, they are known as a hard-working, fun-loving people. A few years ago, everyone spoke French, and looked with vague contempt on outsiders, whom they referred to as *les Americaines*. But World War II brought many Cajuns out into the outside world. That experience and television seem to have taken their toll on the folk culture of Cajun Country. Today, only the old-timers still speak French, although some of the younger generation can understand a little because their grandparents still converse in the language. It looks like the next generation could see the end of Cajuns as a unique cultural entity. This is too bad, but it definitely opens up some fine prospects for retirement alternatives. It turns out that people aren't insular or unfriendly at all. In fact, some of the more hospitable people I've met were in Cajun Country. However, you would have to love small-town living, because that's all there is here--small towns. All of the drawbacks of small towns anywhere are found here.

If you're looking for some Gulf Coast beach property in Louisiana, you are out of luck. Except for a short stretch of sand in the western part of the state, which is humorously referred to as the "Cajun Riviera," most coastal lands are swamps and bayous. The emphasis here is on sports such as fishing and hunting. Duck hunting is said to be fabulous. Beaches start when you get to Texas.

My overall impression of Louisiana it that is a real possibility as a retirement site, either in the cities or in the smaller towns. The people seem more open and less like Deep South stereotypes than you'll find in many other southern locations. People here seem to accept neighbors from other places more readily than in some of the other southern states.

## TEXAS GULF COAST

The Texas coast curves gently around the Gulf of Mexico for over 600 miles, from Louisiana all the way to Mexico. It begins with bayou country, where Spanish moss graces live oaks and cypresses, and ends at the mouth of the Rio Grande in a sandy stretch of seashore that provides sanctuary for birds and nesting turtles. Most of the Texas mainland along the Gulf Coast is uninhabited, with enormous stretches of saltwater marsh known only by wildlife. But flanking the mainland, for most of the Texas coast's 624 miles, are extremely long islands comprised of sand dunes and almost unexplored beaches. Much of the coast is little changed from the days when the French pirate Jean Lafitte used the islands as a base in the early 1800s.

A large percentage of these islands, as well as stretches of the mainland, are designated as wildlife refuges. Here whooping cranes and Kemp's ridley sea turtles are making a comeback after what once seemed almost certain extinction. Turtle eggs from Mexico were planted on the Padre Islands about 20 years ago, and the hatchlings from the experiment have matured and have begun coming ashore to nest in a protected environment. When the new hatchlings start for the sea, they are captured and cared for in special pens until they're old enough to have a good chance at survival.

Both the channel and Gulf sides of the long islands teem with fish. From beaches and piers you can expect to catch redfish, speckled and sand trout, flounder, sheepshead, skipjack, croakers and drum. Group boats offer bay and deep-sea fishing, with charter cruisers available for individual or small-party sport. The offshore game includes tarpon, sailfish, kingfish, marlin, mackerel, pompano, ling cod, bonito and red snapper, among others. By far, fishing is the major sports attraction for retirees who have chosen the Texas Gulf Coast as their homes.

Galveston and Corpus Christi are the only towns of any size along the Texas coast. Corpus Christi is a true city, with a population of 232,000, but Galveston is little more than an overgrown resort town, with around 60,000 inhabitants. Texas City, Freeport and some other towns along the coast are basically industrial, with huge petrochemical plants spoiling the view for those thinking of retirement. However, when you get away from the industrial areas, there are some rather nice residential areas, mainly for workers and executives of the plants.

**GALVESTON**--Galveston was one of my favorite towns of 20 years ago. When I returned to do this survey I was expecting to find astounding changes, as is the rule in most places around the country. To my surprise, Galveston has changed very little from the last time I vacationed there.

The reason for slow change is limited space on Galveston's island, which was filled long ago with houses and businesses. Along the beach, some older homes and buildings are slowly giving way to newer, more urofitable construction, focused on the tourist dollar. But change seems slow in coming and the rest of the town is still the same--old-fashioned and comparatively inexpensive. There are practically no high-rise buildings, either on the beach or in town. Fascinating Victorian homes--some in a poor state of repair, most in fine shape and some positively gorgeous--grace quiet, tree-lined streets away from the bustle of the seashore. Once you leave the honky-tonk atmosphere of Seawall Boulevard, it is hard to believe that you are in one of the major tourist attractions on the Texas coast.

I found several interesting bargains in Victorian homes, complete with gingerbread verandas and Queen Anne towers. The owners had invested enormous amounts of money, modernizing kitchens and bathrooms and updating electrical equipment. Now they are discovering that there is no way to recoup their expenses--the market is too soft. This might be a lesson to those who have always had this dream of renovating an old house: It's expensive. Once you start digging into the defects of an 1887 model home, you might find that the remedies for old age are incredibly expensive. Although I admit that renovation of a Victorian has always appealed to me, I've decided to save myself a bundle and buy one already gussied up with someone else's money. Here, you can buy an enormous Victorian home for as low as $100,000, and it's possible the previous owners have poured that much or more into modernizing and restoration.

Downtown Galveston is as old-fashioned as the rest of the city. The city fathers came up with the idea of capitalizing on nostalgia by turning a portion of downtown into an "old-town" section. Old brick and cast iron fronts with wrought iron balconies give the area a New Orleans French Quarters feeling. Even in the winter, when tourism is slow, downtown Galveston has a special charm. One street has been turned into a pedestrian mall, with restaurants, smart shops and park benches for sunning and people-watching.

There is a surprising intellectual air about Galveston, surprising because it is known mostly as a weekend and vacation resort for Houston, or as a convention center. The University of Texas medical school is in downtown Galveston, as well as a branch of Texas A&M and a community college.

The one thing I found very much different from the days when I used to drive down here from Houston and fish for crab, is that the stretch of 34 miles of sparkling beach that fronts the island is no longer open to automobile traffic. There are plenty of access points, however, where fishermen can surf cast, and there are piers for easier fishing. I fondly remember blissful days and large catches of blue crab, later made into a seafood gumbo at the home of a displaced Cajun who lived in Houston.

Today, the beach outside of town is no longer deserted and wild, but is often lined with ugly, unpainted summer homes that are built on 15-foot stilts to avoid high waves during hurricane weather. All along the Gulf Coast, from Key West to the tip of Texas, you find this stilt construction. Insurance companies insist on new buildings having stilts; it cuts their losses considerably. Some owners successfully disguise the stilts by screening the lower portion of their house, turning it into a garage and storage space. This makes it look like an attractive two-story home. But others don't bother, making stretches of beach look as if they had been invaded by spindly-legged monsters. Since the beach area is pure tourist and most popular during the spring and summer months, it turns into a ghostly place in winter. Few homes are lived in year-round.

**CORPUS CHRISTI**--The other large population area on the Texas coast is Corpus Christi, with 232,000 inhabitants. It's a major deepwater port that, despite being a popular tourist attraction, is large enough to mask the crowds. For the most part, it looks like an ordinary, contemporary city--pleasant and unusually neat. Unlike Galveston, which sits exposed to the whims of hurricane-driven tides, Corpus Christi enjoys the protection of offshore islands. Therefore, construction doesn't have to take into consideration the constant threat of flood; the town has a relaxed look about it. It even has a high-rise downtown section.

Although Corpus Christi is a nice looking city, and has attracted many retirees because of a fair climate, low prices and great beaches, it is still a large town. Too large for my liking, with its share of traffic congestion. Still, there are many advantages to living there, particularly for those who are into the ever-present Gulf Coast sport of fishing. And it's a fairly safe town to live in.

By the way, don't be misled by crime statistics, particularly when dealing with towns that have a heavy influx of seasonal tourists. I've been told that sometimes up to 100,000 tourists, many of them college students, flock to Corpus Christi and Mustang Island to celebrate spring break. As you can imagine, the police are busy arresting drunks, breaking up fistfights and stopping exuberant youngsters from destroying motel rooms. All of these offenses are reflected in the crime rates for the area, but they are crimes that don't really affect ordinary people who neither live in nor frequent the tourist areas. This book assumes that you, as a retiree, can refrain from engaging in fistfights with college students.

**NORTH PADRE ISLAND**--Corpus Christi and Mustang Island--the northern part of the Padre Islands, across the Laguna Madre--are the closest resorts to San Antonio. Because so many people from San Antonio vacation here and maintain summer homes, Corpus Christi and Mustang Island are often referred to as annexes of San Antonio. Port Aransas is the only town on Mustang Island. It's small, with a year-round population of about 2,000, although summer tourism can push this considerably.

Here, the familiar stilt houses abound, some of which can be purchased quite inexpensively. I saw several in the low $30,000 range. Some look nice, but most have a temporary air about them, as if their owners hate to put much maintenance into them, just in case a hurricane might make it a waste of time.

The islanders like to brag about their low crime rate. "There are only two ways off the island," they point out, "either by ferry to the mainland, or by the bridge to Corpus at the other end of the island. No one expects to commit a serious crime and make a getaway." When a crime is committed, the police immediately shut down the ferry and place a roadblock at the bridge. Another thing they like to brag about is the fishing, claiming that Mustang Island is "where they bite every day." This is probably a good thing for the retiree who loves to fish, because there is very little else to do on Mustang or North Padre Island.

Once you leave Port Aransas, the island is very sparsely populated. Long stretches of dunes and beach line the Gulf side, with lagoons and marsh facing the mainland. Except for a few tourist condos and some private homes, the rest of the island is left to the sea turtles and birds. If you keep driving south you find yourself on Padre Island, and the road abruptly ends, with no more pavement for another 80 miles.

**SOUTH PADRE ISLAND**--Very different from the northern end of the island, South Padre Island is almost pure tourist, with condos, hotels, and rental units competing for space with restaurants and souvenir shops. Although it looks like a city when first viewed from the causeway that crosses the Laguna Madre from Port Isabel, there are only 791 year around residents, according to the *State of*

*Texas Travel Handbook.* Almost nothing looks like a residential area. The built-up part of the island covers a small portion of the southernmost tip, and then becomes dunes and beaches, inhabited by RV owners and campers out "boondocking."

Developers may have been a little over-optimistic about the future of the island, because they overbuilt. High-rise, luxury condos, motels and duplexes sprouted quicker than buyers could be found. The result is that some great buys were available when I stopped off there in 1987. Example: Some luxury units that had been built to sell for $400,000 had been on the market for over three years with no takers. They were being sold at auction for $70,000 and under.

South Padre Island lies at the most southern latitude of anywhere in the continental United States except for the Florida Keys. As you might expect, it has a Florida-like climate, but enjoys a lower summer humidity. Its beaches are endless and gently sloping--great for swimming and surf fishing. No wonder it attracts its share of snowbirds in the winter and sun-lovers in the summer, although winter seems to be the slowest season.

Rentals are at a low in the winter season, and almost everything you see on the islands is for rent. This would be an excellent place to spend a winter while checking out retirement possibilities in nearby Rio Grande Valley. (See next chapter.)

**PORT ISABEL**--I suspect that the reason so few people actually live on South Padre Island is that Port Isabel (pop. 3,800) is right across the causeway. Many people prefer to live in Port Isabel and make the short drive to take advantage of the pleasures of Padre Island without paying premium prices for property. Another advantage to living is Port Isabel is that the island acts as a barrier against storm-driven seas. High stilt construction isn't necessary.

Here is where you can park your RV if you insist on having water and electricity hookups, rather than "boondocking" out on the island. There are several large parks that are full most of the year. And here is where you find the residential areas for people who work on the island. The town is neat and comfortable. Housing is quite reasonable, and rentals are surprisingly low, with two-bedroom houses often listed at $200 a month.

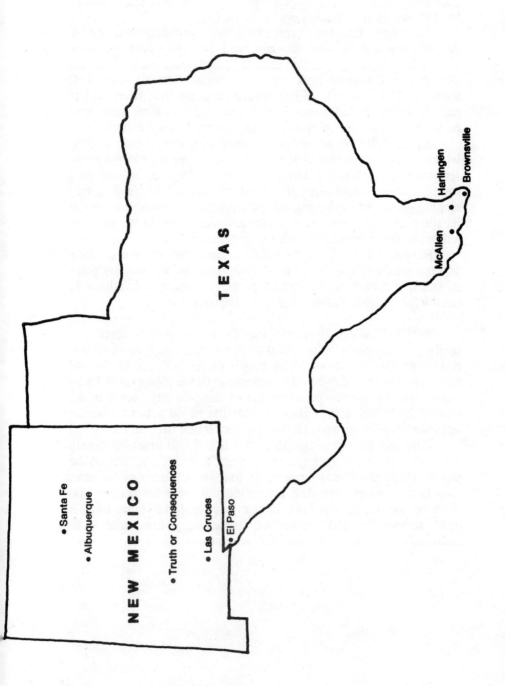

CHAPTER THIRTEEN
_____

# *Texas and the Rio Grande Valley*

You don't have to be told that Texas is one enormous state. But if you give a Texan the chance, he'll remind you of it anyway. The fact is that the state is almost as large as Texans claim, and that's pretty darn big. Not only is it large, it boasts some of the prettiest scenery in the country--as well as some of the most boring. The altitude, climate and scenery vary so between parts of the state that an appetizingly wide range of retirement alternatives are available.

The northern Panhandle region can be one of the coldest places imaginable in the winter, and one of the hottest places this side of Death Valley in the summer. At least it seems that way to me. On the other hand, the southern extreme of the state is as close to west coast Florida as you could hope for. You can find some of the driest and some of the dampest climates in Texas, large cities and small villages. East Texas reminds me of Tennessee, and the mountain country north of Austin is amazingly scenic. There's plenty to look at in retirement choices in Texas.

## THE RIO GRANDE VALLEY

The Texas Gulf Coast ends at Port Isabel, but it's at this point where one of the most important and fastest growing of all Texas retirement areas begins, the Rio Grande Valley. Here, the famous Rio Grande empties into the sea after its 1,900-mile trip from Colorado, down through New Mexico and along the Texas-Mexico border. Each winter, several hundred thousand people journey here to soak up sunshine and enjoy what they call, "the Poor Man's Florida." Most head for that stretch of valley from the Gulf beaches westward to Rio Grande City, about 90 miles inland.

Retirement here isn't something new. For years, midwestern farmers spoke of the legendary warm winters along the Rio Grande, where "perpetual summer" is an apt description. When snow and ice gripped their fields with bitter winter cold, farmers arranged for someone to feed the livestock, hooked a trailer to the pickup and started off for a winter of retirement in the Lower Rio Grande Valley. There, orange groves, palm trees and frequent 80-degree, sunshiny days made for pleasant living, while ice, sleet and snow paralyzed the farming country. And, best of all, living there was (and is) cheap. Local people used to joke that "the farmers come down here with a five-dollar bill and a pair of overalls, and don't change either one the whole winter."

You don't hear that joke nowadays. Winter residents are big business in south Texas. And they aren't all farmers, either. Today, winter refugees arrive with pockets full of Social Security and pension money. More and more come each year. Ten years ago, about 50,000 snowbirds wintered in the valley each year, but today the estimated number tops 200,000. They pump well over $200 million into what would otherwise be a sagging economy. So many people flock into the area that they are commonly called "Winter Texans."

Many border towns are famous for being rather dreary places, with rundown shacks, unemployment and boarded-up storefronts. This picture has been particularly true since the collapse of the Mexican economy and the demise of Texas oil industry. The devalued Mexican peso makes everything on our side of the border too expensive for Mexicans, so they no longer stream across to shop in U.S. stores. The result has been disastrous for some border cities.

But, thanks to retiree money, this stretch of border along the lower Rio Grande Valley is distinguished by an obvious air of prosperity. Businesses buzz with activity, restaurants and stores teem with customers. Residential areas look as modern and as well kept, or better, than just about any place in Texas I've seen.

Everyone agrees that the prosperity here is due to Winter Texans' money. One bank reports that 20 percent of its deposit growth for the last six years is "snowbird money." Another bank admits that one-third of its deposits are from transplanted and temporary Texans. The city of McAllen estimates that 25 percent of its winter sales-tax revenue comes from Winter Texans. And one bank there even flies a Canadian flag alongside an American flag to acknowledge the importance of the growing number of northern neighbors who winter here.

## RVs POPULAR WITH WINTER TEXANS

Recreational vehicles are the primary residences of these Winter Texans. Mobile homes rank next in popularity. It seems that everywhere you look, new parks are replacing citrus groves or vegetable fields. As best as I can tell, there are over 500 parks in the Brownsville-Harlingen-McAllen area, many with several hundred spaces each. The parks compete with each other for business by offering organized social activities. Pancake breakfasts, square

dances, ice-cream socials, all the things that get people to mingle and make friends with each other are offered in hopes of luring the Winter Texans back the following year.

The retirees, with typical midwestern friendliness, tend to organize extensive social lives on their own as well. Bicycling clubs, bridge parties and adult education classes are just a few of their activities. Especially popular are Spanish classes. With Mexico just across the river, the Winter Texans have ample opportunity to practice their language skills and have a lot of fun bargaining for treasures in the shops in Old Mexico. The merchants there are just as pleased at this flow of midwestern and Canadian dollars as their U.S. counterparts. Everyone goes out of their way to make the visitors feel welcome.

Incidentally, one of the popular organized activities here is touring Mexico. People go in motor caravans (sometimes taking their RVs with them), or by chartered bus or on regularly scheduled flights. In fact, a high percentage of tourists you'll meet in Mexico, particularly in the northern part of the country, are winter residents of the Rio Grande Valley on excursion. In the summer, when it heats up, the permanent valley residents seek relief in the cool mountains of Mexico. Towns like Saltillo, Guanajuato and San Miguel de Allende are within easy driving distance. Excellent housing is available in these picturesque towns--rock-bottom prices--prompting many Texas retirees to establish yet another retirement haven.

Winter Texans have done more than organize socially; they've become a political force to be reckoned with. This is easy, because Texas requires only a 30-day residence to become a legal voter. Winter Texans have become involved in several full-tilt political battles, even electing a mayor in one town, and blocking a drug rehabilitation center from locating near three RV parks. With this kind of political clout, you can be sure that local officials pay attention to the needs of Winter Texans.

Besides the warm, Florida-like winters, the other great advantage of living here is the cost of living. As in all border areas, wages are quite low, kept there by the availability of eager workers from "the other side of the river." Low wages usually mean low costs of goods and services. So retirees enjoy an exceptionally low cost of living. Some RV parks charge as low as $50 monthly space rent, including water, electricity and garbage service. Other, more deluxe, places might charge $100 a month, which covers additional luxuries such as 24-hour security, professional landscaping service and cable TV. A similar lot in Tucson would surely cost twice as much, and one in some parts of Florida, four times as much. Conventional housing, apartments and condos begin at bedrock prices, partly due to low-cost construction labor.

Here are a few examples taken at random from the Harlingen newspaper, February 22, 1987: For rent, furnished: One bedroom Apt. $165. Two wks. free rent--1 bdrm. apt. $195. Unfurnished apartments: 2 bdrm townhouse, $350; large 1 bdrm $195. Houses for rent: 2 bdrm house $225, incl utilities; 3 bdr. $325; 3 bdr., 2 ba. $275. Houses for sale: 3 bdr, 2 ba. $39,000. 3 bdr, 2 ba., $32,500. One house was advertised for rent "as is" for $125 a month or $18,000 to buy.

Another area of economy that retirees along the international border enjoy is the cheap medication found in the *farmacias* across the river in Mexico. Over there, most medicines don't require prescriptions and are often manufactured by the same drug companies that distribute in the United States and Canada. The major difference lies in the price. For example, a 30-day supply of Enderal, a common medication for hypertension and heart irregularities, costs about half to a third of what you would pay on the American side of the border. Dental work is still another attraction on the Mexican side. All border towns have dentists who specialize in working on Winter Texans' teeth. The people I've interviewed claim that the work is excellent, and at a fraction of what dentists "back home" charge.

## WINTER AND SUMMER WEATHER

While winters here are summer-like, with highs averaging in the 70s, the summers are *extra* summer-like. Highs average in the 90s for the three summer months, with lows around 75 at night. At first, this doesn't seem excessive, but coupled with an average relative humidity of 75 percent, this means real summer. With this high humidity, evaporative coolers are worthless, so you must depend on refrigeration-type units. This extreme summer weather is why 200,000 people choose to be Winter Texans and make an exodus when the temperatures begin to rise.

Nevertheless, more and more of them are converting into permanent residents. According to the U.S. government, the number of Social Security checks being sent to the Rio Grande Valley is up by 16 percent over a three-year period. And twice as many of the RV and mobile home park spaces are occupied year-round as were

10 years ago--about 20 percent have exchanged their Winter Texan status for "Year-round Texan" status.

What surprises me was the number of Rio Grande immigrants who at one time lived in Florida, and later changed to Texas. Of course, the ones I interviewed owned RVs, so making the change in migration patterns wasn't all that traumatic. One couple explained, "We decided we liked the people we meet here better than in Florida. It seemed as if everyone in Florida came from Connecticut, New York or New Jersey. They just didn't seem as friendly as folks from the Midwest, as we are."

Another couple complained about the crowds in Florida. "Sure, there are a lot of RVs crowded together here," admitted one ex-Florida retiree, "but the streets and highways are a pleasure to drive on in Texas. And, besides, everything in Florida seems like it costs twice as much."

In many ways, this part of Texas does look like Florida. Plenty of palm trees, fragrant citrus blossoms, bougainvillaea and other flowering shrubs provide a distinctly tropical flavor. However, temperatures can drop, suddenly and dramatically. Many palm trees and acres of citrus orchards still show damage from the severe freeze of 1983. Some palms look as if they aren't coming back at all. But one retiree said, "A cold snap like that happens once every few years, that's true. But where I come from, it happens every year and lasts the whole damn winter long!"

A final benefit of living here, one that is constantly pointed out by local boosters, is the low crime rate. Robberies, for example, are less than one-fourth the national average. I'm convinced that this area would look even safer if we could exclude arrests and incidents involving dope smuggling and illegal aliens, none of which directly threaten retirees.

As a temporary retirement area, the Rio Grande Valley would put you in a lot of good company if you decided to become a Winter Texan. For those of you who can stand the heat and don't mind hanging around the kitchen, the valley wouldn't be too bad as a year-round retirement site. But, let's follow the Rio Grande upstream for a look at some other interesting possibilities.

**EL PASO**--Just over four centuries ago, in 1581, the first Europeans pushed their way north and found an easy crossing or "pass" across the sometimes sluggish, sometimes wild, Rio Grande. They called the place "El Paso del Norte." When Spain, and then Mexico, relinquished their claims to the crossing, the U.S. Army established a post there to protect American settlers from marauding Indians and oversee the growing business of international trade between Mexico and the United States. Over the years, El Paso grew from a dusty cow town into a modern city of over 500,000. It's by far the banking and commercial center along the 1,933-mile U.S.-Mexico border. A growing number of retirees are discovering that this city has plenty to offer.

El Paso has several good things going for it. First of all, the climate is quite mild, with summers that seem much cooler than those of the lower Rio Grande Valley. Here, you can usually get out in July or August and play a game of golf without the threat of sunstroke. That would be all but impossible downstream, around Brownsville or McAllen. The difference is Brownsville's humidity of 75 percent, compared to El Paso's 36 percent.

Another thing that makes El Paso attractive is the proximity of Ciudad Juarez, across the Rio Grande. Juarez is more than just another border town like Reynosa or Matamoros; it is truly a city. It's even larger than El Paso, with an estimated population nearing a million inhabitants. Juarez's downtown section, close to the border, is a bit grungy, with honkytonks and topless bars, an occasional good restaurant, plus the usual bordertown curio and souvenir shops. But when you get away from the old downtown section, there are several modern areas, with broad boulevards, nice restaurants and clothing stores.

Naturally, one of the attractions of Mexican border towns is the cheap prices. Many retirees come across the border to do shopping every week. Items like instant coffee, which costs about $1.00 for four ounces, would price out at least $2.50 on the Texas side of the border. Other grocery items are priced similarly. Fruits and vegetables are at giveaway prices; unfortunately, you can't bring them across the border. A liter bottle of Domecq's Presidente brandy (one of the best you can buy anywhere) costs around $3.00.

El Paso is also unique for its blend of Mexican and Anglo cultures, something not found in the lower Rio Grande Valley. Here, instead of keeping rigid lines between English and Spanish, between Mexico and the United States, we find a pleasant mixture of Texas and Chihuahua. Restaurant menus on both sides of the border reflect these influences. El Paso restaurants typically offer dishes like *menudo* or *chiles rellenos*, while Juarez restaurants are famous for their steak-and-lobster dinners. Radio programs from both sides of the border often mix Spanish and English transmissions in the same program.

This blend of American modern and old Mexican charm gives El Paso its distinctive character. From the downtown section, wide streets branch out in all directions, and Interstate 10 moves traffic quickly and efficiently. City traffic is remarkably light. Commercial buildings are modern and crisp, without a lot of the garishness and mirrored walls that seem to be the vogue in some cities. As you move toward the outskirts of the city, you can't help but be impressed with the neatness and cleanliness. Most of the residences are single-family, one-story homes, mostly of brick. In the newer sections of town you find "ranch-style" homes, and others showing the influence of nearby Mexico, with arches, inside patios and atriums.

In the newer sections, away from downtown, you'll also find a profusion of apartment buildings. Apparently they're overbuilt, because you'll see signs everywhere advertising special deals to entice renters. Some offer the first month's rent free, or free utilities for the first year, or color televisions. The best part is the advertised rents: They start at $200 a month. Where I come from, that's a gift!

Actually, it was in El Paso that I first conceived the idea of doing this book. I was visiting a friend who had an almost-new apartment on a hill overlooking El Paso and Ciudad Juarez in the distance. It was December and just cool enough that a fire in the fireplace seemed appropriate, yet warm enough that we didn't bother to put on sweaters when we went outside to tend the barbecue. We both had worked on the El Paso newspapers, so I wasn't too surprised when he returned there to live when he retired because we both enjoyed working there. I asked him why he chose El Paso over some of the other places he'd worked in and had liked. San Francisco, for example, or Fort Lauderdale--I know his wife had loved both of those places--or why not retire in their home town in Connecticut?

He smiled wryly as he looked around the apartment. "You know what a place like this would cost us in Connecticut, or in Florida?" Before I had a chance to guess, he went on, saying, "At least $750 a month, that's what. My entire Social Security check would have to go to make the rent. We'd have to dig into savings every month to buy food. We wouldn't be able to enjoy living there if we had to live like paupers."

His wife nodded agreement. "The secret to low-cost retirement is cutting back on housing," she emphasized. "Our rent and utilities here come to about $250 a month. I figure that leaves us with $500 that we don't have to spend on housing. That $500 buys the groceries and pays most of the bills. Actually, we could easily live on Jim's Social Security check if we had to."

Their apartment was nice, I had to admit, and I'm sure that it would have cost much more than $750 a month where I come from. Because labor costs are low, Susan has a cleaning woman do the apartment once a week. Also, they manage to eat out at a nice restaurant at least weekly.

Until that moment, I had always assumed that living on Social Security automatically meant abject poverty. I assumed that it was all but impossible to live graciously in the United States on Social Security alone. Clearly, it's possible in Latin America or in some places in Europe, but in the United States? Yet, here they were getting by nicely, enjoying retirement without feeling deprived. With my own retirement not too far away, the rusty gears in my head began cranking and the idea of a retirement book started grinding away.

## FRIENDLY PEOPLE

Texans are famous for their friendliness and hospitality, but El Paso hospitality is more than Texan. As in many growing areas of Texas, the people here come from all parts of America. Sometimes I get the distinct impression that native Texans are in the minority in El Paso. One reason for this homogeneity of population is the military influence around the town. Air Force and Army personnel, when on a tour of duty here, easily come to think of El Paso as one of their retirement possibilities. They like the cleanliness and neighborliness of the city, the affordability of real estate, and they recognize the cultural and recreational advantages of retirement here. Of course, being military, they also consider the convenience of the PXs and excellent free medical facilities.

When I worked in El Paso, I found it exceptionally easy to make friends. People are just naturally friendly there. When you stop someone on the street to ask for directions, chances are you will find a Boston or a Chicago accent rather than a Texas accent. But unlike in many northern and eastern cities, where you are likely to be ignored, the person will be helpful, maybe even going with you to make sure you find your destination.

When I asked people why they retired in El Paso, the usual answer included the weather and that there is plenty to do. Besides golf, tennis and the usual sports, there are bullfights and horse racing across the river plus many organized activities by senior citizens' clubs and organizations. Just as retirement clubs in McAllen and Brownsville organize tours into Mexico, so do their El Paso counterparts. An interesting variation is to take a Mexican train for excursions. Old-fashioned trains, complete with Pullmans, dining and club cars, make their way down into Mexico for ridiculously low fares. Sometimes a group of retirees will get together and charter its own car, each party getting a private room with bath, and go through the famous Copper Canyon route in Chihuahua.

## UPRIVER INTO NEW MEXICO

LAS CRUCES--Up river from El Paso, and only 45 minutes by interstate highway, is the town of Las Cruces (pop. 45,000). This is another popular place for retirees, with a high number of residents over 65. It's the largest city in southern New Mexico, despite its small population. But it's large enough for most shopping needs, and there is even a theater and a symphony, and it's small enough to avoid the drawbacks of urban living.

The town is nestled in the fertile Mesilla Valley, which draws irrigation waters from the Rio Grande. It's almost surrounded by mountains, some rising to over 9,000 feet. Las Cruces is a pretty place to live as well as a pleasant one. Summers are hot, but the winters, like El Paso's, are sunny and mild. Humidity is higher, at 50 percent, probably because of the large amount of nearby irrigation farming.

Like El Paso, rents and property costs are low. However, competition from students at the New Mexico State University can force rents upward, particularly around the university campus. Like all college towns, Las Cruces enjoys participation in the school's cultural and entertainment events.

TRUTH OR CONSEQUENCES--Farther up river, about 70 miles, we come upon a town with a silly name. Bordered on one side by dramatic mud and sandstone bluffs, Truth or Consequences (pop. 5,200) squats among sagebrush and a great desert landscape. Despite its name, it turns out to be a practical retirement spot for desert lovers. Nearby is a long lake that was created by damming the Rio Grande some 70 years ago. So, in the middle of the New Mexico desert, we find a great place for fishing and water sports. Mobile homes seem to be the order of the day, with a good measure of RV parks for winter snowbirds.

Modest two-bedroom mobile homes start about $25,000 and up, and they can be placed on residential lots. Basic two-bedroom home prices begin around $35,000, and a nice two-bedroom apartment will rent for about $200 to $300 a month. Clearly, this is an affordable town.

Snowbirds can be an appropriate term here, because when I visited here in January, I saw remnants of a recent snowstorm. "Very unusual weather," protested several residents of Truth or Consequences. "Usually it's warm and sunny here." Sure, that's what they all say. But apparently summers are cool enough to attract a large following of year-round retirees.

Among the advantages pointed out by residents is the mild weather, water sports and active senior citizens' center clubs. Certainly there are adequate services and shopping, but the nearest large medical center would be either Las Cruces or Albuquerque. There is a small hospital, however, with an intensive care unit and an emergency room, with helicopter service for burn and trauma victims. Golf may be played year around on two local courses, and tennis, bicycling and other outdoor sports are enjoyed year-round. Hiking and camping are available in the nearby mountains.

Originally, this place was called Hot Springs. Hot, volcanic water runs beneath the town, which residents tap for hot tubs and heating. Obviously, the town was named for these hot springs. But back a few decades, when the radio show "Truth or Consequences" was popular (remember?), the town fathers saw a way to garner a little nationwide publicity by making a deal with Ralph Edwards, who was master of ceremonies. They agreed to name the town *Truth or Consequences* if he would come there to broadcast a show. That was the height of the town's silly season I suppose. It does have a comfortable, small-town atmosphere, but since just about everyone is from somewhere else, there's an openness to strangers not generally found in towns like this. It looks like a pleasant town for quiet retirement, but I'm not sure I'd want the name of the town on my personal stationery.

**ALBUQUERQUE**--High in the desert, sitting on the east bank of the Rio Grande at an altitude of over a mile, Albuquerque is a fast-growing retirement area. The combination of altitude, dry air and mild temperatures are exactly what many people look for in a place to live. It almost never hits 100 degrees, and almost never sees zero. With 43-percent humidity average and 30 percent in the afternoons, the weather seems even milder. July is the hottest month of the year with an average high temperature of around 90 degrees. But the July evenings average only 66 degrees, so air conditioning seems truly redundant here. One retiree reported that he cuts his heating bills considerably with his woodburning stove. "It never gets so cold that a little fire won't warm things up," he said.

Rainfall is a scant 8 inches per year, so the yearly average of sunny weather is a brilliant 78 percent. And the best part is that the winter months of December and January are the sunniest. It's a two-season year, with about 11 inches of snow expected every winter. It doesn't stick around for long, though, because winter days usually see 50 degrees by noon. Muggy days and long, drizzling spells are just about unknown in Albuquerque. Summers can become quite dry, however, causing the mighty Rio Grande to dwindle to a muddy trickle. Once, when Will Rogers was giving a talk in Albuquerque, he cajoled: "Why, you folks ought to be out there right now irrigating that river to keep it from blowing away!"

Albuquerque's biggest drawback is that its name is difficult to spell. The problem with spelling started back in 1706 when the Spanish Duke of Alburquerque decided that this spot, where the old Camino Real crossed the Rio Grande, would be a great place to have a town named after him. But, when they put up the city limits sign, somebody left an "r" out of his name. So, it's been Albuquerque ever since. And schoolkids have been having trouble spelling it ever since. Sure seems like there should be at least one "k" in there somewhere.

With Mexican independence from Spain and later annexation by the United States in 1846, the town began growing. Since it was a crossing for two branches of the famous Santa Fe Trail, and later for a railroad, numerous travelers passed through on their way "West." Many of them paused long enough to decide that they liked Albuquerque, and they stayed. Today it's the crossing of Interstates 25 and 40 that bring travelers, and many are staying once they discover how great the town is for retirement.

The city has taken pains to preserve some of the historic parts of town. This was possible partly because the coming of the railroad in 1880 moved the "downtown" away from the original plaza, thus sparing it from development. Today the area now known as Old Town offers fine restaurants and shops, but keeps the historic flavor of the Old West. Old adobe buildings and museums cluster about the Duke of Alburquerque's village.

The downtown section is clean, modern and amazingly prosperous looking. Everything looks polished and tastefully designed. A pedestrian mall completes the picture of a pleasant city center. The rest of the metropolitan area is also quite pleasant, with many homes designed in an adobe style and lots of huge shade trees in the older areas of town.

Albuquerque is the metropolitan hub of New Mexico. As a high-technology center of the Southwest, it attracts people from all over the country to work and live here. This in part accounts for the prosperous look of the city. The University of New Mexico (25,000 enrollment) accounts for much of the rich cultural offerings of the city. There's a full calendar of lectures, concerts, drama and sporting events. The campus, on the southern part of town (east of downtown), is quite pleasant, and there are numerous classes which interest senior citizens.

Albuquerque is not only the metropolitan hub, it's also in the center of a lot of scenic and recreational country. Almost any direction offers interesting day trips to cultural and scenic marvels. The city enjoys a view of the snowcapped, 10,000-foot Sandia Mountains on the east and a chain of extinct volcanoes on the west. The "Turquoise Trail" (Highway 22) to the north takes you through the old mining towns of Golden, Madrid and Cerillos. To the south on "Mission Trail" (Highway 14) are the Indian pueblos of Gran Quivira, Abo and Quarai. Many Zuñi pueblos are within easy visiting of Albuquerque, and there are Mescalero and Jicarilla Apache, and Navajo reservations not too far away.

Skiing is great, with over 11 facilities within striking distance. Sandia Peak (15 miles northeast of Albuquerque) has lifts that go up to over 10,000 feet. Hunting, fishing, prospecting and rock-hunting are all great outdoor pastimes here. But all outdoor activities don't require going out into the wilderness. For the horse racing fans there are seven tracks, with events starting off at Downs at Albuquerque in January.

## HOUSING

In Albuquerque, over 70 percent of the dwellings are single-family homes. Compared to some parts of the country, Albuquerque prices aren't cheap, but you can buy a pretty nice three-bedroom home for $65,000. Older ones are advertised sometimes as low as $45,000. Mobile home park and apartment rents are moderate.

A particularly beautiful residential area is out of town, near the Sandia Peak Tramway, the longest continuous aerial tramway in the world. The houses here are constructed with nature in mind, each designed to fit in with the gnarled juniper trees, rocks and boulders, and look as if they grew there naturally rather than being built by humans. There's a great view of the city from here. Prices aren't cheap, with prices starting above $100,000, but worth it.

Because of the high numbers of retirees living there, many retirement complexes are available. They seem like pretty good deals. For example, one apartment-type complex offers a studio unit with weekly maid and linen service for $630 monthly *including three meals a day!* It's located in a nice section of town and is near shopping. The quoted rate is for a single person; a couple pays a percentage more.

Places like this assume that you are in good health and capable of getting around without help. Other retirement complexes offer health care as an integral part of the retirement services, and you can expect to pay more. Some of these places require that you buy into the complex for $30,000 on up, plus a monthly fee of around $600 (or more, depending on the size of your apartment). But this is lifetime care, which means that nursing care is included if and when it becomes necessary.

**SANTA FE**--Fifty-nine miles northeast of Albuquerque is the city of Santa Fe (pop. 68,000). This is a town of history. It's the oldest capital city in the United States, founded in 1610 by Don Pedro de Peralta. Santa Fe was a thriving little community 10 years before the Pilgrims made their landing at Plymouth Rock! Santa Fe has been a capital city for over 375 years.

Here you'll find the oldest private house in the United States and the oldest public building in the country, the Palace of the Governors. This building was used as a headquarters when General Kearney captured Santa Fe during the Mexican-American War in 1846. Incidentally, this was the first foreign capital ever captured by the U.S. armed forces.

This is not only a town steeped in history and culture, but it has residents who work very hard at keeping it that way. Strict building codes insist on all new construction being of adobe or adobe-looking material; all exteriors must be of earth tones. This preserves the distinctive Spanish Pueblo style for which Santa Fe is famous. Occasionally one sees a home that was built in the days before the zoning codes, and the blue or white building sticks out like the proverbial sore thumb. At first I felt that the shades of sand, brown and tan were too somber, but after while, I grew to like the atmosphere.

Retirement here is big business. In fact, other than tourism and art, retirement is almost the only industry. The economy is tied to services dealing with tourists, retirees and the art colony. Art is truly important in the everyday life of Santa Fe. There are hundreds of painters, writers and craftsmen, and there are almost 200 galleries full of their treasures. The old plaza in the heart of the city is usually lined with street artisans displaying jewelry, paintings, leather goods and all kinds of quality artwork. Local Indians bring intricate silver and turquoise jewelry here to sell in the plaza.

With such an emphasis on art and culture, it comes as no surprise that Santa Fe has an exceptionally rich offering in this regard. A highly regarded opera company performs in a unique outdoor theater. Fortunately, Santa Fe's weather seldom interferes with the performances. The 1987 season listed five operas during July and August. There are concerts by The Orchestra of Santa Fe, a chamber music festival, the Chorus of Santa Fe, the Desert Chorale and the Santa Fe Symphony. Then there are numerous theater and drama presentations by The New Mexico Repertory Theatre, the British American Theatre Institute, the Armory for the Arts, the Santuario de Guadalupe, the Community Theatre and the Greer Garson Theater. If these aren't enough cultural events, then there are various fiestas and festivals throughout the region and even a rodeo every summer. And, the horses are running at Santa Fe Downs from May to Labor Day.

## COOL, BRISK CLIMATE

"When I get up in the morning, I know there's going to be sun," said a man who retired in Santa Fe after living most of his life in northern Illinois. "It makes a big difference in my life."

Actually Santa Fe is just about tied with Albuquerque for percentage of sunshine. Almost 300 days a year should be at least partly sunny. There is more rain here, though, about twice at much at 15 inches a year, and there's three times as much snow, with about 33 inches. The result is that Santa Fe is greener. You'll find a true four-season year here with winters a little longer and a little cooler than in Albuquerque; not by much, four or five degrees. But summers are remarkably cooler. Average highs in July and August just barely top 80 degrees. Be prepared to wear a sweater on every summer eve-

ning. The temperature typically drops to below 50 degrees at night!
All summer long! For those of you who can't stand to perspire, or
who hate air conditioning, this might be perfect.

The reason for this cool summer climate is the altitude.
Perched high in the foothills of the Sangre de Cristo range, Santa Fe
is at 7,000 feet. Even younger people can notice breathlessness, fa-
tigue and headaches with relatively minor exertion. The idea is to
allow yourself time to acclimate to the higher altitude. If you should
have heart, lung or other medical problems, it's best to check with
your doctor before selecting such a high altitude for retirement.

Housing is curiously mixed in price in Santa Fe. Generally, it is
more expensive than Albuquerque, particularly for nicer housing.
But there are some inexpensive places, although not as many as
there could be. Typical quality housing sells for about $85,000 per
unit, about $20,000 more than in Albuquerque. The problem is that
Santa Fe has such a reputation as a retirement and artist's center that
the outsiders have bid up real estate to an unusual level. "It's getting
so that we natives can't afford to live here, anymore," lamented one
hometown resident. And she is pretty much right. Several houses
were advertised at over $500,000. Occasionally one will come on
the market at $65,000, but these are exceptions; most listings are
over $100,000. Several condos were advertised at around $50,000.
Rentals tend to be high, with $400 being a rather low end for an
apartment or duplex. $500 to $600 is more common. Rentals are at a
premium here. There are a couple of pretty good retirement
residences, but my understanding is there can be a waiting list.

All in all, my analysis of Santa Fe as a retirement possibility is
that it's a town that's best for people with moderate to affluent
means, folks with deep interests in art and culture, and those who
like cool, crisp, sunny weather. It's a great ambiance for writers or
artists who need the company of kindred souls.


## MORE ABOUT TEXAS

We've covered the Rio Grande country, now let's take a look
at other parts of Texas. Again, it's an enormous state with many
places suitable for retirement. An entire book could easily be written
to cover it all. Let's look at a couple of other examples: San Antonio
as an illustration of central and west Texas and as a military-
retirement spot; and Nacogdoches as an example of east Texas.

SAN ANTONIO--Although more in the south-central part of the state, San Antonio (pop. 885,000) is considered by many people as "West Texas" because of its climate. West Texas is dry, and from here on west is the kind of country one expects from the western United States, with brush, cactus and sandy soil. In the summer plants tend to become golden brown, whereas East Texas gets rain all summer long and stays green. To the west of San Antonio is an interesting section known as the "Texas Hill Country," centered around Fredericksburg, which I believe has great potential for a future retirement boom. San Antonio is considered to be at the edge of the Hill Country. It's a pleasant, wooded area of spring-fed streams, with a nice climate.

Settled in 1718 as a military post and a mission, San Antonio was slow in growing. Its original colonists were from the Spanish Canary Islands, to whom many Texans proudly trace their roots. But once Mexico gained its independence, immigrants began coming from all over the world. Mexico encouraged settlement, and soon waves of Irish, Polish and Germans began settling around San Antonio, as well as plenty of Americans from Tennessee and Louisiana. From the very beginning, San Antonio had a cosmopolitan makeup.

This is the home of the famous Alamo, where the heroic defenders stood fast against the army of General Santa Anna (who was also the president of Mexico). All died rather than surrender. The interesting thing was that all of the defenders, from Jim Bowie to Davy Crockett, were Mexican citizens! They had sworn allegiance to Mexico and had become citizens as a condition for immigration.

Today, the Alamo is a fine museum, and together with the nearby San Antonio River shopping-and-restaurant area, has become a prime tourist attraction. This has done a lot to keep urban decay from the heart of the city.

The weather here is warmer than Albuquerque, with highs in the summer in the mid-90s. But summer nights are delightful with temperatures always in the low 70s; just right for shirt-sleeve evenings and for sleeping under a sheet. The humidity is fairly moderate, so the summers are quite tolerable, and swamp coolers work efficiently. The nice thing about San Antonio weather is the winters. The temperature almost never drops below freezing at night and is almost always in the mid-60s even in the coldest month of January. For all practical purposes, there is no winter. Snow? Forget it. Rain? Only about 25 inches a year.

## GOOD LIVING CONDITIONS

The cost of living here is generally low. Residential areas have built up on the fringes of the city, leaving the central area (the older section) pretty much untouched. Homes in this older part of town are bargains, sometimes in the low $30,000s. But much of it is probably not suitable for the majority of retirees. Most prefer to live in the outer rings of subdivisions, out near one of the dozens of new shopping centers. In these newer areas, three-bedroom homes can be bought from $50,000 on up. My brother, a retired Air Force colonel, bought a place for $65,000 that would cost two to three times that in many areas of the country.

Rentals are similarly inexpensive. Apartments start at $300 a month and houses from $400. One reason for the abundance of rentals is the enormous military population which is continuously on the move. Rentals have been built like mad to try to keep up with the floating residents. The bases are on all sides of town, so chances are that one of your neighbors will be in the military should you choose to live in San Antonio.

Since its beginning as a presidio some 280 years ago, San Antonio has carried a military tradition. Today, there are *four* Air Force bases and an Army post. Brooks Air Force Base has one of the finest medical facilities in the country. This alone is an attraction to military retirees, and would draw them even if San Antonio weren't such a nice place to live. Fort Sam Houston is the Army post where the famous Geronimo and his renegade Apaches were confined for a while. Kelly Field, Lackland and Randolph Air Force bases complete the enormous military complex. My understanding is that there are almost 70,000 service personnel and at least twice that many retirees and their families living around San Antonio or towns in the Texas Hills.

San Antonio has more than its share of retirement communities and residences, simply because it has such a large percentage of retirees. But I'd like to describe a different type of complex, one which is limited to military personnel. Called Air Force Village, this large complex is conveniently located across the highway from Brooks Air Force Hospital. The resident here must buy into the complex with a "founder's fee" which starts at $27,265 for a one-bedroom, one-bath unit, up to $73,150 for a deluxe two-bedroom, two-bath, 1,100-sq. ft. apartment. Then with a $325 to $871 fee (depending on the size of the quarters) the resident is entitled to weekly maid service, weekly physician visits, transportation, all utilities and meals. If it's needed, home health care and food delivered to the apartment is provided, as well as 24-hour nursing home care. It's a once-in-a-lifetime deal.

The facilities are top-notch and as spic-and-span as you would expect from a military retirement complex. My impression is that most of the residents are Air Force officers, but it's possible for other military retirees to enter. But it's academic at this point, since there's a waiting list at this particular facility.

**EAST TEXAS--NACOGDOCHES--**Towering pines, rolling hills, vast blue lakes, cypress swamps and Spanish moss; these are characteristic of east Texas. There are bayous, alligators and scented wildflower blossoms galore. East Texas is a showcase of luxuriant nature. All of this is far from the stereotype of Texas as sagebrush and cowboys. Clearly, it's closer to being part of the Deep South. Plantation homes express the life-styles of Old South elegance. This was the first area of Texas to be settled by pioneers from Tennessee and Louisiana, so it's no surprise that their new homes looked the same as the ones left behind.

Much of this country looks great for retirement to me. But one town in particular appealed to my eyes. This is Nacogdoches (pop. 30,000). I visited here in spring 1987, and the town attracted my attention favorably. It seems to be vigorous, prosperous and modern, with none of the run-down qualities that some sleepy Texas towns can have.

My suspicions about this area being good for retirement were confirmed when I learned that Nacogdoches was named one of the top 10 cities in the United States to live by *U.S. News and World Report* in 1982.

Nacogdoches started as a Spanish mission back in 1716 and became a military outpost later. An old Spanish stone fort still stands there, on the campus of Stephen F. Austin State University. The university has 12,000 students and contributes to the cultural atmosphere of the city, and retirees take advantage of this. Also important to retirees are two excellent hospitals and a senior citizen treatment center.

Housing is downright affordable here. Because of an expected expansion of the university, optimistic builders overdid things. The result is an oversupply of housing. Two-bedroom apartments can be found from $175 to $250 a month, and houses for just a little more. Three-bedroom houses are going for as low as $45,000. A retirement complex called Pine Lake Estates offers units from $337 a month, with a lot of services thrown in.

254   *Retirement Choices*

The weather here is typical Deep South: Hot, muggy summers and mild winters. But one retiree there said, "But we make up for it the rest of the year. Things are green and beautiful all year-round. We have flowers blooming until late November." This part of the country catches about 42 inches of rain a year, enough to keep things pretty without making things soggy.

The city seems to have just about everything a person would need, but in case you get itchy for a big city, Dallas is a three-and-a-half hour drive, and Houston is two-and-a-half hours to the south. Add another hour, and you can be at the Galveston beach.

CHAPTER FOURTEEN

# The Ozarks and Tennessee

Next to Florida, Arkansas is the fastest growing state for retirees. It has been estimated that 80 percent of the state's growth comes from people 65 and older. Almost a fifth of the population is over 60! Retirees choose this part of the country for several reasons besides the exceptionally low cost of living. Arkansas enjoys a mild, four-season climate, low taxes, extremely low crime rates, inexpensive property and friendly people who welcome tourists with sincerity. Additionally, the Ozarks--where most choose to retire--are famous for picturesque, low mountains, with clear-running streams and sparkling clean air.

Over the past few years, an enormous influx of retirees has changed Arkansas from a sleepy, mid-southern state into a retirement mecca for more and more people. The overwhelming majority of these immigrants come from midwestern or northern states. For this reason, newcomers don't feel the social isolation in Arkansas that they might in more insular Deep South states like Mississippi or Alabama. A person from Detroit or Chicago feels immediately at home in the friendly atmosphere of Arkansas, and has no problem forming camaraderie with others from his part of the country and his social class.

As an example of retiree population boom, the little town of Heber Springs, a few miles north of Little Rock, reports that population grew from 2,500 in 1962 to over 6,000 today. The vast majority of the newcomers were pensioners. Bank deposits jumped more than twentyfold, from $4.4 million 25 years ago to well over $100 million today. As more retired people moved into town, retail sales climbed dramatically, as did service-type jobs for local people. The townspeople readily acknowledge the advantages of having lots of new neighbors who put pension dollars and Social Security money into circulation. The more the dollars circulate, the more prosperous becomes Heber Springs.

One couple in Fairfield Bay (on Greers Ferry Lake, north of Little Rock) originally retired in Florida. But after a few years there, they visited this little Ozark town, and soon after, decided to move to Arkansas. The wife explained, "We got tired of worrying about crime in Miami. It was as bad as living back home in Chicago. And here, our property taxes are at least $2,000 a year less than in Chicago, even though our house is twice the size and quality as the one we sold when we retired."

The new population is bringing other things besides new money; it's bringing new political balances. Since many retirees are well-to-do, they tend to be more conservative politically. This traditionally Democratic state is gaining more Republicans daily, much to the delight of the Republican party workers. A state party official says, "When I started campaigning in north Arkansas in the '60s, it was like pulling teeth to find people to come out and help you. This movement of new faces into the state has had a tremendous impact on Arkansas politics. People in the Republican party are no longer considered carpetbaggers."

Another political impact comes from the state legislature. Always sensitive to such a large bloc of voters, the lawmakers spend more money per capita on services for elderly than any other state in the country. This results in some very active senior citizens organizations which take full advantage of state and federal monies.

The retirement industry in Arkansas has become a big business. Retirement complexes are popping up all over in the northern part of the state in an effort to keep up with the demand. Land is inexpensive, so developers can buy huge tracts of forested hills, and create some lakes and a golf course or two, all at a fraction of what land alone might cost in some places. And the country is scenic, so outside of clearing away enough woods to plant a home or a mobile home, there isn't much landscaping to be done. This permits developers to put more into quality housing and recreational facilities.

A surprising number of people plunk down cash to pay for their new places. Often the equity in their old homes covers all expenses of a new and better home, without the need for financing.

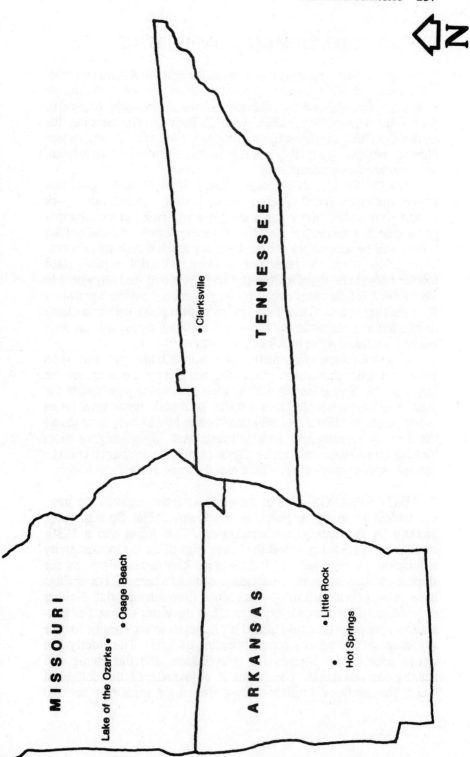

## HERMETICALLY SEALED COMMUNITIES

A point that real estate salesmen for certain Arkansas retirement communities often make, sometimes not too subtly, is the almost complete absence of minorities. Some of the more expensive places are hermetically sealed, with 24-hour guards manning the entrances. The salesmen will emphatically deny there is any racism implied, but they invariably manage to make a point of the whites-only nature of their community.

The Ozarks are mobile home country. If you're looking for that kind of life-style, you'll have no trouble finding a mobile home park to suit your tastes. Many parks advertise vacancies in the newspaper, a clue that spaces are plentiful and inexpensive, and that mobile homes will be reasonably priced. Monthly space rentals usually cost from $50 to $100, the latter rate including all utilities paid. Used mobile homes are about as low-priced as you will find anywhere in the country, for the simple reason that you are not paying a premium for a parking space. There are a few run-down parks for extra-cheap living, but as a rule, the mobile home facilities are as nice as anywhere I've seen--yet at rock-bottom prices.

If you want the convenience of a mobile home, yet want it on your own land, this is the place for you. Except for some of the larger towns, few areas restrict the kind of housing you choose for your land. Many people place a trailer or mobile home on a lot as living quarters while they build their home. More often, they install the unit as a permanent living arrangement. Some mighty nice-looking farms nestle in Ozark valleys, complete with barns, chicken houses, woods and pasture, with a mobile home as the farm house.

**HOT SPRINGS**--One of the more attractive areas of the state, yet typical in many respects, is the town of Hot Springs (pop. 38,000). A fascinating combination of 1920s resort and a 1980s small city, Hot Springs sits at the lower edge of the Ozarks, as pretty a location as you will find anywhere. The town clings to the sloping-to-steep sides of a mountain canyon where 45 hot springs have poured forth steaming water since time immemorial. Neither drought nor rainy seasons seems to affect the water's flow. For generations, people who could afford it journeyed to the springs to take advantage of the water's reputed healing qualities. The elderly and infirm soak in the springs for rejuvenation, and the young and healthy for relaxation. The bonus is enjoyment of the delightful Ozark surroundings. Fresh mountain air and the smell of pines and sassafras trees probably aid as much as the mineral waters. The magic waters are reputed to heal everything from rheumatism to constipation. Maybe, but the water tastes just like water to me, no smell or flavor, nothing odd floating in it, just as water is supposed to be.

For decades Hot Springs held a reputation as a gambling and nightclub attraction for those in the know. The wealthy came to play roulette and slot machines in the fancy casinos. They could rub elbows with the elite of the crime syndicate, who also vacationed in Hot Springs. Everything was first class. It was a kind of mid-country Las Vegas. Restaurants, hotels, businesses catered to the visitors who came for casino action first and hot springs second.

Today, casino gambling is gone. Visitors are once again the elderly and infirm who make the pilgrimage to bathe in soothing water. But these days, there's a new breed of visitor, the visitor who decides to become a resident, the visitor who brings retirement money instead of gambling money.

Hot Springs, like many other Ozark areas, boasts new, quality senior citizens complexes and excellent mobile home parks. It also offers some excellent buys in homes and condos. The local newspaper listed a "fixer-upper" two-bedroom home for $17,900, and a three-bedroom lakefront home for $39,000. Rentals are outrageously cheap. Three-bedroom houses rent for $300 or less a month, many for $200 to $275. Furnished apartments seem to be plentiful, ranging from $150 to $300 a month. Some are advertised as weekly rentals, a great way to see if you like a town without living out of suitcases in a motel.

**HOT SPRINGS VILLAGE**--One of the more impressive of these retirement complexes is Hot Springs Village, a self-contained community about 15 miles from the city of Hot Springs. It isn't particularly inexpensive, but it's certainly first-class and gives you your money's worth. Condos start at $60,000 and houses from $85,000 for new units. Compared to retirement complexes I've seen in Arizona, Florida and California, however, these homes are great values.

This development started with about 21,000 acres of Ozark foothill wilderness, rolling to steep hills, covered with hardwood forest and a scattering of pines. Roughly one-third of the property has been converted into lakes and golf courses (four of them). Another third of the land is in homesites, and the remaining third in forest that is not to be developed. The architectural planning is unique in that almost all of the homesites are arranged so that none of the houses will ever have another lot touching its backyard. Every backyard has either forest or golf course at its edge.

In order to keep from having the property open to the public, the developers chose to build and maintain their own roads. This way, they have complete control of who gets into the complex. They've managed to get their own division of the county police force to patrol the roads. Because of this, and because there are very few juveniles living there, crime is said to be virtually non-existent.

## OTHER ARKANSAS TOWNS

Like the Missouri Ozarks to the north, there are numerous small towns in northern Arkansas where living is quiet and attractive for those who demand little in the way of cultural stimulation. Crime is negligible, property is cheap and neighbors are friendly. Good farmland can be purchased for $1,500 an acre, including fences. Some have retirement communities and retirement population from out of state, and some don't.

If you are a city person, the problem here is that you may not find the company of people from your own background and interests. This may not be important to you, particularly if all you want out of retirement is peace and quiet, a place where you can grow vegetables, have a milk cow and a few laying hens. You can be sure that your neighbors will be pleasant, but will you have anything in common? I looked at a lovely Arkansas farm of 36 cleared acres, fenced, with a live stream winding through the property and a modern three-bedroom, two-bath brick home, all for an asking price of $110,000. Of course, I'm not particularly interested in farming, but when I discovered that the farm was in a dry county, my interest dissolved into powder. Dry farming isn't in my bag of tricks.

## DRY COUNTIES

When selecting a retirement spot in a small town, one of the things you might consider is whether the county permits the sale of alcohol. Many counties in Arkansas, Texas, Missouri, Illinois, Kentucky and other states give counties the right to prohibit booze.

Now, maybe you don't drink and you feel such an arrangement is perfectly all right because it won't affect you. Yet there are some things you may not have considered about living in a dry county.

For one thing, maybe you've been used to dining out once or twice a week. You like to go somewhere nice, with a steak-and-lobster menu, and other treats. You can be sure that where there are no liquor licenses, you will almost never find a "good" restaurant. Typically, the best restaurant in town will consist of a formica counter and a row of chrome-and-plastic booths. The featured special of the evening will be chicken-fried steak and mashed potatoes. Don't misunderstand: I love chicken-fried steak, once in a while.

Another thing to consider is that when a county votes to go dry, you can be sure that the local church organization is all-powerful and persuasive. Dry counties don't happen, they are achieved by skillful and sometimes coercive political action by one or more churches. If you feel comfortable in a community where a couple of preachers and their congregations direct politics and control public morals, then fine. Me, I have a hard enough time minding my own morals.

And, finally, never think that making a county dry stops drinking. It simply means that people will drive 10 or 20 miles to the next county, have a few snorts, load the trunk with beer, then happily weave their way back home. Young people, not having cocktail lounges or bars around, tend to do a lot more driving around and drinking in their automobiles. What's prohibited always has more attraction for youth.

All in all, I think you'll find that northern Arkansas offers some fine retirement spots. It will take some on-the-spot investigation and a bit of living experience, however. Different towns vary widely in their advantages and disadvantages, in the kind of people they are home to, and in the convenience of their shopping and recreational activities.

## MISSOURI OZARK TOWNS

Ozark country covers much of the southern part of Missouri as well as northern Arkansas. The main difference lies in the heavier population farther north, particularly as you get closer to Kansas City and St. Louis. There, population pressures push more and more people into the northern fringe of the Ozarks. With good highways, property here is within commuting distance for many who want to escape the hassles of city living.

But even with more people moving here, the Ozarks still haven't grown crowded, nor will they ever likely be. One reason the

Ozarks country has been spared is that its land, lush and green as it looks, isn't particularly good for farming. Much of the countryside is in small, rounded mountains that give the Ozarks their character. The country is full of rocky hillsides, unsuited to plows and farm machinery. Even in the level valleys, much of the land is of decomposed limestone, brick red and reluctant to yield rich crops. Hickory trees, pines and oaks do well, however, covering an immense area with marvelous forests. To be sure, there are plenty of small farms carved out of the woods, and crops are grown, but it's obvious that farming isn't the big business enterprise here as it is in other parts of Missouri.

If the land were as fertile and productive as the Mississippi River floodplains, you'd probably see the Ozarks denuded and planted in soybeans and wheat for export to Russia or someplace. The happy fact is that most of this country is wild and beautiful, open mostly for recreational living. And the closer to mid-state you get, the better the shopping and service facilities. Land is cheap. The farther into the mountains, the cheaper it gets. There are some beautiful wild and scenic rivers, particularly the Current River, which runs as impressive and free as it did a thousand years ago.

Years ago, before the development of retirement communities, most "outsiders" who owned Ozark property had rustic accommodations, often log cabins, and used them as summer retreats or as fall hunting lodges. Most cabin owners lived in St. Louis or other large cities and prized their backwoods hideaways, wanting to keep things just as rustic as possible. Kerosene lamps and wood stoves were part of the ambiance. Local residents were remarkably isolated from the outside world, with accents that marked them indelibly as "Ozark." Some communities are still this way, tucked into narrow valleys and separated from civilization by miles of gravel roads. But today, television and paved roads have exposed even the most remote areas to our modern-day ideas of civilization.

As in Arkansas, developers are taking advantage of low property costs and free scenic values to attract retirees. Several new complexes are underway near scenic Lake of the Ozarks. This is a large, man-made lake formed by the construction of Bagnell Dam on the Osage river back in the 1930s. For years, the lake was simply a place where people went to pitch a tent or rent a crude cabin and do some bass fishing. The lake is 94 miles long, with over a thousand miles of shoreline. But today, with good highways and pressures from people looking for retirement havens, things are changing. Houses, condos and mobile home parks are sprouting up, and many of the purchasers are senior citizens. Since it is in between St. Louis and Kansas City (a little closer to Kansas City), the lake attracts retirees from both cities.

I investigated one retirement development on the lake, near the town of Camdenton (pop. 2,300). Called Autumn Village, the development consists of single-story, brick homes constructed in four-plex. The quality seems good, and for a price of $59,000 to $77,000, you get air conditioning and such appliances as microwave, dishwasher, washer/dryer and refrigerator. The development features a large clubhouse, a boat launch, an RV parking area and is adjacent to a country club that has tennis courts, an 18-hole golf course and a restaurant.

The developer admitted that there were many nearby condos and homes for sale, possibly at lower prices than in Autumn Village, and rentals at very low cost. But he pointed out that the population of the area varies from none in winter to too many in the summer. "This presents problems of loneliness in winter and overcrowding in the summer," he said. "Since a lot of homes in the lake area are second homes, you find summer kids and friends crowding in for vacations. And, even when one of these developments has a clubhouse, on rainy days it's taken over by children." He was quite proud of the social program that Autumn Village had developed.

Many more ordinary developments are being built on the shores of the lake, and some older homes, both on the lake and a few miles inland, are bargains. The farther away from the lake you go, the fewer pressures there are from vacationers, making property less expensive. The tourist aspect seems to be a mixed blessing. On the one hand, it creates a demand for better services--shopping, restaurants and the like. This attracts retirees from larger cities and raises the social level of the area from provincialism. But it does bring erratic waves of population. Even though residents sometime complain about this, I think that they don't know what crowds are until they visit Fort Lauderdale during semester break.

## CLIMATE

Every retiree I talked to in the Ozarks mentioned the four-season climate as one of the pluses of living there. "I like to know what time of year it is," said one lady who had lived in California for some years before retirement. "Here, I get the feeling for the seasons. Summer is nice and warm, fall is beautiful and colorful, winter is short and merciful, and then comes spring!" She sighed in ecstasy. It was springtime when I was interviewing people there.

The average highs for December are over 50 degrees, and snowfall is infrequent, but pretty. But make no mistake, it is winter, and there will be ice on the puddles in the mornings. Still, it doesn't begin to compare with winters farther north. Summers are humid, but not unbearable, with 92-degree highs normal. There is enough rain in the summer to keep things looking green and fresh in the Ozarks, enough water to keep streams flowing and fishing good year-round. While summers aren't exactly seashore cool, they compare favorably when measured against the steambath summers of St. Louis or Kansas City.

## TENNESSEE

Western Tennessee, in some ways, is much the same as the adjacent parts of Missouri and Arkansas. This is farming country, with broad stretches of flat to rolling land, fields hedged with rows of trees, neat and prosperous-looking farmhouses, barns and silos. The smaller towns look pretty much like any in Middle America. Memphis and Little Rock are the larger cities in this area. They have their good points to be sure, but my feeling is that they offer little more in the way of retirement advantages than most other midwestern and mid-southern locations. However, as you travel east in Tennessee, the country changes, gradually growing more scenic with every mile. You're heading toward the Appalachian Mountains. Before long you find yourself in foothill country. And I mean *country*.

Some of the smaller towns I've visited in backwoods Tennessee are the most isolated places I've ever seen in the United States. I recall getting lost and ending up in a little town tucked away between two forested hills. I stopped to ask directions how to get back to the main highway. I couldn't have generated more curiosity on the part of the natives had I come from outer space. (In a way, I suppose, I had.) From the general store, the gasoline station, the pool hall and several white frame houses, people poured out on the street to stare at me. The staring eyes weren't hostile, just dumbfounded that someone from "outside" would come to visit. This was probably the most exciting event to happen in several days. When a couple of men tried to explain to me where I took the wrong turn that sent me to their village, I had difficulty understanding their

English. It was thickly accented with an archaic "southern drawl" that clearly had its roots in early English settlers from the 18th century.

As an anthropologist, I was immediately fascinated. Apparently the surrounding hills had severed this little hamlet from the leveling influence of television. When this happens, people not only tend to retain their accents in the original, pure form, but they also hold onto customs, beliefs, legends and behavior patterns that are virtual gold mines for anthropological research. I felt positive that I would have had a great time trying to worm my way into the social structure of the village. What a paper I could write! It wouldn't be easy, because people seemed quite shy and uneasy talking to a "fur-riner."

But, I don't think I'd care to retire there. The town had fewer than 1,000 residents, most of whom wore either bib overalls or sun-bonnets. Since few readers of this book are deeply into anthro-pological research, I don't imagine many would be willing to put up with the exaggerated isolation in a village like this. Being an out-sider might be a novelty at first, but after a while it could get pretty darn lonely.

As I traveled through other parts of Tennessee and Kentucky, I discovered that insular villages like this aren't all that rare. Yes, the scenery is fantastic, with picturesque log cabins, overgrown with moss and vines. Land prices and housing are next to free. The weather is mild, with four clearly defined seasons, and not too frigid in the winter. Still it takes a certain type of personality to "fit in" with a community like this. The point is: Don't assume that because the cost of living is low, housing prices are cheap, and the FBI crime statistics look good you've found your retirement goal. Yet, if you come from a small town, particularly a small southern town, you might enjoy living here.

**CLARKSVILLE**--Don't get the idea that all of Tennessee is like this, any more than all of Arkansas or Missouri are back-woodsy. A particularly pleasant part of Tennessee, one where even New Yorkers wouldn't feel out of place, is a town near the Ken-tucky border, about a 40-minute drive northwest from Nashville. It's called Clarksville. The population is 70,000, large enough to be a city, yet small enough that friends are constantly honking greetings to each other as they drive around town. Shopping malls and com-plexes are as large and complete as you could hope for in a much larger city, yet the clerks are as friendly and helpful as in a smaller town.

The thing that takes Clarksville out of the realm of backwoods, inbred communities is the large U.S. Army installation in Fort Campbell, just across the border in Kentucky. Not only are the people perfectly used to a multi-faceted cultural mix, but many residents themselves were once outsiders who lived in Clarksville as part of the military. As in other areas with large military installations, when retirement decisions are made, the pleasant times spent in Clarksville weigh heavily on the balance scales.

Fort Campbell is the home of the 101st Airborne "Screaming Eagles." Here is the training ground and base of the only air assault division in our armed forces. The helicopter is the primary means of transport, and there is a high degree of pride among the soldiers. About two-thirds of the base's 105,000 acres are in Tennessee, butting against the Clarksville city limits. But since the post office is in Kentucky, that state has the honor of claiming Fort Campbell. Military retirees enjoy base PX privileges and Army hospitalization benefits. The fort, almost a city in itself, has a post population of 37,432, with a post-exchange as large as a shopping center, plus seven on-post schools for military dependents. Military and retirees come from all parts of the country, and contribute much toward making the area cosmopolitan.

The town was named after General George Rogers Clark, the famous Indian fighter and Revolutionary War hero. Situated on the bluffs of the mighty Cumberland River, where the Red River joins in, Clarksville lay along the natural transportation route of early pioneers traveling west from North Carolina. The settlers found good farming land on level-to-gently-rolling terrain. The town quickly became a center of tobacco and cotton agriculture. One standout feature of the countryside is the presence of tobacco barns. Ancient-looking, tall, built of loosely spaced boards, these barns are for curing chewing tobacco and snuff. During the season, aromatic wisps of smoke filter through the barn's boards as hanging sheaves of tobacco are smoke-cured and prepared for market. It smells so good, I sometimes almost wish I chewed tobacco. But I tried that once when I was about 13 and was cured instantly of that habit.

The early-day prosperity of the tobacco plantations shows clearly in the beautiful antebellum mansions in town. Set back from the street among magnificent oaks and magnolia trees, surrounded by acres of lawn, these old homes are among the best preserved in the South. This idea of large lawns carries right over into today's housing styles. Big lots are in. Humble, two-bedroom homes often sit on enormous lots with awesome expanses of lawn--awesome because of the amount of energy people spend there to cut the grass. Yet they all tell you with straight faces that they enjoy yardwork. Another awesome aspect to homes in this part of Tennessee is the price. Housing is downright cheap.

One factor contributing to a robust renter's market is the military presence and the abundance of inexpensive rentals it encourages. Monthly apartment rentals range from less than $100 to $300, and houses from less than $200 on up. From a May 2, 1987, copy of the *Clarksville Leaf-Chronicle* come the following rental examples: Unfurnished apartments: Large two-bedroom, air-conditioned, washer & dryer, $240. Two-bedroom near hospital, $200. The most expensive apartment listed was for $300, one which was near Fort Campbell. Unfurnished houses: Two bedrooms, downtown, air conditioning, $200. Three-bedroom brick, $375. Four-bedroom brick, two baths $350. The highest rental offered was $450 for a three-bedroom brick with stove, refrigerator, dishwasher and full basement.

Homes for sale included: Three-bedroom brick on one acre, two storage buildings, spa, apple trees, $35,000. Two-bedroom frame with full basement, garage, air conditioner, $17,500. Three-bedroom brick on six acres, fenced pasture, plus farm buildings, $38,000. The most expensive home advertised was a four-bedroom brick, two baths, on a cul-de-sac for $67,950. Farm property is particularly low-priced, with acreage often going for less than $1,000 an acre. A 35-acre piece, just two miles from the city limits--with a barn, well and ponds--was priced at $40,000. Another farm, near the famous Between the Lakes area, was priced at $49,000, for 89 acres and a log home. For the serious farmer, there was a 160-acre spread with a house, buildings and city water for $135,000.

I have a friend who is a contractor in Clarksville. He says, "I can build you a three-bedroom brick home with a basement and a two-car garage for $35,000." He showed me some he had constructed, and they were impressive, indeed. The secret to low-cost construction here is low wages. "I pay my foreman $11.00 an hour," he explains. "That's because he knows everything from electrical to carpentry. Bricklayers are happy to work for $9.00 an hour, carpenters for $8.00. Plumbers get $12.00." When I told him what plumbers earn in my neighborhood, he wouldn't let me near any of his workmen for fear I might accidentally mention it. There's an interesting method of building garages in this area. Most homes are built of brick, with the garage attached to one side as an integral part of the house. The garage doors are then located in the rear, with a circular drive going around the house. This makes the house look much larger than it actually is. This sense of large homes on large lots gives Tennessee a look of class that belies the actual cost of property.

Clarksville has plenty to do considering its size. Austin Peay State University is located here, with an active theater department that produces five shows a season, ranging from comedy to serious theater, and even musicals. A Jazz Festival is held in March, and a Spring Opera in May. Guest artist recitals are offered throughout the year, with admission free to the public. Fort Campbell has an entertainment services office and it produces seven theatrical productions a year, open to the public. There are three golf courses, three boat ramps and three community centers. Nashville is less than an hour away by interstate highway, with its many attractions, sports and recreational opportunities. Most famous among them is the Grand Ole Opry and Opryland, heavily attended by tourists, and obligatory when out-of-town guests come to visit.

The Cumberland River is another major source of recreation. Running between majestic bluffs, the river is scenic and placid, offering great boating. Houseboats are numerous, engaged in leisurely fishing and cruising along hundreds of miles of river and lakes. There are plenty of coves and wooded banks on which to tie up and spend a few quiet days.

Thirty miles to the west of Clarksville is the little town of Dover and the gateway to the Land Between the Lakes. This is a 170,000-acre wilderness area that stretches over a narrow peninsula, 40 miles between Kentucky Lake and Lake Barkley. Almost 90 percent of this area is in unspoiled forest, with just a few scattered farms and some facilities for boat launching, hunting and fishing. Some of the retirees from Clarksville have moved into Dover, mostly because of the exceptionally low housing costs, peaceful living and proximity to hunting and fishing in the Land Between the Lakes.

The Cumberland joins with the Tennessee River here, and this is the site of Fort Donelson National Military Park, where General Grant made a great breakthrough in the Civil War by bringing the war into southern territory for the first time. Dover is an interesting town, but verges on being provincial since it is a long way from any big city. It's about a two-hour drive to Nashville from Dover over winding roads.

East from Nashville, along Interstate 40 or southeast on Interstate 24, brings you to the blue ridges of the Appalachians and some truly beautiful country. This country is similar to the North and South Carolina areas described in Chapter 9. The Great Smoky Mountains National Park straddles the line between Tennessee and North Carolina, with nearby Asheville and Knoxville the major population centers.

CHAPTER FIFTEEN
_____

## *Unusual Retirements*

While most people tend to retire close to home, others prefer to move away for at least part of each year. But a few--those with a more keenly developed sense of adventure--search for alternatives full of challenge and excitement. After all, for the first time in your life, you are free to do anything you want. *Anything.* You can go anywhere you please. You don't have to explain, you don't have to apologize to *anybody.* Why not take advantage of this freedom? Why sit in a dreary living room, your eyes glued to a TV set, growing older with each episode of *Family Feud* or *Wheel of Fortune?* There's a world of adventure out there, just waiting for you to gather the nerve to give it a try! Of all the retirees I've interviewed, the most vibrant, the most youthful were those who chose to pack adventure and travel into their lives. "When you're having fun, you don't have time to grow old," is the way one lady put it. "It takes a little courage to get started but, oh, is it ever worth it!"

Okay, you will have some income, probably not a bundle, maybe just Social Security. What can you do with that? Plenty! All it takes is a little spunk and your creative imagination to enjoy a life that will be the envy of everyone you know. You can travel about the country, visiting places you've only read about, making new friends at every turn, enjoying nothing but good weather, and doing it all on your Social Security check! You can travel to many fascinating foreign countries, learn new languages, enter totally new worlds, and maybe *save* a little money from your Social Security check. In fact, later we're going to investigate an alternative that offers safe, fulfilling adventures abroad, all expenses paid! You can save *all* of your Social Security check and receive a cash bonus besides! Your potential for creative retirement is unlimited.

It appears obvious to me that the most dangerous pitfall of retirement is a television set. Far too many people, young and old, spend far too many hours staring at colored pictures on a screen. Statistics on how many hours a day children watch TV are frightening. But at least when the kids aren't sitting in front of the tube, they are running about, leaping and playing, getting some exercise. But older TV junkies tend to get little exercise outside of changing channels. Statistics show that senior citizens spend surprisingly little time running about and even less time leaping. Television watching can be the cause of physical disintegration, and a shortened retirement--not to mention a boring retirement.

Therefore, allow me to present my favorite chapter on retirement alternatives. This part of the research was most enjoyable, in large part because the kind of people who choose interesting retirement alternatives tend to be interesting, happy people. Yet most hadn't been particularly adventuresome before retirement. They couldn't *afford* adventures, not while raising children and working at jobs to keep up the house payments and expenses. A fast and hectic three-week vacation was the best they could manage, then back to the drudgery of the workaday routine. Then, before they had time to think, they were retired, and suddenly free. No more nine-to-five routine, no more three-week vacations.

This chapter looks at three alternative lifestyles for retirement. Check them out and see if they possibly coincide with some of your dreams, or fit your personality. They aren't impossible, and they don't have to be expensive.

## LIVING ON WHEELS

Not a new concept, but certainly a growing one, is traveling the country in recreational vehicles (RVs). Most people look upon RVs strictly as weekend or vacation affairs. That's understandable, because that's all the time most people can afford to spend in them. But a large number of retirees (who are on permanent vacation) use RVs as periodic homes, sometimes as *permanent* homes. Most pack up their summer clothes and head for Arizona or Florida each winter, parking their "rigs" in the warm sunshine until spring thaws out the ground "back home." But a growing number are opting for full-time living in trailers or motor homes. Part-time or full-time, it's fun, and it's inexpensive (if you *want* it to be inexpensive).

Initial investment in an RV varies widely, from cheap to outrageous, all depending on the customer's pocketbook and needs. Some of today's rigs are so luxurious, with furnishings so well designed, they make staying at home seem like living in a slum. Other rigs are old, plain-looking and cheap. But they're livable. You can pay well over $100,000 for a super-equipped diesel motor home, or $750 for a two-wheel camping trailer. The essential features are wall-to-wall floors and a roof that sheds water. From there you can add all sorts of extras, from microwave ovens to bidets. I understand some travelers have put as much as $250,000 into their "rigs." The main thing is that your rolling home be comfortable and homelike.

The most obvious advantage in movable housing is that you can choose your favorite climate, your favorite season in your preferred geographical location. When the climate begins to change or the season draws to a close, or you become bored with the scenery, you simply start your engine and move on to the next location.

Another often-stated advantage is that it's easier to visit friends and relatives who are scattered around the country. One couple I interviewed has two sons living on the West Coast, a son in New Jersey and a daughter in Miami. "We make it a point to spend a month each year visiting," explained June, a petite brunette who helps drive the 30-foot motor home. "We never wear out our welcome, and we have our own home. We don't have to interfere with our children's privacy by staying in their house."

So, you like to fish? No problem--find an RV park where you can back your rig up to the riverbank, unhook your boat trailer and send your husband after bait. Want to visit cities? Most large towns have RV facilities somewhere near the center. If not, simply park your rig in a supermarket parking lot, flick on the TV and you are home for the evening. Ocean beaches, mountain forests, fishing streams, New England villages--the whole world is at your windshield. Even foreign travel is possible--there are RV facilities anywhere you look in Mexico, or at least anywhere you would care to travel with an RV. Winters find huge numbers of RVs camping along the Pacific coast south of the border, while summers see them headed for Canada. I met one couple who owned a VW camper and are proud of having traveled through Europe, South America, and even through India, shipping their camper by freighter from place to place.

I hear you saying, "What? *Me*--leave all my 'things' and become a homeless nomad? How can I possibly get by without a home?" Most traveling people have roots somewhere, even if it's just a storage facility where they store their "things." And, if you've ever traveled for a few months at a time, as I have, you quickly learn that all of those belongings you have stuffed around the nooks and crannies of your house aren't essential. My last trip was a 10,000-mile, 10-week jaunt in which I had to keep clothing and "things" to a bare minimum. I developed a system of regular visits to the laundromat and cleaners so that I would never run short of clean clothes. I got along just fine on a suitcase of clothing. When I returned home, I had almost forgotten about all the clothes hanging in my closet. I certainly didn't miss them!

## FULL TIME VS. PART TIME

The majority of RVs on the road are temporary (or "part-timers," as the RV crowd terms them). Their owners keep a homebase somewhere--a house or a mobile home--as a permanent address, and then use their RV for long-term travel. They look on this as a sort of leisurely vacation extension of their retirement scheme. Others are truly serious about RV living, and spend full time traveling about the world, carrying their homes with them. These adventurers have turned the concept of RV living into an interesting subculture, complete with their own clubs, social networks and even their own news magazines.

The largest club for RV owners is known as "Good Sam." You'll know when a person belongs to Good Sam, because there's usually a funny-looking emblem stuck on his rig, a cartoon of a man with a halo over his head. With 560,000 members in the United States and Canada, it's supported by both casual and serious RVers. An offshoot of *Trailer Life* Magazine, the Good Sam club furnishes emergency road service for RVs, something other insurance companies are reluctant to do. A monthly magazine called *Hi-Way Herald* goes to all of the members, giving news of local chapter events, jamborees, caravans and an action line to help solve members' problems. There's even a travel agency, and caravans venture up to Alaska, and down to Mexico. They offer discounts for repairs, parts and campgrounds. Mail forwarding, trip routing, and a lost-pet service is provided for members. This club is a must for RV enthusiasts. The address is: Good Sam Club, Box 501, Agoura, CA 91301; 800-423-5061. (*Trailer Life* also publishes another magazine called *MotorHome*.)

The most important club for "full-timers" is an organization called Escapees, or S.K.P., as they call themselves. The national headquarters is at Rte #5, Box 310, Livingston, TX 77351. The club publishes a monthly news magazine, *Escapees*, which brings news of where members are heading for the season, new places to park, tips on equipment maintainence and hints for making life easier for people who make their homes in moveable tin boxes. People write in to tell where they are and what they've been doing so their friends can keep in touch with them. An S.K.P. member told me, "We feel like we're part of a large, close-knit family. Another service of the club is a mail forwarding and message service. An 800 telephone number takes phone messages from friends and relatives and the messages are retrieved by calling the same number. Mail is forwarded automatically."

Kay Peterson, one of the founders of Escapees, has written several books on RV living, one called *Home Is Where You Park It,* and another titled *Full Time RVing, Is It For You?* (RoVing Press, Box 2870, Estes Park, CO 80517). Another important book is *Guide to Full-Time RVing,* by Don Wright (published by Trailer Life, Agoura, Calif. These books are musts for anyone thinking about a mobile life-style alternative. The books explain how to choose your moveable home, what life is like in a home on wheels, adjusting to a life among strangers, just about everything you might want to know. But don't get the idea that this is a lonely life, or a homeless existence. People are more neighborly "on the road" than they ever would be at home. Kay Peterson says, "We can live on the road and still have our pets. We can still grow plants. We can still cook gourmet meals. We can still make our own clothes or carry a portable workshop with us. We are not homeless. We are, in fact, the ultimate homemakers who make everywhere we go *home."*

## RV PEOPLE ARE SPECIAL

That should be self-evident. It takes a certain type of person to want to pack everything into a motor home or trailer and leave his life behind for the open road. You don't have to be a gypsy, but you have to have some of that gypsy spirit of adventure. My first introduction to an S.K.P. member came in Grants Pass, Ore. There, at an AARP meeting, I met a delightfully interesting lady named Beulah who maintained a duplex in Grants Pass as a summer home base and used a 28-foot motor home for her "roving manor." Beulah wasn't quite the type I had figured for a snowbird, because she was a wisp of a woman, small and shapely, a retired school teacher from Hawaii who, surprising to me, had just celebrated her 74th birthday. I'm convinced that the active, interesting life she led contributed to her looking so youthful. As a widow, she felt she faced a rather lonely existence if she didn't get out and face the world. So she investigated RV living, and the opportunities it presented for making friends and a social life. She decided to join S.K.P. and become a winter snowbird. Then she discovered another travel organization, this one for single people just like her, called "Loners on Wheels" (or LoW). "These two clubs made a big difference in my life," she said enthusiastically. "I have a support group of instant friends wherever I go. Luckily, I found a reliable tenant for my duplex, one who watches over things while I'm gone, and every October, I just close up my half of the duplex and away I go!" She drives her motor home clear across the country to Florida and back every year. But to Beulah, the fun is in traveling to and fro as much as just being in the destination site. She explained that it takes at least a month each way. "I've made so many friends that almost every campground I stop at, someone knows me."

Beulah gave us tips on where to seek out other "full-timers" and "part-timers" and where to interview people. "A great place to start," she said, "is at *Slab City*. You will see a full spectrum of RV people. Some will have $100,000 rigs and others will have piles of junk. They've made a winter RV *city* there. I stay there at least a week every year, on my way to Florida. I just love it!"

Where in the world is Slab City? It's a 600-acre piece of desert a few miles east of Nyland, Calif., near the Salton Sea. This used to be the training quarters of General George Patton during World War II. All that's left is a network of paved roads and a lot of concrete slabs where barracks and other buildings used to be. I arrived there in January, when the population was at its peak. (It's all but abandoned in the summer.) My estimate would be around a thousand RVs parked in this sagebrush and sand expanse. Some parked away from others, as if seeking solitude, while others clustered together in small "neighborhoods."

I interviewed several people and I received similar answers from all: "This is our winter home, and we hope it will never change." What about security? "We feel safer here by far than in the city. Here, we all watch out for each other. If a troublemaker tries to move in, he either changes his attitude or leaves because of isolation. No one steals or vandalizes, even though we might leave our rigs here for a week or two while we go visiting elsewhere."

Most RVs were clustered together in groups of three or four, and many displayed a conversational grouping of chairs under a shady awning as an open invitation for people to drop in for a visit and a chat. When I remarked about how friendly everyone seemed, one man said, "That's the way it is everywhere with snowbirds. If you don't like neighbors, you won't like RV living."

"What will my family say?" is a question that comes up, particularly in the case of single women. One woman, who left her home in New England to travel full-time, said, "My daughters don't like the idea. They miss being able to drop in and visit any time they care to. And they miss not having me to help them with their little problems. But I figure that I've spent enough of my life raising them, and now it's my turn to enjoy life. Besides, if I didn't travel, I'd never get the chance to see my grandchildren. Two are in Texas and one is in California."

## BOONDOCKING

This kind of RV living is known as "boondocking," that is, living in the open with no electrical or water hookups. Also, with no rental expense. Each vehicle is self-contained, with water tanks, a septic holding tank and battery power for electricity. Every other week or so, it's necessary to go into town to renew the water supply and to dump the holding tank into an RV disposal. Several people boasted solar electric systems to keep a steady charge on their battery system. A lightweight panel sits on the roof of the living quarters and changes the sun's rays into electrical energy that runs the lights, television, water pumps and cooling fans. One unit I looked at had two batteries and two panels which generated a 6-amp charge for a 100-watt system. Being independent is one of the main sources of pride for "boondockers."

Loners on Wheels maintains a social center and headquarters in Slab City, as well as at other popular rendezvous. Every afternoon there's a "happy hour" around a fireplace in the center of the LoW area, and by night they hold campfire get-togethers, potlucks, cards and other activities designed to draw people together socially. Almost every one of the LoW members I met that day were of retirement age, and most were widowed. My impression was that at least 40 percent were women, many of whom, like Beulah, didn't want to sit around feeling lonely and sorry for themselves. "I am only 56 years old," said one lady, a registered nurse who works every summer in Ohio. "I want to go places and meet people, and I want to do it now, while I have plenty of energy to enjoy traveling."

Loners on Wheels also publishes a newsletter so people can keep in touch with each other and keep up with the latest news.

"But, don't get the idea that we're a bunch of swinging singles," one man cautioned. "We expect people to conduct themselves properly around here. If anyone acquires a live-in traveling companion, both of their memberships are automatically canceled." The club members stress that they don't try to dictate or monitor anyone's conduct when they're away from official LoW functions, but they do insist on adherence to club rules while there. Often friendships blossom into romance and into marriage, at which point they don't need LoW anymore. This looks to me like a great way for single or widowed people to meet. They obviously must have a lot in common to both be adventuring in RVs.

I did get a feeling of peace and tranquility, not only in Slab City, but in several other sites popular with RV retirees. The nearby Salton Sea is perfect for RV boondocking, with both state park facilities and private locations around the lake's shoreline. Government Bureau of Land Management sites cost $25 for unlimited, year-round use, or $3.00 per day. Private parks quoted prices from $8 a day to $100 a month, including electricity. One small place on the Salton Sea beach asked $50 a month. I'm sure some are probably higher. Unfortunately, there's a rumor going around that the government recently sold the Slab City site to a developer, so this most famous "boondock" rendezvous could soon be history. But never fear, the determined RVers will surely find a substitute location for their winter sojourn.

## CONVENTIONAL RV LIVING

For a sizeable group of people, half the fun of RV living is in boondocking, but the vast majority of RV enthusiasts opt for more luxurious accommodations. Yes, they might stay overnight or for a day or two in free, or low-cost spots while on their way to their destinations, but most choose their long-term accommodations in developed parks. They insist on good laundry and shopping facilities, swimming pools, Jacuzzis, shuffleboard courts, and even golf courses. An all-important part of a good park is the clubhouse. Here's where you go for a cup of coffee and meet your neighbors. Parties, bingo, craft classes and group tours are just a few of the organized activities available there. The better RV parks often charge from $180 to over $200 a month in some areas. "That's less than our winter utilities used to cost when we stayed home all winter," said a lady from Minnesota. "So, now we just weatherproof the place, and forget it until the snow melts."

## WHAT ARE THE PROBLEMS WITH RV LIVING?

There are some stumbling blocks to full-time RV living. Perhaps the biggest is compatibility. A couple who get together quite well under normal circumstances can come unglued unless they're compatible. When the hubby had his workshop in the basement and his bowling team a couple of nights a week, and when the wife had her bridge club and evening classes at the community college, things were fine. They kept out of each other's hair. Suddenly they are spending a *lot* of time together, and they have to do it in the confines of a small RV. The unit becomes smaller and smaller as arguments grow bigger and bigger. Before planning a long trip together, better try out a few shorter ones to make sure you can get along.

Often a couple fondly remembers the enjoyable times with that vacation trailer, back in the days when they would spend their vacations traveling to the lake or to the shore. The kids loved it and the vacations always seemed to be too short. But now the kids are grown up. The vacation is now full-time. After the first euphoric weeks of traveling, the novelty can wear off. If the wife starts to watch soap operas all day, while the husband opens his first beer at 10 o'clock in the morning, you can bet their RV retirement isn't going anywhere. Boredom is precisely what we are trying to avoid.

This problem can be remedied by finding as many friends and outside interests as you can in your travels. This may require a complete change in your life-style. But, after all, this is what retirement should be about: Change. Instead of spending your time indoors, as you used to back home to escape the freezing cold or steamy summers, you can now spend more time outside in the sunshine. Fortunately, the other RVers tend to do just this. You have an unequaled opportunity now to make new friends, find new interests and hobbies and to break the patterns of your past life. If you can do this successfully, you have a great retirement potential in RVs. If you can't, you had better consider another alternative which will be more compatible with your TV schedules.

But the surprising thing about RV travel for most people is how quickly they adapt to smaller spaces. "We don't feel at all cramped," said one man, "because we spend so much time away from our motor home. I play golf three or four times a week, and my wife is into all of the things they have going at the clubhouse." She added, "It seems like the only time we spend at home is sleeping and having our meals."

Another common problem arises when one person wants to

travel and the other one doesn't. This, too, can spell disaster. The decision to be a RV retiree has to be mutual, the excitement shared by both people. Maybe this is why singles groups like Loners on Wheels are so successful: There is only one person to please.

Some people find that living space is too confining for long-term living. They are used to having a lot of elbow room and many possessions. For most people, this isn't much of a problem; before long, they realize that most of the "things" they prize so much are things they seldom use. These prizes are usually packed away in a closet somewhere in the first place. They are comforted by the fact that somewhere, "back home," their things are safely stored, waiting for that moment when they are really needed.

There's an interesting solution for those who are serious about RV travel, but who don't want to abandon the possessions they've collected over the years, or who *need* to own land. They buy a lot in a "co-op" and build a home base. Typically a co-op is formed by 100 or more RV enthusiasts pooling their money to buy some land. Then they pool their labor and develop it into a park at a fraction of the cost that a developer would have to pay. Then each member owns a lifetime lot where he can park rent-free for the rest of his life. He can rent his space while he is gone or sell it like any other piece of property if he decides to change his life-style. A lady who owns a space in the co-op in Livingston, Texas, says, "I could use this place for the next 20 years and get all my money back, and probably a profit besides."

## CO-OP PARKS

The problem of what to do with belongings is solved by co-op members who build a storage shed next to their RV. Sometimes the additions are quite elaborate, with a large living room, and maybe sleeping accommodations, in addition to storage. When the motor home or trailer is connected to the structure, you have an instant kitchen and bedroom. I've even seen some *two-story* affairs, with a large garage-like space to park the RV in when the owners aren't traveling.

The cost of a membership in a co-op varies with the location. One in Lakewood, New Mexico, charges $1,300 for a full-hookup on a 50'x60' lot. When the lots are sold out, you get on the waiting list for someone wanting to sell. Co-op members pay their own metered electricity and a fair share of taxes, insurance, a manager's salary and other operational costs. Split 100 ways, the monthly costs are minimal. Many co-ops keep costs down by renting spaces they've reserved for that purpose to travelers and temporary residents. Also, most members allow their lots to be rented when they aren't there; the manager handles this for them. All management decisions are made by vote of the members.

This concept of club-owned parks makes much more sense to me than some of the commercial membership campgrounds that are being pushed so strongly nowadays. Some of these campgrounds charge as much as $9,000 for a membership, plus a hefty monthly fee for maintenance and profits for the developers. People who buy in here don't really *have* anything for their money, and they feel obligated to spend their time at that park rather than travel. When they do travel, they feel restricted to other membership campgrounds within the same organization, where they are charged additional fees. And, instead of having a say in the rules of the park, they must follow rules set down by a corporate executive who doesn't live there. If members decide to go somewhere else, they can't rent their site for extra income. For $9,000 and the monthly fee, an RV can do a lot of traveling.

Not all snowbirds are retired. There are some who work at trades that permit them to move from job to job. Construction workers are one example, but there are many other possibilities. All larger cities have temporary agencies such as Kelly Girl or Western Girl-Western Man, who are always looking for short-term workers. Many resort areas need seasonal help, particularly in maintenance, food service or management assistance. Sales jobs are often ideal for seasonal work. Many firms and businesses need extra help during the snowbird season, but not when everyone goes home. This kind of job pays little, that's true, but since it costs less to live in an RV you don't *need* as much money. Many retirees take on temporary jobs just for the fun of having a new job every season.

While RV travel isn't for everyone, it's certainly a plausible option. Many people are doing it, more every day.

## PEACE CORPS

You'd like to travel, to live in a foreign country? You are retired, but would love to have some meaningful, fulfilling work to do? Consider the Peace Corps. It isn't as off-the-wall as it might seem at first glance. Many older Americans are having the time of their lives, and at the same time participating in programs that affect literacy, health, hunger and help promote world peace, friendship and sharing. Retired singles and couples have put their expertise to work in Africa, Asia, South America, Central America and the Pacific Islands.

Perhaps you've always been under the impression that Peace Corps volunteers are a bunch of youngsters who are having an adventure between college and going to work. Not so. The Peace Corps is very interested in older Americans. No other single group in this country has the years of leadership, skills, experience and proven ability of our senior citizens. You have an enormous reservoir of work experience and wisdom which will be lost if you don't share it with grateful people in developing countries. And, unlike the United States, where the emphasis is on youth, most countries respect and appreciate age.

Besides the wealth of expertise and experience that older Americans have to offer, they are usually in a better position to *afford* being a Peace Corps volunteer. A youngster right out of college has to think about money, usually big money to repay the costs of his education, or to get started in the job market. But a retired senior citizen with Social Security, and maybe a company pension coming in, isn't stymied by the low compensation paid by the Peace Corps. Actually, many older Peace Corps volunteers bank their entire Social Security, pension and interest income while they are on their two-year tour of duty. Peace Corps volunteers receive living expenses and a monthly stipend to cover incidental needs, so there is no need for them to spend savings or other income. In addition, $175 per month is put aside and given to them at the end of the typical two-year assignment. This $4,200 per person comes in handy for making a transition back into life at home. The compensation you receive from the Peace Corps doesn't affect your Social Security earnings any more than does unearned income from savings annuities, dividends or pensions.

Here is a terrific opportunity to make a contribution to peace, to utilize your life's experience helping others, and to have the *time of your life*. If you're married, odds are that your spouse also has some much-needed skill, so there's a chance that the two of you might go overseas as a team.

What kinds of skills are needed? The following needs are listed in the Peace Corps booklet, "Older Americans and the Peace Corps."

**AGRICULTURE:** Men and women with farm experience are needed to work in:

| | |
|---|---|
| --crop development | --plant protection |
| --soil science | --agriculture education |
| --agriculture economics | --animal husbandry |
| --community agriculture | --farm mechanics |
| --beekeeping | --rural youth projects |

**ENGINEERING:** Engineers are needed in:
--water and sanitation engineering
--road and structural building

| | |
|---|---|
| --architecture | --urban planning |

**MATH AND SCIENCE:** Volunteers are needed to work in:

| | |
|---|---|
| --mathematics | --symbolic logic |
| --general science | --biology |
| --chemistry | --physics |
| --botany | |

**HOME ECONOMICS AND NUTRITION:** Volunteers are needed for:
--diet planning
--school lunch programs
--commercial handicrafts production
--vegetable and small animal production
--demonstration of proper food use and storage
--counseling in mother and child nutrition
--sanitation and health projects

**SKILLED TRADES:** Some of the needs are for:

| | |
|---|---|
| --cabinetmakers | --carpenters |
| --electricians | --masons |
| --mechanics | --metalworkers |
| --plumbers | --welders |

**EDUCATION:** Qualified teachers are needed in:

| | |
|---|---|
| --primary education | --physical education |
| --secondary education | --library science |
| --special education | --secretarial training |
| --industrial arts | --teaching English |

**COMMUNITY DEVELOPMENT:** Volunteers are needed to:

--improve local craft marketing
--upgrade women's self-sufficiency projects
--increase employment opportunities in rural areas
--set up small businesses, cooperatives and other income-
generating projects

**FORESTRY AND FISHERIES:** Men and women are needed
with:
--commercial fishing experience --forestry experience
--mechanical training        --business training.

These are by no means all of the skills desired. If you have
something to offer, don't hesitate to write the Peace Corps and make
them a proposition.

## CASE STUDIES

Listed here are some of the experiences of senior citizens who
elected to participate in the adventure of the Peace Corps. They
came from my interviews with retirees and from the booklet "Older
Americans and the Peace Corps."

Virginia Spray, a peppy 71-year-old from Kansas, retired from
27 years of teaching school. She bought an RV and traveled about
the country for a while as a member of Loners on Wheels, but decided to try something a bit more exotic. She joined the Peace
Corps. Her volunteer assignment was to conduct teacher-training
workshops. She began by visiting local schools in a town not too far
from Monrovia, the capital of Liberia on West Africa's Ivory Coast.

"What I found in one school was 60 children sitting on logs in
one room. There were no textbooks." Virginia began collecting old
books from the U.S. school where she had taught and gave them to
the students. In addition to teaching and teacher-training, she
worked with a former Peace Corps volunteer to produce teaching
materials. She edited and proofread textbooks for Liberian schools.
She would change the vernacular to standard English and corrected
informational mistakes.

Her home was a mudblock house which she shared with another volunteer. They cooked on a kerosene stove and got their water
from a hydrant. People called her "Old Ma," a term of endearment.
"I had a marvelous experience. Age is so looked up to, you suddenly
feel important again," she recalled enthusiastically.

Another volunteer, George Wrenhold, 68, is helping small
farmers in Barbados plan irrigation systems. He points out that the

Peace Corps has helped him to be "uncommonly healthy. I haven't missed a meal or a day's work." George lives by himself in a small cottage, does all his own shopping, laundry and cooking. "I eat lots of locally grown vegetables and salads," he says.

Mary Le Baron, at the age of 61, having raised nine children, began looking for a change, something satisfying, something that would narrow the space between peoples. She accepted an appointment in Honduras as a teacher/counselor/friend to 69 girls who live in a group center. Mary lectures in Spanish on nutrition, cooking, gardening techniques, sewing and crafts, as well as teaches English. Her goal is to help these young women go into business for themselves. She lives in a three-bedroom home with a family of three, of whom she says, "We share a common bond in feeling that family is the most important element in life and that love and affection are natural and necessary." Mary believes that she has learned to be happier with a small success--to value herself more as a person than she did before the Peace Corps.

Albert Fitchett, who joined at the age of 65, says, "Anyone who doesn't want to get old and who wants to give back some of the knowledge acquired over his business life should join the Peace Corps."

Bea Alford served as a Peace Corps volunteer when she was in her 70s. "Experience and skills that have been gathered all your life are the best things to take with you," she says.

And Jane Carter, a Peace Corps volunteer at age 54, says, "Life was never lonely, because for two years it was shared with a town full of people. What a closeness with each other and a oneness with our Maker those moments gave us."

## PEACE CORPS BENEFITS

The Peace Corps points out that there are some major benefits of becoming a volunteer. Perhaps for the first time in your life you will be measured by your accumulated life's experience rather than how much you can earn each month. You can live with dignity and purpose in a culture where your age is respected and looked upon as an asset. This respect and knowing that your work is appreciated renews vigor and vitality. And finally, you have the adventure of creating a new and exciting life. What more could you ask of retirement?

## HOW IT WORKS

Here are some of the details about being a Peace Corps volunteer:

SAFETY--Safety is the highest priority. The Peace Corps monitors volunteers' environments constantly. If there's any doubt about safety, volunteers are immediately evacuated.

HEALTH CARE--The focus is on prevention, with every possible safeguard taken to provide quality health care. Volunteers undergo complete physical and dental exams, are given immunizations, preventive medications and health care training. Every country has a medical officer with access to qualified local doctors and medical facilities.

LIVING ALLOWANCE--Covers basic expenses such as food, housing and incidental expenses. Modest but comfortable housing is provided.

TRAINING--Technical and language training is provided during an intensive 10-12 week program. Volunteers' expenses are covered during this training, and their $175-a-month savings plan starts with training. Cross-cultural training gives volunteers an in-depth acquaintance with the customs and traditions of the country where they will live and work.

VACATION AND TRAVEL--Volunteers accrue vacation at the rate of two days per month, which can be taken as the work situation permits. Most Peace Corps workers take the opportunity to visit neighboring countries, travel adventures they could never dream of in ordinary retirement. Friends are permitted to visit as long as they don't interfere with the work schedule.

For further information or an application, write to Peace Corps, Room P-301, Washington, D.C. 20526; or call, toll-free, 800-424-8580, ext. 93.

## RETIREMENT IN THE SUN

Now here's an alternative that, chances are, you have never considered before: Retirement in a naturist park. "Naturist" is a modern day word for "nudist," in case you are wondering. Before you drop this book in horror, hang on, because later I'll give you a few insights as to what the naturist lifestyle is and what it is not.

But first, a description of the facilities and advantages of living in a naturist park. Let's take a look at one of the better ones, a place called Cypress Cove, located in Florida about midway between the Atlantic and the Gulf of Mexico. It's a beautiful setting on a 50-acre lake, shaded by live oaks and towering pines, with home sites incorporating Spanish-moss-festooned trees and natural shrubbery

into their landscaping schemes. This is basically a luxury mobile home park, but with a special, country club atmosphere. There's an especially nice heated swimming pool, a large Jacuzzi hot tub, eight tennis courts, paved roads for bicycle riding and jogging, plus boating and fishing in the lake.

Everything is first-class, with a landscape crew always busy mowing, trimming and shaping things up. Incidentally, your rent includes mowing your lawn, so if you like to travel, you don't have to worry about your place looking shaggy when you return. What's the rent for one of these luxury lots? From $125 to $165 per month--and that includes TV cable and water. You must buy the mobile home - of course. A new, two-bedroom, double-wide starts at about $42,000, the same as you might pay for a mobile home in an ordinary park, but with facilities and freedom never achieved in an ordinary park. Older units are also available from time to time. Cypress Cove is like living in a year-round swim-and-racquet club. In addition, there is a small store and a first-class restaurant with a full-service bar, and lots of friendly, interesting people.

One of the advantages to private park living is the high level of security. Unlike most mobile home parks, a naturist park is tightly controlled. People can't wander in at their leisure. Some condos, apartments and mobile home parks do have guards who observe comings and goings, but seldom actually check anyone out to see if he or she actually belongs there. And too often the guards are off duty at night, when they're most needed. But a naturist park entrance is closely monitored 24 hours every day, and you can believe that people can't enter unless they can produce identification and prove they have business being there. And sometimes even this isn't enough; if the gatekeepers think a person looks questionable, the gates won't open. Cypress Cove residents all listed the tight security as one of the best parts about living there. "I never lock my bicycle," said one lady, "I leave it by the curb and never think anything about it. And unless I'm leaving for a day or two, I never lock my home. It's too much of a hassle having to carry a key." No pockets, if you know what I mean.

## WHAT KIND OF PEOPLE ARE THEY?

Now that you have a description, let's talk about the kind of people who live in a naturist park. If you've never been to one, you may picture a group of young, superbly built swinger types. You are in for a surprise. At Cypress Cove, 90 percent of the permanent residents are retired! That means you won't have any trouble finding someone with more wrinkles than you, or with a bigger tummy than your spouse's. Of course on weekends and after working hours, younger families, including children, come to enjoy the pool, volley ball, or just relaxing in the sun. You can see it isn't just for retired couples.

My research shows that the type of people found in naturist parks tend to be better educated and in higher income brackets than average. They also seem to be well-traveled and more adventurous, which probably accounts for their willingness to try this unusual life-style. I also found the average person in this kind of setting more interesting and alert.

People who have never tried a naturist park typically have many misconceptions and often apprehensions at the thought of trying it. But naturists universally tell you that after your first immersion, usually within 15 minutes, you totally forget about what your body looks like, and you find that it doesn't matter; nobody cares!

I interviewed a couple who moved to Cypress when they both retired from teaching school in Fort Wayne, Ind. "It's amazing how quickly you stop noticing that others are not clothed," said the wife, "and how quickly everything seems so natural. I was reluctant to visit one of these places, but after that first day, I wanted to come back as often as I could. So when we retired, we naturally thought about Florida, and about Cypress Cove."

Another lady, a widow from Montreal, explained why she enjoys this life-style. "All my life, I believed that my body was misshapen," she explained, "a little too much here and not enough there. But when my husband and I joined a club in Canada, suddenly I discovered that it doesn't matter! Everybody has some little imperfections, and they allow them to become horrible deformities by dwelling upon them. Becoming a nudist lifted the weight of shame and insecurity and added tremendously to my feeling of freedom, not to mention my self-confidence." Having said this, she ran off to the tennis court for her lesson from the club tennis pro.

## ISN'T IT SEXY?

A common misconception about nudism is that it must be erotic and sexually stimulating. This is understandable, since in our society we seldom see someone of the opposite sex without clothing unless we are about to have sex or unless the other person is behaving in a sexually provocative manner. It's sort of like Pavlov's famous dog, who salivated at the sound of a bell, because the critter connected the bell with food. But after a while, later in the experiment, when the bell sounded and no food was forthcoming, the dog ignored the bell. The reaction was extinguished. Similarly, the eroticism of nudity is quickly extinguished when you see naked people working in a garden, riding a bicycle, or polishing a car, just doing ordinary things, with sex far removed from their thoughts. By the way, if you've never experienced swimming in the nude, you're missing something. Why would anyone wear a swim suit in a hot tub? Sort of like taking a bath with your socks on.

Although Cypress Cove is considered one of the better naturist parks, there are other places around the country, possibly one in your neighborhood, where you can try out this free, natural way of living. You needn't invest in a mobile home to see if you like it.

Naturists are inveterate RV fans. All naturist clubs have RV connections, and every day sees trailers, campers and motor homes coming and going, as well as a good share of tents being pitched. Because a naturist park's security system is generally so tight, people feel perfectly safe in leaving a tent with belongings in it, or an unlocked RV while they go fishing or swimming, or into town for supplies. Many parks have rental trailers, cottages or even condos for daily, weekly or monthly rental. For those without RVs, this is a great way to try out the life-style, and to see what kind of members a club might have.

Typically, a couple who considers this retirement style will travel about the country, either camping or in an RV, investigating the various parks and facilities. Tents are common and inexpensive if you'd rather not invest in an RV. Cypress Cove, for example, has 160 camping and RV spots, all with water, sewer and electrical hookups. For $186 a month (including utilities), you can set up and enjoy unlimited swimming, boating, fishing, tennis or just lazily working on your suntan. How can you beat that?

As you might guess, the naturist way of life is one that naturally lends itself to part-time retirement. Many of the motor homes, travel trailers and campers you'll see in these parks are seasonal travelers. Couples who want to flee the rigors of Minnesota or Canadian winters pack up their necessities in the RV and head for California or Florida to enjoy swimming and volleyball for the winter. Retirees who have their winter headquarters in Tucson or Florida head north for the summer to Oregon, Canada or perhaps Minnesota. There they can enjoy the benefits of naturism and not be committed to owning a second home. And, there are others who have their southern and northern parks, commuting back and forth whenever the weather begins to change. Parks with residential facilities can be found from coast to coast and from Canada to the Mexican border. You have quite a selection to choose from. There are naturist parks in 40 states and in six Canadian provinces.

By the way, you notice I keep referring to *couples*; don't they have singles? Yes, but on a limited basis. Most clubs accept single women without hesitation, but often discriminate against single men. Their rationale is that they prefer to keep a family-type environment. They also claim it's easier to screen couples for character rather than a single man. However, some clubs will accept single male applications and others will provided there is a matching single lady applicant, thus keeping a balance of membership. If a single male wants to join, he had better be prepared for rigorous screening as to his character. It isn't impossible, it's just necessary to hunt for a club that's taking applications. Once a member of the American Sunbathing Association, his membership card will usually be accepted anywhere. Generally, married couples have no problem visiting a club to see how they like it without having to join.

A naturist style of retirement isn't for everyone, of course, but don't laugh it off too quickly. You might discover that you and your spouse are among those who fall in love with this way of life. For more information, write: American Sunbathing Association, 1703 N. Main St. Kissimmee, FL 32743-3396.

## CHAPTER SIXTEEN

# *Foreign Retirement*

Retire to a foreign country, enjoy exotic foods, strange new scenery, learn to speak a foreign language? Does that sound too wild for you? It really isn't; people just like yourself do it all the time. You need a slight sense of adventure to get started, but once you do, you'll find that the zest of foreign living and the challenge of meeting every day's cultural surprises will sharpen your wits and your interest in life. It's not for everyone, you understand, but if you have that need to expand, this is one way to go!

Ask why people retire to foreign countries and you will receive varied answers, but the most common are the exhilaration of living in a new and stimulating environment and the bonus of a low cost of living. The financial advantage of living abroad can be considerable, but that's not a valid goal in itself. There are places in the United States where you can live *cheaply*, if that's all you're after. The important factor is the *quality* of the life-style available. Ask almost anyone who has retired in Mexico, Spain, Costa Rica, anywhere, and they will tell you, "After living here for a while, I'd stay even if it weren't a bargain!"

But the fact remains, in many foreign countries a person with dollars in his pockets can live in a style way beyond what the same dollars would normally permit in this country. It isn't that things are necessarily cheap in other countries, rather things are *expensive* here. When you transfer your dollars into a foreign currency, some wonderful things happen because of the exchange rate. Your Social Security checks can change from a subsistence-level pension into a truly magnificent income. Your income becomes enviable in the eyes of the local people.

A highly skilled toolmaker working full time in England expects to clear the equivalent of $7,500 a year, and a Spanish

automobile mechanic $3,900. Most Social Security recipients get
much more than that annually. In Mexico, a school teacher earns the
equivalent of $71 every two weeks. A bank teller there will pull
down $3,600 a year if he's lucky. In the spring of 1987, a doctor in
Mexico charged me $3.00 for an office visit, which included minor
surgery. He thought he was doing quite nicely. In this country, a
doctor would charge $30 for the office visit, and then refer you to a
specialist for the surgery. It isn't that things are cheaper in foreign
climes; things are expensive here.

In February 1987, I interviewed a native of Seattle who had
recently moved to Guanajuato, Mexico. I asked how he was making
out financially.

"Great," he replied enthusiastically. "My main income is my
Social Security check, which is just $770 a month. I have a two-
bedroom apartment in a nice section of town, which costs $140. In-
stead of having to pinch pennies, I manage to put almost 300 bucks
of Social Security in the bank every month!"

This man is a widower who had been feeling particularly lonely living in Seattle. He decided to give Mexico a try after making a
trip there and finding that the North American colony was full of
open, friendly people. "At home, my money barely kept the ends
from fraying," he pointed out. "I would never have thought about
getting married again, but here I can afford to do it." (He had met a
lady from Vancouver, and they were negotiating at the time.)


## FOREIGN HEALTH CARE

Surprising as it might seem, some people are moving to Canada for retirement. Prices aren't much lower there than in the United
States, and taxes are considerably higher, but there is one definite
benefit there that few people talk about. That is the terrific benefits
provided by the government health insurance program. Medical
treatment is just about free. The catch is that you must acquire official permanent resident status. Great Britain, Ireland and Sweden,
among other countries, also enjoy government-sponsored hospitalization. Again, you have to check with each country to learn the
details. Some are understandably reluctant to let outsiders come in
and free-ride on tax-paid benefits. But all countries have private
doctors available--and, since there is so much competition from
government *free* doctors, you can be sure that their fees will be far
more reasonable than in the United States.

While we're talking about medical care in foreign countries, we should mention that Medicare doesn't pay off overseas. That's the bad part. But the good part is that most countries have excellent medical care, and at a low cost. Should you contract some serious problem that you might not want to trust a local doctor with, it's quite easy to hop on a plane for the United States (or to Canada if that's your country) and use your medical insurance back home. My experience was wonderful when I went to the hospital in Costa Rica in 1985. My hospital bill was less than $30 a day, which included three of the best meals I've ever eaten anywhere in Costa Rica. If I had opted for a four-bed ward instead of a private room, the cost would have been just a little over $10 a day! For a complete physical, including electrocardiogram, blood and urine tests, and a full set of X-rays, I paid $50. That included the doctor's fee, and I was given the X-ray films (they belong to the patient in some countries, not the doctor, as it is the case here).

Why would medical care in a third-world country be so inexpensive? Actually it isn't inexpensive; medical care in the *United States* is expensive. The reason is simple: Since the United States is one of the few countries in the world without government-sponsored medical care, there is little or no competition in the medical industry. If hospitals have empty beds, they simply raise the room rates to take up the slack. If an area has too many doctors, they raise their fees to make sure they earn a good living. But in a country where medical care is all but free, the doctors and hospitals in private practice have to compete. Their rates and fees have to be competitive, and the quality of care has to be better than at public clinics.

When doing research on my other books, I queried hundreds of North Americans living in foreign countries about how they felt about the local medical care. Almost all replied that they were quite satisfied, and that if they faced a serious operation they would seriously consider having it done locally rather than return to the United States. One man, who lives in San Miguel de Allende, Mexico, told of his wife's hysterectomy, which she had done in San Luis Potosi. "It cost about $350," he said, "and as far as we were concerned, the care was as good as we could have possibly gotten in the States. By the time we used up our deductible and paid the difference between Medicare and $800 a day for the hospital, we would have been into several thousand dollars back home." Incidentally, that $350 figure included surgery and a four-day stay in the hospital to recuperate. Round-trip airfare to a hospital in the United States would have cost about the same as the total operation did in Mexico.

## WHERE DO AMERICANS RETIRE AND WHY?

By far the largest number of U.S. and Canadian citizens who decide to retire in a foreign country choose Mexico. About 150,000 choose to live there.

Although Mexico is not technically "overseas," and although Mexico is our next-door neighbor, it's the most *foreign* country of all the retirement choices. Let me explain. North American culture is essentially *European* in nature because, after all, most of our customs, beliefs and modes of behavior came from Europe. But Mexico is different in many subtle and exotic ways. First, there is the legacy of ancient traditions from feudal Spain, in turn, colored by centuries of Moorish occupation. Added to this is the heavy influence from 19th century France, when Maximilian and his French troops occupied Mexico. French philosophy reigns paramount among intellectuals in the country even today. All of this rests upon, and sometimes merges with, a base of ancient, pre-European civilizations. Aztecs, Mayas, Zapotecs and other indigenous traditions still influence ways of behaving and modes of thinking in Mexico. To this day, many villagers all over the country retain the tongue spoken by their ancestors. Some country folk still worship pre-European gods, referring to the Virgin Mary as *Tonantzin*, who was the earth goddess to whom ancient priests dedicated their human sacrifices.

So, Mexico blends all of these cultures into something uniquely Mexican. You'll find Southern European friendliness blended with Indian politeness and reserved courtesy. The language is Spanish, almost indistinguishable from that spoken in Valencia, Spain, from where most early colonists came, yet it's sometimes colored with Aztec and Mayan words. The resulting cultural tapestry is neither European nor Indian, neither modern nor ancient. It's *Mexico!* If you want to live in a foreign country, Mexico is the most foreign of all.

The North American colony in Mexico is large, indeed, with many thousands living there on a full-time basis. The largest group is centered around Guadalajara and Lake Chapala, with more than 30,000 living there full-time. Nobody knows exactly how many Canadians are living in Mexico because the Canadian government doesn't keep count. Rest assured there are plenty of them. The North Americans have formed their own branches of fraternal organizations, such as Elks, Lions and Moose lodges, American Legion and VFW posts, even their own chambers of commerce.

There are English-language weekly newspapers, printed in Guadalajara, San Miguel de Allende and Ensenada, as well as an excellent English language daily newspaper from Mexico City.

There are so many "gringos" living there that many don't bother to learn Spanish. This is surely a shame, because these people are missing out on a lot; it's as if they were partial deaf-mutes. But the point is, a place like Mexico is a great place to give foreign living a try without having to immediately face the hurdles of language. Time enough to learn Spanish as you learn to love the country and the people.

Some North Americans turn up their noses when you mention popular retiree places like Lake Chapala or San Miguel de Allende. You'll hear them say, "Well, if I ever retire in Mexico, it won't be someplace the gringos have spoiled," or, "If I wanted to live in the middle of a bunch of *ugly Americans*, I'd simply stay at home." Others say, "I want to go to the *real* Mexico, someplace where the culture hasn't been ruined by U.S. dollars." But, you'll seldom hear someone who actually has *lived* in Mexico talk this way.

## YOUR SOCIAL LIFE

One of the important advantages of a town with a large American colony is the very fact that there are people there with whom you can develop relationships. You can have English-speaking neighbors. You have someone with whom you can discuss current events, argue politics, play cards or turn to for help in an emergency. A few years ago, Don Sherwood--a popular West Coast radio-television personality--decided to chuck his career to go live in an exotic, isolated Mexican fishing village. The natives were down-to-earth, friendly folk, living on the bountiful fruits of the tropics. Best of all, they were neither spoiled by U.S. dollars nor corrupted culturally. Don found himself in a situation that many of us only dream of. His employers were so worried that he might come out of retirement and work for another broadcasting network that they insisted on paying him a salary, forever if necessary, if he would agree to come back to them should he give up retirement.

Don loved this development. Now he could lounge forever on a hammock in the shade of a palm tree, enjoy an unspoiled culture and friendly people, free of all financial worries. The people in the village loved him. He had everything in the world he had ever dreamed of. But there was one thing lacking: Social contact. His

Spanish was sufficient, but not advanced enough so he could hold deep, meaningful conversations. After a while, he realized that he was lonely. Regretfully, he abandoned his friends in the village, returning to a place where he could fully communicate. Eventually he returned to broadcasting, even though he would have been paid his salary anyway.

The important point here is that it takes a certain type of personality to truly enjoy an "unspoiled" foreign situation. Not only that, you need more than a *desire* to participate in the native culture. You also need the *ability* to participate. This is true whether we're talking about France, Greece, Costa Rica or even Great Britain. I happen to speak fluent Spanish, so I feel perfectly at home wherever that language is the rule. I can argue politics, philosophy, football or economic theory with the best of them and enjoy it thoroughly. Brazilian, Portuguese and French aren't that difficult for me, either. But, there comes a time when the sound of my native "NBC" English sounds as sweet as a tinkling brook does to a trout. Being in "unspoiled" parts of the world, absorbing the fragrance of an ancient culture, is marvelous experience. But then after a week or two, it's time to move on.

So, pay little attention to the person who urges you to steer clear of towns with large gringo communities. Instead, go to these places and discover for yourself. Check out the popular retirement places like Guadalajara, Oaxaca, San Miguel de Allende, the seacoast towns of Mazatlan, Puerto Vallarta, Acapulco, and on the other side of the continent, Cancun and Playa del Carmen. If you happen to be one of those rare individuals who can get by with little English-speaking contact, then there are many delightful towns high in the mountains or down in the tropical lowlands where retirement can be a true adventure. The people living in these towns and villages are incredibly friendly and accepting, and the prices for rent and food are low, low, low. But these are for people who either already know Spanish, or who are determined to learn by "total immersion" in the culture. I urge newcomers to find a location where there are other English-speaking retirees living, people to whom you can turn for advice and help getting "into the groove."

One further note on places being "spoiled" by too many dollars. What does this really mean? Once my wife and I were renting an apartment from an American retiree in Tequisquipan. We made an arrangement to have his maid spend one hour a day cleaning our apartment, doing laundry and washing yesterday's dishes. The agreed upon rate amounted to 35 cents an hour in our money. We felt this was shamefully low. We insisted on paying the lady 70 cents for the hour. Our host was furious with us. We were "ruining things for the people who have to live here!" Perhaps we did ruin things for the unfortunate gringos who feel that 35 cents an hour is enough to pay anyone. I can live with that on my conscience. Seventy cents an hour meant nothing to us or to any of the moderately wealthy North Americans we knew in the town, but it meant a hell of a lot to the smiling, appreciative maid.

Just as in the United States, a community benefits when retiree money comes into circulation. Having affluent gringos conspire to keep that money from being put into circulation, or to keep the local economy depressed for their own selfish benefit seems pretty close to being ungrateful guests in an accepting foreign country.

## "TOURIST TRAPS"

You'll hear people warn you to stay away from "tourist traps" in Mexico. What is a tourist trap? A tourist trap is simply an extraordinarily nice place to visit. It's so nice that loads of tourists go there to enjoy. If it were a boring place, there wouldn't be any tourists, yet it would still be boring. Something which surprises many people is that resort towns such as Acapulco or Mazatlan are not necessarily the super-expensive, jet-set places they're made out to be. At least, they don't have to be. In Acapulco, for example, the vast majority of tourists are *Mexican* families on vacation, not dollar-rich gringos. These Mexican tourists simply cannot afford the $65- to $185-per-day rooms that travel agents happily book for their clients. Mexican families look for rooms that cost less than $10 if they can. (For many Mexicans, school teachers for example, $5 is a day's wages.) And of the almost one million people who live in the area around Acapulco, very few can afford to rent an apartment or a house for much over $100 a month. Two hundred dollars a month secures a nice place, often with a breathtaking view of the bay. Don't expect to find bargains on the beach, however, because that's where the gringos go. Get a few blocks away, or perhaps up on a hillside, and start looking.

In my other books, I advise people to rent rather than buy, at least in the beginning. There are several solid reasons for this, one of which is the legalities of buying property. It can be done, but there are many restrictions and problems. For example, in Mexico, a foreigner cannot legally buy property on the ocean. They do, of course, through a maneuver of buying through a bank and leasing it back. It's legal, I suppose, but I would want the deal closed by a good lawyer. My own view is that rents are so inexpensive in Mexico, I can't see the advantage in buying something out of my own pocket. Yet many people have the time of their lives buying 300-year-old colonial mansions and restoring them, or building a "dream house" with a view of the Caribbean. A contractor in Guanajuato assures me that he could build a colonial-style home, with two bedrooms, two baths, with a large interior patio, for less than $30,000 U.S. But I pointed out to him that I was renting a place just like that for $225 a month. It wouldn't make sense for me to put up $30,000 to have something I already had for almost nothing. By the way, when you buy real estate in Mexico, the terms are almost always cash on the old barrelhead. But I plead with you, don't buy anything until you are positive you need to.

Despite this advice, many readers have written, asking for names of Mexican real estate people whom they may contact. Some want to buy a house, even before they visit their target retirement site. Obviously, I would be in a poor position to recommend a sales company when I don't deal with them in the first place. Aside from that, we must realize two things. First, that a reputable real estate broker is in the business of selling property and isn't likely to enter into a pen-pal relationship with strangers. His or her job is to *show* houses, not write letters about them. Secondly, it makes as much sense to buy a house in Mexico by mail as it does to buy one in Miami by mail. Another common request is for addresses of retirees in Mexico, so the respondent can write for information and advice on relocating. That's something that will never happen. The average person has so much inertia that writing Christmas cards to relatives is a chore. So, forget about their sending chatty letters to perfect strangers. Subscribing to one of the English-language newspapers will give you adequate information about housing costs, servant's wages and things of that nature.

Mexico, like many foreign locations, is a great place for retirement. But there are a few advantages to choosing Mexico for retirement over most other countries. The major advantage, one which almost all retirees point out, is Mexico's proximity and accessibility. If you want to go home to visit the grandchildren for Christmas, you simply hop into your automobile and go. When the family or friends feel like visiting you, catching an economy flight to Puerto Vallarta or Cancun is no big deal. But how often does the average American visit Europe? Mexico is also ideally suited for part-time retirement. Many, many people, instead of snowbirding in Florida or the Los Padres Islands, choose to drive a little farther and snowbird in Mexico. Some also do this in Costa Rica or Europe, but they usually leave their autos at home. Finally, a big advantage is obviously financial. The cost of living in Mexico is at its lowest in years, and from all indications, it will stay that way for some time to come.

## CLIMATES

Mexico offers you a wide choice of climates. Along the Pacific Coast are the well-known resorts, Mexico's Gold Coast. Mazatlan, Puerto Vallarta, Manzanillo, Zihuatanejo, Acapulco, Puerto Escondido and Puerto Azul. Just south of Puerto Azul is a beautiful area known as Huatulco. This is targeted for government development into a new tourist mecca, created from scratch the way Cancun was developed on the Caribbean side of Mexico. These coastal towns enjoy tropical winters of sunshine and warmth, and summers with enough overcast to keep things from becoming hot. Tourist accommodations will be more or less expensive, but renting a house or apartment away from the tourist zones can be surprisingly inexpensive.

For those who prefer temperate climates over tropical, the solution is simple: Travel a few hours up into the mountains to the large central plateau, and you find permanent spring. Guadalajara's temperature varies just a few degrees all year around (low-to-mid 70s) with flowers growing in profusion in January and February. Lake Chapala, Oaxaca, Morelia, Cuernavaca and other temperate towns are quite popular with retirees, and each has active retiree organizations. Several towns publish newsletters or weekly newspapers, to keep the foreign community aware of what's happening.

When you get into the even higher latitudes, with towns like San Miguel de Allende or Guanajuato, the spring-like climate is sometimes broken by a few cool, crisp days in January; that is the extent of their winters. Very few days require a sweater. The town squares are always frequented by Americans in shirtsleeves reading today's issue of the *Mexico City News*, or practicing Spanish with local people.

As in the United States, retirees find that getting involved in volunteer work is a highly rewarding activity. This is particularly true in Mexico, and the volunteer work is directed at helping Mexican people rather than toward helping other retirees. Several active retiree organizations are involved in setting up libraries in small villages, helping handicapped children, helping poor families organize small handicraft industries and medical clinics; all sorts of things to help the local population. The payoff comes in the attitudes of the villagers toward North Americans. "Gringo" becomes a term of endearment as people regard them as unselfish, kind and generous people. Besides helping others in doing volunteer work, you also meet other quality people like yourself and make friends, something badly needed when living in a foreign setting.

If you're going to live in a foreign country, you'll probably want to start learning the language right away. Don't get the idea that you can "pick up the language" simply by listening to it. You have to *study*! The way to do this is enroll in a school, or *instituto* and take a class. My advice is to do this immediately upon arrival. You'll meet other newcomers and more than likely start making a circle of friends from the start. Usually these schools also have programs where volunteers teach English to the local people. This is an excellent way of meeting people outside of the foreign community, a chance to make contacts which could be valuable later on.

Yes, Mexico is an incredibly inexpensive place to live. But the fact is that even if Mexico weren't such a bargain financially, it would still be a wonderful place to live. Those of you who've visited there as a tourist can vouch for the beauty of the beaches, the verdant mountains, and the gracious, friendly people. Being able to have all of this and live for $400 a month is an added bonus. The $400 a month figure is the minimum amount that Don Merwin and I figured a couple would need to live in modest comfort in Mexico. We calculated this after an extensive survey in which we interviewed by mail and in person hundreds of retirees to see how much they spent for essentials. If you're interested in finding out more about retirement in Mexico, pick up a copy of CHOOSE MEXICO from your library or bookstore, or order one from Gateway Books.

## OTHER LATIN AMERICAN COUNTRIES

COSTA RICA--Mexico is the closest foreign country to us, and the closest country where the $400 figure seems valid. But there are many other places where North Americans go to retire on a limited budget. Let me again stress that inexpensive living is only part of it. Much more important is the *quality* of your retirement life. High on your priority list should be personal safety, cultural and social activities, recreation and neighborliness of the country.

One of my favorite countries, Costa Rica, fulfills all of these criteria. In addition, the panoramic beauty of the country is absolutely breathtaking. Costa Rica enjoys one of the most varied climates imaginable. From dense, tropical jungles to rain forests, to eternal spring highlands, and finally, to cool mountains that remind one of Switzerland in the summer, Costa Rica has it all. Most people live in the high central valley, where temperate breezes from the Pacific continually sweep over the mountains to keep the air crystal clear--never cold, never hot, never smoggy. When you feel like to visit a verdant, tropical ocean beach, you have your choice of either the Atlantic or the Pacific--either is just a few hours' drive away.

It's a little country, with fewer than 2.5 million people, but here you'll find the largest percentage of North American retirees in any foreign country. There are about 15,000 U.S. citizens living in Costa Rica, and the government goes out of its way to welcome them. The benefits of having retirees bringing dollars into the country are obvious. If you choose to retire here, you'll receive substantial tax breaks and other incentives from the government. Unlike Mexico and some other countries, Americans are encouraged to go into business, or buy farm properties. There's plenty of room for expansion in Costa Rica and always room for more North Americans. We're well liked there.

One of the things that makes Costa Rica so comfortable and attractive to North Americans is that Costa Ricans think and act like we do. Their fierce dedication to democracy is legendary. Because the country is so small, they can afford to have a "town hall" type of democracy that the United States hasn't had for a long time. An individual's voice carries more weight in a smaller democracy. Here, the president drives his own car (a Honda), lives in his own home (an ordinary bungalow). He is as accessible and responsible to the voters as is the mayor of a typical U.S. city. Elections are open, free and wildly celebrated. Each voter knows his decision counts.

Costa Rica is the most affluent country in Central America, with one of the highest standards of living in this hemisphere. There is almost no apparent poverty, and even the most humble neighborhood is clean and livable. It's a country of independent farmers and small businessmen, without the extremes of rich and poor of other countries.

In Costa Rica, there are absolutely no controls over elections, with parties from extreme left to radical right campaigning hard. But the middle-of-the-road, democratic candidates always win by landslides. To make sure that there are no military coups d'etat, the people abolished the army in 1948. Instead they have a civilian police force that wears military uniforms and carries weapons, but is under strict control of the civilian government. Since their job is not to protect the government from people who don't like the government, the Civil Guard devotes its energies to maintaining law and order.

Is there a danger of the Nicaragua problem spilling over into Costa Rica? Ask this of the average Costa Rican citizen, and his reply will be an amused smile. "Our only neighbors, Nicaragua and Panama, can't even handle their own problems at home," the Costa Ricans point out. "They would be insane to go to war with another country. Nicaragua particularly would love to be as rich and as free as we are. They never have been free, but we hope some day they can solve their problems and enjoy democracy as we do."

It's important to note that many Costa Ricans helped with the struggle against the Somoza dictatorship in Nicaragua. The country rejoiced when General Somoza was finally kicked out. Today, many Costa Ricans are volunteering as teachers and health workers. This doesn't mean they approve of a Marxist dictatorship next door, just that they recognize the need to help their less fortunate neighbors.

The main reason that Marxist politicians cannot garner any significant vote is that Costa Rica is prosperous, and the voters optimistic. The fact is, people don't opt for communism except as a last resort. While there are a few wealthy families in Costa Rica, there are very few, and by the same token, few families live in abject poverty. Costa Rica's middle class is proportionally huge. The government, instead of wasting money on military spending and corruption, invests in schools, hospitals, roads and other works for the improvement of the standard of living. The educational system is one of the finest in the world, and the functional literacy rate is higher than that of the United States.

All of this contributes to the Costa Rican personality of optimism, openness and dedication to equality. It's this personality that also makes Costa Rica attractive for Americans; the people think and act very much as we do. This is important. When the social structure of a country is highly stratified, with barriers between various economic and social classes, you'll find people rarely make close friends across class lines. This was part of Don Sherwood's problem when he tried to become part of Mexican village life. His status was far too high for humble villagers to feel at ease with his friendship. In a class-conscious society, Americans don't fit into any of the traditional class distinctions. Poor people consider you higher in class and education, therefore unapproachable. The wealthy aren't sure if you're in a higher or lower class, so they feel uncomfortable accepting your friendship. But this isn't the case in Costa Rica or in some South American countries. Costa Ricans shake your hand, look you in the eye and accept you for who you are rather than how much money or how many university degrees you have. A Costa Rican will invite you to dinner at his home. In Mexico this rarely happens; you might be invited to dine at a restaurant, but not at home.

## OWNING PROPERTY

Ownership of property in Costa Rica is much easier than in most other countries, Mexico, for example. Here you don't even have to have government permission, much less residency status. Because the records are centralized, it's relatively easy to determine whether a piece of property is free and clear before you buy it. There seems to be a rash of Americans who have purchased "survival" farms in the countryside. Typically, this would be about 50 acres, with some coffee, bananas, a vegetable garden, some chickens, a pig or two and a milk cow. Usually there's a trout stream that generates electricity and a "peon's house" for the caretaker and his family. They figure that in the event of a nuclear holocaust, they will simply slip on down here and wait things out.

Frankly, I am cool to the idea of survival farming. But the idea of having a caretaker to do the work takes some of the sting out of owning a farm. I much prefer to live in the capital city of San Jose. Technically, it's a city, but practically, it's an overgrown small town. Except for the downtown section, most buildings are of one or two stories and tastefully designed. Even the downtown buildings are rarely taller than two stories. To illustrate how much it is like a small town: Many of the streets away from the city center don't have names, and neither do the houses have street numbers. The mailman knows where everyone lives in the neighborhood, so it's no big deal.

What about expenses? Costa Rica isn't as inexpensive as Mexico, but it's ridiculously cheap compared to the United States. By my calculations, a bare-bones monthly budget for a couple to live in Costa Rica would be close to $600 U.S. dollars. I hate to make a budget estimate for someone else, because I know people who spend $600 a month on entertainment and imported cognac. But figure it like this: $600 a month is about two to three times what a Costa Rican school teacher earns. If he can live decently on his salary, you should do quite well. I've always said that I don't care to be a millionaire, as long as I can live like one. And in Costa Rica, I can live like one. None of the restaurants are out of my price range, rents are affordable, and what I consider the world's most beautiful beaches are there for all to enjoy--the rich and the poor, and me.

Like Mexico, Costa Rica has ocean on both sides, with tropical lowlands immediately next to the beaches. There is a high central plateau that enjoys permanent spring weather. It's hard to envision a more even climate. Summer or winter, noon-day temperatures are in the mid 70s, and at night, the high 60s to low 70s. The reason for these mild, even temperatures is that the country is narrow and warm, westerly breezes from the tropical Pacific continually course across the mountains to warm and cleanse the air.

It's hard to imagine a setting more beautiful. Everything is lush and green, with flowers which seem to glow in the immaculately clear mountain air. Huge trees sometimes seem to explode with colorful blossoms. Verdant mountains ring the capital city of San Jose and its pleasant little suburbs. Coffee farms climb the hills and mountain slopes, their tender shrubs shaded by banana leaves. Many Americans own a dozen or so acres of coffee and use the income to supplement their living. Some do quite well. Some also are experimenting with other crops in the tropical lowlands, such as black pepper, macadamia nuts and breadfruit. On the western side of the country, the lowlands are lush with grass and, as you might expect, heavily populated with cattle. The beaches on both coasts are gorgeous. People who've traveled all over the world tell me that some of the prettiest beaches of all are in Costa Rica.

## LANGUAGE SCHOOLS

By the way, this is an excellent country in which to learn Spanish. There are several highly regarded schools that specialize in intensive courses for North Americans. This is not only a great way to learn, but it is also a unique cultural experience. Typically, a school will place you with a non-English speaking family where you are given a room, and you take breakfast and dinner with the family. A bus picks you up and takes you to school for six to eight hours of instruction and practice. The usual class is seldom larger than five students. All of this, including room and board, laundry, tuition, transportation to and from the airport, comes to as little as $600 a month! My favorite school there is Lingua Conversa. Its tuition is a little higher than the others, but the setting is beautiful: A ranch house high above San Jose with a stunning view.

If I sound prejudiced toward Costa Rica and the Costa Rican people, that's because I am. I can highly recommend it for full- or part-time retirement.

## SOUTH AMERICA

Most North Americans have a distorted vision of South America. They conjure an image of poverty, overpopulation and primitive living conditions. If this is your image, you have a pleasant surprise ahead of you. Some of the most modern, affluent and undercrowded places in the world await you on the other side of the equator. My favorite countries there are Uruguay and Argentina.

Both countries are clean, modern and have exceptionally low crime rates. Since people observe the European custom of late night dining, the streets of large cities are full of people strolling along leisurely at 2 or 3 o'clock in the morning, without the worry that would accompany a late-night stroll in many U.S. cities. In Chicago, strolling the streets after midnight is called "lurking" or "prowling." I've been invited to dinner in several Buenos Aires homes, and after the dinner is concluded (usually after 10 or 11 pm) the children go outside to play in the park, sometimes staying out until after midnight. I can remember as a child being allowed to play outside after dark, but that's a thing of the past in the United States.

Why would anyone choose South America for retirement? There are benefits and drawbacks. First the benefits: Since the seasons are reversed in the Southern Hemisphere, Argentina and Uruguay enjoy summer while we are having winter. December, January and February are the same as June, July and August would be up north. I've enjoyed several "second summers" by spending them in Buenos Aires and Punta del Este.

Understand, there's a big difference between warm winter weather and honest-to-goodness *summer*. It can be warm in Florida or Arizona in the winter, but it's still *winter*. The sun goes down around 5 o'clock in the afternoon, and you need a sweater in the evening. Many trees shed their leaves, standing around like skeletons, and the songbirds pack up their music and head for Costa

Rica or Argentina. On the other hand, January in Buenos Aires is pure summer delight. The sun hangs around until after 9 o'clock, birds sing, evenings are for shirt-sleeve sidewalk cafe dining and tango music. Yes, there's much more to summer than just warm weather.

A second advantage is the price structure. Prices here are almost as low as they are in Mexico. But the standard of living is much higher. The average wage earner earns abut $400 a month and does okay on that. The living costs are low enough that even with airfare from the United States or Canada, it's possible to enjoy an extra summer every year and not spend any more than if you had gone to Florida for the winter. For example, in Buenos Aires I stay at a small, family-style hotel on beautiful Avenida de Mayo. It's an older place, but the employees are friendly and helpful. Last year the daily charge for a double room, with a balcony that looks out over the avenue, was less than $8.00. For two people. Laundry was another $2.00 dollars a week.

The drawback is, like all South American countries, there's a language problem. Fewer natives there speak English, and there are not yet as many North Americans living there.

## ARGENTINA AND URUGUAY

Argentina is a place where you had better sharpen your Spanish skills or be prepared to be lonely if you plan on staying permanently. Argentine Spanish, by the way, has a couple of minor differences from standard Spanish. Basically, differences are in the way of pronouncing the sound "y" and in using a "vos" form of grammar for familiar usage. Once your mind adjusts for these differences, there is no problem other than some Italian slang words that people love to use. But, if you are just going south for the second summer season, you can struggle along. There's always somebody who is willing to try out their high school English and help you. Also, if you stick to the tourist spots, there are always English-speaking workers around.

In Uruguay, Punta del Este is the most modern and luxurious city I've ever seen. Relatively new, and built by and for millionaires from all over the world, Punta del Este is not only modern and spiffy, but it's incredibly inexpensive for we lucky persons with dollars to spend. A few years ago, this wasn't true, but with hyperinflation and Latin American debt problems, prices in dollar terms have plummeted. A dinner in an elegant restaurant will cost $3.00 and a taxi ride just about anywhere in town $1.50. A luxury condominium that cost $100,000 to build five years ago can be purchased today for less than $20,000, or rented for $300 a month. Is it crowded? Well, just drive 15 minutes from the center of Punta del Este and you'll find beaches that seldom endure the imprints of human feet.

Uruguay is the second smallest country in South America, about the size of Missouri, but its population is only 2.8 million, about 60 percent that of Missouri's. With a third of its citizens living in the capital, Montevideo, the rest of the country is really underpopulated. It isn't because it's a wasteland, either; Uruguay is one of the richest agricultural lands, acre-for-acre, anywhere in the world. But with the "green revolution" in agricultural production and the lessening demand of world food markets, people are leaving the rural areas and either moving to Montevideo or leaving the country entirely.

The same economic conditions prevail in Argentina, across the wide Rio de la Plata from Uruguay. Prices are ridiculously low, but the country is astonishingly rich at the same time. In my trips there I've visited many people in their homes, from all walks of life and in all sections of the country. I'm always amazed at the high standard of living, not very much different from how Americans live. One difference is that in Argentina I don't see slums, obvious poverty or street people. Well, yes, there are working-class barrios of modestly priced homes and apartments, but they aren't what I'd classify as "slums." Come to the United States and I'll show you slums!

Buenos Aires, one of my favorite towns, is a fascinating combination of Paris, Barcelona and Naples. The people are predominantly of Italian origin (about 70 percent), and often learn to speak Italian at home before learning Spanish. So the connection with Italy is obvious, as is the Spanish heritage in the style of Barcelona. But it's the outdoor cafes and the exuberance for life, as well as some of the architecture, that reminds one of Paris. British industrialists and immigrants contributed much to the Argentinian way of life, with more British citizens living here than in any other place outside the Commonwealth except South Africa. Polo and cricket are big here. It's been said that, "Argentinians are a people who think in Italian, speak Spanish, act like Englishmen and wish they were French."

There's even one interesting section of western Argentina where many of the people speak German. This is an area of rolling foothills 400 miles northwest of Buenos Aires area that is reminiscent of the Black Forest in Germany. The survivors of the WWII German battleship Graf Spee were stranded in Argentina after their ship was scuttled in the Rio de la Plata. When they discovered this place, near Cordoba, which reminded them so much of home, they decided to stay. When the war was over, they sent for their families and began recreating the Black Forest in South America.

My sister-in-law comes from Argentina. She lives in Los Angeles now, and she has introduced me to many other Argentinians who have immigrated to this country. When I ask them why they chose Los Angeles to live, they invariably reply, "Because Los Angeles is so much like Buenos Aires." And this is true in many respects. Both towns are big and sprawling. Both towns have similar climates--as a matter of fact, Buenos Aires is as far south of the Equator as Los Angeles is north. The big difference in climate is that it rains during the summertime in Argentina, keeping things green all year, whereas it just about never rains in the summer in Los Angeles. Oh yes, one more point: Buenos Aires has *no* smog! Ever.

Like North Americans, Argentinians are open and friendly, almost aggressively friendly. Stop someone on a Buenos Aires street and ask for directions, and you'd think that person's main goal in life was to make sure you arrive at your destination. You will have no problem making friends in Argentina, even if you don't choose the country for year-around living.

Unlike Uruguay, Argentina is enormous. If you can imagine the country superimposed on a map of the Northern Hemisphere, it would stretch from Puerto Vallarta in Mexico on up to Fairbanks, Alaska. To go by train from Buenos Aires to the ski resort of Bariloche takes two days and a night, and Bariloche is only about halfway down the country! Put it this way: Argentina is more than seven times the size of California, yet with a population approximately the same as California. People there often lament, "One of our problems is we don't have enough people." When I try to point out that not being overcrowded is a benefit rather than a detriment, I receive puzzled stares in return. If Argentinians had their way, Buenos Aires would spread from the Brazilian border to the Antarctic.

If Costa Rica, Argentina or Uruguay sound like subjects you'd like to know more about, go to your library for a copy of my book CHOOSE LATIN AMERICA (better yet, buy a copy). This book discusses other retirement spots in Brazil, Chile and other Latin American countries.

## EUROPEAN RETIREMENT

Recently the dollar has fallen against European currencies, and has drained away much of the financial advantages of living in Europe. My guess is that this is a contrived situation, one that will correct itself over time. In the meantime, living costs in Great Britain are similar to the United States. Most other countries are even higher, making the United States look like a cheap place to live in comparison.

Two European countries still look like good bets for retirement: Spain and Portugal. Prices have gone up there, of course, as the dollar has fallen. But both countries started from a much lower base. You can still rent a nice apartment in Spain or Portugal for from $150 to $200. Four hundred dollars will rent a villa, maybe with a view of the Mediterranean or of the Atlantic. Restaurant meals are half to a third of what they would cost back home. Europeans know this, and make Spain and Portugal their vacation playgrounds. Another thing that's bringing foreigners into Portugal, particularly, is the potential of land appreciation. In 1990, Spain and Portugal will become full members in the European Common Market. At that time there will be a common exchange of people and money, and almost no restriction on property ownership. Some expect at least a 20-percent appreciation.

Most Americans go to the southern Mediterranean coast of Spain for retirement, congregating around the Costa del Sol. However, this can be quite crowded at times, with tourists coming from all over Europe. Housing costs can go out of sight for those who don't lease. Farther north along the Mediterranean are some delightful towns and villages that escape a measure of the tourist crush. But with the region's balmy weather and low prices, no place totally escapes the crush of visitors. The mild coastal Mediterranean weather is the drawing card. When you travel inland, on Spain's arid interior plateau, the summers are oven hot and winters are bitter cold and long. So you can understand why the verdant Mediterranean coast, with its balmy winters, is so attractive.

The Costa del Sol is a wondrous landscape of cement highrises, night clubs and tourist-supported businesses. Even though it is crowded, it has managed to retain some of its old charm. Brightly colored flowers, blazing white Mediterranean-style buildings, outdoor cafes and cool Mediterranean breezes remind you constantly of why the Costa del Sol is Scandinavia's winter playground and a summer playground for the rest of Europe and the Americas.

I particularly like the *Costa Brava* toward the French border. The coastline there reminds me a great deal of California's Big Sur country, with rugged cliffs looming over surf-washed beaches. The people here speak *Catalán*, which sounds like an odd combination of old Spanish and French. Even street signs and some newspapers are printed in Catalán. But when people discover that you are a foreigner, they will speak Spanish so you can understand. If you can't speak Spanish, there's almost certain to be someone who can help you. Look around for a Swede or a German; they study a lot of English and Spanish in school.

American retirees are well organized in Spain, with at least five "American Clubs" quite active. There is even a monthly magazine, called LOOKOUT, which is a must for anyone thinking about retirement in Spain. The cost of a one-year subscription is $26. The address is LOOKOUT, Puebla Lucia, 29640 Fuengirola, Malaga, Spain.

## MEDICAL CARE IN SPAIN

Spanish medical care is said to be spotty. One problem is that many doctors and nurses don't speak English. Spanish education hasn't stressed learning foreign languages as other European countries have. (Neither has the United States!) The foreign community decided to do something about this and formed an organization they call Fundacion para Estudios de Enfermeria (Foundation for Nursing Studies, or FEE). Located in Malaga and run by people from the United States, the Netherlands, Britain and Spain, the organization provides English training for nurses. Classes are given twice a week, and prizes awarded to the best students. FEE operates on volunteer labor and donations from foreign residents. If you have a few extra pesetas to pass around, you might consider giving them to FEE.

One of the officers of an American club in Spain has this to say about health care: "Come on over and enjoy your retirement, but when you see medical problems coming, go home!" This is excellent advice for almost any foreign country, particularly one where you are unfamiliar with the language. There is nothing more frustrating that to be in a hospital with a pain in your stomach and are unable to tell the doctors or nurses what your problem is. Not only is it frustrating, it can be highly dangerous. Before a doctor can diagnose your problem and prescribe the correct medication, he needs to know your symptoms.

Aside from that, being an invalid in a foreign country puts an unnecessary burden on your fellow expatriates who may feel obligated to help out. In addition, there is always a question whether anyone will even *feel obligated* to help you.

Always, at least in the back of your mind, you should keep medical alternatives viable. If you have a history of heart problems, it wouldn't be an overwhelmingly great idea to retire someplace three or four hours from a cardiac center. This is only common sense; you don't need a book to point this out to you. On the other hand, if you are in reasonably good health and have no hint of impending medical trouble, it would be equally foolish to choose your retirement location solely on the basis of nearby medical facilities. If your health is that delicate, perhaps you have no business retiring in a foreign country. Stick close to your doctor and your hospital.

# PORTUGAL

Mention retirement in Portugal and the Algarve immediately comes to mind. That's the most popular place for foreigners. Some live around Lisbon, but the Algarve, Portugal's southern coast, remains unique. The weather is perfect, with clear, sunny skies all summer long. More than 150 miles of perfect beaches, sometimes backed by rocky cliffs, are washed by the deep blue waters of the Atlantic.

The rush is on with investors buying up as much of the coastline as they can. The thought of a rapid appreciation is luring them on. Some of the world's rich and super-rich enjoy mansions with views of the blue Atlantic's waters. Of course, this has pushed prices up, but not entirely out of reach of us ordinary Americans. Fortunately, regional officials have taken a clue from the cement jungle at Costa del Sol. They've severely limited the construction of multistory buildings. Anything that might block views of the ocean is prohibited. An interesting thing about real estate in Portugal I think I should pass along: When you purchase a house it's taken for granted that the house is *furnished*. That means everything from bedroom sets to silverware, pots and pans, even linens.

One common problem with foreign living is diminished in the Algarve. Learning Portuguese isn't absolutely necessary for survival. There are so many British living here that English is almost a second language. Still, you need to enroll in a school, not only for the sake of learning the language, but to meet other retirees and to begin building your network of friends.

There's a publication from Algarve which is also desirable for information about retiring in Portugal. Write to Algarve, Rua 25 Abril, 8400 Lagoa, Algarve, Portugal. In Lisbon, there's an organization called the American Club. Among other things, it holds a monthly luncheon and invites speakers, both native and foreign. Of course, the club sponsors the annual Fourth of July celebration for the expatriates.

I know several people who are retired in Spain and Portugal, and they enjoy it very much; in fact, they rave about living there. Once, when I was interviewing a Brazilian consular official about retirement in that country, the official said, "When I retire, I'm going to Portugal!" That tells me something. But even though I know that retirement there is a practical matter, I don't feel competent to give any deep advice on the matter. If you are seriously interested in finding out the complete story, you might contact Jane Parker at Retirement Explorations in Saratoga, Calif. Jane conducts tours to Spain and Portugal, shows people around, introduces them to local retirees, shows them houses and apartments, and generally acquaints them with many facets of living in Spain or Portugal. By the way, she offers a similar service for potential retirees to Costa Rica.

## AUSTRALIA

Australia is another underpopulated country which is attracting retirees. An obvious advantage in retiring there is that the people there speak English. The Australian government welcomes retirees who have "transferable assets sufficient to establish a home in Australia and to provide adequately for their futures."

This means that you have to have sufficient funds to support yourselves and be able to contribute to the economy. This is certainly understandable, particularly since retirees get in on the national health system. Almost all of your essential medical and hospital costs are covered. One problem is that, since Australia loosened up its immigration policies two decades ago, there has been a flood of settlers who have put a strain on the health system.

Australia's cultural traditions are typically British, from the corner pubs and fish and chip shops to the parliamentary squabbles in Canberra, the capital city. But the wave of immigration in the last seven or eight years has brought in people from all over the world, giving Australia a cosmopolitan flavor. People from

Pakistan, India, Vietnam and China, as well as from Europe and the Americas, have come in force. In fact, a fifth of the population today are immigrants. Sydney is particularly rich in foreigners. Only 25 percent of the high school students there speak English as their first language.

This immigration boom is causing some controversy. Some fear loss of jobs, racial tensions or other problems. But so far, the immigrants have had a positive effect on Australia's economy.

Australia has a lot to offer as a retirement spot. There are tropical beaches in northern Queensland, with jungles and sugar cane fields, plus great deep-sea fishing. Twenty-five hundred miles southwest is Perth (pop. 980,000) in a more temperate climate, said to have the best weather in Australia. Canberra (pop. 260,000) is located inland, southwest of Sydney, and is a culture center, with museums and an art colony.

Sydney seems to be the most popular site for retirement. It's by far the largest city, with over 3.5 million people, and has an exceptionally active retired community. Another town that caters to retirees is a resort town on the coast called Nambucca Heads. It's said that 40 percent of the residents are retired.

## AUSTRALIAN COST OF LIVING

Australia isn't particularly inexpensive, but clearly less costly than the United States. Housing is comparatively inexpensive. The median price of a home in Perth, for example, is under $40,000. And, you must be prepared to buy a home, because in order to become a retiree, you must provide evidence that you have enough money to buy a house, or else convince the Australian consulate that you will have other, suitable accommodations. The income requirement is a minimum of $270 a week for a couple, or $200 a week for a single person. To become a retiree, you must also be over 55 years old.

Taxes are high. The high tax bracket starts somewhere around $15,000, and is 46 percent. On the other hand, you don't pay U.S. taxes, and there are no state taxes. Also, the taxes cover the excellent medical care that's provided by the government.

If affordable retirement in an interesting country where everybody speaks your language seems appealing, you might want to write to or visit one of the Australian consulates and investigate further. They are located in New York, Chicago, Los Angeles and San Francisco.

## FINANCIAL PITFALLS

Don't get the idea that you can pack your belongings and move to a foreign country and find everything lovely. You have to keep your eyes on the local currency and you mustn't go investing in everything that comes along just because someone makes it sound good. There are entirely too many fast-talking gringos who will try to get you to invest in tapioca mines or spaghetti plantations.

Another thing you must keep your attention on is the banking situation. Devaluation can be one of the biggest ingredients for financial disaster, or it can be a bonanza, depending on how you approach the problem. Remember, for every loser there's a winner in the devaluation-inflation game. As a person with dollars, you have a good chance of becoming a winner.

In some countries where the inflation is high, interest rates are also high. At one time Argentina was paying 25 percent per month interest. That's right, *per month*. But with a 23 percent per month inflation rate, you can see that you couldn't get rich. Mexico is currently paying over 90 percent per annum for peso accounts, but with an annual percentage rate of 100 percent, this leaves you somewhat in the hole. Listen with a very skeptical ear when someone encourages you to invest in a country where a lot of surprises have been pulled on investors in the past. If you want to learn how to protect yourself, read my book CHOOSE LATIN AMERICA (Gateway Books, San Francisco, 1986), which also goes into great depth about retirement living in Mexico, Costa Rica, Uruguay, Brazil, Argentina and other South of the Border countries.

But does this mean that you ought to stay away from countries with high inflation rates? Not at all. Far from being a detriment, inflation can work for you if you take advantage of it. What does it matter if the price of dinner is $3.00 or 36 million pesos? If a dollar buys 12 million pesos, it doesn't matter at all. Your money is in dollars, and if you're smart, you change only enough every week (or every day) to take care of your needs. What happens if the value of the peso (or cruziero, or colon, or whatever) drops drastically? This just means you can buy more of them with your dollars. Actually, there's usually a lag between the currency of a country dropping and an inevitable raising of prices. This lag is where the real bargains can be found. The bottom line of this discussion is: Keep your money at home in dollars or in some liquid asset. Sure, if you have a few bucks you want to invest, and you want to take a chance on collecting some of that 90 percent interest, go right ahead. Better yet, I can get you a good deal on a geranium mine...

Taxes are another item you need to watch for in foreign retirement. Some countries tax even your Social Security payments, so if you have a lot of income, this might be a consideration. One piece of good news is that the United States has agreements with many foreign countries that permit you to credit your taxes against each other so that you only pay one set of taxes (the higher of the two). Countries who co-operate are Great Britain, Canada, Ireland, Greece, Germany and France. Another piece of good news is that many countries, such as Mexico and Costa Rica, don't tax earnings from outside their countries.

CHAPTER SEVENTEEN

# *Retirement Considerations*

An important part of retirement planning is health care. The question of what might happen when illness strikes should be one for which you seek solutions before it happens. What kind of community facilities will be available to you and your spouse? What kind of attitudes do state and local officials have toward helping the elderly? While these aren't necessarily the prime considerations, they should figure into your decision making.

## SENIOR RESOURCE CENTERS

During the research on this book, I visited many senior citizen centers. Some were nothing more than a couple of rooms where friends meet to play cards, have potluck dinners, and socialize. Others were quite elaborate, with full-time staffs working seven days a week. The better ones have medical personnel and services. A good senior center can make a big difference in your life; if not the day you move into the town, surely later on, when you may need some of the services. As an example of one of the better facilities, I'll present the Humboldt Senior Resource Center in Eureka, Calif.

The resource center is located in a large, three-story Victorian building on a quiet Eureka side street. The receptionist informed me that this was once the grammar school for Eureka and that she had gone from kindergarten through eighth grade there. She was a volunteer worker, and obviously quite proud of the resource center. "I feel as if we are all one big family helping one another," she said as she took us on a tour. "Fortunately, we have local politicians who are sensitive to our needs. They always manage to come up with enough money to keep us going."

Each of the three floors, as well as the basement, is fully utilized, with everything from arts and crafts classrooms and a library, to rehabilitation services (physical, speech and occupational) by registered therapists. The fully equipped exercise room is well used, as is the kitchen where hot, nutritious lunches are served.

"From 50 to 100 people every day drop in to talk to friends, have lunch and exercise, or maybe go on one of our outside trips," our guide pointed out. "If they don't have transportation, we see to it they get here. If it weren't for this kind of center, many of these people would be lost." If a person is unable to ride a regular bus because of a disability, or is over 70 years old, a "Dial-A-Ride" transportation service is provided.

Among the social activities offered are cards, bingo and pool. There are monthly dances, sing-alongs, exercise sessions, video movies and creative writing classes. Other activities include: tax assistance, bus tours around the county, arts and crafts, even Mah-Jongg. Most of these activities are organized and undertaken by volunteer workers.

The director of the center stressed that while social activities are extremely important to the elderly, the most important service the center can provide is keeping people from being institutionalized. "People not only have a much better quality life in their own homes than in an institution, but it's much, much less expensive." It costs from one-half to two-thirds more to place a patient in a nursing home, he pointed out. Home-delivered meals, home repair, referral services, respite care--all of these things make it possible for a person to live in the dignity of a home environment. With today's technology, many techniques and procedures are just as easily administered at home as in hospital settings. So home health aides can visit to give medications or injections to bedridden patients. Registered nurses provide services such as cardiovascular care, cataract care, chemotherapy and intravenous antibiotic therapy, sterile dressing changes, plus a host of other services that would otherwise mean spending time and money in a hospital or nursing facility.

Across the street is the Alzheimer Resource Center where over 25 patients come every day, come to be with friends, have a hot meal and exercise. If it weren't for the Resource Center, many would be institutionalized. Another benefit is family members who must care for the patient get a break from around-the-clock responsibilities. R.S.V.P. volunteers perform some of the most appreciated services of all by coming to the aid of family members who serve as caregivers for invalids. They visit the homes to give counseling, help with household tasks, and take care of the invalid while the often-harassed relative has a chance to get away for a few hours. It's a most satisfying way to spend some of your time, by helping people who *really* need and appreciate the helping hand.

The Eureka Resource Center isn't restricted to the city of Eureka, but also has branches in Fortuna and McKinleyville. They serve people throughout the county. The center isn't unique, there are many others like it around the country, but it's an example of one of the better, if not the best. Fortunately, the state of California has lots of tax dollars it can afford to spend on Medicare supplements (MediCal), and to help establish and maintain senior centers. Taxes are high in California, so the financial backing is there. What happens when state and local governments don't have a large tax base, don't have the money to spend? Sometimes this means the local senior center is just a cardroom and a refrigerator. But not necessarily.

## BOOTSTRAP HEALTH CARE

Let's look at another senior center, in another state. Oregon doesn't have the huge industrial base for tax revenues that California does, and its major industry, lumber, has been floating in the doldrums for several years. Tax money is scarce, and money available for senior citizen services is even scarcer. To Oregon's credit, it does provide as much as it can, probably scrimping in other areas to take care of the elderly.

Since the money just isn't there, Oregon tries to fulfill its duties by utilizing volunteer workers. This not only does the job, but the volunteers profit through increased social networking. Don Bruland, a state senior citizens coordinator in Central Point, Ore., stressed that, "the chances of a person ending up in a nursing home here are much less than almost anywhere in the country. We emphasize *home* care, with volunteer workers to relieve the family." The state of Oregon saves a lot of money in the process. He figures that it costs about $800 minimum to keep a patient in a nursing facility for a month, whereas it only costs $341 to provide similar care in the person's own home. Sometimes it isn't possible to provide adequate at-home care, in which case the state tries to find private family foster care homes, which they can do for an average of $192 a month, one-fourth the cost of a nursing home. He further stated that 80 percent of aging parents can be cared for by relatives if they receive assistance from volunteers and some state resources. Granted, these figures for nursing care are quite low, but they are kept that way by careful oversight by state employees. This should be a model for other public health care agencies to study.

## POLITICAL ACTION FOR HEALTH CARE

Perhaps your political philosophy has always been against tax supported national health care, and you've always heard politicians and private enterprise shout "socialism" any time the subject is mentioned. But maybe you should examine your dogmatic stand and see if the huge profits being made by the private sector are justified. Perhaps you should consider the cost in human misery to the people who are at or below the poverty line and have to spend from one-quarter to one third of their meager income on doctors, hospitals, and nursing homes.

Reject slogans and hysteria fostered by politicians and the private health care industry. Instead, take a look at the profit motives and draw your own conclusions.

For example: According to a recent newspaper article, the board chairman of a large for-profit hospital chain, was paid $18.1 million in 1985, making him the *second highest paid executive in the United States*.

I'm quite sure that people in this salary bracket wouldn't want to see that nasty "socialized medicine" sink its claws into the health care business. Neither would another head of a hospital corporation who happily accepted a salary increase from a paltry $1.4 million to a more comfortable $2 million. That same year, still another health-care executive accepted a salary boost of $1.1 million, pushing his yearly take to $6.4 million!

The list goes on and on, with executives pulling down fat salaries while millions of Americans are worried about how to pay their medical bills. Salaries of chief executives in the pharmaceutical industries averaged $982,000 in 1984, up *28 percent* over the previous year. Working people that year averaged 4-percent pay hikes. So you see, there is a vested interest in the medical care industry to keep things just as they are.

## ARE SENIOR CITIZENS AFFLUENT?

You've probably seen statements in newspapers to the effect

that the elderly today are unusually affluent, and figures are often quoted to prove that few elderly live in poverty. Presumably this means that cutting a little off their Social Security or from Medicare insurance won't hurt. Spokesmen for certain groups make the claim that we are "enriching older Americans at the expense of the young." They claim that Medicare and cost-of-living increases in Social Security have pushed elderly people into the lowest poverty rate of any age group. It appears that some people would like to change this and put a little more poverty into our lives.

As the old saying goes, figures don't lie, but liars do figure. The way the government calculates, a couple under 65 is counted as poor if their income is less than $7,231 per year. But a couple *over* 65 isn't considered poor unless their income is less than *$6,503*. The rationale for this is that people over 65 don't need as much to live on, because their homes are paid for, and they don't have to support children or have job-related expenses. This is a convenient way to figure the poverty line, because most couples receive a little bit more than $6,503 from Social Security, so this automatically boosts them from the ranks of the poor into the ranks of the affluent. The magnificent sum they receive translates to $125 a week. If this isn't poverty, I don't know what poverty is!

Don't think this is a matter of semantics--there are individuals and organizations out there campaigning against benefits for elderly and urging cuts in Social Security and Medicare. One group, calling itself Americans for Generational Equity (AGE) seems to be concerned that we are spending too much on the elderly and not enough on children. A key supporter of the group is Senator David Durenberger (R-Minnesota) who helped launch AGE. Durenberger denies that the group is anti-elderly, rather that its thrust is defending the interests of the young. The group worries about the government's trillion-dollar budgets and future generations who must pay off the staggering debts we are running up. We must applaud government officials for worrying about debt, but I could applaud much louder if they would simply stop spending trillions they don't have instead of looking to cut back on benefits for the elderly.

According to Christopher Connell (*Monterey Peninsula Herald*, Monterey, Calif., April 26, 1987), AGE is well funded and lobbies strongly for cutbacks in social programs for the elderly. Connell says, "Most of its $270,000 budget comes from corporate sponsors, primarily banks, insurance companies, defense contractors and other major corporations." Can you see the vested interests here? Defense contractors not wanting to cut the deficit by trimming billion-dollar contracts? Insurance companies, fearful that improved Medicare would cut into their lucrative premiums on health insurance? Rather, they want to take it out of the hides of those who have been paying taxes and premiums all their lives.

Granted, the young people of today aren't affluent. I don't know about your neighborhood, but young people weren't affluent when I was a boy, either. But it's faulty logic to claim there is unemployment among youth because we spend too much money on the elderly. That's like saying young people are unemployed because we spend too much money for farm supports. This is a separate problem and should be addressed as such. The national debt is caused not by Social Security, which is paying its way, but by wild, reckless spending by the government, and worsened by huge tax cuts for corporations and the wealthy.

Another insidious goal of some politicians is to place Medicare on a "need" basis. That way, only poor people would qualify and the plan would save money. One of the beautiful things about Medicare is that it is a "safety net," something to protect your family and your estate should a last, final illness put you into the hospital for weeks on end at $1,000 a day. When Medicare came along, the elderly no longer needed to hoard their resources for that eventuality. They were able to spend money on themselves and retirement, instead of saving it for doctors and hospitals. Of course, proponents of this "need" basis deny that they are taking away the safety net. Actually, what they propose is to lower that safety net to ground level. Thus, you couldn't begin to collect benefits until private health care people have wiped out your bank account, leaving you and your spouse in poverty.

Become an activist, right now! Don't wait until you retire. Check on your representatives' stances on these important issues and let them know that you are checking .

# APPENDIX

## TAXES

Taxes vary from state to state, with places like Arizona taking a larger bite from your pocket than Alabama or Arkansas. States like Texas and Louisiana can bank on oil revenues to keep taxes lower, and states like Florida can't get its citizens to go along with higher taxes.

If you are in a high tax bracket, clearly, higher taxes could be significant. But if you are like most retirees, your income will be lower, so taxes won't be all that serious. But, to my way of thinking, taxes are just one of many factors to consider when making retirement decisions. Giving too much weight to them would be irrational. The important goal is finding a pleasant, quality retirement location. Remember, most senior citizen benefits are financed with tax money, and states or localities with low taxes have less to spend.

According to the Advisory Commission of Intergovernmental Relations, the tax burdens of the states discussed in this book are ranked as follows (from highest taxes to lowest):

1. Arizona
2. Colorado
3. California
4. Oregon
5. Nevada
6. Georgia
7. Missouri
8. New Mexico
9. Florida
10. North Carolina
11. Louisiana
12. South Carolina
13. Mississippi
14. Texas
15. Tennessee
16. Arkansas
17. Alabama

The average tax burden in Alabama is about $365, the lowest taxed state, as compared to $795 in Arizona. Of course, you must take into consideration that the per capita income in Arizona is higher. But deciding to retire in Alabama over Arizona simply to save a few dollars a year would be a foolish decision, unless you determined that Alabama has everything you want in the way of retirement and Arizona lacks something.

## SUMMER AND WINTER HIGHS AND LOWS FOR SELECTED CITIES

| | DEC HIGH | DEC LOW | JAN HIGH | JAN LOW | FEB HIGH | FEB LOW | JUNE HIGH | JUNE LOW | JULY HIGH | JULY LOW | AUG HIGH | AUG LOW |
|---|---|---|---|---|---|---|---|---|---|---|---|---|
| Augusta, GA | 58.7 | 34.1 | 56.7 | 34.0 | 60.5 | 36.1 | 89.6 | 66.7 | 90.8 | 69.9 | 90.2 | 69.0 |
| Albuquerque | 47.5 | 24.9 | 46.9 | 23.5 | 52.6 | 27.4 | 89.5 | 59.7 | 92.2 | 85.2 | 89.7 | 63.4 |
| Austin, Tex. | 63.1 | 41.7 | 60.1 | 39.4 | 63.8 | 42.7 | 91.6 | 71.3 | 95.3 | 73.0 | 95.9 | 73.0 |
| Biloxi-Gulfport | 62.6 | 46.2 | 60.7 | 45.5 | 63.6 | 47.2 | 87.9 | 73.2 | 89.3 | 74.5 | 89.6 | 74.2 |
| Brownsville | 72.4 | 53.4 | 69.5 | 51.0 | 72.7 | 54.1 | 90.6 | 75.0 | 92.8 | 75.9 | 93.0 | 75.7 |
| Charleston | 60.8 | 37.7 | 59.8 | 37.3 | 61.9 | 39.0 | 87.7 | 68.1 | 89.1 | 71.2 | 88.6 | 70.6 |
| Charlotte | 52.5 | 32.4 | 52.1 | 32.1 | 54.9 | 33.1 | 86.4 | 65.3 | 88.3 | 68.7 | 87.4 | 67.9 |
| Chattanooga | 50.9 | 31.4 | 49.9 | 30.5 | 53.4 | 32.3 | 87.5 | 64.5 | 89.5 | 68.1 | 89.0 | 67.0 |
| Chicago | 35.3 | 21.6 | 31.5 | 17.1 | 34.6 | 20.1 | 80.5 | 60.3 | 84.4 | 65.1 | 83.3 | 64.1 |
| Chico, CA | 55.0 | 36.7 | 53.3 | 35.7 | 59.1 | 38.4 | 89.0 | 56.4 | 96.5 | 60.7 | 94.5 | 58.2 |
| Colorado Springs | 43.1 | 18.9 | 41.0 | 16.1 | 43.6 | 18.9 | 78.1 | 51.1 | 84.4 | 57.0 | 82.4 | 55.8 |
| Columbia, SC | 57.9 | 34.1 | 56.9 | 33.9 | 59.8 | 35.5 | 90.3 | 67.3 | 92.0 | 70.4 | 91.1 | 69.4 |
| Columbus, GA | 59.0 | 36.3 | 57.8 | 35.9 | 60.9 | 37.8 | 89.9 | 67.5 | 90.8 | 70.4 | 90.8 | 69.8 |
| Corpus Christi | 69.3 | 48.9 | 66.5 | 46.1 | 69.8 | 49.3 | 91.2 | 73.6 | 94.4 | 75.2 | 94.8 | 75.4 |
| Denver | 46.2 | 18.9 | 43.5 | 16.2 | 46.2 | 19.4 | 80.1 | 61.9 | 87.4 | 58.6 | 85.8 | 57.4 |
| Eugene, OR | 47.4 | 35.6 | 45.6 | 33.1 | 51.7 | 65.2 | 74.1 | 48.7 | 82.6 | 51.1 | 81.3 | 50.9 |
| El Paso, Tex. | 57.1 | 30.9 | 57.1 | 30.2 | 62.5 | 34.3 | 94.9 | 65.8 | 94.5 | 69.9 | 92.7 | 68.2 |
| Ft. Myers, Fla. | 75.9 | 53.6 | 74.7 | 52.3 | 76.0 | 53.3 | 90.4 | 71.6 | 91.1 | 73.7 | 91.4 | 71.4 |
| Galveston | 62.7 | 51.4 | 59.4 | 48.2 | 51.4 | 50.9 | 85.2 | 77.5 | 87.4 | 79.1 | 87.5 | 78.9 |
| Honolulu | 80.3 | 67.1 | 79.2 | 65.3 | 79.2 | 65.3 | 85.6 | 72.2 | 86.8 | 73.4 | 87.4 | 74.1 |
| Jacksonville, Fla. | 65.5 | 45.1 | 64.5 | 44.5 | 66.9 | 45.6 | 88.3 | 73.1 | 90.1 | 72.0 | 89.7 | 72.3 |
| Las Vegas, Nev. | 56.7 | 33.7 | 55.7 | 32.6 | 61.3 | 36.9 | 97.2 | 67.4 | 103.9 | 75.3 | 101.5 | 73.3 |
| Little Rock | 52.0 | 31.1 | 50.1 | 28.9 | 53.8 | 31.9 | 89.3 | 66.9 | 92.6 | 70.1 | 92.6 | 68.5 |
| Los Angeles | 66.5 | 47.3 | 63.5 | 45.4 | 64.1 | 47.0 | 70.3 | 58.6 | 74.8 | 62.1 | 75.8 | 63.2 |
| Medford, OR | 44.2 | 31.1 | 44.2 | 29.0 | 51.8 | 30.7 | 79.4 | 49.1 | 89.5 | 53.8 | 87.8 | 52.9 |

| | DEC HIGH | DEC LOW | JAN HIGH | JAN LOW | FEB HIGH | FEB LOW | JUNE HIGH | JUNE LOW | JULY HIGH | JULY LOW | AUG HIGH | AUG LOW |
|---|---|---|---|---|---|---|---|---|---|---|---|---|
| Miami | 76.6 | 60.1 | 75.6 | 58.7 | 76.5 | 59.0 | 88.0 | 73.9 | 89.1 | 76.5 | 89.9 | 75.8 |
| Minneapolis | 26.6 | 10.6 | 21.2 | 3.2 | 25.9 | 7.1 | 77.1 | 56.8 | 82.4 | 61.4 | 80.8 | 59.6 |
| Mobile | 63.0 | 42.8 | 61.1 | 41.3 | 64.1 | 43.9 | 89.8 | 70.7 | 90.5 | 72.6 | 90.6 | 72.3 |
| Nashville | 49.6 | 31.1 | 47.6 | 29.0 | 50.9 | 31.0 | 87.5 | 65.7 | 90.2 | 59.0 | 89.2 | 57.7 |
| New York | 41.4 | 29.5 | 38.5 | 25.9 | 40.3 | 26.4 | 80.5 | 62.6 | 85.2 | 68.1 | 83.4 | 66.4 |
| New Orleans | 64.2 | 45.3 | 62.3 | 43.5 | 65.1 | 46.0 | 89.6 | 71.2 | 90.4 | 73.3 | 90.6 | 73.1 |
| Norfolk, VA | 50.6 | 34.0 | 48.8 | 32.2 | 50.0 | 32.7 | 83.5 | 65.6 | 86.6 | 69.9 | 84.9 | 68.9 |
| Orlando | 71.4 | 51.5 | 70.5 | 50.1 | 71.8 | 51.3 | 89.3 | 71.1 | 89.8 | 72.9 | 90.1 | 73.5 |
| Phoenix | 66.5 | 38.5 | 64.8 | 37.6 | 69.3 | 40.8 | 101.4 | 67.7 | 104.8 | 77.5 | 102.2 | 77.1 |
| Pittsburgh | 37.3 | 23.6 | 35.4 | 30.9 | 37.4 | 21.3 | 79.5 | 57.8 | 82.5 | 61.2 | 80.5 | 59.4 |
| Portland, ME | 34.9 | 16.5 | 31.2 | 11.7 | 33.3 | 12.6 | 73.2 | 51.1 | 79.1 | 56.9 | 77.6 | 55.1 |
| Raleigh, NC | 51.9 | 30.5 | 51.1 | 30.1 | 53.2 | 31.1 | 85.6 | 63.1 | 87.7 | 67.2 | 86.8 | 66.2 |
| Reno | 46.3 | 19.6 | 45.4 | 18.3 | 51.1 | 23.1 | 80.4 | 42.5 | 91.1 | 47.4 | 89.1 | 44.8 |
| Sacramento | 52.4 | 38.3 | 53.1 | 37.2 | 59.1 | 40.4 | 86.3 | 54.7 | 92.9 | 57.5 | 91.2 | 56.9 |
| Santa Barbara | 64.2 | 39.3 | 62.7 | 38.3 | 63.6 | 40.3 | 69.7 | 49.5 | 71.8 | 52.4 | 72.1 | 52.5 |
| Savannah | 62.1 | 38.7 | 61.1 | 38.7 | 63.6 | 40.5 | 89.3 | 68.8 | 90.8 | 71.3 | 90.3 | 70.9 |
| San Antonio | 64.4 | 41.8 | 61.6 | 39.8 | 65.6 | 43.4 | 92.4 | 72.0 | 95.6 | 73.8 | 95.9 | 73.4 |
| San Diego | 66.2 | 55.4 | 64.6 | 45.8 | 65.6 | 47.8 | 71.1 | 59.9 | 75.3 | 63.9 | 77.3 | 65.4 |
| San Francisco | 56.5 | 42.9 | 55.3 | 41.2 | 58.6 | 43.8 | 70.2 | 53.0 | 70.9 | 54.0 | 71.6 | 54.3 |
| Seattle | 45.4 | 35.5 | 43.4 | 33.0 | 48.5 | 36.0 | 69.0 | 50.6 | 75.1 | 53.8 | 73.8 | 53.7 |
| Shreveport | 58.9 | 39.4 | 56.8 | 37.8 | 60.4 | 40.6 | 90.1 | 70.2 | 93.5 | 72.8 | 93.8 | 72.5 |
| Springfield, MO | 45.7 | 26.3 | 43.2 | 22.6 | 47.5 | 26.5 | 84.2 | 62.9 | 89.0 | 66.5 | 88.9 | 65.2 |
| Tallahassee | 65.2 | 41.3 | 64.2 | 416.5 | 66.4 | 43.1 | 90.4 | 69.6 | 90.6 | 71.5 | 90.4 | 71.7 |
| Tampa-St. Petersbu | 72.1 | 51.2 | 70.5 | 50.1 | 71.8 | 51.7 | 89.9 | 72.1 | 90.1 | 73.7 | 90.4 | 74.1 |
| Tucson | 64.8 | 39.1 | 63.5 | 38.2 | 67.0 | 39.8 | 97.9 | 66.2 | 98.3 | 74.2 | 95.3 | 72.3 |

# CITIES RANKED FOR AMOUNT OF SUNSHINE

| | Relative Humidity | Sunny Days | Inches Rain | Inches Snow | Pct. Good Weather |
|---|---|---|---|---|---|
| Las Vegas............ | 29 | 300 | 4 | 1 | 82.19 |
| Phoenix................ | 36 | 295 | 7 | 0 | 80.82 |
| El Paso............... | 39 | 294 | 8 | 5 | 80.54 |
| Tucson................ | 38 | 287 | 11 | 2 | 78.63 |
| Santa Barbara.... | 74 | 285 | 12 | 0 | 78.08 |
| Albuquerque........ | 43 | 283 | 7 | 11 | 77.53 |
| Chico, Ca............ | 68 | 276 | 26 | 1 | 75.61 |
| San Diego........... | 68 | 267 | 21 | 0 | 73.15 |
| Sacramento......... | 66 | 265 | 17 | 0 | 72.60 |
| San Francisco..... | 75 | 265 | 21 | 0 | 72.60 |
| Ft. Myers............ | 76 | 264 | 54 | 0 | 72.32 |
| Honolulu............. | 67 | 264 | 23 | 0 | 72.32 |
| Los Angeles........ | 71 | 258 | 12 | 0 | 70.68 |
| Reno.................... | 50 | 255 | 7 | 27 | 69.86 |
| Colorado Spr....... | 49 | 249 | 16 | 40 | 68.21 |
| Miami.................. | 75 | 248 | 60 | 0 | 67.91 |
| Denver................ | 53 | 246 | 16 | 60 | 67.3ǝ |
| Orlando............... | 74 | 241 | 51 | 0 | 66.02 |
| Tampa................. | 74 | 238 | 49 | 0 | 65.20 |
| Brownsville.......... | 76 | 234 | 25 | 0 | 64.10 |
| Tallahassee......... | 76 | 233 | 62 | 0 | 63.83 |
| New York............ | 65 | 232 | 40 | 29 | 63.56 |
| Austin, Tex.......... | 67 | 231 | 33 | 1 | 63.28 |
| New Orleans........ | 77 | 229 | 57 | 0 | 62.73 |
| San Antonio........ | 67 | 227 | 28 | 0 | 62.19 |
| Jacksonville, Fl.... | 75 | 226 | 54 | 0 | 61.91 |
| Columbia, SC...... | 73 | 223 | 46 | 2 | 61.09 |
| Corpus Christi...... | 77 | 222 | 29 | 0 | 60.82 |
| Raleigh, NC......... | 71 | 220 | 43 | 7 | 60.27 |
| Biloxi, Miss......... | 77 | 219 | 59 | 0 | 60.00 |
| Augusta.............. | 72 | 217 | 43 | 1 | 59.45 |
| Mobile................. | 73 | 217 | 67 | 0 | 59.45 |
| Savannah............ | 74 | 217 | 51 | 0 | 59.45 |
| Shreveport.......... | 71 | 217 | 45 | 1 | 59.45 |
| Columbus, Ga...... | 73 | 216 | 51 | 0 | 59.17 |
| Springfield, Mo..... | 70 | 216 | 40 | 15 | 59.17 |
| Little Rock.......... | 70 | 215 | 49 | 5 | 58.90 |
| Charleston........... | 76 | 214 | 52 | 0 | 58.63 |

# CITIES RANKED FOR AMOUNT OF SUNSHINE (Cont.)

| | Relative Humidity | Sunny Days | Inches Rain | Inches Snow | Pct. Good Weather |
|---|---|---|---|---|---|
| Charlotte | 69 | 214 | 43 | 6 | 58.63 |
| Chattanooga | 72 | 213 | 52 | 4 | 58.35 |
| Norfolk | 71 | 212 | 45 | 7 | 58.08 |
| Nashville | 71 | 210 | 46 | 10 | 57.53 |
| Portland, Mn | 74 | 205 | 41 | 74 | 56.16 |
| Galveston | 78 | 203 | 42 | 0 | 55.61 |
| Minneapolis | 69 | 200 | 26 | 46 | 54.79 |
| Chicago | 67 | 197 | 34 | 40 | 53.97 |
| Medford, Or | 67 | 196 | 21 | 8 | 53.69 |
| Pittsburgh | 68 | 161 | 36 | 45 | 44.10 |
| Eugene, Or | 77 | 158 | 43 | 7 | 43.28 |
| Seattle | 74 | 136 | 39 | 15 | 37.26 |

# CHAMBERS OF COMMERCE

Following is a list of various chambers of commerce in various towns to which you might want to write for further information. If the address you want isn't here, simply address your letter to Chamber of Commerce in the town you wish to contact, and it will be delivered. Don't expect too much from these organizations. In doing research on this book, I tried to visit every chamber of commerce office that I could. I was surprised at the different attitudes from the various offices. Most were enthusiastic and extremely helpful but a few showed absolute boredom and lack of interest. When writing the chambers of commerce for information, I received stacks of material from some offices, and no reply from others. Some wanted money before they would even send me even a pamphlet about their town. The problem is that many offices are run by volunteer help who may or may not care whether retirees come there or not. Others are primarily in the business of selling tickets for local attractions, and if you aren't going to buy something, they aren't interested in talking to you.

**ALABAMA**
Business Council of Alabama: P.O. Box 76, Montgomery, AL 36195
Fairhope: 327 Fairhope Av., Fairhope, AL 36532
Mobile: P.O. Box 2187, Mobile, AL 36652

**ARIZONA**
Ajo: P.O. Box 507, Ajo, Ariz. 85321
Arizona Chamber of commerce: 3215 N. 3rd St., Suite 103, Phoenix, Ariz. 85012
Arizona City: P.O. Box 5, Arizona City,Ariz. 85223
Bisbee: P.O. Box BA, Bisbee, Ariz. 85603
Bullhead City: P.O. Box 66, Bullhead City,Ariz. 86430

Flagstaff: 101 W. Santa Fe Av., Flagstaff, Ariz. 86001
Green Valley: P.O. Box 566, Green Valley, Ariz. 85614
Parker: P.O. Box 627, Parker, Ariz. 85344
Phoenix: 16042 N. 32nd St., Suite D-17, Phoenix, Ariz. 85032
Scottsdale: P.O. Box 130, Scottsdale, Ariz. 85251
Tempe: 504 E. Southern, Tempe, Ariz. 85282
Tucson: P.O. Box 991, Tucson, Ariz. 85702
Wickenburg: P.O. Drawer CC, Wickenburg, Ariz. 85358
Yuma: P.O. Box 230, Yuma, Ariz. 85364

ARKANSAS
Arkansas State C. of C., 911 Wallace Bldg., Little Rock, Ark. 72201
Camden: P.O. Box 99, Camden, Ark. 71701
Heber Springs: P.O. Box 630, Heber Springs, Ark. 72543
Hot Springs: P.O. Box 1500, Hot Springs, Ark. 71902
Little Rock: One Spring St., Little Rock, Ark. 72201
Texarkana: P.O. Box 1468, Texarkana, Ark. 75504

CALIFORNIA
California State Chamber of Commerce, P.O. Box 1736, Sacramento, CA 95808
Alpine: P.O. Box 69, Alpine, CA 92001
Arcata: 780 7th St., Arcata, CA 95521
Bakersfield: P.O. Box 1947, Bakersfield, CA 93303
Big Bear Lake: P.O. Box 2860, Big Bear, CA 92315
Brawley: P.O. Box 218, Brawley, CA 92227
Calexico: P.O. Box 948, Calexico, CA 92231
Capitola: P.O. Box 234, Capitola, CA 95010
Chico: P.O. Box 3038, Chico, CA 95927
Desert Hot Springs: P.O. Box 848, Hot Springs, CA 92240
El Centro: P.O. Box 3006, El Centro, CA 92244
El Cajon: 109 Rea Ave., El Cajon, CA 92020
Escondido: P.O. Box C, Escondido, CA 92025
Eureka: 2112 Broadway, Eureka, CA 95501
Fortuna: P.O. Box 797, Fortuna, CA 95540
Garberville: P.O. Box 445, Garberville, CA 95440
Grass Valley: 248 Mill St., Grass Valley, CA 95945
Healdsburg: 217 Healdsburg Av., Healdsburg, CA 95448
Indio: P.O. Box TTT, Indio, CA 92202
Jackson: P.O. Box 596, Jackson, CA 95642
Laguna Beach: P.O. Laguna Beach, Box 396
Lindsay: P.O. Box 989, Lindsay, CA 93247
Los Angeles: 2020 Avenue of the Stars, Los Angeles, CA 90067
Marysville: P.O. Box 1429, Marysville, CA 95901
Mt. Shasta-Dunsmuir: 300 Pine St., Mt. Shasta, CA 96067
Ojai: P.O. Box 1134, Ojai, CA 93023
Palm Springs: 190 W. Amado Rd., Palm Springs, CA 92262
Paso Robles: P.O. Box 457, Paso Robles, CA 93447
Pismo Beach: 581 Dolliver St., Pismo Beach: CA 93449
Redding: P.O. Box 1180, Redding, CA 96099
Salton City: P.O. Box 5185, Salton City, CA

San Diego: 110 W. C St., #1600, San Diego, CA 92101
Santa Barbara: P.O. Box 299, Santa Barbara, CA 93102
Santa Cruz: P.O. Box 921, Santa Cruz, CA 95061
Sun City: P.O. Box 37, Sun City, CA 92381
Tahoe City: P.O. Box 884, Tahoe City, CA 95730
Ukiah: P.O. Box 244, Ukiah, CA 95482
Ventura: 785 Seaward, Ventura, CA 93001
Yucaipa: P.O. Box 45, Yucaipa, CA 92399

COLORADO
State of Colorado C. of C.: 1860 Lincoln St. #550, Denver, CO 80295
Aspen: 303 E. Main, Aspen, CO 81611
Colorado Springs: 100 Chase Stone Center, Colorado Springs, CO 80901
Crested Butte: P.O. Box 1288, Crested Butte, CO 81224
Denver: 1860 Lincoln St., Denver, CO 80295
Grand Junction: P.O. Box 1330, Grand Junction, CO 81502
Gunnison: P.O. Box 36, Gunnison, CO 81230
Steamboat Springs: P.O. Box 774408, Steamboat Springs, CO 80477

FLORIDA
State of Florida, P.O. Box 11309, Tallahassee, FL, 32302
Apalachicola: 45 Market St., Apalachicola, FL, 32320
Boca Raton: P.O. Box 1390, Boca Raton, FL 33432
Boynton Beach: 639 E. Ocean Ave., # 108, Boynton Beach, FL 33435
Bradenton: P.O. Box 321,Bradenton, FL 33506
Cocoa Beach: 400 Fortenberry Rd., Cocoa Beach, FL 32952
Coral Springs: 7305 W. Sample Rd.,Coral Springs, FL 33065
Daytona Beach: P.O. Box 2775, Daytona Beach, FL 32015
Delray Beach: 64 S.E. 5th Av., Delray Beach, FL 33444
Ft. Myers: P.O. Box CC, Ft. Myers, FL 33902
Ft. Walton Beach: P.O. Box 640, Ft. Walton Beach, 32549
Gainesville: P.O. Box 1187, Gainesville, FL 32602
Jacksonville: P.O. Box 329, Jacksonville, FL 32202
Key Largo: Centre of Key Largo, Key Largo, FL 33037
Key West: P.O. Box 984, Key West, FL 33040
Kissimmee: 320 E. Monument Av., Kissimmee, FL 32741
Lakeland: P.O. Box 3538, Lakeland, FL 33802
Marathon: 3330 Overseas Hwy., Marathon, FL 33050
Melbourne: 1005 E. Strawbridge Av., Melbourne, FL 32901
Miami: 900 Perrine Av., Miami FL 33157
Naples: 1700 N. Tamiami Tr., Naples, FL 33940
Ocala: P.O. Box 1210, Ocala, FL 32670
Orlando: P.O. Box 1234, Orlando, FL 32802
Palm Beach: 45 Coconut Row, Palm Beach, FL 33480
Panama City: P.O. Box 1850, Panama City, 32402
Pensacola: P.O. Box 550, Pensacola, FL 32593
Plantation: 7401 N.W. 4th St., Plantation, FL 33317
Pompano Beach: 2200 E. Atlantic Blvd., Pompano Beach, FL 33062
Port St. Joe: P.O. Box 964, Port St. Joe, FL 32456
St. Augustine: P.O. Box Drawer O, St. Augustine, FL 32085

St. Petersburg: 100 2nd Av. North, St. Petersburg, FL 33731
Sanibel Island: P.O. Box 166, Sanibel Island, FL 33957
Sun City Center: P.O. Box 5203, Sun City, FL 33571
Tallahassee: P.O. Box 11309, Tallahassee, FL 32302
Tampa: 5118 N. 56th St., Tampa, FL 33610
Vero Beach: P.O. Box 2947, Vero Beach, FL 32961
West Palm Beach: P.O. Box 2931, West Palm Beach, FL 33401
Winter Haven: P.O. Box 1420, Winter Haven, FL 33882

GEORGIA
State of Georgia C. of C.: 575 N. Omni Intl., Atlanta, GA 30335
Atlanta: P.O. Box 1740, Atlanta, GA 30301
Augusta: P.O. Box 657, Augusta GA 30903
Brunswick-Golden Aisles: P.O. Box 250, Brunswick, GA 31520
St. Simons Island: Neptune Park,St. Simons Island, GA 31522
Savannah: 301 W. Broad St., Savannah, GA 31499
Sea Island: P.O. Box 747, Sea Island, GA 31561
Tybee Island: P.O. Box 491, Tybee Island, GA 31328

LOUISIANA
Baton Rouge: P.O. Box Box 3217, Baton Rouge, LA 70821
Houma: P.O. Box 328, Houma, LA 70361
Lafayette: P.O. Box 51307, Lafayette, LA 70505
New Orleans: P.O. Box 30240, New Orleans, LA 70190

MISSISSIPPI
Gulfport-Biloxi: Biloxi, MS 39533
Natchez: P.O. Box 1403, Natchez, MS., 39120

MISSOURI
Missouri Chamber of Commerce: P.O. Box 149, Jefferson City, 65102
Cabool: P.O. Box 285, Cabool, MO 65689
Cape Girardeau: P.O. Box 98, Cape Girardeau, MO 63701
Columbia: P.O. Box 1016, Columbia, MO 65205
Excelsior Springs: 101 E. Broadway, Excelsior Springs, MO 64024
Jefferson City: P.O. Box 149, Jefferson City, MO 65102
Osage Beach: P.O. Box 193, Osage Beach, MO 65065
Sunrise Beach: Hwy. 5, Sunrise Beach, MO 65079

NEVADA
Nevada Chamber of Commerce: P.O. Box 2806, Reno, NV 89505
Carson City: 1191 S. Carson St., Carson City, NV 89701
Las Vegas: 2301 E. Sahara Av., Las Vegas, NV 89104
Reno: P.O. Box 3499, Reno, NV 89501
Virginia City: P.O. Box 464, Virginia City, NV 89440

NEW MEXICO
Albuquerque: P.O. Box 25100, Albuquerque, NM 87125
Las Cruces: P.O. Box 519, Las Cruces NM 88005
Santa Fe: P.O. Box 1928, Santa Fe, NM

Taos: P.O. Box I, Taos, NM 87571
Truth or Consequences: P.O. Box 31, Truth or Consequences, NM 87901

NORTH CAROLINA
Asheville: P.O. Box 1011, Asheville, NC 28802
Black Mountain: 201 E. State St., Black Mountain, NC 28711
Brevard: P.O. Box 589, Brevard, NC 28712
Chapel Hill: P.O. Box 2897, Chapel Hill, NC 27515
Charlotte: P.O. Box 232785, Charlotte, NC 28232
Durham: 201 N. Roxboro St., Durham, NC 27702
Greensboro: P.O. Box 3246, Greensboro, NC 27402
High Point: P.O. Box 5025, High Point, NC 27252
Raleigh: P.O. Box 2978, Raleigh, NC 27602
Wake Forest: P.O. Box 728, Wake Forest, NC 27587

OREGON
Brookings: P.O. Box 940, Brookings, OR 97415
Ashland: P.O. Box 606, Ashland, OR 97520
Bend: 164 N.W. Hawthorne Av., Bend, OR 97701
Coos Bay: P.O. Box 210, Coos Bay, OR 97420
Corvallis: 420 N.W. Second St., Corvallis, OR 97330
Eugene: P.O. Box 1107, Eugene, OR 97440
Florence: P.O. Box 712, Florence, OR 97439
Gold Beach: 510 S. Ellensburg, Gold Beach, OR 97444
Grants Pass: P.O. Box 970, Grants Pass, OR 97526
Klamath Falls: 125 N. 8th St., Klamath Falls, OR 97601
Medford: 304 S. Central, Bend, OR 97501
North Bend: P.O. Box B, North Bend, OR 97459
Portland: 221 N.W. 2nd Ave, Portland, OR 97209
Reedsport: P.O. Box 11, Reedsport, OR 97467
Springfield: P.O. Box 155, Springfield, OR 97477

SOUTH CAROLINA
State of South Carolina C.of C: P.O. Box 11278 Columbia, SC
Abbeville: 104 Pickens St., Abbeville, SC 29620
Aiken: P.O. Box 892, Aiken, SC 29802
Beaufort: P.O. Box 910, Beaufort, SC 29901
Charleston: P.O. Box 975, Charleston, SC 29402
Columbia: P.O. Box 1360, Columbia, SC 29202
Hilton Head Island: P.O. Box 5674 Hilton Head, SC
Myrtle Beach: P.O. Box 2115, Myrtle Beach, SC 29578
Rock Hill: P.O. Box 590, Rock Hill, SC 29731

TENNESSEE
Chattanooga: 1101 Market St., Chattanooga, TN 37402
Clarksville: P.O. Box 883, Clarksville, TN 37041
Dayton: 305 E. Main Av., Dayton, TN 37321
Gatlinburg: P.O. Box 527, Gatlinburg, TN 37738
Johnson City: P.O. Box 180, Johnson City, TN 37605
Memphis: P.O. Box 224, Memphis, TN 38103

TEXAS
State of Texas: 1012 Perry Brooks Blvd., Austin, TX 78701
Aransas Pass: 452 Cleveland, Aransas Pass, TX 78336
Bandera: P.O. Box 171, Bandera, TX 78003
Brownsville: P.O. Box 752, Brownsville, TX 78522
Bryan: P.O. Box 726, Bryan, TX 77806
Corpus Christi: P.O. Box 640, Corpus Christi, TX 78403
El Paso: P.O. Box 9738, El Paso, TX 79987
Fredericksburg: P.O. Box 506, Fredericksburg, TX 78624
Harlingen: P.O. Box 189, Harlingen, TX 78551
Lufkin: P.O. Box 1606, Lufkin, TX 75901
McAllen: P.O. Box 790, McAllen, TX 78501
Nacogdoches: P.O. Box 1918, Nacogdoches, TX 75963
San Antonio P.O. Box 1628, San Antonio, TX 78296
Port Isabela: Padre Island: P.O. Box 2098, Port Isabela, TX 78597
Texarkana: P.O. Box 1468, Texarkana, TX 75504

## ABOUT THE AUTHOR

John Howells, born in New Orleans, raised in suburban St. Louis, but a Californian by choice, has traveled the country, working on newspapers from coast to coast and border to border. He worked on 40 daily newspapers in his career, and in the process, learned much about living in various sections of the country. He has worked as a Linotype operator, English teacher, silver miner, travel and feature writer, and has authored books on travel-retirement living in Mexico and Latin America, as well as one on prospecting for gold. He received his B.A. in Anthropology and M.A. in Mexican-American Graduate Studies from San Jose State University.

# BIBLIOGRAPHY

BOYER and SAVAGEAU. *Places Rated Almanac.* Rand McNally, New York, 1985

CHAPMAN, ELWOOD N. *Comfort Zones.* Crisp Publications, Palo Alto, Calif. 1985

COOLEY and MORRISON. *The Retirement Trap.* Doubleday & Co. Garden City, NY, 1965

DICKINSON, PETER A. *Retirement Edens Outside the Sunbelt.* E.P. Dutton, New York, 1981

HALLOWELL, CHRISTOPHER. *Growing Old, Staying Young.* William Morrow, New York, 1985

HOWELLS, JOHN. *Choose Latin America.* Gateway Books, San Francisco, 1986

HOWELLS and MERWIN. *Choose Mexico.* Gateway Books, San Francisco, 1985

LEGLER, HENRY. *How to Make the Rest of your Life the Best of Your Life.* Simon and Schuster, New York, 1967

MORRISON, MORIE. *Retirement in the West.* Chronicle Books, San Francisco, 1976

PETERSON, KAY. *Home Is Where You Park It.* RoVing Press, Estes Park, Colo. 1982

WRIGHT, DON. *Guide to Full-Time RVing.* Trailer Life, Agoura, Calif., 1985

ZIMMERMANN, GEREON. *Secrets of Successful Retirement.* Simon and Schuster, New York, 1963

# LIST OF MAPS

# GEOGRAPHICAL INDEX

**O**ur books are available in most bookstores. However, if you have any difficulty finding them, we will be happy to ship them to you directly.

Mail us this coupon with your check or money order and they'll be on their way to you within days.

| | | |
|---|---|---|
| RETIREMENT CHOICES<br>   For the Time of your Life | $10.95 | _____ |
| CHOOSE SPAIN<br>   Leisurely Vacations or Affordable Retirement | 11.95 | _____ |
| CHOOSE MEXICO:<br>   Retire on $400 a Month | 9.95 | _____ |
| RV TRAVEL IN MEXICO<br>   The Complete How-to-do-it Book | 9.95 | _____ |
| GET UP AND GO:<br>   A Guide for the Mature Traveler | 10.95 | _____ |
| CHOOSE LATIN AMERICA<br>   A Guide to Seasonal and Retirement Living | 9.95 | _____ |
| THE GRANDPARENT BOOK<br>   A Commonsense Guide | 11.95 | _____ |
| TO LOVE AGAIN:<br>   Intimate Relationships After 60 | 7.95 | _____ |

**Subtotal:** _____

Add $1.50 for postage and handling for the first book,
$ .50 for each additional one. _____

**California residents add sales tax.** _____

**Total Enclosed:** _____

❂ ❂ ❂

Name_____

Address_____

City_____State_____Zip_____

Books should reach you in two or three weeks. If you are dissatisfied for any reason, the price of the book(s) will be refunded in full.

**Mail to : Gateway Books • 13 Bedford Cove • San Rafael, CA 94901**